THE MASTER PLAN

BRIAN H. FISHMAN

The
Master Plan

ISIS, AL-QAEDA, AND THE JIHADI STRATEGY

FOR FINAL VICTORY

Yale

UNIVERSITY PRESS

NEW HAVEN & LONDON

Yale University Press books may be purchased in quantity for
educational, business, or promotional use. For information, please
e-mail sales.press@yale.edu (U.S. office)
or sales@yaleup.co.uk (U.K. office).

Set in Scala type by Westchester Publishing Services.

Printed in the United States of America.

Library of Congress Control Number: 2016944655
ISBN 978-0-300-22149-7 (hardcover : alk. paper)

A catalogue record for this book is available from the British Library.

This paper meets the requirements of ANSI/NISO Z39.48-1992
(Permanence of Paper).

10 9 8 7 6 5 4 3 2 1

To the children of war, who have seen more than they should

CONTENTS

DISCARDED

THE ATTACKS CAME IN QUICK SUCCESSION ACROSS the globe. On Metrojet Flight 7K9268 from the Egyptian resort town of Sharm el-Sheikh to Saint Petersburg, Russia, a bomb tore through the plane's skin, rapidly depressurizing the cabin and killing all 224 people on board. Three weeks later, a double suicide bombing in a Beirut neighborhood dominated by Shia Muslims killed forty-three people. The following night, a multi-pronged attack in Paris killed 130 people, many inside a local concert hall.

All of those attacks were claimed by the Islamic State, which in late 2015 controlled a swath of territory in Iraq and Syria the size of the United Kingdom, containing a population of more than six million people, and collecting revenue of approximately $80 million per month. The Islamic State called itself the "Caliphate," with supposed religious and political authority over every Muslim on earth. It enforced that grandiose vision by brutally killing anyone in its way, most of whom were Muslims the Caliphate disavowed as apostates. Islamic State "provinces" sprung up in Libya, Egypt, Afghanistan, Nigeria, and beyond, ensuring that destroying the group would take years, if not decades. No government on earth recognized the Islamic State as a sovereign entity, but the most dangerous terrorist organization in the world was, de facto, its own country.

For many in the West, the Islamic State's emergence as a global force was a surprise. It seemed to come from nowhere in the cauldron of the Syrian civil war and immediately transform into a global threat.

But the Islamic State did not emerge from nowhere. The Islamic State's leaders celebrated the institution's tenth anniversary in June 2016, identifying its founding in October 2006. And even prior to that, a senior al-Qaeda leader living under a permissive form of house arrest in Iran framed a seven-stage master plan that began with the 9/11 attacks and called for the declaration of a caliphate in Syria between 2013 and 2016. If not a blueprint for events to come, the proposal has proved a startlingly prescient prediction of future events.

There are many ways to tell the history of the Islamic State: as an ideological movement, as a product of the Syrian civil war, as part of a broader social backlash against the century-old division of the Middle East into modern nation states. All of these lenses have their own value, and the rise of Zarqawiism as a distinct strain of jihadi thought deserves particular attention.

At its core, however, this book is not a history of ideas; it is a history of people and the strategic and operational decisions they made to create the Islamic State. Zarqawiism is a dystopian cultural movement wrapped around a core set of ideological principles. Those ideological principles are obviously critical, but they should not be removed from the people that conceived and implemented them. Ideas are dangerous, but they do not kill en masse until human beings build organizations to implement them.

Indeed, the importance of jihadi strategy is often overlooked. The master plan that predicted the caliphate would be reestablished in Syria between 2013 and 2016 was the best guide to the Islamic State's future development, but it was not, primarily, an ideological document. Although it was a nod to religious prophecy and was designed to pursue jihadi ideological goals, the master plan was a strategy document not so different from those developed by all sorts of military and political organizations. The end state to be achieved was a function of ideology, but the heart of the master plan was simply a blueprint to get from here to there.

The old cliché about military plans is that they never survive first contact with the enemy. The master plan has proved extremely accurate in some respects, but it is far from perfect. The point of planning, however, is not so much to develop a perfect scheme for action, but to identify critical decision points, risks, and benchmarks. By that standard, the master plan has succeeded brilliantly.

This book is the history of the people who built the Islamic State by implementing elements of that master plan and rejecting others. It also lays a foundation for understanding the Islamic State's future. After all, the master plan's initial vision was not simply to declare the caliphate. After the caliphate was declared, the plan promised a campaign of terrorism like none the world had ever seen, and a jihadi "final victory" by 2020. The Islamic State is increasingly on the defensive in Iraq and Syria, but according to the master plan, the worst is yet to come.

ACKNOWLEDGMENTS

THIS BOOK BEGAN AS THE SYLLABUS FOR AN Advanced Terrorism seminar I taught on the Islamic State of Iraq at the United States Military Academy in 2008. That course was based on research I began at West Point's Combating Terrorism Center (CTC) in 2005. This means, among other things, that I have a decade's worth of people to thank.

First, I owe a great debt to all of my colleagues at the CTC. Thank you to Jarret Brachman, Jeff Bramlett, Bill Braniff, Vahid Brown, James Forest, Alex Gallo, Scott Helfstein, Lianne Kennedy-Boudali, Will McCants, Kip McCormick, Afshon Ostovar, Don Rassler, Reid Sawyer (who recruited me), Jake Shapiro, Thalia Tzanetti, and Clint Watts. Their influence—formally cited and otherwise—is all over this book.

The leadership of the CTC and the SOSH Department at West Point created a wonderful environment in which to learn and work. Thanks to General Russell Howard, General Michael Meese, and General Cindy Jebb. Ambassador Mike Sheehan, Bruce Hoffman, General Wayne Downing, and General John Abizaid offered guidance and inspiration. A special thanks to Colonel Joe Felter, a friend, mentor, traveling partner in two war zones, and co-author for more than a decade.

The CTC functioned only because of donor support. I am thankful to everyone who supported our work, but particularly Vinnie Viola, a West Point graduate.

After leaving the CTC, I landed at New America, a think tank in Washington, D.C., where I tracked the resurrection of the Islamic State of Iraq in late 2010 and 2011. Thanks to Peter Bergen, Steve Coll, Katherine Tiedemann, Andrew Liebovich, and Jennifer Rowland.

I am grateful to the various individuals and institutions that have offered me an organizational home during the writing of this book. To Peter Bergen at New America, Bryan Price at West Point's CTC, Amy Zegart at Stanford's Center for International Security and Cooperation, and Lawrence Rosenthal at UC Berkeley's Center for Right-Wing Studies, thank you.

This book would not have been possible without the support of my agent, Don Fehr, who deftly managed a first-time author's angst, and Bill Frucht, my editor at Yale University Press, who has helped make a very complex story more accessible. Thank you both.

Various people offered support during the research, writing, and editing process. I am thankful in particular for the kindness of Anand Gopal, Matthew Jury, and Alexander Key. Many people have reviewed drafts of this book, and even more have had a major influence on my thinking about the Islamic State and its origins. Thank you to my wife, Jama Adams; my father, Bill Fishman; my mother, Margaret Howes Fishman; my brother, Scott Fishman; and my sister-in-law, Katy Fishman. Bill Braniff, Ryan Evans, Mohammed Hafez, Haroon Moghul, and Craig Whiteside all read full or partial versions of this book, which is far better for their comments. Of course, any remaining mistakes are mine alone.

NOTE ON SOURCES, SPELLING, AND NAMES

IN AN EFFORT TO INCREASE ACCESSIBILITY for readers unaccustomed to Arabic names, I use simplified spelling and inconsistent—but hopefully intuitive—conventions to identify various characters on the second use of their names. For example, Abu Mus'ab al-Zarqawi is referred to as "Zarqawi," but Sayf al-Adl is called "al-Adl." Some individuals are even called by their "first names." Abu Anas al-Shami, for example, appears as "Abu Anas." In all cases, people are identified by the name they were most commonly known by. In rare cases, I have used similar conveniences in reference to the names of jihadi organizations.

The original sources for this book, collected over more than a decade of research on the Islamic State and its predecessors, were all unclassified and publicly available.

Many of the primary sources in this document were captured by U.S. forces on the battlefield and subsequently declassified. Most were drawn from the Department of Defense's Harmony Database, declassified, and made publicly available through the Combating Terrorism Center at West Point (www.ctc.usma.edu).

Many other documents were declassified for use as evidence in criminal trials. By far the most useful of these court releases was the massive collection of documents declassified for the prosecution of Abd al-Hadi al-Iraqi at a military tribunal at Guantanamo Bay (www.mc.mil/CASES/military Commissions.aspx).

Finally, the Central Intelligence Agency has released many documents collected during the raid on Osama bin Laden's safehouse in Abbottabad, Pakistan. These documents are referenced as part of "Bin Laden's Bookshelf" (www.dni.gov/index.php/resources/bin-laden-bookshelf). The work done by the Conflict Records Research Center, before it was defunded, was also invaluable.

Over a decade of research on the Islamic State and its predecessors, I have benefitted from repositories of open-source data as well. This archival work is generally thankless, but it is vital. I am particularly grateful to Aaron Zelin at Jihadology (www.jihadology.net), Aymenn Jawad al-Tamimi (www.aymennjawad.org), Pieter Van Ostaeyen (www.pietervanostaeyen .com), the excellent rotating cast of characters at Jihadica (www.jihadica .com), and the talented folks at the Open Source Center.

A number of the sources in this book were collected on private jihadi web forums, many of which are no longer publicly available. In some cases, I archived these years ago before they were taken down; in other instances, I accessed them through the Internet Archive's Wayback Machine.

KEY CHARACTERS

Abaaoud (Abdelhamid Abaaoud): Belgian recruit to the Islamic State of Iraq and Syria in 2013. Key leader of the Islamic State's campaign of terrorism in Europe. Killed in a shootout with French police in November 2015.

Abd al-Hadi (Abd al-Hadi al-Iraqi): Managed al-Qaeda's guesthouse in Kabul prior to 9/11. Key al-Qaeda interlocutor with Abu Mus'ab al-Zarqawi and al-Qaeda in Iraq. Arrested in Turkey in 2006 and currently imprisoned at the U.S. facility at Guantanamo Bay.

Abu Anas (Abu Anas al-Shami): Key religious leader for Abu Mus'ab al-Zarqawi in Iraq. Onetime acolyte of Abu Muhammad al-Maqdisi. Killed near Abu Ghraib in 2004.

Abu Bakr (Abu Bakr al-Baghdadi): Named emir of the Islamic State of Iraq in 2010. Named Caliph Ibrahim in 2014 by the Islamic State. Alive as of July 2016.

Abu Ghadiyah: Battlefield nickname used by two key individuals. The first was Sulayman Khalid Darwish, a close aide of Abu Mus'ab al-Zarqawi, who was killed in 2005. The second was Turki Badran Hishan al-Mazidh, who was the leading smuggler of jihadis through Syria in 2006 and 2007. He was killed by U.S. Special Operations troops inside Syria in 2008.

Abu Hammam (Abu Hammam al-Suri): Swore allegiance to Osama bin Laden in 1999. Ultimately the military chief of Syrian al-Qaeda affiliate Jabhat al-Nusrah. Alive and managing JaN's military affairs as of July 2016.

Abu Hamzah (Abu Hamzah al-Muhajir): Longtime Egyptian jihadi. Successor to Zarqawi as emir of al-Qaeda in Iraq. Minister of war in the Islamic State of Iraq. Killed in April 2010.

Abu Khaled (Abu Khaled al-Suri): Longtime friend and ally of Abu Mus'ab al-Suri. Named al-Qaeda's representative in Syria by Ayman al-Zawahiri in 2013. Captured in Pakistan in 2005; reportedly transferred to Syrian custody in 2009 by the United States. Assassinated by the Islamic State in 2014.

Abu Umar (Abu Umar al-Baghdadi): Former Iraqi policeman. Kicked out of Iraqi civil service for his extreme views. First emir of the Islamic State of Iraq. Killed in April 2010.

Abu Wa'el (Abu Wa'el): Only Arab member of Ansar al-Islam's original Shariah Committee. Reputed by the Bush Administration to be the link between Saddam Hussein's regime and al-Qaeda. Eventually emerged as a key enemy of the Islamic State of Iraq.

Adnani (Abu Muhammad al-Adnani): Early aide to Abu Mus'ab al-Zarqawi in Iraq; spokesman for the Islamic State and commander of its external operations branch. Alive as of July 2016.

al-Absi (Shakir al-Absi): Founder and emir of Lebanese jihadi group Fatah al-Islam. Killed by Syrian troops in 2008.

al-Adl (Sayf al-Adl): Al-Qaeda's security chief prior to 9/11 and key interlocutor with Abu Mus'ab al-Zarqawi; primary designer of the seven-stage master plan. Spent approximately fifteen years after 9/11 in Iran, but reportedly went free in early 2015.

al-Douri (Izzat al-Douri): Advisor to Saddam Hussein; key leader of Ba'athist elements of the Iraqi insurgency. Alive as of March 2016.

al-Kanj (Bassam al-Kanj): Met Zarqawi during his first trip to Afghanistan in the late 1980s; leader of seminal jihadi uprising in Lebanon in 1999. Killed by Syrian or Lebanese troops in early 2000.

al-Muhajir (Abu Abdallah al-Muhajir): Radical Egyptian preacher active in Afghanistan during the 1990s. Highly sectarian; taught Zarqawi to embrace suicide attacks. Spent nearly a decade incarcerated in Iran after 9/11, but was reportedly released to Egypt in 2011.

al-Shafi'i (Abu Abdallah al-Shafi'i): Founder and emir of Kurdish jihadi group Ansar al-Islam. Captured by U.S. forces in May 2010 and reportedly still in Iraqi custody.

al-Suri (Abu Mus'ab al-Suri): Veteran of the Syrian uprising against Hafez al-Assad, renowned jihadi theorist, and sometime rival of Osama bin Laden. Captured in Pakistan in 2005; reportedly transferred into Syrian custody in 2009. Reportedly still in Syrian custody as of July 2016.

Atiyah (Atiyah abd al-Rahman): Iran-based al-Qaeda leader and ultimately a senior aide to Osama bin Laden. Killed in August 2011.

bin Laden (Osama bin Laden): Founder and emir of al-Qaeda. Killed in May 2011.

Hakaymah (Muhammad Khalil al-Hakaymah): Senior activist in the Egyptian Islamic Group. Fled Afghanistan with Zarqawi. Likely author of *The Management of Savagery* under the pseudonym Abu Bakr Naji. Killed in October 2008.

Hardan (Muhammad Hardan): Longtime Iraqi salafi activist. Mentor to Abu Bakr al-Baghdadi prior to the U.S. invasion. Founder of Iraqi insurgent group the Mujahidin Army; enemy of the Islamic State of Iraq. Alive as of March 2016.

Husayn (Fuad Husayn): Jordanian journalist imprisoned with Zarqawi during the 1990s. Received and published Sayf al-Adl's history of Zarqawi, and draft of the seven-stage master plan. Alive as of March 2016.

Jawlani (Abu Muhammad al-Jawlani): Onetime member of the Islamic State of Iraq; emir of Jabhat al-Nusrah. Alive as of July 2016.

Maqdisi (Abu Muhammad al-Maqdisi): One of the world's most prominent jihadi ideologues; before their estrangement, a mentor to Abu Mus'ab al-Zarqawi. Alive as of July 2016.

Qar'awi (Salah al-Qar'awi): Founded the Abdallah Azzam Brigades at Zarqawi's behest. Married Muhammad Khalil al-Hakaymah's daughter. Wounded by a U.S. drone strike in Pakistan in 2012, Qar'awi is in custody in Saudi Arabia.

Teusant (Nicholas Teausant): American that pled guilty in 2015 of attempting to provide material support to a terrorist organization, namely the Islamic State.

Zarqawi (Abu Mus'ab al-Zarqawi): Jordanian founder and emir of al-Qaeda in Iraq; godfather of the Islamic State. Killed by U.S. forces in June 2006.

Zawahiri (Ayman al-Zawahiri): Al-Qaeda's second-in-command on 9/11; named emir of al-Qaeda after Osama bin Laden's death. Alive as of July 2016.

THE MASTER PLAN

Prologue: The Kandahar Meeting

IN OCTOBER 2001, A LINE OF 135 VEHICLES wound through Afghanistan's southern desert on their way from a lonely camp near Herat, in Afghanistan's far west, to Kandahar.[1] Many of the jihadis in the long column were Syrian or Jordanian, and in driving to Kandahar they were taking a great risk. Unlike most jihadis in Afghanistan, many of these men had brought their families with them, and so there were women and children on the 350-mile journey to the central bastion of Taliban resistance to the United States. American fighter pilots patrolled the skies above, ready to exact vengeance for the carnage of 9/11.

The caravan was guided by a Jordanian who once called himself *al-Gharib*, the Stranger. He was thirty-three years old, was absolutely committed to violent jihad, and had drawn the jihadis and their families to Afghanistan with a vision of establishing a "mini Islamic Society." In the years prior to 9/11 he was also relatively unremarkable—just one of many Arab jihadi leaders in Afghanistan. His name was Abu Mus'ab al-Zarqawi.

Zarqawi was not a member of al-Qaeda and had no prior knowledge of the 9/11 attack. He was not even in Herat on the day of the strike. Rather, he was returning from Iran, where he met with one of his agents living in Europe.[2] Upon learning of the attack, Zarqawi's first response was to rush home; the second was to join forces with other Arab jihadis and the Taliban in an attempt to repel the U.S. counterattack.[3]

This was easier said than done. Many of Herat's residents come from the Shia sect of Islam, rather than Afghanistan's majority Sunni sect, which included the country's Taliban rulers who had grudgingly blessed Zarqawi's project. After 9/11, some local Shia tribes in Herat rebelled against Taliban authority and surrounded Zarqawi's training camp.[4]

Zarqawi might easily have been killed there in Herat if not for the local Taliban governor, Mullah Jihadwal. Zarqawi did not have a good relationship with the Taliban leadership in Afghanistan. His ideology and vision for jihad were far more intransigent than most of theirs. But Jihadwal was different. He was one of the few senior figures in the Taliban to have left Afghanistan for jihad. Whatever he thought of Zarqawi's ideology, which was radical even by jihadi standards, Jihadwal valued Zarqawi's commitment to jihadi revolution. Jihadwal ordered his own nephew to lead the operation to liberate Zarqawi's camp. As one prominent jihadi recalled, the Taliban fighters "stormed the location and killed whoever [they] could, and rescued the brothers."[5] News of Zarqawi's escape quickly reached Kandahar, and the 135-vehicle column was not far behind.[6]

In the last week of November 2001, Zarqawi was invited to a jihadi confab to plan the final defense of Kandahar. The meeting brought together veritable jihadi royalty, including two men that would play critical roles in shaping Zarqawi's future: al-Qaeda's security chief, Sayf al-Adl, and Muhammad Khalil al-Hakaymah, a longtime member of the Egyptian Islamic Group with grand ideas about jihadi revolution.

The gathering was risky. The Taliban could not defend against U.S. airpower, and American spies were thought to be everywhere in Kandahar. The jihadis were paranoid; al-Qaeda's second-in-command, Abu Hafs al-Masri, had just been killed in Kabul by a U.S. missile that the jihadis concluded was directed by local spies that identified his location with a tracking device.[7] So after finishing his noon prayers, Hakaymah stepped outside to check the group's cars for American tracking devices. But as he stood in the courtyard, an explosion ripped through the house behind him, crumpling one wall and collapsing the roof.[8]

In the dust-filled whirl, the jihadis scrambled to find their fellows, even as they feared a follow-on attack. Abu Zubaydah, a Palestinian militant, described finding two men half-buried under the rubble, heavy "dirt and iron" pressing down on their backs.[9] American officials would claim later that Zarqawi was almost killed in the airstrike, but in fact he stumbled from the wreckage with only a few broken ribs.[10] "Indeed," wrote Abu Zubaydah in his diary on November 29, 2001, "all were well, none of them was hurt except for some bruises on the two brothers who were under the rubble."[11]

It was a series of near misses. If Zarqawi had died in Herat or Kandahar in the fall of 2001, many of the events described in this book would not have happened. Jihadism would still be a danger to the civilized world, but the Islamic State as we have come to know it would not exist.

1

The Awakening Stage
(2000–2003)

The awakening stage began with preparation for the September 11
attacks. . . . It ended with the American occupation of Baghdad. . . .
The first stage compelled the Americans to leave their conventional
bases. . . . The Americans and their allies became easy and close
targets. . . . The second important achievement [al-Qaeda] made at
this stage was that its tenets became known everywhere.

Fuad Husayn, *Zarqawi . . . The Second Generation of al-Qaeda*

The Stranger

The godfather of the Islamic State was not known for his introspection,
but if Abu Mus'ab al-Zarqawi's life flashed before his eyes as the Kandahar
safe house collapsed around him, he might have reflected on the strange
series of events that had led him to that moment. Born and raised by a
single mother in the hardscrabble Jordanian town of Zarqa, Zarqawi spent
his adolescence fighting, stealing, and spending time in prison for a range
of offenses, including sexual assault.[1] Zarqawi turned eighteen in 1984, at
the height of the anti-Soviet jihad in Afghanistan, but he was initially un-
interested. Many of his contemporaries were inspired to fight against the
Soviet Union's occupation of Afghanistan by Abdallah Azzam, a Palestinian preacher who declared that jihad against the Soviet Union was an
individual responsibility for every able-bodied Muslim man. At the time,

Azzam's logic—and his success distributing it through books, pamphlets, and tape recordings—was revolutionary. He asserted that Muslim men were obligated to fight in Afghanistan regardless of other social obligations, including familial commitments. The argument motivated thousands of young men to travel to Afghanistan to fight the Soviet Union, but it did not convince Zarqawi to leave his mother behind.

Ultimately, it was Zarqawi's mother, no doubt hoping to keep him out of a life of crime, who enrolled him in religious classes at a local mosque.[2] There, Zarqawi was entranced by the legendary Afghan commander Abdul Rasul Sayyaf, who was visiting Jordan to recruit and fundraise for the anti-Soviet war.[3] Sayyaf was an intellectual who carried a gun, and he dazzled Zarqawi by combining religious rhetoric with battlefield stories of struggle.[4] In doing so, Sayyaf embodied a leadership paradigm combining religious scholarship and battlefield experience that Zarqawi would extol and attempt to emulate for the rest of his life.[5] The principle remains critical to the Islamic State today. Religious rhetoric that is not backed by action is easily dismissed.

In 1989, soon after seeing Sayyaf speak, Zarqawi left for Afghanistan for the first time.

Zarqawi missed his chance to kill Soviets in Afghanistan. The Soviet Union withdrew in February 1989, and the fight had shifted to an intramural bloodbath among Afghans—Muslims—for the future of the country. Zarqawi's first job was to scribble articles for *Bunyan al-Marsous*, a jihadi newsletter published by Sayyaf.[6] Al-Qaeda had been founded in 1988 as an elite organization of former mujahidin, and it recruited some employees of *Bunyan al-Marsous*; Zarqawi, unsurprisingly, was not invited to join.[7]

Zarqawi did not have the experience to join al-Qaeda's first generation. He was just "an ordinary guy, an ordinary fighter," when he arrived for jihad in South Asia.[8] But even senior jihadis recognized that "he was brave" and eager to be at the center of a battle.[9] It was a trait that would serve Zarqawi well until it got him killed.

Zarqawi was also an effective networker during his first trip to Afghanistan. He built relationships with jihadis from Syria, Jordan, and Lebanon that would be extremely useful in ensuing decades.[10] Most importantly, however, he met Abu Muhammad al-Maqdisi.[11]

Zarqawi and Maqdisi were a jihadi odd couple. Zarqawi was the "brave" fighter that reveled in violence; Maqdisi was an intellectual who described himself as "illiterate" with weapons.[12] The two men became partners and rivals, friends and enemies. The crucible of their disjointed relationship was the forge that created much of the intellectual foundation for the Islamic State.

Maqdisi was seven years older than Zarqawi and had been born in the West Bank city of Nablus when it was under Jordan's control.[13] Israel conquered the territory in 1967, and Maqdisi's family fled to Kuwait.[14] Whereas Zarqawi learned lessons in the street, Maqdisi learned them in the library. He was studious and brilliant, and by the time he met Zarqawi, Maqdisi had a reputation as an intellectual hard-liner among jihadis. His absolutism met fertile ground in Zarqawi's search for ideological clarity and personal identity.

Maqdisi's writing is broad and deeply influential among jihadis, but two ideas have been particularly important. First, Maqdisi developed a radical, politicized understanding of *al-wal'a w'al bara'a*—the notion that Muslims should remain loyal to Islam and disavow what is not. For most Muslims, this means striving for justice and avoiding vice, but Maqdisi argued this meant that Muslims should reject political leaders who did not impose his version of shariah. Most radically, he argued that the Saudi ruling family should be disavowed, a position that in the early 1990s was significantly more radical than Osama bin Laden's.[15] Second, Maqdisi argued that democracy was a form of religion because it asserted the sovereignty of human beings over God.[16] Thus, Western calls for democracy were attempts to promote a competing religion, not secular claims that could be embraced alongside Islam.

These were heady ideas for Zarqawi in the early 1990s, and his views on them at the time remain unclear. He wrote little and did not have a clearly defined ideology of his own. Zarqawi was just a well-networked foot soldier in Afghanistan, fighting in several battles that would become legendary for the jihadis that participated in them—the liberation of Khost in 1990 and the mujahidin advance into Kabul when the Soviet-backed government collapsed.[17] History does not record Zarqawi's role in those battles, but they left an impression on him. In 2005, as Emir of al-Qaeda in Iraq, he told a friend that he wished he had been killed during the siege of Khost, "when his soul was more pure and his heart was more kind."[18]

Maqdisi returned from Afghanistan to Kuwait without having seen combat, but warfare soon followed him. Saddam Hussein invaded the small, oil-rich country in 1990, throwing the Middle East into chaos. Saddam was defeated by a coalition of Western and Arab countries, which Saddam tried to divide by raining Scud missiles on Israel. He hoped to provoke an Israeli counter-attack that would engender sympathy for Iraq among Arab populations. The Palestine Liberation Organization (PLO) supported those Iraqi strikes during the war, which inspired Kuwait to expel some 250,000 Palestinian guest workers from Kuwait after the war. Among them was Maqdisi,[19] who left Kuwait for Jordan in 1992 with a chip on his shoulder, a radical vision of ji-hadi revolution, and a small collection of hand grenades.

Zarqawi returned to Jordan from Afghanistan in 1993, and with Maqdisi quickly founded a militant group called Bayt al-Imam (Allegiance to the Imam).[20] It was an extraordinary moment in Jordan, with the first national election in years around the corner and the prospect that Jordan might sign a historic peace deal with Israel. These developments created opportunities for jihadis opposed to both democracy and Israel, but Zarqawi and Maqdisi were unprepared for the cat-and-mouse game of urban terror.[21] Bayt al-Imam tried several ill-fated attacks, but Jordanian authorities swooped in after members attacked a Jordanian border crossing with Israel, likely in an effort to torpedo the ongoing peace negotiations.[22] Both Zarqawi and Maqdisi were convicted on terrorism charges and sent to prison.

Not surprisingly for men with such different temperaments, the two had very different reactions to prison. Maqdisi found confinement diffi-cult, but it was the best thing that ever happened to Zarqawi.

The jihadis in Jordan's al-Jafr prison initially selected Maqdisi as their emir, but his intellectualism was ill-suited for prison life. Maqdisi was a hard-liner on paper but a negotiator in person, and the other jihadis were quickly disillusioned by his accommodating stance toward the prison guards. Mean-while, Zarqawi swaggered around the prison yard "like a peacock," giving and receiving beatings that bolstered his credibility with other prisoners. The former street thug soon replaced Maqdisi as the jihadis' chosen leader.[23]

Zarqawi also confronted his personal demons, including the tattoo of an anchor running up his forearm that testified to a sacrilegious youth of petty crime, alcohol, and prostitutes. Zarqawi's ideological vision was still undefined, but his conviction was deep and he was a man of action. Convinced that his tattoos were un-Islamic, Zarqawi used a razor blade smuggled into the prison by a relative to painstakingly scrape off layer after layer of skin until the anchor was gone.[24] When a doctor expressed horror at this mutilation, Zarqawi responded with understated conviction, "Tattoos are *haram*. Forbidden."[25] For Zarqawi, a man who did not practice what he preached must not actually believe what he said.

Jordan's King Hussein died in 1999, bringing his son King Abdullah II into power. One of Abdullah's first steps was to declare a broad amnesty for political prisoners in an effort to placate Jordan's Islamist opposition. The tactic was not new, either in Jordan or elsewhere in the Middle East, particularly during leadership transitions. When Syrian President Hafez al-Assad died in 2000, his son, Bashar al-Assad, offered a similar amnesty to opposition leaders.[26] Both decisions were celebrated by human rights organizations because many prisoners had been held without trial, but both would also contribute to the ultimate development of the Islamic State.

In Jordan, Zarqawi and Maqdisi went free.

Once out of prison, Maqdisi and Zarqawi's alliance withered. Maqdisi settled into a vocal, but generally peaceful, role criticizing the Jordanian monarchy; Zarqawi was looking for war. Zarqawi was not picky about where to fight, but like many Jordanian jihadis he was attracted to the Chechen revolt against Russia, at the time the most active jihadi front in the world. To get to Chechnya, however, he needed to link up with other jihadis and get the right set of introductions. That meant returning to Afghanistan and Pakistan.

The Jordanian General Intelligence Directorate (GID) questioned Zarqawi and two compatriots, Khalid al-Aruri and Abd al-Hadi Daghlas, as they were leaving the country, but the Directorate did not try to stop them.[27] The trio was also interrogated by Pakistani intelligence when they arrived (GID had tipped off the Pakistanis) and told to leave the country immediately, which they did.[28] Zarqawi and his partners crossed into Afghanistan and arrived in Kandahar—ground zero for the global jihadi movement—in December 1999.

Jund al-Sham

Zarqawi arrived in Afghanistan at a critical, and contentious, moment for the global jihadi movement. In the years before 9/11, fourteen jihadi groups operated under the Taliban's protection in Afghanistan, but they disagreed widely on strategy and ideology. All wanted to implement shariah (God's law) and ultimately to rebuild a transnational caliphate that would unite Muslims globally under a single political authority. But they did not agree what shariah meant in practice or what the optimal strategy for establishing the caliphate might be. The jihadis shared a sense of history and a rough vision of the future, but the evolution of jihadi groups in the 20th century had led them to very different ideological and strategic perspectives. These disagreements and personal power plays among the jihadis in Afghanistan were critically important to Zarqawi because other jihadis considered him a potentially useful ally in their intramural squabbles, which allowed the young Jordanian to quickly ascend into the jihadi elite.

Most of the jihadis in Afghanistan considered themselves salafis, which meant that they aimed to practice Islam as they understood it to be observed by the contemporaries and immediate successors of the Prophet Muhammad. The jihadis celebrated a literalist interpretation of seventh century Islamic practice and dismissed all intervening history and religious evolution. They believed that the political and military strength of early Muslim societies was inherently tied to the practice of Islam by those societies. For the salafi jihadis, the political strength of early Muslims was evidence not just of smart political and military leadership, but divine approval for their practice of Islam.

The salafi-jihadis gathered in Afghanistan came from the Sunni sect of Islam, rather than the Shia branch. The theological difference between Sunni and Shia Muslims dates to a disagreement over who would succeed Muhammad after he died in AD 632. Muhammad's close supporters selected Abu Bakr, the prophet's close friend and advisor, to succeed him and serve as the first caliph. According to Sunnis, this collaborative process

reflected God's will, but another group argued that Muhammad had selected his cousin and son-in-law, Ali, as successor (and have more generally argued that the prophet's successors should descend from Ali's line).
Ali's supporters rejected Abu Bakr's leadership, which is why sectarian
jihadis today call the Shia *rafidah*, or rejectionists. This disagreement was
briefly resolved when Ali was named the fourth caliph by consensus,
which temporarily unified much of the Muslim community. That comity
collapsed, however, when Ali was assassinated by a radical faction known
as *kharijites*, who were incensed by Ali's magnanimous effort to negotiate
with his remaining rivals.

Many, but not all, modern jihadis view Shia Muslims as deviants or
apostates, though they disagree strongly over whether, when, and how to
use violence against them. At the same time, sectarian dynamics often
take on a geopolitical hue in the Middle East, especially because Sunni-
dominated Saudi Arabia and Shia-dominated Iran compete for regional
and global influence.

Partially because many jihadis despise the Shia, they harken to a time
when the Muslim community was relatively unified, during the reign of
the first four caliphs, culminating with Ali. During this period, Muslim
rule expanded from the Arabian deserts north and east to Anatolia, Persia,
and the Levant; and west across North Africa. Ali's assassination in AD
661 gave rise to the Umayyad Caliphate, which was based in Damascus.
The Umayyad reign only lasted for 100 years or so, but it too saw a dramatic
expansion of Muslim rule into southern Spain and east into South Asia.
The Umayyad Caliphate gave way to the Abassid Caliphate in the eighth
century, which ruled for 500 years from a capital in Baghdad. The Abassid
Caliphate eventually suffered territorial losses, but it governed over an explosion of art, science, and literature that was unmatched anywhere in the
world at the time. After the Mongol Empire captured Baghdad in 1258, the
caliphate's seat moved to Cairo until the Ottoman Empire captured Cairo
and the caliphate's seat shifted to present-day Istanbul. The Ottoman Sultans
claimed the title of caliph until 1924 when Kemal Ataturk announced the dissolution of the Ottoman Caliphate and the founding of modern Turkey.

For many Muslims in the Middle East, the secularization of Turkey reflected a broader shift in global power and authority away from Muslims

and toward European, and Christian, societies. The post-World War I accommodation between the British and French divided the modern Middle East into European spheres of influence that left many Muslims disempowered, frustrated, and angry. In 1928, the Muslim Brotherhood was founded in Egypt to rectify this perceived problem. The Brotherhood called for rebuilding the caliphate but focused its energy on introducing Islamic principles into government through national-level organizations.

While the Brotherhood embraced modern governance structures so long as they imposed the Brotherhood's version of Islamic values, another political Islamist movement came to power in Arabia. The Saud family unified the warring tribes of Arabia and established modern Saudi Arabia in 1932, and it did so with the backing of salafi religious preachers that followed the teaching of Muhammad ibn Abd al-Wahhab, an 18th-century salafi thinker who advocated a return to seventh-century social norms. The so-called Wahhabis rejected the modern outlook of the Brotherhood and its willingness to work collaboratively in modern government structures. Wahhabis have dominated Saudi culture and society ever since.

The modern jihadi movement borrows from both the Muslim Brotherhood and the Wahhabi movement, but it did not fully emerge until the Soviet Union's invasion of Afghanistan in 1979. The year 1979 was an extraordinarily tumultuous moment in the Middle East.[29] The Islamic Revolution in Iran brought a theological Shia government to power, which simultaneously frightened and inspired Sunni Islamists that longed for control of state infrastructure. At the same time, a proto-jihadi Bedouin movement briefly captured the Grand Mosque in Mecca, where it flouted both the Saudi government and the Wahhabi clerical establishment that supported it. For these would-be revolutionaries, the corruption and excess of the oil-rich Saudi royal family—and the Wahhabi establishment's support for it—betrayed the religious principles they ostensibly defended. The Soviet invasion of Afghanistan in December 1979 offered an outlet for this revolutionary energy.

Islamist scholars, most notably the aforementioned Abdallah Azzam, called on young Muslims from all over the world to support their Muslim brothers and sisters in Afghanistan against the foreign invaders. Many governments in the Middle East were eager to support the jihad, inspired by the Soviet geopolitical threat, their own sense of religious obligation, and a desire to export the most radical elements of their own societies to a fight far away. The United States, which was pilloried as a land of moral depravity by the jihadis, supported the fight in Afghanistan for geopolitical reasons.

Up to 20,000 foreign fighters (but probably closer to 10,000) joined the jihad against the Soviet Union and its proxies in Afghanistan.[30] When the Soviet Union withdrew in 1989, many simply went home to peaceful lives, but significant numbers did not. These fighters had gained useful military skills, felt empowered by defeating a superpower, and had built relationships with similarly minded fighters from all over the world. Their collective experience fighting as Muslims in the same struggle gave credence to the notion of rebuilding the caliphate, but most of these fighters were drawn back to local fights in their home countries. The vast majority of foreign fighters in Afghanistan hailed from countries with oppressive governments led by corrupt ruling cadres. Many of these governments claimed to rule according to Islamic principles, but the jihadis argued they had been corrupted by power and Western influence. Unsurprisingly, most of the militant jihadi groups that emerged after the Afghan jihad focused first on overthrowing these crooked local regimes, often called the "near enemy." For them, the effort to unite under the caliphate would come later.

Al-Qaeda was different. Founded in 1988, just as the Soviets were withdrawing from Afghanistan, it was initially conceived as a sort of Special Forces brigade to train and support jihadi groups intent on attacking the "near enemy." As time went on, however, bin Laden came to believe that governments buttressed by the United States would never be overthrown. As a result, al-Qaeda's strategic priority shifted toward dramatic terrorist attacks against the United States and the West, known as the "far enemy." The primary strategic purpose of these strikes was to compel the United States not to support the local governments, leaving them susceptible to overthrow by jihadis.[31]

Al-Qaeda's strategy was not widely embraced by other jihadis.[32] Most still believed that the "near enemy" should be the primary target of violence. Only five of the fourteen groups operating in Afghanistan signed on to al-Qaeda's declaration of war against the United States in 1998.

Al-Qaeda's focus on the "far enemy" was a distraction that might unnecessarily create a powerful enemy. Moreover, provoking the United States might put their safe haven in Afghanistan at risk. When al-Qaeda attacked two U.S. embassies in East Africa in August 1998, the United States responded with cruise missiles in both Sudan and Afghanistan. The United States' response elevated bin Laden's fame among jihadis, but the Taliban regime and many of the other jihadis were deeply concerned.[33]

The foreign jihadis in Afghanistan were split on where to prioritize their attacks, and equally divided over their Taliban hosts. On one end of the spectrum were hardcore salafis who believed that Taliban support for Afghan cultural practices, such as decorating graves, constituted apostasy.[34] They were similarly critical of the Taliban's engagement with foreign regimes, including Pakistan and Saudi Arabia. Some of these salafi leaders, including an Egyptian sheikh named Abu Abdallah al-Muhajir who led a research institute near the Khalden training camp in Afghanistan's far east, even opposed Arab jihadis fighting for the Taliban. Bin Laden and al-Qaeda did not go that far—and actively supported military operations with the Taliban. But al-Qaeda did disregard Taliban priorities by conducting attacks on the United States that risked an American backlash that would threaten Taliban rule. At the other end of the spectrum were jihadis who supported the Taliban vociferously. Abu Mus'ab al-Suri, a polyglot Syrian who worked on-and-off with al-Qaeda, and was a veteran of the seminal jihadi uprising against Syrian President Hafez al-Assad in the 1970s and 1980s, thought the Taliban deserved strong support and deference as the only true "Islamic" government in the world.[35]

Although al-Suri and bin Laden agreed on certain principles—including Arabs fighting with the Taliban—al-Suri eventually became one of bin Laden's most important jihadi critics prior to 9/11. Al-Suri had lived in Europe, and led his own small training camp north of Kabul focused primarily on urban fighting.[36] Al-Suri arranged bin Laden's first television interview in 1997, but seemed to regret it after al-Qaeda's 1998 attack on American embassies in East Africa.[37] In a 1999 letter, he and Abu Khaled al-Suri, his longtime friend and collaborator, argued to bin Laden that al-Qaeda was alienating the Taliban. "Our brother has caught the disease of screens, flashes, fans and applause," they wrote, and urged bin Laden to "apologize for any inconvenience" he had created for the rulers of Afghanistan.[38]

Al-Suri was wary of al-Qaeda's elitism and corporate structure. Contrary to bin Laden, who built al-Qaeda into a formal bureaucracy that relied heavily on formal procedures, including expense reports, pay scales, and the like, al-Suri sought to reframe the global jihad as a social movement of loosely connected, radicalized individuals. He grasped the power of the Internet early on to connect widely dispersed individuals and thought that the best way to counter the superior resources of nation-states was a globally distributed social movement. This was not what bin Laden, whose organizational skills made him an increasingly prominent figure among Arab jihadis in Afghanistan, wanted to hear.

Al-Suri's criticism was problematic for bin Laden, but it was not a crisis until he began maneuvering to build his own competing base of support, both within the Taliban regime and among jihadis in Afghanistan. As a strong supporter of the Taliban, al-Suri wanted to control the Arab contingent fighting with Taliban troops north of Kabul, and he wanted to serve as a central coordinating point for new jihadi volunteers from the Levant, a geographic designation corresponding to Jordan, Syria, Lebanon, the Palestinian Territories, and Israel. Some in al-Qaeda worried that he was a threat to their increasingly preeminent role among jihadis in Afghanistan.[39] As one careful jihadi observer put it, al-Suri was effectively saying to bin Laden, "You are not alone in Afghanistan, you are not the only option here. I am here."[40]

Al-Qaeda's concern about al-Suri informed the group's initial engagement with Zarqawi. Abd al-Hadi al-Iraqi, who managed al-Qaeda's guesthouse in Kabul, was on the frontlines of this dispute. One of the few Iraqi members of al-Qaeda at the time, he had a reputation for sociability, but was apoplectic when he came to suspect that al-Suri was trying to poach Syrian fighters from the guesthouse.[41] In an era when reliable recruits were hard to come by, this was considered a major offense. Abd al-Hadi banned al-Suri from the facility and scribbled off a report to his boss, al-Qaeda's military chief, Abu Hafs al-Masri.[42] Other senior al-Qaeda leaders quickly got involved as well, including Sayf al-Adl, the group's feared security chief, who other jihadis remembered was, "very much against Abu Mus'ab al-Suri."[43]

Concerned about a violent clash that would force the Taliban to mediate, in March 1999 Abu Hafs ordered Abd al-Hadi to "assure the brethren" in Kabul that al-Qaeda aimed to de-escalate the conflict with al-Suri.[44] Abd al-Hadi and other al-Qaeda members were to "avoid the brother" and "avoid back and forth dialogue." Instead, Abd al-Hadi was directed to work closely with al-Qaeda's allies and keep them calm.[45] Meanwhile, Abu Hafs took a meeting with al-Suri that assuaged the immediate crisis. In April 1999, he reported to Abd al-Hadi that the situation was settling down. "The brother requests coordination and cooperation," Abu Hafs assured Abd al-Hadi. Al-Qaeda aimed to avoid a clash, and al-Suri "is in agreement with us."[46] Al-Suri also came away from the meeting mollified that whatever "mistreatment" he had suffered, bin Laden had not ordered it.

But even as Abu Hafs mollified al-Suri, al-Qaeda was simultaneously working to undermine him. In early 1999, al-Suri's longtime compatriot Abu Khaled al-Suri quietly reached out to Abu Hafs looking for assistance. Abu Khaled had a distinguished jihadi resume of his own, having been active since the 1970s and serving as a jihadi point man in Istanbul during the early 1990s, where he shuffled jihadis into and out of the seething war zone of Chechnya.[47] Despite his loyalty to al-Suri—the two had been close allies for decades—Abu Khaled needed al-Qaeda's help.[48] His beloved wife fell ill and he hoped that Abu Hafs would "help regarding his travel" to see to her care. For al-Qaeda, it was an opportunity not to be missed. "We helped," Abu Hafs crowed to Abd al-Hadi in March 1999, "and, as far as I know, [Abu Khaled] has abandoned [al-Suri]."[49]

Abu Hafs overstated Abu Khaled's shift, but al-Qaeda's investment in Abu Khaled did eventually pay dividends. Fifteen years later, when bin Laden and Abu Hafs were dead and al-Suri and Abd al-Hadi were in prison on opposite ends of the world, al-Qaeda's new emir, Ayman al-Zawahiri, would appoint Abu Khaled his personal representative in the Syrian civil war.[50]

Turning Abu Khaled was not al-Qaeda's only effort to undermine al-Suri. Al-Qaeda's security chief, Sayf al-Adl, wanted to directly undermine his effort to control jihadis from the Levant.

And that is where Abu Mus'ab al-Zarqawi, the young jihadi from Jordan, came in.

As Zarqawi arrived in Kandahar in December 1999, the Levantine jihadi network was in crisis, and many young Syrian and Lebanese fighters were headed to Afghanistan. Al-Adl seems to have worried they would align with al-Suri, who was one of the few senior Levantine jihadis in Afghanistan. It was a geography where al-Qaeda was historically weak. When Zarqawi arrived in Kandahar, al-Adl seems to have identified an opportunity to kill two birds with one stone. A productive relationship with Zarqawi would allow al-Qaeda to strengthen the jihadi networks in the Levant and sideline al-Suri at the same time.[51] As al-Adl's father-in-law put it, al-Qaeda's embrace of Zarqawi was a rejoinder to al-Suri: "[al-Qaeda] went to [the Levant] with Abu Mus'ab al-Zarqawi, and said to Abu Mus'ab al-Suri, 'We are here, it is not only you.' "[52]

The Levantine jihadi movement was in crisis partially because of an old acquaintance of Zarqawi's. During his first trip to Afghanistan in the late 1980s, Zarqawi met four men who would spend much of the ensuing decade working for the same taxi company in Boston, Massachusetts.[53] The most visionary of the four was Bassam al-Kanj.

As Zarqawi settled into Kandahar, Kanj was prepping for war against the Syrian Army, which was the de facto military authority in Lebanon in 1999. Kanj had built a jihadi force in Dinniyah, near the northern Lebanese city of Tripoli, and envisioned a trans-Levantine uprising that would destroy both the Lebanese and Syrian governments.[54] "In Lebanon, a community can never dominate the others completely and take exclusive power," explained one contemporary salafi leader in Lebanon. "If we want to think about change, we must think on the regional scale, at the level of geographical Greater Syria. Change is only possible at that level."[55]

Visionary does not always mean successful, however. Despite support from international jihadi networks, Kanj's uprising was crushed in the first week of January 2000.[56] Kanj was killed and his supporters across Lebanon and Syria scattered.[57] One of the Boston cab drivers was arrested in Syria and extradited to Jordan where he was charged alongside Zarqawi with conspiring to blow up a series of Western hotels on January 1, 2000.

But many of Kanj's other supporters escaped, including a prominent Syrian logistician named Luai Sakka.[58]

Zarqawi arrived in Kandahar at the perfect moment. Al-Qaeda aimed to sideline al-Suri, and a range of Levantine jihadi veterans were about to flee to Afghanistan looking for a new organizational home.

The Dinniyah failure and al-Qaeda's spat with al-Suri was the backdrop for al-Qaeda's engagement with Zarqawi, but getting to "yes" with the young Jordanian would not be easy. Zarqawi was significantly more radical than bin Laden.[59] Zarqawi opposed Arab jihadis fighting with the Taliban, was deeply sectarian, and thought al-Qaeda had been too slow to disavow the Saudi ruling family.[60]

Zarqawi's extremism and independent streak worried al-Adl, but it was not all bad. He reasoned that al-Qaeda "had disagreements" with many groups that it engaged and Zarqawi's radicalism made him less likely to work with al-Suri, a relative ideological moderate.[61] Al-Adl prepared to meet Zarqawi by reading up on him in *al-Minhaj*, a London-based jihadi magazine that had covered his trial and conviction in Jordan.[62] And he brought another jihadi hard-liner—a former member of the Egyptian Islamic Group who was "not in full agreement with other Sheikhs"—to their first meeting.[63] The message was clear: all sorts of jihadis worked with al-Qaeda, and they did not need to have a completely shared vision.[64]

Indeed, al-Qaeda and Zarqawi did not develop a combined strategic concept until Zarqawi swore allegiance to bin Laden in late 2004. Only then did al-Adl and Zarqawi allies conceive a joint, seven-stage master plan to reestablish the caliphate in Syria between 2013 and 2016. The world would change much by then. The United States would invade Iraq and Zarqawi would emerge as one of the world's most notorious terrorists.

By design or luck, the master plan got a lot right—the Islamic State declared the caliphate resurrected in Syria in 2014—but it was far from perfect. Something else had changed between al-Adl and Zarqawi's first meeting and the time that the master plan was drafted. Zarqawi had developed a much more coherent and forceful worldview, built from the ideas of people like Abu Abdallah al-Muhajir, one of the most radical of Afghanistan's jihadi preachers. It was raw, brutal, violent, and divisive, even among the already fractious jihadis. After his death, Zarqawiism would become the dominant strain of jihadi thought in the world. So even as Zarqawi's descendants in the Islamic State met the most important milestone of the master plan, they found themselves at war not just with local regimes and the United States, but with al-Qaeda as well.

There were hints of this conflict-ridden future in al-Adl's remembrance of Zarqawi's initial meeting with al-Qaeda's leadership, which was authored in 2004 while he was under house arrest in Iran. According to al-Adl, Zarqawi met with bin Laden and Ayman al-Zawahiri, his eventual deputy, but the two sides were so immediately antagonistic that he was required to do some shuttle diplomacy to smooth things over.[65] Over time, al-Adl explained, he was able to negotiate a deal.

Al-Adl's story has been repeated in virtually every journalistic or academic retelling of Zarqawi's engagement with al-Qaeda. But it should not be taken at face value. After all, there is one significant dissenter to this version of events: Osama bin Laden himself.

In a private 2010 letter, bin Laden argued that al-Adl's history had been manipulated by Iranian intelligence. After all, al-Adl had been under house arrest in Iran when he wrote it. Bin Laden alleged that al-Adl's story unfairly defamed Zarqawi and had been designed that way by Iran to undermine the Jordanian. Bin Laden noted inconsistencies in al-Adl's story, most notably the claim that Zarqawi met initially with bin Laden and Ayman al-Zawahiri. Although Zawahiri went on to be bin Laden's deputy and successor, bin Laden accurately noted that al-Qaeda had not yet merged with Zawahiri's organization at the time of the negotiation with Zarqawi. According to bin Laden, Zawahiri would therefore not have been present. Per bin Laden, his second in those meetings would have been Abu Hafs al-Masri, al-Qaeda's military chief.[66] Abu Hafs' prominent role managing al-Qaeda's crisis with al-Suri lends credence to this assertion.

The truth is hard to discern, but it is worth noting that al-Adl's and bin Laden's versions are both subtly self-serving. Al-Adl's exalts his own diplomatic skills by highlighting the undeniable differences between bin Laden, descended from a wealthy Saudi family, and Zarqawi, the street thug from Zarqa. Bin Laden's explanation, however, coming after Zarqawi had emerged as a legendary figure in his own right, downplayed the two men's undeniable differences.

There is no dispute about the ultimate arrangement between al-Qaeda and Zarqawi. Al-Qaeda would arrange start-up money for Zarqawi to build a camp near Herat, along the Iranian border, and provide logistical support through a network of safe houses in the Iranian cities of Tehran and Mashaad. Zarqawi would not join al-Qaeda, but he would complete a special training program at al-Qaeda's facilities near Kandahar.[67] Subsequently, he would provide al-Adl with monthly updates on his progress.

Lastly, al-Qaeda would intercede with the Taliban to ensure Zarqawi would not "face obstacles"—a subtle nod to both Zarqawi's belief that the Taliban were insufficiently Islamic, and a Taliban decision to close jihadi training camps that fostered the most extremist jihadi ideas.[68] Indeed, selecting Herat for Zarqawi's camp was probably designed to manage relations with the Taliban. Mullah Jihadwal, the powerful deputy governor there, was one of the few senior Taliban that had left Afghanistan for jihad elsewhere and was therefore more in tune with the foreign jihadis than most Taliban.[69]

Zarqawi got the better end of the negotiation with al-Qaeda. He received institutional and financial support from the world's most prominent jihadi group while keeping his independence intact.[70] Some reports suggest bin Laden requested that Zarqawi swear allegiance five times, but Zarqawi never did so.[71] For its part, al-Qaeda did succeed in catalyzing a new generation of jihadi militants focused on the Levant—Zarqawi's organization was named Jund al-Sham, or Soldiers of the Levant—and it ensured that those fighters would not rally under al-Suri.[72] Al-Suri and Zarqawi did know each other in Afghanistan, but Zarqawi was never interested in allying with the older Syrian.[73] Zarqawi aimed to lead, not to follow.

Zarqawi's first two recruits at the Herat camp were neither from Jordan, his home country, nor from Iraq, where he would make his name. Rather, they were Syrian, where the Islamic State would one day explode. The first was Sulayman Khalid Darwish (known as Abu Ghadiyah), who would manage the first generation of jihadi logistical networks that moved foreign fighters through Syria to Zarqawi's eventual insurgency in Iraq. The other was Luai Sakka, who had been chased out of Syria following Assad's crackdown on jihadis after Bassam al-Kanj's Dinniyah uprising.

Sakka was born into a Kurdish family from Turkey that had resettled in Aleppo, Syria. A swashbuckling figure by jihadi standards, the erratic

Sakka was a linchpin of the jihadi networks crisscrossing Turkey, Syria, Lebanon, and Iraq.[74] He helped move fighters in and out of Chechnya prior to 9/11, spent months in Germany in late 2000 and early 2001, and claimed that he had helped train the 9/11 hijackers.[75] After his eventual arrest in 2005, Sakka bragged about a whiskey habit to investigators.[76] Sakka's claims were often too outlandish to be taken at face value, but he was well connected and became a critical asset for Zarqawi's nascent movement.

Sakka and Darwish started a trend. When al-Adl journeyed to Zarqawi's Herat camp for the first time, he was pleased to find, "42 men, women, and children."[77] Three Syrian families had just arrived, al-Adl gleefully recounted, including one from Europe (probably Germany).

Zarqawi did not recruit all of the Levantine jihadis in Afghanistan—and sometimes those early allegiances had fateful consequences. A Syrian recruit named Abu Hammam al-Suri pledged *bayah* to bin Laden with a handshake in 1999.[78] He was a skilled prospect; Abu Hammam graduated second in his class at the al-Faruq training camp and was subsequently appointed commander of the Kandahar airport. Fifteen years later, Abu Hammam was still fighting for al-Qaeda; by then, he was back home in Syria, at war with Zarqawi's intellectual descendants in the Islamic State.

Al-Qaeda's financial support to Zarqawi was useful, but its logistical assistance was invaluable. Herat sits very near the Iranian border, which immediately emerged as the most useful vector for new recruits to enter Afghanistan. But if Zarqawi looked at the Taliban askance, he despised the Shia government in Iran. Iran's intelligence service no doubt understood Zarqawi's sectarian disposition, but they also had a policy of tolerating jihadis transiting their territory, especially if those fighters were hostile to the Taliban.[79] In 1998, the Taliban executed eight Iranian diplomats, which prompted Tehran to give Gulbuddin Hekmatyar, a legendary Afghan fighter and opponent of the Taliban, extensive latitude to set up shop on Iranian territory.[80] Sayf al-Adl was quick to capitalize on those networks for use by al-Qaeda and he offered them to Zarqawi.

Al-Adl also reached out to the Egyptian Islamic Group (EIG), which had a better relationship with Tehran than any other jihadi group.[81] The EIG was routed from Egypt in 1997 after massacring dozens of tourists at the Luxor temple complex. "The Egyptian Islamic Group was on better terms [than other jihadis] with the Khomeini government of Iran," wrote Abu Mus'ab al-Suri. "It praised the Iranian Revolution and its ideology . . . [which] gave EIG a safe haven from the crackdown they were experiencing everywhere else."[82]

In 1998, the EIG's leadership "held more than ten meetings to discuss strategic matters" in Tehran and ultimately decided on two courses of action.[83] First, they would sign al-Qaeda's seminal declaration of "War Against Jews and Crusaders," which effectively meant declaring war against the United States.[84] Second, the EIG would send Muhammad Khalil al-Hakaymah—a mid-level operative who had been working for the Voice of Palestine Radio in Tehran—to London with the mission of reviving EIG's propaganda capability.[85] In the meantime, EIG's relationships in Iran were at al-Adl's disposal, and, by extension, Zarqawi's.

Hakaymah was still in London on 9/11, but after seeing the carnage in the United States decided immediately to return to Afghanistan. To get there, like so many Zarqawi supporters before him, he would travel across Iran. His story of doing so is the best insider jihadi tale of Iranian complicity with jihadi transit during this period.

Hakaymah's heart pounded—"he felt [as if] he was conducting a jihadist operation"—as he approached the security checkpoint at Heathrow Airport with his wife and ten children. In the weeks after 9/11, they were traveling on three forged passports from London to Iran, and he was terrified.[86] In the end, though, they were waved through.

After landing in Tehran, Hakaymah contacted Hekmatyar's network, members of which arranged for him to travel to the Iranian border near Afghanistan's Nimroz province. The journey was smooth until his family was arrested by Iranian intelligence along the border.[87] As Hakaymah put it:

[The Iranians] were most interested in Sheikh Hekmatyar's role in smuggling people across the border. At the time, the United States was putting pressure on Iran to close down [Hekmatyar's] operations because [he] had declared jihad and urged [his] followers in Afghanistan to resist the Americans.[88]

Despite his conflict with the Taliban, Hekmatyar opposed the U.S. counterattack to 9/11, and his networks in Iran had garnered U.S. attention as a result. Despite the United States' queries, Hakaymah's confinement was not particularly trying. He and his family were held for a week in a hotel near the border—and then, one morning, the guards simply disappeared.

Hakaymah did not stop to reason why. Instead, he arranged for his family to stay in an Iranian Sunni town and contacted a smuggler. A few days later Hakaymah was trotting along amidst a crowd of gasoline-laden donkeys into Afghanistan.[89]

Hakaymah was eventually united with Zarqawi and al-Adl at the fateful Kandahar meeting where Zarqawi was almost killed in a United States' airstrike, but that was just the beginning of their journey together. In the following weeks, Mullah Omar sounded a general retreat from Kandahar and announced that Arab jihadis would leave Afghanistan before sunrise the following morning. Before dawn broke the next day, Hakaymah, Zarqawi, and twenty-two other senior jihadis—al-Adl was notably absent—boarded the same bus for Pakistan. They almost certainly paid a bribe at the border—guards were charging $100 or more per Arab they let into the country.[90] After crossing the border, Hakaymah, Zarqawi, and the other jihadis split into groups of four, each accompanied by a Taliban guide. Using public buses to escape detection, the world's most dangerous men scattered to safe houses across Quetta, Pakistan.

Two months later, Zarqawi and Hakaymah moved again. In early 2002, Hakaymah arranged for smugglers to move both of them across the Pakistani border into Iran. Zarqawi, Hakaymah remembered, was already "planning to find a way to get his group into Iraq," but the decision was apparently not final until the Jordanian conferred with Sayf al-Adl, who was already settled into an Iranian safe house.[91] Al-Adl was convinced that the United States would invade Iraq and thought that if Saddam's government collapsed, the jihadis could dramatically expand their presence in the heart of the Arab world.

Al-Adl and Zarqawi did not have long to deliberate. The Iranian regime, facing intense pressure from the United States, began arresting jihadis in April 2002, including Zarqawi's longtime friend and confidant, Khalid al-Aruri.[92] Some jihadis, including al-Adl, remained free for a time.[93] The rest, including Zarqawi, scattered.[94]

Writing with the hindsight of Iraq's collapse into chaos, but long before the Syrian civil war began, al-Adl explained the opportunity Zarqawi hoped to seize:

> The security mess that resulted from the collapse of Saddam Hussein's regime provided a good opportunity for the jihadist action to spread in the Iraqi arena . . . Syria and Lebanon will likely face similar circumstances. If they do, that will give the Islamic [groups] a vast area of action . . . [and] provide an opportunity to establish a united Islamic army capable of achieving consecutive victories that will win it major credibility. New leadership for the Islamic nation will emerge that can utilize the capabilities of the nation on the path of blessed jihad. Jihad will enable these leaders to reestablish the Islamic caliphate in society once again.[95]

Zarqawi was moving to Iraq, but from the get-go, his eyes were on Syria, Lebanon, and Jordan.

The ISIS Footprint

Zarqawi crossed from Iran into Iraq's Kurdish Autonomous Region, an area outside the central government's control. He was welcomed there by a Kurdish jihadi group called Ansar al-Islam, and another vibrant young Jordanian jihadi named Ra'id Khuraysat. This period was critical for Zarqawi—and the future Islamic State. Ansar al-Islam provided Zarqawi a platform to build his network in the Middle East, and also showed Zarqawi what jihadi governance might look like. The group was an early adopter of the video and Internet technology that would one day make Zarqawi famous, and the Islamic State possible.

Meanwhile, Zarqawi and Khuraysat were friendly rivals. Like Zarqawi, Khuraysat followed Abu Muhammad al-Maqdisi's guidance in Jordan and left the country in 1999 aiming for Chechnya. Unlike Zarqawi, he actually made it there. After fighting with the jihadi contingent in Chechnya, Khuraysat arrived in Afghanistan in 2000, where Zarqawi tried to convince him to join the camp in Herat.[96] Instead, Khuraysat traveled on to northern Iraq, where he led a small foreign contingent fighting with Ansar al-Islam.[97] There is little record of Khuraysat's jihad in Kurdistan, but Maqdisi thought it was deeply influential. He even credited Khuraysat with founding Tawhed w'al Jihad, the jihadi organization that Zarqawi eventually came to lead and is usually credited with creating.[98]

The Kurdish jihadi community was fractured but well known to al-Qaeda's leadership in Afghanistan. The largest group was led by Mullah Fatih Krekar, a veteran of the anti-Soviet jihad, but the most internationally focused group was led by Abu Abdallah al-Shafi'i, himself a veteran of Chechnya and Afghanistan's training camps. It is not clear whether al-Shafi'i worked closely with al-Qaeda in Afghanistan, but a jihadi map of the al-Faruq training camp in Afghanistan shows a "Kurds Camp" in it.[99] Al-Shafi'i also had strong ties to the Levant, welcoming Syrian and Lebanese refugees from the Dinniyah uprising and embracing Khuraysat when he arrived.[100]

Ansar al-Islam also dabbled in governance in ways that foreshadowed the Islamic State. In territory the group controlled, it banned praying at graves; ordered shops closed during prayers; decreed that women wear a veil and only leave their homes with a male escort; outlawed any "works and words" that are "un-Islamic"; ordered shops to take down all images of women; prohibited listening to music and possessing musical instruments; and proscribed all foreign media, including television.[101] Fifteen years before the Islamic State shocked the world with videos of beheadings, al-Shafi'i had a reputation for decapitating captives.[102] His Shariah Committee made little effort to justify these practices, explaining that people "liked these rules" and they urged Muslims to "continue the implementation of Islamic Law and to spread this all [over the] world."[103]

The Kurdish jihadis were also at the vanguard of the global communications revolution, adopting the digital tools that would make Zarqawi, and then the Islamic State, global phenomena. The group's website was state-of-the-art by 2001 standards. Although it was a one-way tool for posting statements to be consumed, the site included simple dynamic graphics, was replicated simultaneously in three languages, and included an email address to begin two-way communications.

Despite these innovations, the Internet's technological limitations in 2001 curbed al-Shafi'i's ability to use it for propaganda. Broadband Internet was rare in 2001, which made distributing video and audio files online practically impossible. The workaround seems old-fashioned today: Ansar al-Islam printed videos onto CD for manual distribution across the Middle East. "These CDs were extremely important," explained Mohamed Gharib, an Arabic-speaking Kurd who developed propaganda for the group:

> They were our income source—we sent them back up the cash chain to donors. . . . It's not governments, but people from rich countries, Kuwait, Saudi, and Qatar—rich people who would not dare to take part, but sent support to establish Islamic rule. . . . There were groups claiming [to fight] jihad, but just stealing money. So [the donors] ask: "Where is your product? Where is your fighting?"[104]

Jihadis still videotape operations to inform fundraising. But as Internet technology improved, Zarqawi and his successors learned to distribute this content online. Indeed, the Islamic State's propaganda operation today owes much to this chain of innovation. Al-Shafi'i was not the first jihadi to develop a website, but his example seems to have inspired Zarqawi and led to the Islamic State's contemporary propaganda behemoth.

Shortly after 9/11, al-Shafi'i's group combined with Mullah Krekar's to formally create Ansar al-Islam. Given the outflow of jihadis like Zarqawi from Afghanistan to northern Iraq, the consolidated organization raised questions for American intelligence analysts, especially as the Bush Administration began a push for war in Iraq. To what extent was Ansar al-Islam working with al-Qaeda? And, critically, were Ansar al-Islam and Zarqawi a bridge of sorts between Saddam Hussein and the perpetrators of 9/11?

The Bush Administration famously argued that the answer to both of these questions was "yes," most prominently in a speech by Secretary of State Colin Powell at the United Nations justifying the invasion of Iraq.[105] According to the most belligerent proponents of this argument, an Arab member of Ansar al-Islam's Shariah Committee, Abu Wa'el, was both an Iraqi agent and Ansar al-Islam's true leader. Zarqawi supposedly joined

Ansar al-Islam when he arrived in Iraq, and Ansar al-Islam was reputed to have received hundreds of thousands of dollars from al-Qaeda. According to some analysts, Ansar al-Islam even celebrated that connection to al-Qaeda on its website.[106]

Eventually, this argument was widely and convincingly discredited, but there are important bits of truth in it. Ansar al-Islam likely did receive financial support from al-Qaeda.[107] Correspondence in 2007 between the emir of the Islamic State of Iraq (ISI) and al-Shafi'i indicates that Ansar al-Islam requested funding and that Zawahiri viewed the request favorably.[108] Ansar al-Islam did not, however, celebrate that connection to al-Qaeda.[109] Passages from the group's website reputed to acknowledge a connection to al-Qaeda were clearly intended to be sarcastic:

CLAIM 3- The claim that [Ansar al-Islam] numbers more than 1,000 [people], has all sorts of military material, and was sent $150,000 from Osama bin Laden.

REPLY 3- There are more interesting claims than these, e.g. that [Ansar al-Islam] has ties with Iran, Iraq, Sheikh Osama bin Laden etc. We wonder why they forgot the names of other countries and people that are enemies of America.[110]

The link between Saddam's regime and Ansar al-Islam is also suspect. Abu Wa'el was a onetime Iraqi Special Forces officer, and he eschewed the ideological exclusivity of some Kurdish jihadis, which aligned with claims made by some Kurdish prisoners that he was an intermediary between Baghdad and the jihadis.[111] But the CIA placed less credence in those sources than pro-invasion analysts and ultimately declared that it could not determine whether Abu Wa'el was "informing Baghdad of al-Qa'ida associated activities; acting as a liaison between Baghdad, Ansar al-Islam and al-Qa'ida, or is Baghdad's point of contact for assessing Ansar al-Islam or al-Qa'ida."[112] There is no evidence that Abu Wa'el was ever the leader of Ansar al-Islam.

Abu Wa'el never led Ansar al-Islam, but the group did suffer a coup.[113] In February 2003, Abu Abdallah al-Shafi'i deposed Mullah Krekar, who had spent most of the previous two years in northern Europe and recently appeared on television with secular Kurdish officials, the group's most virulent enemies.[114] He would remain a skeptical ally of the Islamic State's progenitors for the next seven years.

The chaos of Kurdish jihadism created a welcoming environment for Zarqawi, but the Jordanian leader did not stay planted in northern Iraq after he arrived in 2002.[115] That year, Zarqawi was spotted in Damascus and the Palestinian camps of southern Lebanon. And although Jordanian officials deny it, jihadis even claim he snuck back into Jordan to attend his mother's funeral.[116]

This growing regional network was busy. On the morning of October 22, 2002, at precisely 7:00 a.m. local time, two assassins stepped out of a rental car in front of a private home in Amman, Jordan. When they got back in the car, Laurence Foley, the head of the United States Agency for International Development (USAID) in Jordan, lay dead with bullet holes in his chest.[117] Three weeks earlier, Zarqawi had given the assassins $18,000 and a mandate to kill an American. The killers selected Foley based on little more than his predictable schedule.

Although Zarqawi funded the assassination, it was primarily planned in Syria. One of Foley's assassins had begun his career in Syria, where he allied with a Syrian-Palestinian named Shakir al-Absi, who would eventually become a critical ally for Zarqawi. In the 1990s, however, al-Absi led a Syrian government–backed jihadi group attacking Israelis and secular Palestinians.[118] Al-Absi was a critical ally for Zarqawi, both because of his logistics networks in Syria, and because he would go on to found Fatah al-Islam, a seminal Lebanese jihadi group with deep ties to both al-Qaeda and the progenitors of the Islamic State.

Zarqawi's network even reached beyond the Middle East. More than a decade before the Islamic State unleashed terrorist attacks in Europe, the group's godfather was building networks there. Zarqawi's most dangerous one was the so-called Tawhed Group, which formed in 2001 under the leadership of Mohammed Abu Dhess, known as Abu Ali, and operated out of the German city of Essen.[119]

It was Abu Ali that Zarqawi was meeting in Iran in the days before 9/11, and he returned to Germany with orders to attack Jewish or Israeli targets.

The group later focused on nightclubs they believed were owned or frequented by Jews.[120] The attacks, however, never occurred. Abu Ali told Zarqawi that "if you ordered me to die, with God's permission, I would do it," but he also repeatedly delayed executing the plot, to Zarqawi's apparent consternation. German authorities rolled up the entire network in 2002.[121]

Even the Tawhed Group's operational failure suggests that Zarqawi's vision always extended much further than Iraq. After all, he tried to organize a terrorist attack in Europe before he fired a shot in Iraq.

In later years, Western analysts would often argue that Zarqawi was dedicated to the traditional jihadi strategy of attacking the "near enemy" in Iraq, and he certainly did devote most of his resources to that goal. But this choice was a matter of circumstance as much as anything. Prior to the U.S. invasion, Zarqawi was building a regional and global network; after the invasion, both the "near enemy" and "far enemy" were on the ground right in front of him.

One of the unheralded moments that contributed to the ultimate establishment of the Islamic State was Ra'id Khuraysat's death in a firefight with secular Kurdish militiamen in late 2002. His demise removed one of the few potential obstacles to Zarqawi consolidating leadership of the Levantine jihadis in Kurdistan.[122]

Even without Khuraysat, however, Zarqawi was not the only jihadi with extensive international ties to arrive in Iraq. In 2002, two Egyptian fighters with long ties to al-Qaeda's second-in-command, Ayman al-Zawahiri, arrived in Baghdad.[123] One, Abu Hamzah al-Muhajir, would eventually follow Zarqawi as emir of al-Qaeda in Iraq. So did Abu Hammam, the Syrian who swore allegiance to bin Laden with a handshake in Afghanistan. His conversations with Zarqawi and Abu Hamzah in Baghdad must have been brotherly, but fifteen years later, Zarqawi's offspring in the Islamic State would mark Abu Hammam for death.[124]

Meanwhile, Saddam's government took a multilayered approach to the jihadis in their midst. Iraq welcomed some fighters as assets to oppose a potential U.S. invasion, but it cracked down on jihadis it believed posed a threat to the regime or might precipitate the U.S. attack. Iraqi intelligence documents indicate that Saddam put Zarqawi in the latter category.[125] Abu Hammam was put there as well. He was arrested in Baghdad and deported to Syria, where he was promptly released.[126] Saddam was afraid al-Qaeda-linked militants in Baghdad might spur an invasion, but the Assad regime in Syria wanted its homegrown militants fighting and dying outside of Syria.

The U.S. invasion of Iraq began on March 21, 2003, with a decidedly complex operation. Turkey denied the United States use of its airspace, so U.S. Special Operations Forces made a long loop from bases in Europe, south across the Mediterranean Sea, east over Israel and Jordan, and then north over the western desert of Iraq to Kurdistan.[127] They called it Operation Ugly Baby.

When the operators finally arrived in Kurdistan, their target was Ansar al-Islam and the Arab fighters who lived with them. The battle was quick. Tomahawk cruise missiles and laser-guided bombs dropped by F-18s devastated the organization. Ansar al-Islam and its Arab partners scattered, some south to Arab-held Iraq, others across the border to Iran.[128]

Iran did not expel the jihadis immediately, though it did eventually push them back into Iraq. The Iranians' flexibility is unsurprising. After all, many of the al-Qaeda members that fled Afghanistan after 9/11 still operated relatively openly in Iran. Sayf al-Adl was living freely in Shiraz when the United States invaded Iraq. He continued to play a key role in al-Qaeda's broader command structure. In June 2002, al-Adl appointed Abd al-Hadi al-Iraqi as commander for all of northern Afghanistan.[129] And in early March 2003, as U.S. troops were charging through southern Iraq, he drafted detailed guidance to Iraqis on how to confront the United States militarily. He praised the Toyota Corolla, for example, because the "car was quick on flat ground; easily maneuverable in mountainous areas; fast, light, and roomy enough for a four-man crew with their full military gear."[130]

Al-Adl's Iranian captors clearly gave him leeway to remain a productive member of al-Qaeda's leadership, but that did not stop others in al-Qaeda from plotting ways to secure his freedom. In late 2003, Abd al-Hadi—who was quickly moving up the ranks in al-Qaeda—reviewed plans to kidnap Iranian diplomats to trade for the release of al-Qaeda prisoners. This was not a onetime tactic; in the years since, al-Qaeda has repeatedly kidnapped Iranian diplomats for such trades. It goes to show that despite al-Adl's relative freedom, Iran's relationship with al-Qaeda was no alliance. Iran's control of senior al-Qaeda members gave it leverage over the jihadis; al-Qaeda hoped to gain some of its own.[131]

Regardless, al-Adl had plenty of opportunity to think big about al-Qaeda's strategy and the opportunity created by Zarqawi's growing network in Iraq. And in the early years of his captivity, at least, he maintained regular contact with the outside world. The result of these machinations was a master plan to finally integrate the Zarqawiists into al-Qaeda, build a near-term strategy to reestablish the caliphate, and, eventually, secure final victory.

2

The Eye-Opening Stage
(2003–2006)

The eye-opening stage began with the occupation of Baghdad . . .
[and] will take three years. . . . Al-Qaeda plans to directly engage Israel in Palestine . . . prioritize preparation for electronic jihad . . .
[and] take Iraq as a base to build an army of jihad . . . [that] will
redeploy in neighboring countries by the beginning of the third
stage.

    Fuad Husayn, *Zarqawi . . . The Second Generation of al-Qaeda*

Stages, Savagery, and the Snake

On February 2, 2015, the Islamic State released a video showing the public immolation of a Jordanian fighter pilot who had ejected while flying
over Syria. After holding Muath al-Kasasbeh for a few months, the pilot's
captors placed him in a steel cage resting in a puddle of gasoline, and set it
alight. It was raw, medieval, and terrible.

Jordan responded to death with death; King Abdullah II ordered that
two Islamic State linked prisoners, including a woman who had been on
death row for nearly a decade, be killed. Sajida al-Rishawi was given a death
sentence for her role in a November 2005 bombing of Western-owned
hotels in Amman. By executing her, Jordan closed a chapter in the Islamic
State's development that reached all the way back to Zarqawi's initial
campaign of terrorism in Iraq.

After the U.S. invasion of Iraq, Thamir Mubarak and Nidal Arabiyat became two of Zarqawi's most important operatives.[1] They were an odd pair. Arabiyat hailed from a prominent family in the Jordanian city of Salt and had joined Zarqawi in Afghanistan in 1999 before moving to Iraq.[2] Mubarak was one of the first members of Saddam Hussein's former regime to join the foreign jihadis who served as Zarqawi's core shock troops. A former Iraqi Army officer from Fallujah, he embraced salafism after traveling to Saudi Arabia for the Hajj, the holy journey to Mecca that every Muslim is encouraged to take once in his or her life.[3]

At first glance, the partnership between Arabiyat and Mubarak is surprising. The two men came from very different backgrounds that seemed to point to different ideological and political outlooks. But just as the foreign jihadis and Ba'athists in Iraq generally agreed on attacking U.S. troops, Arabiyat and Mubarak worked well together on a personal level. Every partnership is built from human relationships that are more nuanced than any ideological text.

In this case, instead of just thinking of Arabiyat and Mubarak as a historical odd couple or as the beginning of a long process of Iraqi military veterans joining Zarqawi's movement, it is better to think of them as family. Mubarak's full name was Thamir Mubarak Atrous al-Rishawi, and he had two sisters. One married Arabiyat; the other was Sajida al-Rishawi, the woman Jordan executed in 2015 after its pilot was burned alive.[4]

Besides their family ties, Mubarak and Arabiyat were strong operational partners. Mubarak had the planning chops and connections of a former Iraqi officer. Arabiyat had been trained as a bomb maker in Afghanistan.[5] Together, the two men would operationalize Zarqawi's first concerted campaign of violence in Iraq and transform the former thug from Zarqa into a globally despised villain.

As Mubarak and Arabiyat were getting organized in the months after the U.S. invasion of Iraq, Sayf al-Adl was holed up with other al-Qaeda leaders and their families at a safe house in the Iranian city of Shiraz. That changed on April 23, 2003, when Iranian security forces raided the home. Most of the men would become quasi-captives in Iranian protective custody.[6]

The Iranians were professional, explained al-Qaeda's former spokesman Suleiman Abu Ghaith to FBI agents ten years later. The al-Qaeda members were not tortured, beaten, or berated after their arrest. But Iran kept them isolated from the outside world for years.[7] According to Abu Ghaith, "There was no system of passing messages outside of where they were incarcerated."[8]

It was a good story. But, Abu Ghaith was either ignorant or he was lying.

The messages arrived in Jordan on forty-two sheets of yellow, grease-proof paper, each of which had been folded so tightly that it was no larger than a cigarette.[9] Reading these notes required carefully unwrapping the deeply creased paper to decipher the handwriting.[10] Sayf al-Adl had written the notes; the man who received them was a Jordanian journalist named Fuad Husayn, who had been jailed in Jordan alongside Zarqawi and Maqdisi in the 1990s for writing articles critical of the Jordanian monarchy.

While Abu Ghaith languished in a solitary prison cell pining for his wife in Kuwait (who would eventually divorce him), al-Adl lived relatively comfortably under house arrest in an Iranian villa. Al-Adl's old role as al-Qaeda's primary liaison to Iran was paying off.[11] Despite his confinement, al-Adl repeatedly passed messages to al-Qaeda members in Saudi Arabia and Pakistan.[12] The courier of those forty-two yellow sheets was a Palestinian that had been jailed with al-Adl decades earlier in Egypt and had been more recently living in Tehran.[13]

Scribbled on those forty-two pieces of paper were two documents: al-Adl's history of Zarqawi's engagement with al-Qaeda, and the master plan—a visionary effort to incorporate the Zarqawiist movement into al-Qaeda's strategic vision.[14]

Integrating al-Qaeda's long-term strategic framework with Zarqawi's action-oriented, near-term focus was no easy task. The result was a vision to establish the caliphate in Syria and, effectively, control the world by 2020. This timeline was a revelation for al-Qaeda, which had long sought to resurrect the caliphate but on a much more protracted, and intentionally vague, timeline.[15]

It was not the first time al-Adl challenged the received wisdom in al-Qaeda. Al-Adl had been one of several senior al-Qaeda figures to oppose the 9/11 attacks (on grounds that it would undermine the Taliban government).[16] He had lost that argument. But now he aimed to build an airtight case for the new strategy, which meant bridging al-Qaeda's skepticism that Muslim governments could be overthrown quickly and Zarqawi's almost unrestrained aggressiveness. "Drawing up a clear plan is one of the divine laws," al-Adl wrote. "Mujahidin should have near-term plans aimed at interim goals and long-term plans aimed at accomplishing the grand objective, which is the establishment of a state."[17] By "long-term" he meant approximately fifteen years.

The master plan is usually attributed solely to al-Adl, but that is somewhat misleading. Husayn published the scheme in a 2005 book about Zarqawi, and al-Adl was indeed "one of the main sources [from which Husayn] got details about Qaeda's seven-stage plan." The others were people "related to Zarqawi and his group."[18] The master plan is best understood as a joint vision for al-Qaeda once Zarqawi's growing movement in Iraq had joined it.

The seven-stage master plan is not the only "strategic plan" that al-Qaeda has offered over the years, but it reflects the tenuous alliance al-Qaeda and the Zarqawiists developed when they merged in 2004. Although it should not be understood as a formal blueprint for every jihadi behavior, the master plan has proven a remarkably prescient vision of future events, especially the Islamic State's declaration of a caliphate.

In 2005 the master plan called for reestablishing the caliphate in Syria between 2013 and 2016, which is precisely what happened.

The seven stages were:

1. *The Awakening Stage (2000–2003)* began with planning for the 9/11 attacks and was designed to provoke widespread conflict between the West and jihadis by compelling the United States to strike at targets in the Middle East. By initiating direct conflict with the United States, al-Qaeda hoped to draw the world's attention to its mission, which in turn would drive recruitment and intimidate enemies. The Awakening Stage was already complete when the master plan was developed, which suggests that this part of the master plan is a bit revisionist. After all, al-Adl opposed the 9/11 attacks because of the effect they would have on Afghanistan, but the master plan frames the strikes in very positive terms.

2. *The Eye-Opening Stage (2003–2006)* began with the United States'
occupation of Baghdad on April 9, 2003, and it was predicted to
last three years. During this period, al-Qaeda aimed to "prolong
the confrontation" with the United States to illustrate that governments in the Middle East were in league with the United States.
Al-Qaeda would build an army in Iraq while establishing small
affiliated cells across the region. It would also initiate direct strikes
against Israel and establish the human and material infrastructure for "electronic jihad."[19]

3. *The Stage of Standing Upright (2007–2010)* would see jihadis expand their networks from Iraq across Syria into Lebanon, and ultimately be able to strike Israel and Turkey directly. The master plan's
focus on the Levant was a function of its most important strategic
insight: that Syria was uniquely vulnerable to jihadi revolution
because the United States would not support the Assad government if it were attacked. This was important because it meant that
Syria was an exception to al-Qaeda's usual rationale for prioritizing attacks on the United States rather than local governments,
which was to compel the United States to abandon regional governments and leave them vulnerable to overthrow. The master
plan's fundamental strategic insight was that there were certain
countries—Iraq, obviously, and Syria—where the United States
did not need to be severed from the local regime. Moreover, the
plan noted, the Prophet Muhammad had discussed jihad in the
Levant occuring after war in what is present-day Iraq. Identifying
this geopolitical exception to al-Qaeda's basic understanding of
power in the Middle East is what enabled the master plan to respect al-Qaeda's broader strategic framework but promise success
on a timeline that made Zarqawi comfortable.

4. *The Stage of Recuperation (2010–2013)* predicted jihadis would overthrow regimes across the Middle East while targeting the United
States economically. The United States, suffering from years of
war, would become "weak, exhausted, and unable to shoulder the
responsibilities of the current world order."[20] The plan explained,
"Step by step, the raisons d'etre of these regimes will cease to

exist"—an accurate, but not causal, prediction of the Arab Spring. "When the regimes gradually disintegrate, al-Qaeda and the jihadi trend will continue to grow. The constant deterioration of US power will be hastened by expanding the arena of confrontation and maneuvering. The United States will be unable to continue supporting the regimes."[21] According to one of the plan's most conspiratorial calculations, al-Qaeda would reveal during this stage the extent to which Jewish economists were buying gold "and other precious metals" to undermine the value of the dollar. These tensions, the plan predicted, would drive a wedge between the United States and Israel even as the regimes around Israel collapsed.

5. *The Stage of Declaring the State (2013–2016)* predicts that the caliphate will be declared in the Levant between 2013 and 2016. According to the plan, "global weakness among the enemies of jihad"— particularly a British-led reversal of the "rising unity of Europe"— would offer jihadis a prime opportunity "to declare an Islamic State—the Caliphate."[22] Indeed, the caliphate was declared in 2014 right on THE MASTER PLAN's timeline. But by then the alliance it was designed for—between Zarqawiists and al-Qaeda—had crumbled.

6. *The Stage of Absolute Confrontation (2016–2018)* was to begin immediately after the declaration of the caliphate, which in practice occurred in June 2014. According to the master plan, the caliphate's declaration would divide the world into two camps and precipitate an unprecedented "all-out confrontation" between "the forces of faith and the forces of atheism."[23]

7. *The Stage of Final Victory (2018–2020)* is not described in detail, but the core concept is that the world's "more than 1.5 billion Muslims" would rally under a single banner to overthrow remaining "apostate" Muslim regimes and destroy Israel. Meanwhile, the caliphate would show the world "the meaning of real terrorism" in order to "terrify the enemy and make them think a thousand times before attacking Muslims." This stage, according to the plan, would culminate in "final victory"—the destruction of Israel and elimination of Western influence over Muslims—by 2020.

At the time of its publication, the seven-stage master plan received little attention in the West.[24] Even Western journalists who studied the plan were skeptical that jihadis would actually abide by it. Their caution was warranted; most al-Qaeda strategic plans go nowhere. Even today, there is no conclusive evidence that jihadi leaders consulted the master plan in their own decision making, though prominent jihadi theorists did use it as a blueprint to assess al-Qaeda's "progress" in Iraq.[25]

Yet even if the Islamic State's progenitors have not consciously followed the seven stages, the plan is a remarkable forecast. Most importantly, it identified Syria as a geopolitical loophole to al-Qaeda's traditional strategic worldview, which prioritized attacks against the United States in order to sever its support for "near enemy" regimes that the group ultimately aimed to overthrow. The master plan, however, identified that Syria was already uniquely vulnerable to jihadi pressure because the United States would not support the Assad regime. The strategic rationale that led al-Qaeda to focus attacks on the United States did not apply in Syria. It was therefore a shortcut to jihadi state building that did not fundamentally reject the strategic analysis that led al-Qaeda to prioritize attacks against the United States. Even if the accuracy of the master plan's timeline has been more coincidental than causal, the document remains strategically prescient and a powerful representation of the strategic compromise that cemented the alliance between Zarqawi and al-Qaeda. As such, it is also a trenchant framework for understanding the processes that led to the Islamic State's declaration of the caliphate in 2014.

The master plan has proved a strikingly insightful strategic vision, but it did not offer a clear operational blueprint. The master plan established goals and landmarks for measuring progress, but if Zarqawi wanted guidance for putting those principles into action, he needed to look elsewhere. Yet even as al-Adl was smuggling notes on the master plan to Fuad Husayn, another jihadi theorist was focused on the operational steps necessary to establish an Islamic State.

The Management of Savagery, released online in 2004 by an author using the pseudonym Abu Bakr Naji,[26] interprets classic concepts of insurgency and state building for a jihadi audience. It argues that jihadis must

exhaust their enemies through protracted violence, destroy established social and political hierarchies with brutal attacks on military and civilian
targets, and thereby create "areas of savagery" that will allow them to build
"Islamic" political systems when people seek an end to violence. Unlike
the master plan, *The Management of Savagery* discusses operational questions of leadership, training programs, target selection, and, ultimately, the
sort of governance an Islamic State ought to provide.

Its core message, however, is that polarizing society through brutal violence is valuable to mobilize a reticent population:

> By polarization here, I mean dragging the masses into the battle such that
> polarization is created between all of the people. Thus, one group of them
> will go to the side of the people of truth, another group will go to the side
> of the people of falsehood, and a third group will remain neutral, awaiting
> the outcome of the battle in order to join the victor. We must attract the
> sympathy of this group and make it hope for the victory of the people of
> faith, especially since this group has a decisive role in the later stages of
> the present battle.[27]

There is no definitive proof of Abu Bakr Naji's true identity, but several
informed sources indicate he was Muhammad Khalil al-Hakaymah, the
Egyptian jihadi that was almost killed alongside Zarqawi and al-Adl in
Kandahar, and subsequently traveled with Zarqawi from Afghanistan to
Pakistan and then into Iran. Naji's identity was an open question for nearly
a decade after *The Management of Savagery* was published, but no less an
authority than Egyptian Islamic Jihad founder Imam al-Sharif claimed in
2014 that Hakaymah was Naji.[28]

The Management of Savagery has long been considered an influential
text among jihadis, but if Hakaymah was the author it takes on added importance. Just like al-Adl, Hakaymah lived in Iran when the book was
published, and just like al-Adl he had ties with the Iranian government
predating 9/11. Moreover, *The Management of Savagery* was first published
by Mu'askar al-Battar, an al-Qaeda propaganda outlet based in Saudi Arabia that published many of al-Adl's articles during the same period.
Hakaymah also knew Zarqawi personally, having escaped with him from
Afghanistan and Pakistan after 9/11. Taken together, the master plan and

The Management of Savagery offered strategic and operational plans for Zarqawi's war in Iraq and beyond. But these were not documents developed remotely from Zarqawi; they were produced by men that knew him personally and were likely in direct communication with him when they were written.

Still, strategic plans and operational concepts are only as influential as the people implementing them—and Zarqawi's early violence in Iraq, during 2003, often appeared more opportunistic than strategic. By early 2004, however, Zarqawi was negotiating to join al-Qaeda while defining a brutal sectarianism that al-Qaeda had previously eschewed. Indeed, both the master plan and *The Management of Savagery* may be best understood not as documents that drove Zarqawi's behavior, but as efforts by jihadis outside Iraq to codify and contextualize the lessons of Zarqawi's early jihad.[29]

This approach is theoretically anathema to the U.S. military, which has a very top-down operational model. Policy drives strategy, which drives operational questions (like logistics), which in turn drives tactics. Zarqawi's approach turned that model on its head. In reality, doctrine often follows tactical innovation even in the United States military. The famous counterinsurgency manual FM 3-24, which informed United States counterinsurgency strategy in Iraq, was backed by theory while codifying best practices that had been used in Iraq previously. For Zarqawi, the tactical pace in Iraq demanded innovation prior to developing a full-fledged strategic or operational vision. Hakaymah and al-Adl's documents filled that gap.

Baghdad fell to U.S. forces on April 14, 2003, but the Iraqi military was not done fighting. Specialized units from a range of military and intelligence agencies had prepared to fight an insurgency against the United States if the Iraqi government fell.[30] These units hid weapons, stockpiled money, trained in underground warfare, and welcomed foreign fighters, many of which were bused into Iraq from Syria where the government eagerly enabled radicalized youth to leave the country for jihad.[31]

The regime's resistance efforts received a huge boost in May 2003 when the Coalition Provisional Authority—the U.S.-backed governing body of Iraq—dissolved the Iraqi army and decreed that senior-level Ba'athists were banned from serving in the new Iraqi government. Not only did this empty the Iraqi administration of skilled officials, it effectively handed over thousands of trained fighters to the insurgents.

The former regime soldiers sorted themselves into a range of insurgent groups, ranging from explicitly secular Ba'athists to various Islamist dispositions. The two most prominent leaders of the Ba'athists were General Izzat al-Douri, Saddam's deputy in the Iraqi Ba'ath Party, and General Muhammad Younis al-Ahmed. After the U.S. invasion, both operated out of Syria, where they were given safe harbor by the government of Bashar al-Assad.

The regime-linked opposition groups were ideologically diverse in part because of the dualistic nature of the regime during the 1990s. Saddam had instituted the "Faith Campaign," which aimed to imbue Iraq's historically secular Ba'ath Party with a distinctly Iraqi version of Islamic identity. The purpose was to unite Sunni and Shia elements of Iraqi society in opposition to both the revolutionary Shiism of Iran and radical Sunni ideologies, including both Saudi Arabia's official "Wahhabism" and jihadi concepts.[32]

The "Faith Campaign" was led by al-Douri, who would go on to be a leading figure in the Iraqi insurgency—and his connections with Islamic elements of society were extremely useful for wrangling the ideologically motivated incoming fighters.[33] Some of the early foreign fighters in Iraq joined Zarqawi, but in the initial wave more joined militant groups built around former regime officials—some of which eventually emerged as the Islamic State's most virulent enemies. Indeed, even though al-Douri sometimes cooperated with Zarqawi and the Islamic State after the U.S. invasion, he has never been a jihadi by Islamic State standards. As late as 2014, al-Douri was still championing Iraqi nationalism and decrying sectarian divisions in Iraq.[34]

The foreign jihadis, including Zarqawi, engaged many of the former regime groups in the early days of the Iraqi insurgency, but most former regime elements worked with other insurgent networks. The jihadis, after all, were not simply trying to roll back the invasion; they envisioned a radically different Iraq and not a return to the status quo ante. As Mohamed Hafez points out, both secular and Islamic organizations pursued "system integration," which in practice meant a return to the old Ba'athist hierarchy, whether defined by the Ba'ath Party's original secular principles or the more Islamic ones.[35] Zarqawi, however, favored "system transformation"—a very different Iraq, not dominated by the old hierar-chies, the United States, or Iran. Rather, a jihadi Iraq, where law came only from God.

Zarqawi's first terrorist attacks in Iraq reflected this focus. They were savage—and scattered across the breadth of his enemies.

Thamir Mubarak and Nidal Arabiyat, Zarqawi's militant odd couple, col-laborated first to bomb the Jordanian Embassy in Baghdad. The explosion killed seventeen people on August 7, 2003, and showed that Zarqawi's grudge against Jordan was far from resolved. The strategy also lined up with a decision by Saddam to direct the Ba'athist underground against "collabo-rators" with the U.S. invasion.[36] For Mubarak, the onetime Iraqi intelli-gence officer turned to jihadism, this alignment must have made working with Zarqawi easier—both his past networks and his ideological convic-tions were aimed in the same direction.

Twelve days later, Zarqawi's agents attacked the United Nations office in eastern Baghdad.[37] A suicide bomber plunged an explosive-laden truck into Baghdad's Canal Hotel, which the UN had used for years before the invasion and had reoccupied only days before the attack.[38] The bomb left twenty-two people dead, including the head of mission, Sergio Viera de Mello. The bomb left a crater five feet deep and twenty feet across.[39]

Several groups claimed responsibility for the attack, including the ji-hadis of Ansar al-Islam, but American officials suspected former regime elements.[40] They pointed out that many of the Iraqi security contractors working at the UN Headquarters had ties to the Iraqi intelligence service and that the attack was perfectly timed and placed to kill de Mello, which suggested an inside job.[41] Key U.S. intelligence analysts later noted that the suicide bombers' safe house was adjacent to compounds controlled by Sad-dam's former Special Security Organization.[42]

In actuality, it was not a question of whether jihadis or former regime elements were responsible. Zarqawi claimed responsibility in 2004 and his group later credited Mubarak—who was both former Ba'athist and a jihadi—for organizing it.[43]

Since ISIS declared itself a caliphate in 2014, observers have debated whether the organization is truly jihadist or effectively a front organization for old Ba'athist operatives.[44] This debate is often myopic. Jihadis and former

Iraqi government officials have collaborated in the Islamic State's predecessors since the earliest days of the Iraq war. This does not, however, imply that the jihadi groups were tools of the wily Iraqis. The jihadis say that Mubarak, for example, rejected the Iraqi regime long before the U.S. invasion, when he recognized the "atheistic nature of the Ba'ath and its President."[45] It is no surprise that veterans of Saddam's security forces eventually ascended to leadership positions in the Islamic State and its predecessors; after all, they eventually came to lead *most* insurgent groups operating in Iraq. Political and ideological disposition aside, these former Iraqi military officials were the people with the skills to be effective insurgent leaders.

Zarqawi embraced some former regime elements, but his vision for Iraq was very different than the Ba'athists—and his next major attack after the United Nations would prove it. This was the strike that informed and embodied the polarization strategy eventually described in *The Management of Savagery*.[46]

In January 2013, nearly ten years after the UN Headquarters attack, a man named Muhammad Jarrad was killed in al-Suwayda, Syria. His death was little different from thousands of others in the horror of the Syrian civil war, except for one thing: Muhammad Jarrad was Abu Mus'ab al-Zarqawi's brother-in-law.[47] Zarqawi met and married Jarrad's sister in Kabul, Afghanistan, in 2000, when she was just thirteen.[48] Despite their close ties to Zarqawi, neither Muhammad nor his sister left a mark on history like their father, Yassin Jarrad. It was Yassin that Zarqawi tapped in 2003 to commit one of the most important terrorist attacks since 9/11. Like many of Zarqawi's early attacks in Iraq, Thamir Mubarak planned it, and Nidal Arabiyat is thought to have built the bomb.

Their target was a key Iraqi Shia leader, Ayatollah Muhammad Bakir al-Hakim. Hakim fled to Iran in 1979 at the beginning of the Iran-Iraq war and had only briefly returned to Iraqi soil in the years since.[49] But he was not idle during exile. Hakim founded the Supreme Council of Islamic Resistance in Iraq (SCIRI) and its militia, the Badr Corps, which worked directly with Iran's Revolutionary Guard Corps (IRGC) to fight Saddam's government.

Returning to Iraq in May 2003, Hakim was greeted by crowds in the Iraqi city of Basra chanting, "Yes, yes to Islam. No to Saddam. No to America."[50]

Hakim quieted the crowd and described a relatively measured agenda. "We don't want the Islam of the Taliban," he explained, "nor the Islam of extremists, nor of those who have become like Americans. We want the Islam of God's prophet, our great Islam, the Islam of moderates."[51] Hakim had deep ties to Iran that likely would have been problematic for the United States over the long run, but in post-invasion Iraq, he was a voice for political temperance.

Zarqawi, of course, did not see Hakim as a moderate; he saw the ayatollah as an Iranian puppet and an apostate. Despite Zarqawi's continued reliance on logistics networks traversing Iran, he increasingly focused on attacking Iraq's Shia. In 2003 that meant killing one of the most important political leaders in the country.

For Shia Muslims, there are few places in the world more holy than the Iraqi city of Najaf. After the fourth caliph, Ali, was assassinated in AD 661, he was buried in Najaf and the immense Imam Ali Mosque complex grew up around his grave. For Shia Muslims, it is a place of pilgrimage, remembrance, and devotion.

Some 1,300 years after Ali's death and only a few months after his own return to Iraq, Ayatollah Hakim delivered a sermon at the Imam Ali Mosque calling for unity among Shia Muslims and productive engagement with the United States. Zarqawi had other plans. At 2:15 p.m. on August 29, 2003, just as Ayatollah Hakim was exiting the shrine, Yassin Jarrad drove a truck bomb into the former exile's motorcade. The explosion left ninety-five people dead, including Ayatollah Hakim.

Killing Hakim was strategy, not nihilism. *The Management of Savagery* advocated social polarization as a means of gaining recruits—and Zarqawi's attacks on Iraq's Shia were his method to operationalize that strategy. Zarqawi believed Iraq's Shia were implacably hostile to Sunnis, and that most Sunnis were oblivious to that danger. In a letter to Osama bin Laden dated February 2004, he explained that Iraq's Sunnis were "absent, even though present . . . they look forward to a sunny tomorrow, a prosperous future, a carefree life, comfort, and favor . . . and are thus easy prey for cunning information [media] and political enticement."[52]

Zarqawi's strategy for changing their attitude was to provoke the Shia— approximately 60 percent of Iraq's population—into openly attacking

Sunnis, who would then have no choice but to turn to jihadis for support. As he put it in his letter to bin Laden:

> [the Shia] are the lurking snake, the crafty and malicious scorpion, the spying enemy, and the penetrating venom. . . . [They are also] the key to change. I mean that targeting and hitting them in [their] religious, political, and military depth will provoke them to show the Sunnis their rabies and bare the teeth of the hidden rancor working in their breasts. If we succeed in dragging them into the arena of sectarian war, it will become possible to awaken the inattentive Sunnis as they feel imminent danger and annihilating death at the hands of these Sabeans.[53]

If al-Adl framed the strategic master plan and Hakaymah (cum Naji) the operational framework, Zarqawi's sectarian vision was the work plan in Iraq.

Zarqawi's sectarianism aligned conceptually with *The Management of Savagery*, but it was far from universally accepted among jihadis. Nonetheless, Zarqawi prioritized killing Shia out of both hatred and strategy: he thought Shia "apostasy" was more deplorable than the original disbelief of American infidels, and he also believed the Shia were more dangerous over the long run. The United States, Zarqawi reasoned, would ultimately leave Iraq, but the Shia were fundamental to Iraqi society and represented Iranian influence, apostasy, and a persistent danger that would never simply withdraw.[54]

Zarqawi's strategy has not been an unmitigated success, but by 2014 it had produced dividends almost unimaginable in 2003—a reconstituted "caliphate" with control over a territory the size of Great Britain.

The relationships undergirding Zarqawi's strategy were riddled with paradoxes. Even as Zarqawi and his successors targeted Shia Muslims in Iraq, they relied on networks in Shia Iran—including al-Adl and Hakaymah—to communicate with al-Qaeda, and networks in Alawite-led Syria (a sect that includes many Shia beliefs) to import foreign fighters. And even as Iran and Syria tolerated the jihadi networks, they bolstered Shia militias fighting the Zarqawiists. Indeed, the killing of Ayatollah Hakim opened the door for a new generation of Shia militants in Iraq, shepherded by some of Iran's most practiced agents. Since the Syrian civil war began in 2011, those Shia militias have become the backbone of militant opposition to the Islamic State in both Syria and Iraq.

Zarqawi's contradictory relationship with Iran, and his tenuous relations with insurgent groups composed of former regime loyalists, came to the forefront in 2004 when the Islamic Army of Iraq (IAI) kidnapped an Iranian diplomat south of the city of Karbala. The IAI, which was dominated by former Iraqi military officers, hoped to exchange him for prisoners still held from the Iran-Iraq war, but Zarqawi—consistent with the strategy al-Qaeda's Abd al-Hadi al-Iraqi had approved in 2003—aimed to trade him for jihadis held by Iran after 9/11.[55] The final arrangement is unclear, although the IAI turned the diplomat over to Zarqawi in early 2004. Zarqawi's group subsequently released him, but claimed there was no quid pro quo with the Iranian regime.[56] Still, it seems highly unlikely that Zarqawi would have released him without getting something in exchange, although that may have simply been lenience in moving messages or people across Iran.

Zarqawi never credited either the master plan or *The Management of Savagery* for driving his efforts in Iraq, but his operational approach was consistent with both. Zarqawi grew famous in the West for his brutality, but that spectacle masked the strategy inherent in his violence. Brutality intended to provoke Iraq's Shia population instantiated the polarization model outlined in *The Management of Savagery*, and Zarqawi's long-term vision always focused squarely on reestablishing the caliphate. As a jihadi biographer wrote of Zarqawi in 2005: "His intent is not just to liberate Iraq from the filth of the Crusaders; our Sheikh goes further than that. He dreams of an Islamic Caliphate guided by the Prophet that would reestablish God's law."[57]

Mergers and Antagonisms

Zarqawi was convinced that Shia were apostates, but his sectarian attacks caused consternation among al-Qaeda's leaders, who feared that killing Muslim civilians would repulse the wider Muslim population. This was a consequential disagreement, because in early 2004 Zarqawi finally began negotiating seriously with Osama bin Laden about whether to formally join al-Qaeda. The substantive question of whether to kill Shia civilians was only one hurdle to a more comprehensive alliance. There were logistical problems as well, most importantly how to communicate reliably and securely from Pakistan to Iraq.

Bin Laden's point man in South Asia for communicating with Zarqawi was well accustomed to intra-jihadi negotiations: Abd al-Hadi al-Iraqi, the ethnically Kurdish former Iraqi Army officer who had managed al-Qaeda's guesthouse in Kabul prior to 9/11.[58] Although Abd al-Hadi is not a familiar name to most Westerners, he was a high-profile figure in al-Qaeda. After 9/11, he managed al-Qaeda's military operations in Afghanistan and had a hand in external operations as well.[59] Abd al-Hadi regularly reported back to bin Laden, and he was part of a critical al-Qaeda meeting where the group's future was determined in the months after 9/11.[60]

Al-Qaeda's counterparty in the Levant varied over time, but one of the first was Luai Sakka, Zarqawi's first recruit when he established the Herat camp. In 2003, Sakka played middleman between Zarqawi, al-Qaeda, and local Turkish jihadis to plan a series of terrorist attacks in Istanbul. That summer, he also passed a request from Zarqawi to Abd al-Hadi requesting money and supplies for the jihad in Iraq.[61]

Abd al-Hadi was hesitant to assign sparse resources to such a mission, in part because he did not fully trust his own intermediaries to success-fully complete the journey to Iraq. He needed more information on what was happening in Iraq—and fast. Abd al-Hadi's first move was to dispatch a Kurd named Abdallah al-Kurdi to Iraq. But al-Kurdi did not have the gumption of his boss. He was averse to combat and was considered "soft"— the worst sort of emissary to engage Zarqawi.[62] Kurdi's ultimate fate is unknown, but after refusing to "engage in any [military] activities" in Iraq his days as a credible messenger to Zarqawi were over.[63]

Having chosen poorly with al-Kurdi, Abd al-Hadi settled on another courier, Hassan Ghul. A longtime jihadi operative from the Pakistani province of Baluchistan, Ghul was trusted and battle-tested. Abd al-Hadi hoped Zarqawi would respect him.[64]

Indeed, Ghul's conversations with Zarqawi were more productive than al-Kurdi's. When Ghul and Zarqawi met in January 2004, Zarqawi bluntly explained his strategy for Iraq.[65] Only by inciting a sectarian bloodletting, he argued, could jihadis hope to rally Iraq's Sunnis en masse. He would keep assassinating Shia political and religious leaders until that sectarian war began. Ghul relayed the message to Abd al-Hadi, who was disturbed by the suggestion and was "opposed to any operations in Iraq that would promote bloodshed among Muslims."[66] As Ghul later told CIA investigators, Abd al-Hadi "counseled al-Zarqawi against undertaking such operations."[67]

Neither Zarqawi's strategic plan nor the unreliable courier system inspired Abd al-Hadi's confidence. Fortunately, there were many al-Qaeda members in Pakistan eager to travel to Iraq to fight. So Abd al-Hadi "tasked [Ghul] to discuss this issue with Zarqawi and to recon the route" for more fighters to make the journey to Iraq.[68] For a man with Zarqawi's independent streak, sending more operatives to Iraq was a sensitive subject, but Zarqawi was open to the idea and even requested specific individuals with skills that he thought would be useful.[69]

Perhaps inspired by Zarqawi's seeming openness to al-Qaeda members joining the fight in Iraq, Abd al-Hadi proposed something even more radical: he would personally come to Iraq. Whether this was a spur of the moment suggestion or an idea endorsed by al-Qaeda's leadership, Zarqawi's interest in new recruits did not extend to al-Qaeda leaders more senior than he. Perhaps worried about an implicit challenge to his leadership, Zarqawi rebuffed the suggestion, explaining to Ghul that, "this was not a good idea, as operations in Iraq were far different than those Abd al-Hadi was conducting in Afghanistan."[70]

For the time being, Abd al-Hadi did not push the issue.

Ghul facilitated a productive conversation between Zarqawi and al-Qaeda's leadership, but he failed at a courier's most important task: not getting caught. Kurdish forces seized Ghul as he began the journey back to Afghanistan.[71] Buried among the digital detritus he carried was a seventeen-page memo authored by Zarqawi himself. It was a letter to bin Laden, and it advocated nothing short of all-out sectarian civil war in Iraq.[72]

American forces in Iraq captured Umar Izz al-Din on January 31, 2004. He was only a teenager when he arrived in Iraqi Kurdistan three years earlier, hoping to travel through Iran to Taliban-controlled Afghanistan. That plan collapsed when Iranian security services refused him entry, so he stayed in

Kurdistan and joined Jordanian jihadi leader Ra'id Khuraysat's militant group. When Zarqawi arrived in 2002, Umar signed up immediately.

Umar's fate was a mystery for the better part of a decade. In 2003, jihadis claimed he had been "martyred," even though the Jordanian government charged him alongside thirteen others, including Zarqawi, of plotting terrorist attacks against American interests in Jordan.[73] The ambiguity was perhaps hardest on his parents, who did not know whether they should mourn the death of a son or continue to pray for his well-being. Umar's father explained his frustration in 2005: "My son is a young man, barely 17 years old. A juvenile. When he left he still needed education. . . . He wanted to go to Afghanistan to fight . . . I was told that he was killed. Then I was told that he was imprisoned in Abu-Ghraib."[74]

It is difficult to imagine the pain of a father whose son has disappeared on a foreign battlefield, but it is easy to understand the anger he felt toward the men who lured him there. Umar's father was certainly aggravated in early 2004 as he waited for information about his son's fate.

Umar's father, however, was no ordinary man. He was Abu Muhammad al-Maqdisi, Zarqawi's first ideological mentor, and the most prominent jihadi-salafi ideologue in the world.[75] With Umar's fate unclear, and discouraged by the brutal but seemingly undirected violence in Iraq, Maqdisi released an open letter criticizing Zarqawi for sacrificing young Muslim lives without a more coherent strategy in place. "An individual might be forgiven for arbitrary or disorganized action that is not governed by a plan or 'strategy,'" he wrote, but militant leaders have a responsibility to develop a strategy commensurate with the sacrifices they demand from their followers. Perhaps thinking of Umar, he went on: "[I]f a group acts arbitrarily, like an individual, without a well-defined plan it means the group does not respect its own efforts and does not care about the life of its youth."[76]

The ensuing debate between Zarqawi and Maqdisi fundamentally shaped Zarqawi's long-term worldview and, ultimately, the ideology and cultural ethos of the Islamic State. The dispute is easily understood through very different lenses. Zarqawi was a man on the battlefield negotiating with a mentor far away; Maqdisi was a thoughtful scholar concerned by Zarqawi's impetuous and deeply violent interpretation of Islamic and jihadi principles. Zarqawi was a young man rebelling against his only real father figure; Maqdisi represented the jihadi clerical mainstream against a violent, populist interlocutor.

These frameworks make sense, but so does this: Maqdisi was the father of a missing son and Zarqawi was the commander who had risked that son's life for what seemed like no good reason.

Maqdisi's criticism of Zarqawi reflected an older conflict between the two men. When Zarqawi favored emigration and open warfare after he and Maqdisi were released from Jordanian prison in 1999, Maqdisi argued for peaceful confrontation with the Jordanian government. Even then, the disagreement was not just intellectual; they were competing for a limited pool of recruits, most of whom, including Maqdisi's son Umar, followed Zarqawi's path. Afterward, Maqdisi frankly expressed his dismay that the emigration "left the [Jordanian] arena empty" of young jihadi activists.[77]

The yin and yang of action and intellectualism that made Zarqawi and Maqdisi such an intriguing partnership ultimately tore their relationship apart.

It is easy to understand why Zarqawi wanted to leave Jordan. For him, walking the tightrope of nonviolent (or mildly violent) jihadi opposition to the Jordanian state would have been a recipe for failure and more years in prison; emigrating to Afghanistan played to his leadership skills and pre-dilection for action. Maqdisi was much better disposed for striking a politi-cal balance in Jordan, but even he has spent the years since 1999 in and out of Jordanian prisons, including time in 2004 on charges of plotting to kill U.S. soldiers.[78]

During those same five years, Zarqawi transformed himself into the world's most recognizable villain aside from Osama bin Laden. But Maqdisi treated him like a middle school student gone awry. "Some people," Maqdisi pedantically reminded the leader of the world's most violent terrorist organ-ization in 2004, "do not learn from the experiences of others and continue to act without rhyme or reason. A happy person is someone who respects his age and knowledge and learns from the experience, lessons, and mistakes of others."[79] Zarqawi, unsurprisingly, was in no mood to take counseling.

Maqdisi still treated Zarqawi like the small-time jihadi who led their group in prison, not as the man who had negotiated with al-Qaeda, run his own training camp, escaped Iran, prepped the assassination of an American diplomat, and was now one of the most wanted men in the world. In September 2004, Maqdisi criticized Zarqawi's use of suicide bombings (a practice they both opposed while in prison together) and challenged his qualifications based on a distinctly 1999 version of his resume: "The superficial and limited experience of leading a small group in prison should not affect an organization's armed action. . . . Religious zeal, loyalty, emotions, and enthusiasm . . . does not, under any circumstances, replace the help of seasoned people who have the experience, wisdom, and knowledge. Beware of arrogance."[80]

The Jordanian government clearly relished Maqdisi's criticism of Zarqawi but feared the elder man's broader influence. In December 2004, after publicly criticizing Zarqawi the second time, Maqdisi was quickly acquitted of plotting to kill Americans in Jordan. For many jihadis, it looked like a quid pro quo. Maqdisi was released in July 2005, but after he gave an interview to Al Jazeera a week later, Jordan had him back in jail.[81] Maqdisi was one of the world's most influential jihadi thinkers, and he was genuinely critical of Zarqawi, but he also could only speak when the Jordanian government allowed it.

In mid-2005, Zarqawi struck back at his former mentor, and in doing so established a core principle of Zarqawiism. Zarqawi acknowledged that the mujahidin "are not immune to mistakes and failure," but he was sharply critical of scholars who condemned jihadis in the field from the safety of another country. "The ones who avoid battle," he lamented, "attack [jihadis] with sharp tongues and theorize about the cause of their defeat." For Zarqawi, such critiques were hollow and ill-informed, no matter the religious or scholarly credentials of the source; intellectualism meant nothing without action; credibility was a function of one's willingness to face personal risk on the battlefield. Ideologues and theorists should be "at the battlefront, waging war, experiencing the sweet and the sour and the pressure the mujahidin face; pressure that even mountains could not sustain."[82]

At its core, Zarqawi's argument was radically populist. The jihadi ethos that jihad against a foreign invader was *fard ayn*—mandatory on able-bodied Muslims—laid the groundwork for this idea. Indeed, al-Qaeda embraced some of this ethos because it urged young Muslims to reject the dominant social, political, and religious hierarchies that supported them. But al-Qaeda's leadership and scholars like Maqdisi still respected the notion that religious scholarship was valuable and that scholarly knowledge should guide jihadi military and political policy. They rejected the dominant political and religious structures of the modern Middle East, but looked to a different, antiestablishment set of elites for guidance.

Zarqawi rejected that basic idea. For him, "religious knowledge" that was not reflected in action was not actually knowledge. And since he believed that violently fighting for Islam was the supreme expression of both devotion and religious understanding, then religious scholars who did not join the jihad must not actually understand Islam as they claimed to. For Zarqawi, it was fundamentally contradictory to assert that Maqdisi was the world's most senior jihadi cleric and "illiterate" in the use of weapons. In Zarqawi's understanding, the highest form of religious worship was to fight on God's behalf, so Maqdisi clearly did not understand Islam as he claimed.

Maqdisi was not on the battlefield himself, but his son Umar was. And while Zarqawi was measuring ideological credibility by proximity to the battlefield, this was a minority view among Muslims generally and even most jihadis. Maqdisi was trying to reassure followers that his scholarly objectivity was uncompromised by the ambiguity over his son. When asked by a journalist about losing Umar to Zarqawi's jihad, Maqdisi was stern: "I will speak to [Umar] as I speak to all our mujahidin brethren. My speech to the mujahidin in Iraq and my opinion on what is taking place in Iraq is what I say to my son."[83]

City of Mosques

In January 2014, ISIS fighters raised a black flag over the center of Fallujah, an Iraqi city of 300,000 people sitting on the north bank of a bend in the mighty Euphrates River. Capturing Fallujah was more than just a battlefield triumph for those jihadis; it was a homecoming of sorts. Ten years earlier, before the two iconic battles that would etch Fallujah into the minds of thousands of American soldiers and Marines, Zarqawi's Shura

Council gathered there to make one of the most far-reaching decisions by a jihadi group in history.

As Abu Anas al-Shami, the head of Zarqawi's Sharia Committee, put it:

> [A]t Abu Mus'ab al-Zarqawi's orders, the military council met in [Fallujah] to review the situation. . . . The conclusion was painful. We found that in a year of jihad we had not achieved anything on the ground. No one could find a speck of land where he could take refuge. . . . We hid during the day and snuck around like rats at night. Everyone had left their homes. Families were pulled apart; houses were stormed; heroes were chased. . . . Everyone felt a sense of total failure. . . . A change in the operational plan was mandatory. So we decided to transform Fallujah into an invincible fortress for Muslims and off-limits to the Americans. They would be terrified to set foot inside. They would leave it horrified and hunted, carrying their wounded and dead.[84]

Abu Anas' story was partly after-the-fact justification for the killing and immolation of four American security contractors on March 31, 2004.[85] The men were ambushed on the outskirts of Fallujah, dragged out of their cars, lit on fire, and mutilated. Their bodies were dragged through the streets before being hung from the trestles of a bridge over the Euphrates. At least one man was decapitated.[86]

Even Abu Anas seemed disturbed by this degree of viciousness. "It was an outbreak of rage that deafened the ears to the voice of Shariah and reason," he explained, neither defending nor denouncing the immolation and mutilation.[87] Rather, Abu Anas cited Islamic scripture for and against both practices. Most importantly, however, he reminded critics that, "Knowledge is protected only if knowledgeable men protect it."[88] It was a Zarqawi-ist distillation and embrace of battlefield logic. Essentially: war is hell.

Abu Anas was writing at a delicate political moment. When Zarqawi's group, Tawhed w'al Jihad, decided to hold territory in Fallujah, it did not speak for all of Iraq's insurgents, or even all its jihadis. The majority of Iraq's insurgents were still tied to the former regime and focused on Iraqi independence and sovereignty, not the transnational goals espoused by Zarqawi. Zarqawi's closest ally was Ansar al-Sunnah, a group created in late 2003 when the Kurdish Ansar al-Islam united with various Arab jihadi factions.[89] But Ansar al-Sunnah remained defiantly independent of Zarqawi's authority.[90]

Zarqawi's first goal after deciding to hold territory in Fallujah was to unite the various factions there "under a single banner of jihad." It was a job much easier said than done—the groups differed on strategy, theology, and leadership—and it fell to Abu Anas, the head of Zarqawi's Shariah Committee.[91] But Abu Anas was a skilled diplomat, and he succeeded in bringing many groups together in an umbrella organization called the "Mujahidin Shura Council," which would coordinate the various insurgents fighting in Fallujah.[92]

The first battle of Fallujah, which was precipitated by the mutilation of those four contractors, was Zarqawi's defining political moment in Iraq. In large measure due to Abu Anas' work, Fallujah's defenders rebuffed the first U.S. assault on the city, which enhanced Zarqawi's status among Iraqi insurgents and strengthened his hand in the ongoing negotiation with al-Qaeda.

Despite being trained as a scholar, not a soldier, Abu Anas stayed in Fallujah to fight, thereby cementing his own legend and reinforcing Zarqawi's belief that theologians should hew to the battlefield, not the library. Abu Anas was not, however, a natural warrior, much to Zarqawi's amusement. Prior to the battle, Zarqawi often joked that Abu Anas could not be a fighter because no true jihadi would wear such decrepit shoes. If Abu Anas was going to be on the frontlines, he needed better. Abu Anas dug in his heels. The shoes were a gift from a friend in Medina, he claimed, and they had sentimental value. He would not give them up.[93]

During the first battle of Fallujah, however, Abu Anas lost control over his footwear. Fighting in a narrow alley in the Julan district, he was suddenly face-to-face with an American Humvee and stumbled backward into a house, frantically pulling the trigger on his AK-47. Uninjured except for his ringing ears, he escaped through a back door as the Humvee withdrew. Abu Anas did not claim to have hit any American soldiers; the only casualty from this small engagement was one of the infamous shoes, which lay where it fell in a Fallujah alley.

After the battle, Abu Anas' first call was to Zarqawi. Your wish has finally been granted, he joked. Abu Anas would finally get shoes worthy of a proper jihadi, which, in a nutshell, is what Zarqawi valued most in a spiritual advisor.[94]

Zarqawi's position in Fallujah also offered him safe haven from which to connect with jihadis from around the Middle East. Many jihadis arrived from Lebanon, including a group of veterans from the short-lived Dinniyah uprising of Bassam al-Kanj, the former Boston cab driver.[95] Their organization was a splinter of Asbat al-Ansar, a larger Palestinian jihadi group based in the Ayn al-Hilweh Palestinian refugee camp in Lebanon. Neither Asbat al-Ansar nor the splinter group were focused on the Palestinian territories, however. They had a broader vision that was reflected in the new group's name—Jund al-Sham (Soldiers of the Levant), the same as Zarqawi's supporters in Herat, Afghanistan.

Jund al-Sham was never a large organization, but it adopted the strategic vision of Kanj's Dinniyah uprising and conceptualized the Levant (Greater Syria) as a single area of operations. In 2004, the group was focused primarily on building relationships—and it described its immediate priority as "sending brothers to Iraq for training and bringing them back."[96] Over the long run, it wanted to overthrow the Syrian government.

Jund al-Sham was not the only group developing links with Zarqawi. Perhaps the most intriguing connection Zarqawi made in Fallujah was with a Saudi named Salah al-Qar'awi. "We became very close," explained Qar'awi in 2010, "and [Zarqawi] assigned me some tasks outside of Iraq."[97] Qar'awi's claim of friendship with Zarqawi sniffs of self-aggrandizement, but it may be accurate. After Zarqawi's death, Saudi authorities came to believe that Qar'awi assumed guardianship of Zarqawi's newborn son and raised him as his own.[98]

After fighting in Fallujah, Qar'awi left Iraq to pursue Zarqawi's "tasks," but he was arrested by Syrian authorities and deported to Saudi Arabia. In 2004, the Saudi authorities saw no reason to hold him—and let him go. It was a mistake; Qar'awi subsequently traveled to Iran to engage al-Qaeda leaders there, and founded a jihadi group called the *Abdallah Azzam Brigades*, which claimed intermittent terrorist attacks across the Middle East. In 2009, he was named one of the most wanted men in Saudi Arabia.[99]

Qar'awi was a literal and figurative link between Zarqawi and the al-Qaeda cadre in Iran. He was close to Zarqawi and married the daughter of Hakaymah, Zarqawi's traveling companion out of Afghanistan, and the pseudonymous author of *The Management of Savagery*.

Indeed, the Abdallah Azzam Brigades had a bifurcated focus—on Lebanon and Egypt—that parallels Qar'awi's relationship with Zarqawi and Hakaymah. Whereas Zarqawi aimed to extend his network into Lebanon, Hakaymah pined for revolution in Egypt. Hakaymah was particularly supportive—and used his own growing influence to champion the Abdallah Azzam Brigades' operations in his homeland, both in a long history of jihad in Egypt that he published and on his website, *The Promise Keepers*.[100]

Like Jund al-Sham, the Abdallah Azzam Brigades was never a large jihadi organization, but it filled a unique niche in the jihadi universe linking Zarqawi's jihad in Iraq and al-Qaeda's broader regional aspirations.

U.S. and Iraqi forces retook Fallujah in November 2004, but the jihadis' 10-month domination of the city was a tremendous strategic success for Zarqawi.[101] It revealed the insurgents' strength when unified and elevated Zarqawi into a leading role. Before Fallujah, many jihadis were integrated into militant groups led by former regime elements; after Fallujah, Zarqawi was the undisputed leader of jihadis in Iraq.

The battle also revealed nascent Iraqi frustration with the jihadis. Even Abu Anas' glorified retelling describes Fallujah residents berating jihadis for bringing destruction to their city and laments that the Muslim Brotherhood-affiliated Iraqi Islamic Party got credit for the battle among many Iraqi Sunnis.[102] It was one thing to unite Iraq's insurgents for a single battle; keeping them unified was another story entirely.

The insurgents squabbled locally over who would claim credit for Fallujah, but Zarqawi was winning the global propaganda battle hands down. In 2004, the Internet was redefining communications, and Zarqawi embraced that revolution. In his first major online audio statement, released in January 2004 just before the first battle of Fallujah, Zarqawi claimed responsibility for a series of major attacks, including the UN Headquarters

bombing and the assassination of Ayatollah Hakim in Najaf. Most importantly, he trotted out the most durable recruiting theme in the Islamic
State's history: recapturing lost dignity. Zarqawi argued that Muslims were
being humiliated by Western imperialism and the depravity of local governments, and that the solution was to participate in jihad in order to cast
off oppressive and un-Islamic rule.[103]

The theme of restoring dignity was central to Zarqawi's early propaganda, which often seized on contemporary events to illustrate broader
points. Two of the most damaging events were the abuse of prisoners at the
Abu Ghraib prison and the case of Abeer Qassim Hamza al-Janabi, a
fourteen-year-old Iraqi girl who was stalked, raped, and murdered by
American soldiers.[104] Zarqawi's propaganda demanded the release of Muslim prisoners and questioned the masculinity of Muslim men who failed
to defend Muslim women. The crimes by American service members
played directly into this narrative.

Tawhed w'al Jihad's digital propaganda campaign was shaped by the
technology of the time. Long before social media, web forums and broadband enabled widely distributed networks of jihadi supporters to amplify
propaganda developed by militant groups. Broadband Internet, just gaining wide acceptance in 2004, dramatically increased the size of files that
could be transmitted online. This paved the way for digital audio and video
distribution that was not possible a few years earlier. In 2001 Ansar al-
Islam printed CDs to distribute video of its attacks to potential funders;
three years later that was increasingly unnecessary. A video or audio file
uploaded in Iraq could be downloaded anywhere in the world seconds later.
At the same time, web forums enabled Internet users to do much more
than just receive information posted on a site: they could interact with each
other. This was a revelation for sports fans, hobbyists, and political groups
globally; it also enabled jihadi supporters to consume propaganda and exchange their ideas in a digital environment.[105]

The new digital tools were not foolproof: intelligence services might take
down propaganda or a rush of jihadis downloading a video might cause a
site to crash. One of Zarqawi's most notable digital supporters stepped in
to resolve these challenges. Younis Tsouli was a Moroccan-born British
citizen who fancied himself a digital James Bond. He called himself

Irhabi 007 (Terrorist 007) online and would repost Zarqawi propaganda so that others could download it.[106] To prevent disruptions, Tsouli would upload an audio or video to multiple file-sharing sites and then post duplicate links to the same video on jihadi web forums.[107] Compared to modern streaming video and social media distribution, Tsouli's system seems rudimentary, but it worked. With jihadi messages distributed across numerous sites, the propaganda could not feasibly be removed from the web and single sites were less likely to crash.[108] Tsouli's method was soon ubiquitous for all forms of jihadi propaganda.

In May 2004, Tsouli's system was put to the test when Zarqawi appeared in a video online—this time wearing a black mask and standing behind a kneeling captive in an orange jumpsuit like those worn by prisoners at Guantanamo Bay.[109] The kneeling man was Nick Berg, an American businessman who had been captured in Iraq.[110] In a scene that eerily foreshadowed Islamic State executions in Syria a decade later, Zarqawi proceeded to roughly behead Berg with what appeared to be a large kitchen knife.

Like the parade of Islamic State beheadings in Syria a decade later, Zarqawi's assault on Berg riveted the global media. Not only was the attack brutal; there was video.

But the beheading was far from unique.[111] Over the next five months, Tawhed w'al Jihad claimed at least nine other beheadings, including those of Americans Jack Hensley and Eugene Armstrong and British citizen Ken Bigley. Like Berg, Hensley, Armstrong, and Bigley were shown kneeling in orange jumpsuits before they were killed. The other beheadings—doubtless no less tragic to the victims' families—got less media attention in the West: they included two Turkish citizens, a Bulgarian, an Egyptian, and a Korean. Numerous Iraqis probably suffered the same fate, but their deaths were not broadcast to the world.[112] Most of the time, Zarqawi's Iraqi victims were simply shot in the back of the head.

Zarqawi was not the only name-brand jihadi to embrace beheadings in 2004. Luai Sakka also claimed to have supported several beheadings in Iraq.[113] Arrested while planning an attack on an Israeli cruise ship in Turkey, Sakka claimed to have personally presided over the 2004 beheading of British engineer Ken Bigley.[114] Sakka was prone to exaggeration, so investigators considered him unreliable. However, when confronted in court with

a gruesome beheading video of Turkish truck driver Murat Yuce in northern Iraq, Sakka knew precisely what to expect. "Now they are going to cut
off his head," Sakka said in court, leaning forward toward the screen. "In a
minute I am going to remove the pistol so the blood does not get on it.
Blood destroys the inside of a pistol."[115]

Many jihadis celebrated Zarqawi's "revival of the beheading tradition"
precisely because it generated so much resentment in the West. Zarqawi
"shocked the western public," crowed the author of a long treatise posted
on jihadi web forums in May 2005.

> When they saw the Emir of Tawhed w'al Jihad standing in front of the cam-
> era and personally beheading the American infidel Nicholas Berg as a re-
> sponse to the Abu Ghraib crimes, and to demand the release of women
> held in the Christian prisons. . . . The Sheikh of the Slaughterers repeated
> his feat with Eugene Armstrong, whom he beheaded with his own hands,
> and then left the other infidels to be decapitated by his friends.[116]

The "beheading tradition" was not universally supported by jihadis, but
key leaders endorsed it. Al-Qaeda in the Arabian Peninsula's official magazine *Sawt al-Jihad* (Voice of Jihad) celebrated Zarqawi and argued that
beheading was acceptable not just for Westerners but even for "infidel
Arabs."[117] On the English-language *Tibyan* web forum, used extensively by
British jihadi sympathizers, a forum reposted a widely cited judgment by
Abu Muhammad al-Maqdisi arguing that beheading was a humane alternative to torture.[118] That rationale was considered good enough.

In 2014, when the Islamic State aimed to make a splash in the global
media, its leaders did not need much creativity to know how to garner attention. The blueprint—beheading Westerners wearing Guantanamo-
style outfits on camera—had been laid out for them a decade earlier.

Al-Qaeda in Iraq

Zarqawi's increasingly prominent role among Iraqi jihadis enhanced his
position with al-Qaeda, which still had no overt presence in Iraq. Their
negotiations culminated on October 15, 2004, just before the second battle

of Fallujah, when Zarqawi swore *bayah* (allegiance) to Osama bin Laden in a statement released online. It had been almost five years since the two first met.

Zarqawi's *bayah* subordinated him to bin Laden, but Zarqawi made clear that the negotiation had not been one-sided. In a public statement released online, Zarqawi explained that he was swearing allegiance only because his "respected brothers in al-Qaeda understood the strategy of Tawhed w'al-Jihad in the land of the two rivers . . . and their hearts opened to our approach."[119] In other words, the campaign of brutality and sectarianism would continue. Zarqawi certainly did not moderate his brutality to get an agreement; in the six-months before he swore *bayah* to bin Laden, Tawhed w'al Jihad publicly claimed at least ten beheadings.[120]

Bin Laden celebrated Zarqawi's *bayah* in a cheerful public statement released online on December 28, 2004. It papered over concerns within al-Qaeda about Zarqawi's sectarian strategy and is a reminder that al-Qaeda, despite objecting to Zarqawi's most extreme crimes, heartily endorses mass killing, including Muslims that collaborate with "infidels" in any way. As bin Laden put it:

> Supporting America or [Iraqi Prime Minister Ayad] Allawi's renegade government, or [Afghan President Hamid] Karzai's government, or [Palestinian President] Mahmud Abbas' government, or any other renegade government in their fight against the Muslims is tantamount to infidelity and a cause for excommunication. Included among those are the owners of companies and the workers who transport fuel, ammunition, food supplies, and any other needs. Everyone who aids and supports . . . [infidels] in any way has defected from Islam and must be fought.[121]

Al-Qaeda's leadership ultimately pressed Zarqawi to be more nuanced in his targeting, but its objection was a matter of degree: both Zarqawi and bin Laden endorsed bloody campaigns against Muslim civilians. They just disagreed about the scope of the killing.

There were still important strategic and ideological differences between al-Qaeda and Zarqawi, but practical considerations made an alliance attractive. Bin Laden was impressed by the jihadi resistance in Fallujah and compared fighters there favorably to "the nineteen" who had conducted the 9/11 attack. Zarqawi wanted the al-Qaeda imprimatur to attract recruits and donations. At the same time, al-Qaeda knew that Zarqawi was the most prominent jihadi leader in Iraq; if jihadis there were going to unify, Zarqawi would need to lead the movement. Bin Laden's statement urged all "Islamic" groups in Iraq to follow Zarqawi and declared for the first time that supporting the jihad there was a religious obligation.[122]

Zarqawi and bin Laden never formally announced a joint strategic plan, but al-Adl's seven-stage master plan, developed around the time of Zarqawi's *bayah*, and with the input of Zarqawi advisors, was likely intended as that document. Bin Laden was more wary than many in al-Qaeda about the utility of declaring Islamic States, but he could not argue that Zarqawi's focus on building the caliphate in the near-term was a surprise. "It will be Prophethood as long as God wills," Zarqawi explained in his *bayah* to bin Laden, "then it will be the caliphate in the path of the Prophet. . . . Hopefully, we will be the ones to accomplish this task."[123]

Zarqawiism

As Zarqawi squabbled with Maqdisi and negotiated with al-Qaeda, he began to delineate a distinct jihadi ideology and organizational ethos. A decade later, it continues to define the Islamic State.

Zarqawi's dogma was rebellious, populist, and inherently violent. Zarqawiism is perhaps best understood more as a hyper-violent, antiestablishment ethos than a formal ideology, but it is ultimately distinguished by two core ideas:

- An extremely narrow vision of what it means to be a "true Muslim," such that the vast majority of the world's Muslims are considered apostates deserving death. This contrasts with mainstream jihadi thinking, including in al-Qaeda, which argues that most Muslims have forgotten the true faith and must be brought back to it. In contrast, Zarqawiists and the Islamic State assume that most people in the world are legitimate targets of violence, even those who profess to be Muslim.

- A dramatic redistribution of ideological and political authority from a rarified class of religious scholars to frontline jihadis, who by committing to violence for their faith are considered better Muslims. This redefinition of political and ideological authority both insulates the Islamic State from external criticism and justifies the group's targeting of laypeople they deem infidel or apostate. Whereas many jihadis, including al-Qaeda at times, argue laypeople should be exempt from violence and only their leaders targeted, Zarqawiists hold laypeople personally responsible for their "apostasy."

Zarqawi's populism was grounded in the jihadi movement's most controversial question: under what conditions was it acceptable to kill Muslims, either intentionally or through indiscriminate weapons like large car bombs? Islamic scripture and tradition prohibit Muslims from killing other Muslims, including a Muslim ruler. Jihadis address this prohibition through *takfir*, effectively the excommunication of someone deemed so unjust that they must not actually be Muslim. Once someone has been declared *kafir*—an infidel—they may be killed.

The modern jihadi conception of *takfir* is built on the teaching of Ibn Taymiyya, a thirteenth-century Damascene scholar who rallied Muslims to fight against the Mongol Empire's charge through South Asia, Persia, and present-day Iraq. In 1258, the Mongols even burst into Baghdad, then the capital of the Abbasid Caliphate. This was a titanic event in the history of Islam—a shock greater than any suffered at the hands of Europeans during the Crusades.

The Mongol Empire had conquered vast swaths of territory once controlled by the caliphate when it captured Baghdad, but Islam captured the hearts of many of those invaders. The Mongols embraced Islam, and many converted to the local faith. But for scholars like Ibn Taymiyyah, who lived just beyond the Mongol Empire's reach in Damascus, the Mongols still represented a huge threat. The challenge for Ibn Taymiyyah was building a theological argument for war against an empire whose leadership had embraced Islam.

The answer was *takfir*, which in Ibn Taymiyyah's conception was a careful process of analyzing Mongol governance and religious practice to distinguish it from "true" Islam. Thereby war was justified against Baghdad's

new rulers. Centuries later, jihadis borrowed Ibn Taymiyyah's arguments
to justify violence against numerous leaders across the Muslim-majority
world. But in doing so, they confronted a slew of difficult questions. How
bad must a leader be to be declared *kafir* (non-Muslim)? How broadly does
that declaration apply? Only to the leader? To the army? To all government
employees? Anyone who does not join the rebellion? And, critically, who is
qualified to make such a declaration?[124]

Zarqawiism differs from al-Qaeda, and the jihadi mainstream, over
both who should be subject to violence and who was qualified to make that
decision. Although bin Laden endorsed the notion of killing an unjust regime's supporters, Zarqawiism claimed that anyone who "refrains from
carrying out any obligation of shariah" could be declared an infidel.[125] Abu
Hamzah al-Baghdadi, a key member of Zarqawi's Shariah Committee, explained that this was "a piece of Islamic learning that every Muslim should
know, so that those who perish will do so knowingly and those who find
salvation will know why they are saved."[126]

Most jihadis, including al-Qaeda, approach *takfir* as a question of identifying the specific individuals or classes of people that it is acceptable to
kill. And because this is such a difficult and weighty decision, jihadis traditionally defer that judgment to people with extensive religious and political training. This framework is built on the assumption that if individuals
or classes of people are not identified as licit targets of violence, then they
should be left alone.

Zarqawiism inverts that assumption, effectively presuming that violence and killing are generally justified. The pressing question is identifying those classes of people that should be excepted from violence. As
Zarqawi put it, "[T]here are three categories of people on earth."[127] The first
are Muslims "who embrace Islam," meaning they do not refrain "from
carrying out any obligation of Shariah."[128] The second category includes
"those at peace with Islam and Muslims through custody or truce."[129] This
might include People of the Book—Jews or Christians—that have agreed
to special restrictions in order to live under jihadi rule. The third category,
Zarqawi explained simply, "includes everyone else living. . . . Every infidel
on the planet who does not make peace with Islam and Muslims through
custody, truce, or safe conduct, is a warrior infidel. There is absolutely no

protection for him, unless his killing is forbidden to start with, such as children and women."[130]

Practically speaking, both Zarqawiists and al-Qaeda support violence against wide swaths of the world, including many Muslims. But they differ on when to target Muslims with violence. Whereas Zarqawiists, including the Islamic State, effectively endorse violence against anyone that does not actively support them, al-Qaeda generally only condemns Muslims that actively support "apostate" or "infidel" governments.[131] This difference extends even to the Shia. Both al-Qaeda and Zarqawiists consider Shia Muslims deviants, but al-Qaeda aims to kill only senior Shia religious and political leaders and to "reform" laypeople. Zarqawiists, including in the Islamic State, aim to kill all Shia regardless of their political or educational position.

Put another way, the fundamental difference between al-Qaeda and the Islamic State is that al-Qaeda's leaders believe that most people who call themselves Muslims actually are, whereas the Islamic State's leaders do not. The Islamic State believes that many—perhaps most—of the people who consider themselves Muslims are in fact apostates and should be killed. Both al-Qaeda and the Islamic State aim to ultimately lead the entire umma—or global community of Muslims—but they disagree on how big that population actually is.

This leads the Islamic State and al-Qaeda to embrace vastly different operational models. Both recognize that they are fringe movements among Muslims, but whereas al-Qaeda aims to rally Muslims to its cause en masse, the Islamic State thinks its first mission is to sort the "true" Muslims from the "apostates".

Sayf al-Adl, the driver of the seven-stage master plan, does not seem to have fully grasped this aspect of Zarqawiism. The plan assumes that the world's "1.5 billion" Muslims will unite under a reestablished caliphate and in doing so generate tremendous geopolitical power. But Zarqawi in 2006—and the Islamic State in 2016—argued that most of those people were in fact apostates who should be killed. For them, the umma includes far fewer than 1.5 billion people. This is a disastrous position for al-Adl's master plan because the relatively few remaining "true" Muslims would necessarily wield much less power.

Al-Adl's master plan was designed with Zarqawi in mind, but not Zarqa-wiism.

Maqdisi also failed to understand Zarqawi's vision of a much smaller *umma* and urged the younger man to get guidance from religious scholars regarding *takfir* as a result. But Zarqawi was already beginning to define anyone who advocated temperance as an enemy, and because he considered participation in violent jihad the preeminent indicator of religious knowledge, Zarqawi's own reasoning compelled him to federate the authority for *takfir* to those who "understood" Islam best—not scholars in a library but soldiers on the frontline.

Indeed, the Islamic State's willingness to kill laypeople, not just leaders within "apostate" movements, is the flipside of this ideological populism. Whereas al-Qaeda was willing to pardon laypeople led astray by ideologues and political leaders, the Islamic State aimed to hold them accountable for their "apostasy."

This anti-elitism is a defining feature of Zarqawiism, and it is inextricably linked to Zarqawi's conflict with Maqdisi. The younger Jordanian tried to avoid confronting his former mentor, but ultimately abandoned that forbearance. "Do not listen to a deceitful person," Zarqawi thundered in a September 2004 audio statement, "speaking under the guise of an adviser to dissuade you from seeking martyrdom or victory."[132] Zarqawi responded even more directly in July 2005: "The injustice inflicted by kinsmen is more painful than the impact of a sharp sword."[133]

More important than passive-aggressive personal barbs was Zarqawi's building of an argument to undermine the scholarly credentials that were the basis of Maqdisi's authority in the jihadi movement. The battlefield, Zarqawi argued, offered the only meaningful certificate of ideological and scholarly authority. "Throughout history, scholars were at the forefront of jihad," he argued in 2005. "They did not preach to the nation about the rules of jihad and then fail to undertake jihad as a duty. . . . The [historical] jihadi scholars carried the Book [Quran] and sword in their hands on the front line. . . . A scholar living in the land of infidels away from the arenas of jihad and the real situation of the mujahidin should not issue fatwas."[134]

Zarqawi returned to this theme often. In 2006, he explained the conviction that "true knowledge comes not from memorizing texts, publishing, preaching, leading teach-ins, or issuing fatwas. . . . Whoever has a share of knowledge while giving up the major religious duties for the sake of ensuring safety, taking rest, loving worldly life, or submitting to the unjust, he has betrayed the message and lost the trust. Therefore, he has deviated from the bounds of good knowledge, and separated from the blessed caravan of good knowledge. . . ."[135]

Zarqawiism's emphasis on action over scholarship as the foundation for ideological authority was carried on after his death. All of his successors have emphasized that trustworthy jihadi scholars must be on the front-lines of jihad. For example, Abu Umar al-Baghdadi, the first emir of the Islamic State of Iraq (ISI), proclaimed in April 2007 that "when we proclaimed the State of Islam as a state of emigration and jihad, we did not lie to God or the people . . . we are more capable of understanding God's tradition in this jihad. The source of this understanding is the blood of the mujahidin, both migrants and local supporters."[136]

Even Zarqawi's personal sense of identity enabled him to sustain criticism from scholars like Maqdisi. In the late 1980s Zarqawi called himself *gharib*, the stranger. The nickname recalled a widely recounted saying of Muhammad: "Islam began as a stranger, and it will be a stranger again. Blessed are the Strangers."[137]

But Zarqawi took the *gharib* identity to an extreme: criticism was not simply to be disregarded; it actually confirmed that he was on the right path. Public disparagements were a test of commitment to God's will. Muhammad had been similarly tested, Zarqawi reasoned, so his group must not compromise its values because "true" Muslims were "the good few among the evil many. Those who oppose them are more than those who obey them, but [the true Muslims] are the ones who reform people when they become corrupt."[138]

The *gharib* identity continues to steer the Islamic State today. It dovetails with the Islamic State's strategy to sort the Muslim community into apostates and "true" Muslims and explains why both Zarqawi and the Islamic State embrace brutal tactics despite widespread criticism. As the former street thug put it: "The supposed Muslim who follows the pure creed but who refrains from jihad is corrupt and immoral. A Muslim who carries out jihad for God but who is influenced by heresy is better than the [Muslim] with no resolve who does not take part in jihad."[139] In essence, violent jihad is a religious trump card.

It is an unsurprising sentiment from a former street thug and pimp who felt such shame that he cut a tattoo off his own arm. And it helps explain why the Zarqawiist Islamic State has been so successful pulling in recruits with criminal histories. Zarqawiism is an ideology of redemption.

Zarqawi had a particular person in mind when he described his ideal jihadi scholar. Abu Anas al-Shami, the jihadi scribe of Fallujah, was thirty-four when he joined Zarqawi in Iraq, shortly after the fall of Saddam Hussein. A Palestinian born in Jordan, Abu Anas studied at the Islamic University of Mecca and was an acolyte of Maqdisi, who considered him a star student.[140] In late 2002, Abu Anas resigned his academic position and left for Iraq,[141] where Maqdisi hoped he would moderate Zarqawi's more extreme tendencies.

Instead, Abu Anas quickly embraced Zarqawi's battlefield logic, arguing for war against the Shia and confrontation with apostates, and decrying scholars who "sold the nation very cheaply to leaders of perversion."[142] Zarqawi eventually listed Abu Anas as one of his greatest influences, but not because of his religious training. Rather, Zarqawi explained, "his manliness made an impression on me."[143] Zarqawi used Abu Anas' conversion to taunt Maqdisi, claiming that the elder jihadi's criticism of their operations in Iraq had pushed Abu Anas to tears.[144]

Jihadis obsequiously celebrate their leaders' deaths, spinning unbelievable stories of courage, portent, and joyous self-sacrifice. But even by that standard, the memorials for Abu Anas were over the top. He was killed near the infamous Abu Ghraib prison, ostensibly while leading a raid on the facility. The jihadi version is that the moonlight shimmered against his face before the raid advanced, revealing holy determination in spite of deathly premonitions. The jihadis insist that he vowed to lead the assault despite his lack of military training, and they chronicle the tears of his soldiers when Abu Anas did not return.

Whatever actually happened, Abu Anas' death was another blow to Maqdisi's influence on Zarqawi, as well as a personal loss. Maqdisi did not sugarcoat his displeasure, writing, "A man that reaches Abu Anas' maturity and level of education must not be used in such an operation, regardless of the justification. . . . [Abu Anas] was free to make his choice, if he wanted martyrdom. But I, as an official, would not have sent him on such a mission."[145] It is often lost on observers that by 2004 or so, Zarqawi did not particularly care what Maqdisi would have done.

Maqdisi is often considered Zarqawi's most important intellectual influence, but Zarqawi himself told a different story. One of Zarqawi's commanders recalled the jihadi leader pointedly excluding Maqdisi from a list of his biggest ideological influences. Zarqawi, he claimed, said, "I have never been influenced by a scholar in my life, as I was influenced by Sheikh Abu Anas al-Shami and Sheikh Abu Abdallah al-Muhajir."[146]

Indeed, if Abu Anas was the quintessential warrior-scholar, it was Abu Abdallah who defined Zarqawi—and the Islamic State's—embrace of sectarianism, brutality, and suicide tactics that have come to define Zarqawi-ism's adherents.[147]

It is hard to imagine a time when Zarqawi, who applied assembly-line principles to suicide bombing, opposed their use; but he did. Throughout their imprisonment in Jordan, Maqdisi and Zarqawi opposed suicide bombings (a position that put them at odds with Jordanian supporters of the Palestinian Islamist group Hamas).[148] Maqdisi was the driving force for this perspective (though his position too has changed over time), so it is unsurprising that Zarqawi's view evolved when he traveled to Afghanistan in 1999. As he put it:

> I believed that such operations [suicide bombings] were unacceptable when I was in Afghanistan during the Soviet invasion and before having met al-Maqdisi. When I met him, my conviction aligned with his proclamations. When we left jail and returned to Afghanistan I met Sheikh Abu Abdallah al-Muhajir. We discussed Islam's position on martyrdom operations, and the sheikh approved of them. I read his valuable research and listened to his cassette tapes. Not only was I convinced that such operations are acceptable, I came to prefer them. By God, this is the blessing of knowledge and the meeting of scholars.[149]

Abu Abdallah al-Muhajir did not just reorient Zarqawi's thinking on suicide bombings.[150] As the shariah official at the Khalden training camp

in Afghanistan, he took many radical positions that marked him as an extremist among the Arab jihadis in Afghanistan. Al-Muhajir taught that
Shia were apostates, championed beheadings, and criticized Arab jihadis
for fighting alongside the Afghan Taliban, who he considered insufficiently
Islamic.[151] Abu Mus'ab al-Suri represented the most pro-Taliban wing of
the international jihadis in Afghanistan, and al-Muhajir held down the
other end of the spectrum.[152]

Al-Qaeda viewed al-Muhajir and many recruits at Khalden as extremists—
and the Taliban shut down the Khalden Camp in 1998 for the extreme
views taught there.[153] Zarqawi, however, picked up where Khalden left off.
He was so impressed by al-Muhajir that he invited the scholar to teach at
his training camp near Herat, a program that he reported, "had a very
positive influence on the brothers."[154]

To the dismay of some of his supporters, al-Muhajir softened his anti-
Taliban rhetoric when they threatened to kick him out of the country.
Nonetheless, his harsh views made a lasting impression on Zarqawi and
the future Islamic State.[155] Zarqawi ordered copies of al-Muhajir's writing,
most famously a book called the *Jurisprudence of Jihad* (known colloquially
among jihadis as the *Jurisprudence of Blood*) to be distributed among the
insurgents during the occupation of Fallujah. In 2012, the *Jurisprudence of
Jihad* began to appear in Lebanon as the Islamic State prepared for overt
war in Syria, and when the German journalist Jurgen Todenhofer was
allowed to travel through the Islamic State in 2013, he reported that the
Jurisprudence of Jihad was the first book the Islamic State had printed.[156]

Indeed, Zarqawi's advisors in Iraq were convinced that if al-Muhajir had
made it to Iraq, Zarqawi would have made him head of his Shariah Committee. Instead, he was among those jihadis captured and held in Iran.[157]

Zarqawi himself referenced al-Muhajir in a May 2005 statement explaining his use of mass-casualty attacks, including those that killed Muslims accidentally:

> The core of this statement is based on research by our mujahid Sheikh
> Abu Abdallah al-Muhajir, may God protect him. . . . There can be no doubt
> that God has ordered us to fight and kill the nonbelievers in every possible
> way. The mujahidin are therefore able to use all means to take the souls of

the nonbelievers, cleanse their filth from the earth, and prevent the harm they would cause Muslims. . . . This is permissible even if it means killing a number of Muslims that happen to be near operations for some reason. . . . There is no doubt that killing a Muslim is evil, but sometimes you cannot avoid this evil when fighting a bigger evil.[158]

Indeed, Zarqawi's fidelity to al-Muhajir's ideas in 2005 illustrates the limits of his *bayah* to Osama bin Laden six months earlier. Despite the covenant with al-Qaeda, Zarqawi continued to draw explicitly on a jihadi intellectual tradition that had been hostile to the Taliban and al-Qaeda prior to 9/11.

Al-Muhajir was an important influence on Zarqawi, but he never operated in Iraq, so Abu Anas' death left an outsized hole in al-Qaeda in Iraq's (AQI) Shariah Committee. The man who replaced him was a young scholar named Abu Hamzah al-Baghdadi, who became a forceful propagandist, releasing pamphlets inside Iraq, and pushing audio and video statements to the web. He was the first Iraqi to serve as an international proponent of Zarqawiism.

Abu Hamzah al-Baghdadi was also the first AQI scholar not to simply describe the caliphate as a goal to be achieved, but to outline how it might be governed. In a forty-eight-page book released in June 2005, Abu Hamzah al-Baghdadi explained that, "this group aims to restore the rightly-guided caliphate in accordance with the prophet's policy and method."[159] But then he went a step further and argued that whoever was selected Caliph must descend from the Prophet Muhammad's tribe of Quraysh.

Abu Hamzah al-Baghdadi's commitment to a Qurayshi assuming the role of Caliph was widely held among jihadis, but had thus far been absent from AQI proclamations. It was based on a story about how the Prophet Muhammad's "worldly successor" was selected. Muhammad was born into the Qurayshi tribe from the city of Mecca, but he fled to Medina with a small band of followers when the Qurayshi hierarchy cracked down on his growing religious movement. He recruited many more supporters in Medina, which led the Medinans to suggest that they select two successors upon the Prophet's death—one of Muhammad's original followers of Qurayshi descent, and another from Medina.

Muhammad's original Meccan companions rejected that idea, arguing "the Arabs will only follow a man from the Quraysh tribe."[160] According to Abu Hamzah al-Baghdadi this implied an obligation, not a matter of preference. After all, he reasoned, if "the selection of a successor from Quraysh was not an obligatory duty, the [Prophet's companions'] argument would not have prevailed."[161]

It took another sixteen months before AQI declared an Islamic State, and more than nine years before that Islamic State declared itself The Caliphate. During that time, the so-called Islamic State has had two emirs: Abu Umar al-Baghdadi and Abu Bakr al-Baghdadi, who is currently considered the Islamic State's Caliph. Both claim to descend from the tribe of Quraysh.

There is a paradox built into Zarqawiism. The ideology exalts the near-term establishment of the caliphate, but it also takes the antiestablishment position that because violence implies the truest understanding of Islam, relatively low-level people must be empowered to make far-reaching religious decisions.[162] This populist dogma is a double-edged sword. On the one hand, it empowers adherents and recruits to reject political and religious hierarchies that do not support violence; on the other hand, the Islamic State aims to build a political and religious hierarchy of its own. The contradiction is that Zarqawiism provides the intellectual basis for internal factions to reject those new structures.

In this respect, Zarqawiism is essentially the logical outcome of classical jihadi ideas preached during the anti-Soviet jihad. Nelly Lahoud, in *The Jihadis Path to Self-Destruction*, argues that classical jihadi ideas introduced the theological rationale for rejecting Muslims that did not support specific forms of violence. She predicted that this would eventually produce an unstable jihadi movement characterized by intra-jihadi violence. Zarqawiism is that hyper-violent ideology and the Islamic State is that jihadi movement.[163]

The Islamic State's embrace of Zarqawiism has far-reaching implications. First, the movement is prone to internal fracture. If every adherent is encouraged to reject hierarchy that contradicts their conscience, then every member of the Islamic State is empowered to disobey the leadership. Of course, most will not, but Zarqawiism is nonetheless a shaky foundation on which to build a government, let alone one that supposedly has the reach of a caliphate.

Moreover, Zarqawiism discourages the Islamic State from settling into a peaceful status quo with its international neighbors. Zarqawiism argues that religious and political legitimacy is primarily a function of participating in war. Although Zarqawi held out the possibility of truces, he also argued that Muslims could not truly fulfill their obligation to God without fighting. As a practical matter, it means that the Islamic State will always remain at war.

Zarqawiism values both the personal salvation offered by the practice of violence and the collective end state that violence aims to achieve. Zarqawiism's adherents believe that time on earth is a testing ground for a longer and more important existence after death. Although Zarqawi was not primarily focused on end-times prophecies, the Islamic State celebrates his references to eschatology, and his successors introduced apocalyptic prophecies into the group's overall vision.[164] The Islamic State's English-language magazine, *Dabiq,* is named after a town in Syria that Islamic prophecy names as the site of an end-times battle between Islam and forces of disbelief.[165] Every issue of *Dabiq* begins with a Zarqawi quote: "The spark has been lit here in Iraq, and its heat will continue to intensify—by Allah's permission—until it burns the crusader armies in Dabiq."

The mystery of Umar Izz al-Din, Abu Muhammad al-Maqdisi's son, was resolved in June 2010.[166] Umar had not been killed in 2003 during the initial attack on Iraq. Rather, U.S. forces captured him on January 31, 2004, just before the first battle of Fallujah. He spent most of the next seven years in American prisons in Iraq before being released in 2009, as the United States was drawing down its forces.[167] He immediately returned to the fight, moving to the jihadi stronghold of Mosul before actually being killed in late May or early June of 2010.

It is not clear if American forces knew Umar's true identity while he was in prison. He passed himself off as Iraqi, and few other prisoners knew that he was the son of one of the most prominent jihadi thinkers in the world.[168] Anonymous or not, Umar apparently kept busy. According to a letter to his father, he memorized the Quran in Camp Bucca and led a prisoner uprising against the American guards. Nonetheless, Umar's greatest contribution to the jihadi cause was probably the anxiety his disappearance created for his father, which sharpened the confrontation with Zarqawi and fostered the antiestablishment ethos of Zarqawiism that has nurtured the Islamic State.

Zarqawi's *bayah* to bin Laden temporarily papered over their ideological and organizational disagreements. Al-Qaeda's core operated as a small, elite organization with a big-tent ideology. It aimed to work with a wide range of Islamist militants, even those with whom it disagreed on key issues. Zarqawi had a stricter conception of what made a good Muslim and objected to working with militants who did not meet that standard. But he also imagined a more accessible, populist organization than al-Qaeda had been traditionally. Al-Qaeda was built as a special operations task force, with fewer than 200 members on 9/11, and its leaders did not intend it to grow significantly larger. Zarqawi aimed to build a conventional army.

Despite these differences, al-Qaeda's leaders hoped to align Zarqawi's strategy with their own. Fuad Husayn's book on the "second generation of al-Qaeda"—which contained al-Adl's seven-stage master plan—was serialized in the London-based Arabic newspaper *Al Quds al-Arabi* in May 2005. Shortly thereafter, Ayman al-Zawahiri, al-Qaeda's second-in-command, sketched a very similar four-stage plan in a letter to Zarqawi dated July 9, 2005. The stages were:

1. Expel the United States from Iraq;
2. Declare an Islamic emirate, "then develop it and support it until it reaches the level of a Caliphate";
3. Extend "the jihad wave to the secular countries neighboring Iraq"; and
4. Confront Israel.[169]

Zawahiri's letter contradicts the notion that al-Qaeda envisioned developing a caliphate only in the distant future. Rather, the expedited timeline favored by Zarqawi, and codified in the master plan, had gained favor with Zawahiri as well:

> If our intended goal in this age is the establishment of a caliphate in the manner of the Prophet and if we expect to establish its state predominantly—according to how it appears to us—in the heart of the Islamic world, then your efforts and sacrifices—God permitting—are a large step directly towards that goal. So we must think for a long time about our next steps and how we want to attain it.[170]

Of course, Zawahiri may have rhetorically supported Zarqawi's near-term goal of a caliphate in order to focus his attention on an even more urgent problem: the potential for infighting among Sunni militants in Iraq, especially if the United States were to leave precipitously. Zawahiri remembered the dramatic American withdrawal from Vietnam, the Afghan civil war after the Soviet Union withdrew, and the Taliban's challenge of relating to everyday Afghans. "We don't want to repeat the mistake of the Taliban," Zawahiri explained, when it failed to "have any representation for the Afghan people in their ruling regime, so the result was that the Afghan people disengaged . . . from them."[171]

To avoid that outcome, Zawahiri proposed establishing an Islamic emirate to prevent infighting among Sunnis and ensure that the jihadis were ready to govern when the United States withdrew from Iraq.[172] The idea sounded good, but Zawahiri would come to regret it.

United States' forces came across a copy of Zawahiri's July 2005 note to Zarqawi in the home of AQI's Baghdad emir, which they raided in September of that year.[173] In an unusual move intended to publicize Zawahiri's concern about the brutality of Zarqawi's military campaign in Iraq, the U.S. Director of National Intelligence released a copy of the letter to the public the following month. Zawahiri famously admonished Zarqawi to "avoid any action that the masses do not understand or approve," and argued that al-Qaeda is "in a race for the hearts and minds" of the global community of Muslims. Zarqawi's brutality, he explained, would drive far more Muslims away from al-Qaeda than it would attract.[174]

The formal split between al-Qaeda and the Zarqawiists was still nearly a decade away, but Zawahiri and Zarqawi were already speaking different languages in 2005. Zawahiri was concerned with slowly winning over the world's Muslims en masse, but Zarqawi simply disagreed with that vision. For Zarqawi, the primary challenge was to separate "true" Muslims from apostates, so revulsion among Muslims to his brutality only helped clarify who his enemies were. Moreover, Zarqawi was in an increasingly strong position to ignore Zawahiri. In 2003, Zarqawi had requested funds from al-Qaeda through a courier; in 2005, Zawahiri's letter requested money from Zarqawi.

For some observers in the West, Zawahiri's disapproval of Zarqawi's tactics seemed too convenient; they wondered if the letter was a forgery.[175] Western scholars were not the only skeptics. An AQI spokesman claimed that the letter had "no foundation except in the imagination of the politicians of the Black House and their slaves."[176]

It is not clear whether Zarqawi genuinely believed the letter to be fake or not. It is possible that the U.S. forces intercepted the letter in transit and Zarqawi never saw it until the United States released it. But a more likely scenario is that Zarqawi was employing a subtle stalling tactic, designed to give Zarqawi plausible deniability as he ignored Zawahiri's direct instructions. Whatever the case, the letter's authenticity would ultimately be confirmed by al-Qaeda, but only after Zarqawi directly disobeyed its guidance.

The Bride

On August 7, 2005, a gray 1985 Mercedes carrying three men crossed into Jordan from Iraq.[177] It looked like any other vehicle, but this particular Mercedes had a specially retrofitted gas tank that allowed one half to hold gasoline and the other to be used as a storage space. In that special compartment were seven 107-millimeter Katyusha rockets.[178]

It was not the first time that Zarqawi used this sort of tactic. A year earlier, his fighters in Iraq smuggled themselves into Jordan inside large tanker trucks as part of a plot to detonate chlorine bombs in Amman. Jordanian authorities disrupted the plot, which they said would have killed tens of thousands of people.[179]

Perhaps because that ambitious strike had been prevented, the men in the gray Mercedes aimed for something smaller. The group stopped in

Amman to survey the American embassy, but decided that it was too hardened to make a good target. So they traveled south to Aqabah, a Jordanian port city on the Red Sea that abuts the Israeli port of Eilat. After noticing two American ships, the USS Kearsarge and the USS Ashland, in the Israeli port, the men set their rockets to launch from a rented workshop and fled back to Iraq.[180]

On the morning of August 19, 2005, three of the rockets launched toward U.S. ships in Israeli territory, and the rest failed to fire. None hit their intended targets, though an errant explosion killed a Jordanian soldier.[181]

The attack was mostly ineffective, but it was an important political statement because it illustrated Jordan's vulnerability and represented an attack on both Israel and the United States outside of the core battlefield in Iraq. Both AQI and the Abdallah Azzam Brigades, the group founded by Salah al-Qar'awi (Zarqawi's Saudi compatriot from Fallujah and husband to Hakaymah's daughter), claimed responsibility for the attack. Although the strike was directed from inside Iraq, the Abdallah Azzam Brigades' claim had some credibility; over the previous year it had claimed responsibility for killing more than 100 people in bloody attacks targeting Israelis at the Egyptian resort cities of Taba and Sharm al-Sheikh.[182] Either way, Zarqawi was extending his influence outside of Iraq.

Thamir Mubarak, mastermind of Zarqawi's strikes on the UN Headquarters in Baghdad and of the assassination of Ayatollah Hakim, died early in the first battle of Fallujah.[183] When AQI memorialized him it noted, among other plaudits, that he came from a family in which all of his brothers were wanted by the United States.[184] It turns out, however, that it was not one of the brothers that would be the family's most infamous jihadi. Rather, it was a sister.

Sajidah Mubarak Atrous al-Rishawi was 35, unmarried, and frustrated in her ambition of being a suicide bomber. So on the evening of November 4, 2005, Sajidah's cousin escorted her to a discreet ceremony where she was introduced and wed to Ali Husayn ali al-Shammari.[185] Their coupling would be short-lived. The next day, the newlyweds crossed into Jordan from Iraq with two other men. The three men used legitimate passports, but Sajida employed a forged Iraqi passport to hide the connection to her notorious family.[186]

It was a terrible honeymoon.

On the evening of November 9, Ali bent down in the rented house they shared in Amman and carefully attached a suicide belt to his bride. After a brief consult with their housemates, the couple strolled into the night and then into the lobby of the Radisson SAS Hotel, one of Amman's nicer venues. The hotel hosted a wedding nearly every day, and like many in the lobby, Sajidah and Ali were dressed for a celebration. They crossed the lobby and stepped into a crowded ballroom where a wedding reception was ongoing. Sajidah paused, then pulled the detonator cord on her suicide vest.

Nothing happened. Panicked and angry, Ali ordered her back into the lobby and then climbed on top of a table and exploded. Ali's vest, like Sajidah's, was made with a military-grade explosive called RDX and enclosed in a jacket of metal ball bearings designed to produce as many casualties as possible.

Thirty-six people were killed at the Radisson SAS that evening, including both the father of the bride and the father of the groom. Not far away, Sajidah and Ali's partners were committing similar atrocities. One bomb exploded at the Grand Hyatt and another outside the Days Inn. All told, more than sixty people were killed.

Panicked, Sajidah fled. But she did not make it far. She was arrested at the home of distant family, relations of Thamir Mubarak's partner-in-crime, Nidal Arabiyat. The partnership between Mubarak and Arabiyat was a key kernel of Zarqawi's initial campaign of terror in Iraq, and its legacy continued.[187]

The following morning, AQI triumphantly claimed responsibility for the hotel attack. "Let the tyrant of Amman know that the protection wall for the Jews . . . and the backup military camp to the armies of the Crusaders . . . is now a target for the mujahidin," they crowed. Their gleeful mood would soon change.[188]

Not long after claiming responsibility for the Amman attacks, AQI took the unusual step of releasing a second statement. The group's tone had shifted. Instead of unadulterated triumphalism, they tried to justify the target selection. The targeted hotels, AQI claimed, were "favorite spots for intelligence activities, especially for the Americans [and] the Israelis," and were "a secure stage for the dirty Jewish tourists . . . to practice their whoredom and fornications at the expense of the blood and sufferings of Muslims."[189] The bold talk, however, could not hide the fact that AQI was playing defense.

Public opinion in Jordan shifted dramatically after the attacks. Sajidah al-Rishawi, having escaped the murder-suicide pact that killed her husband, could not escape public humiliation at the hands of Jordanian authorities. She was immediately shown on television, despondently opening her celebratory clothes to reveal the ineffectual suicide vest. The message was clear: AQI might have killed on a massive scale, but it employed miserable women to do so. It was hardly the vision of brave Muslim soldiers that Zarqawi and al-Qaeda hoped to project.

A week after the bombing, Zarqawi himself released an audio statement defending the attack. He explained that Israeli embassy employees lived at the Radisson and that AQI meant no harm to the Jordanian people, who "are more beloved to us than ourselves and our own offspring."[190] For all of Zarqawi's talk about polarizing Muslim society, he understood that there were limits and that he had crossed one. Now, he was trying to walk back the mistake.

The November 2005 attack on the three Western hotels in Jordan was Zarqawi's most dramatic strategic mistake. Public support for al-Qaeda in Jordan plummeted from 56 percent in 2003 to 20 percent in 2007.[191] Ten days after the attack, seventy-five members of Zarqawi's al-Khalayilah clan released a statement in four newspapers disowning the jihadi leader. "He is not related to Jordan, has never drunk its water or sought its shade," they charged, "because a Jordanian does not aim his arrow at his own people. We disown him until judgment day."[192] It was exactly the reaction that Zawahiri's letter to Zarqawi had warned about.

Al-Qaeda's leaders were livid.

Civil Wars

"Policy must be dominant over militarism," wrote Atiyah Abd al-Rahman to Zarqawi three days after the Amman bombing. "Readying the brothers . . . and preparing them to be messengers between you and the leadership here is more important than . . . sending the brothers for some operations like the recent operation of the hotels in Amman."[193] Like al-Adl, Atiyah was an al-Qaeda commander in Iran, where he managed the group's communications. A rising star in al-Qaeda, he aimed to link Zarqawi more tightly with al-Qaeda's leadership.

Atiyah was frustrated because Zarqawi had flouted the substance of Zawahiri's letter of July 9, 2005, and his deputy had called it an American forgery. To the contrary, Atiyah reported, the Zawahiri letter released by the U.S. Director of National Intelligence was "genuine," and it "represents the thoughts of the brothers, the Sheikhs, and all of the intellectual and moral leadership here."[194]

Atiyah urged Zarqawi to engage a broader range of advisors in Iraq, even those with "unorthodox" religious views. All of this was necessary, he reminded Zarqawi, because "you, as a leader and a jihadist political organization who wants to destroy a power and a state and erect on its rubble an Islamic State, or at least form the building block [sic] on the right path, need all of these people."[195] He ordered Zarqawi to stop all attacks outside of Iraq without explicit permission from al-Qaeda's senior leadership.

At the time, Atiyah's letter was the harshest repudiation of Zarqawi that al-Qaeda's leadership had ever delivered—and Zarqawi took it seriously. He was not a total rogue actor, and he fell in line *almost* immediately.

On the evening of December 27, 2005, two Katyusha rockets fired from southern Lebanon fell harmlessly into northern Israel. Israeli warplanes responded the next day by targeting a camp used by the People's Front for the Liberation of Palestine—General Command (PFLP-GC), a Palestinian terrorist group backed by the Syrian regime.[196] The PFLP-GC never claimed responsibility, but on December 29, 2005, AQI did, calling it "fulfillment by the mujahidin of their oath to Osama bin Laden."[197] The Lebanese army continued to point at the PFLP-GC. Two weeks later, Zarqawi personally reiterated AQI's responsibility.[198]

This was the first time an al-Qaeda affiliate claimed responsibility for an attack on Israel proper (as opposed to the U.S. warships in harbor at Eilat).[199] Perhaps AQI was lying, though it did claim the attack twice. Perhaps the strike was simply a target of opportunity. But it is worth noting that the strike was consistent with the 'Eye-Opening Stage' of the master plan, during which jihadis were to begin "direct confrontation with the State of Israel in Palestine."[200]

Despite claiming the external strike on Israel, Zarqawi was bringing his operation in Iraq in line with the instructions in Zawahiri's letter.

Zawahiri worried that the al-Qaeda brand was increasingly counterproductive in Iraq, and he urged Zarqawi to develop something more appealing to Iraqis. On January 15, 2006, al-Qaeda in Iraq's spokesman announced the establishment of the Mujahidin Shura Council (MSC), which was composed of AQI and several small insurgent groups.[201] The generic name aimed to obscure AQI's dominant role in the consortium and recall the halcyon moment of Sunni militant cooperation in Iraq—the "Mujahidin Shura Council" that Abu Anas al-Shami put together in 2004 to coordinate the defense of Fallujah.

Zawahiri thought it would be more appropriate to have an Iraqi as the ostensible leader of jihad in Iraq, so someone called Abdallah bin Rashid al-Baghdadi, an unknown, was named the MSC's emir.[202] Zawahiri fretted that Zarqawi's media presence would alienate local Iraqi allies, so Zarqawi dramatically reduced his visibility. Between July and December 2005 he issued ten major media statements; in the following six months he released just three.[203]

AQI and the other constituent groups in the MSC re-branded immediately. The MSC logo appeared on public statements and Abdallah bin Rashid al-Baghdadi announced the coalition's first big military campaign, a series of sectarian assassinations that it called 'The True Dawn Contest.'[204]

The MSC even pulled in some new allies. Over the long term, the most important proved to be a highly sectarian group based in Iraq's Diyala Province called the Army of the Followers of the Sunnah and Collective (AFSC). The small group officially joined the MSC several weeks after the initial announcement, but had clearly been following Zarqawi's guidance long before then.[205] The group had an unusually sophisticated vision for jihadi governance that was premised on borrowing Western governing principles, but its most important feature was the bright young emir of its Shariah Committee, Abu Bakr al-Baghdadi. Eight and a half years later, he would be anointed Caliph Ibrahim, emir of the Islamic State and ostensible global leader of all Muslims.

In January 2006, however, Zarqawi was still the primary jihadi authority in Iraq, and he was trying to prevent a complete break with al-Qaeda's leadership. He had revamped AQI's media strategy to align with Zawahiri's instructions, and hoped Zawahiri was primarily concerned with style, not substance. After all, Zawahiri had urged Zarqawi to stop displaying so much brutality, but he did not ask Zarqawi to stop killing prisoners, only that they be shot rather than beheaded.[206]

Zarqawi hoped to continue his sectarian polarization strategy, but in ways that aligned with Zawahiri's media guidance. So it was no surprise that as AQI prepared one of the most important and far-reaching sectarian attacks of the Iraq war, it also decided not to claim responsibility.

In retrospect, it is also unsurprising that al-Qaeda was considering directly challenging Zarqawi's leadership of AQI.

The al-Askariyya Shrine in Samarra, Iraq, was originally built in AD 944 to honor Ali al-Hadi and his son Hasan al-Askari, whom Shia Muslims consider the 10th and 11th successors to the Prophet Muhammad. The shrine was covered with a brilliant golden dome in 1905, which enhanced its already prominent place in Shia religious and cultural life. By many accounts it is the third holiest location for Shia Muslims in Iraq. In February 2006 it became the site of the most important bloodless attack of the Iraq war.

While the city of Samarra slept on the morning of February 22, 2006, a longtime Zarqawi supporter from Tunisia was frantically wiring explosive charges inside the al-Askariyya Shrine.[207] The Tunisian, with two Iraqis and four Saudi fighters, had overpowered the shrine's guards, locked them in a closet, and set to the task of destroying a 1,100-year-old holy site.[208]

The Tunisian's bomb exploded before dawn, destroying the golden dome but killing no one. The attack on al-Askariyya was meant to incite, not to kill, and it succeeded. The following day, authorities in Baghdad found fifty-three Sunni men in civilian clothing bound and blindfolded, with bullet holes through the backs of their heads.[209]

Consistent with its new media policy, Zarqawi and the Mujahidin Shura Council disavowed the al-Askariyya bombing and accused the Iraqi government and Iranian-backed militias of staging the attack to justify a crackdown on Sunnis.[210] Several other Sunni militant groups released a rare joint statement echoing the Mujahidin Shura Council and excoriating the Iraqi government for tolerating retaliatory attacks against Sunni mosques.[211] In Iran, the Supreme Leader, 220 members of Parliament, and a parade of religious leaders blamed the United States.[212] Perhaps most importantly, the most senior Shia cleric in Iraq, Grand Ayatollah Ali al-Sistani, who has often been a voice for moderation in Iraq, called for Shia militias to defend shrines from further aggression.[213] In the days after the Samarra bombings, this opened the door for sectarian retribution by a slew of Shia militias that even Sistani could not control.

In short, Zarqawi's long-sought sectarian civil war was finally happening.

The Tunisian was arrested and interrogated in June 2006, and he revealed that the al-Askariyya bombing mastermind was a Samarra native named Haitham al-Badri, who before the U.S. invasion had come from a wealthy family with extensive connections in Saddam's Iraq.[214] Al-Badri joined the insurgency shortly after the U.S. invasion and after initially working with Ansar al-Sunnah, the successor to Ansar al-Islam, aligned with Zarqawi.[215]

Al-Badri's shift is notable because Zarqawi never trusted Ansar al-Sunnah, despite its ideological similarities with AQI. His precise concern is unclear, but he may have worried about the group's embrace of some former members of Saddam's security structure. In later years, Zarqawi's successors would go to war against breakaway factions of Ansar al-Sunnah. The godfather of the Islamic State was probably worried it was infiltrated.

Interestingly, al-Qaeda was far less worried about Ansar al-Sunnah's ideological and political purity. In his letter to Zarqawi after the Amman bombings, Atiyah urged the Jordanian to "consult with your mujahidin brothers who are with you in Iraq, such as our brothers Ansar al-Sunnah and others, no matter your worries or reservations about them."[216]

There is no evidence that Zarqawi followed that particular instruction, but al-Qaeda engaged the group directly, despite Zarqawi's misgivings. A few weeks after Zarqawi created the MSC, but before the al-Askariyya bombing, al-Qaeda's "Special Committee for Mujahidin Affairs in Iraq" drafted several letters to Ansar al-Sunnah's leadership. On January 26,

2006, it suggested that Ansar al-Sunnah should "unify" with AQI but understood that the group would only do so "after reforming the situation of AQI."[217] Three days later, the committee sent another letter, assuring Ansar al-Sunnah's leadership that Osama bin Laden's first priority was "unity" with Ansar al-Sunnah and urging that "all the obstacles standing in the way must be removed."[218]

One of those obstacles may have been Zarqawi himself.

Indeed, al-Qaeda was taking practical steps to resolve the issues with its troublesome affiliate in Iraq. Al-Qaeda's second letter to Ansar al-Sunnah, dated January 29, 2006, reported that it had "taken a blessed step toward improving the conditions by sending an honorable brother and a virtuous Sheikh" to Iraq.[219] Al-Qaeda did not name its emissary, but noted that "you know him very well."[220]

Al-Qaeda's leaders, distant from the battlefield, frustrated by inadequate communications, and confounded by Zarqawi, had only had a few bullets with which to influence events in Iraq. In the wake of Zarqawi's biggest strategic misstep, the Amman hotel bombings, they pulled the trigger on a big one.

It would be months, however, before al-Qaeda's emissary could possibly make a difference on the ground in Iraq. And in the meantime, all hell was breaking loose.

The al-Askariyya shrine bombing inaugurated the sectarian fight that Zarqawi was hoping for. Sunni insurgents and Shia militias, some operating within the purview of the Iraqi army, massacred one another on the streets of Iraq's cities. Neighborhoods that had been diverse for years were purged by militants happy to torture, behead, and brutalize their victims with everything from power tools to battery acid. It was exactly the fight that Zarqawi described in his 2004 letter to Osama bin Laden.

But holes in Zarqawi's approach appeared immediately. He hoped that open sectarian warfare would compel terrified Sunnis to embrace AQI. But AQI's brutality, violent clashes with other militants,[221] and efforts to monopolize long-established tribal smuggling routes created friction with other Sunnis even before the al-Askariyya bombing.[222] After al-Askariyya, the Sunni tribes faced a massive backlash from Shia militant networks, just as Zarqawi hoped. But AQI did not have the power to defend them. Iraq's population is 65 percent Shia; Zarqawi had picked a fight he could not win.

On April 24, 2006, Zarqawi appeared in a video propaganda piece in which he taunted the United States, exalted "the mujahidin," and decried collaborators with the Iraqi government, which he argued was controlled by Iran.[223] Zarqawi presented himself as a true military commander, walking with jihadis in the desert and firing an assault rifle. It was his first appearance on video in Iraq without a mask.

American troops were not surprised to see the video when it appeared online. Only a week earlier, British commandos raided an AQI safe house and uncovered a large cache of weapons and documents, including an unedited version of Zarqawi's video and an M4 rifle with a grenade launcher that strongly resembled a weapon that appeared in the video.[224] The unedited version of the video was replete with misfires and outtakes. One of Zarqawi's aides even grabbed the scorching business end of an M249 automatic weapon after it had been fired. After the final video was released, American commanders released those outtakes and ridiculed Zarqawi for his amateurism, even disparaging his New Balance sneakers.[225]

The snark was a purposeful effort to convince Sunni fighters that Zarqawi was not a competent soldier, but it was probably ineffective.[226] After all, most Iraqi militants did their fighting in civilian clothes, and the jihadi community remembered Abu Anas al-Shami, who had grown famous for wearing the shabby shoes that Zarqawi teased were no good for combat. The United States was ridiculing Zarqawi's tennis shoes, but the jihadis' most storied martyrs wore even more inappropriate footwear.

The intelligence operation to track Zarqawi was more effective than the effort to discredit him. Only months after British commandos collected the raw video, a U.S. unmanned aerial vehicle was circling north of Baghdad, near Baqubah, its camera trained on an isolated home surrounded by palm trees.

Zarqawi was alerted to the danger at the last second. He had survived a moment like this once before, five years earlier in Afghanistan. With that knowledge, he burst through the front door of the house and began to sprint. But moments later, two 500-pound bombs dropped from a U.S. F-16 exploded behind him. The concussion knocked him forward, crushing his internal organs. When troops from the elite U.S. Delta Force arrived shortly thereafter, Zarqawi was still clinging to life. The last thing he saw may have been the face of a U.S. soldier.[227]

Zarqawi was found after an AQI administrator, captured in the raid that uncovered his raw video footage, named Zarqawi's spiritual advisor. A task force under U.S. Joint Special Operations Command tracked the advisor for weeks, using drones to follow his movements, until he traveled north from Baghdad toward Baqubah. When the drone's camera caught him greeting a shadowy figure that looked like Zarqawi, U.S. commanders decided to strike.[228]

Zarqawi's mystique as a survivor compelled the U.S. military to publicly release bloodied photos of his face to prove his demise. The intent was to demystify a jihadi who stood second only to Osama bin Laden in global prominence. But Zarqawi's supporters did not focus on the blood. They claimed that Zarqawi looked as if he were smiling in death; some even detected a hint of a halo around his head.

Zarqawi was dead, but Zarqawiism would live on.

Zarqawi's death prompted remembrances and eulogies from jihadis around the world. The most important came from Ayman al-Zawahiri, who had been deeply critical of Zarqawi for a year. On some level, Zawahiri must have been relieved by Zarqawi's death, but he was nonetheless obsequious in his praise for the younger man. "It does not matter when we die," Zawahiri explained. "What matters is how we die . . . the commander of the martyrdom-seekers died a martyr."[229]

But it was Zawahiri's instruction to Zarqawi's followers still in the fight that was most important. "You must establish an Islamic state in Iraq," he urged, "then make your way towards captive Jerusalem and restore the caliphate."[230]

3

The Stage of Standing Upright
(2007–2010)

U.S. and European outrage at the current Syrian regime . . . will undermine the Syrian regime's ability to manage domestic security. . . . The *Jund al-Sham* concept was proposed in Afghanistan many years ago. . . . The young men who built it have returned to Syria and Lebanon. Some are currently in Iraq. . . . By the end of this stage, al-Qaeda intends to have completed preparations for direct clashes with Israel.

Fuad Husayn, *Zarqawi . . . The Second Generation of al-Qaeda*

Declaration of Independence

The man called Husayn gazed out across al-Marjah Square in central Damascus. His eyes settled on a man standing across the square, who looked like one of the four Libyans he had come to meet. But Husayn sensed that something was wrong. The Libyan was lingering near an empty car that looked suspiciously like those from Syria's feared internal intelligence service, the Mukhabarat. But that was just one problem. Husayn was equally concerned about why the Libyan wanted to meet here, just down the block from Syria's Ministry of Interior.

Husayn called his partner, Abu Hafs. Everything was wrong, he said. First, the Libyans had failed earlier to arrive at the appointed meeting spot, and then they had failed to call Husayn's cell phone to explain the delay. Husayn called one of them instead, but the Libyan claimed his group had run out of money and could not pay for a taxi. The Libyan suggested that Husayn and Abu Hafs collect the men in downtown Damascus; after some debate, Husayn and Abu Hafs agreed, despite the fact that the meeting point was almost literally in the shadow of the Ministry of Interior. Now the man Husayn believed was their contact was hanging out right next to a Mukhabarat vehicle.

Abu Hafs told Husayn to relax. Newly arrived recruits in Syria, like these four, were often ignorant about what to expect, and there were so many Mukhabarat running around Damascus that the car in al-Marjah Square was probably just a coincidence.

Abu Hafs and Husayn went ahead with an adjusted plan to collect the Libyans, despite the obvious risks. Perhaps there was money involved; perhaps they did not want to report failure; perhaps Husayn later fabricated the whole story. It is hard to know, because the report Husayn wrote for his superiors focused more on what happened than why.

The plan went like this: Husayn would walk in front of the "Libyan," make eye contact and listen for his accent to make sure that the man was actually Libyan. If he was, Husayn would call his cell phone again and direct him to Damascus' al-Hamidiyah Souq, which was several blocks away. Named after the Sultan who built it in 1780, al-Hamidiyah Souq is an immense covered shopping arena with congested side alleys, swirling crowds of shoppers, and eighty-year-old bullet holes in the iron roof from the 1925 rebellion against the French. Al-Hamidiyah would be a good place for Husayn and Abu Hafs to collect the Libyans unnoticed or, if needed, escape surveillance. While Husayn directed the Libyan, Abu Hafs would watch from a distance to see if they were followed.

Husayn crossed into the open and strolled in front of the would-be Libyan, listening intently. The man's Libyan dialect was clear and Husayn immediately felt more at ease. He retreated a bit, looked out across the square, and called the Libyan's phone as planned, instructing him to move across the square to his right. The Libyan complied, but slowly. Trailing behind him, clear as day, was another man whom Husayn immediately identified as Mukhabarat.

Husayn knew he was vulnerable. This was supposed to have been an easy pickup, but it was turning into something much more dangerous. He regretted having left his gun at home that morning. He hissed into the phone, telling the Libyan he was being followed and urging him to move faster. But the Libyan would not speed up, even with the intelligence agent obviously trailing him. Husayn concluded that "he was a collaborator or was under arrest and they were using him as bait," so he hung up and called Abu Hafs to warn him.[1] But the Libyan and his Mukhabarat fellows had identified Abu Hafs. Per Husayn's report, they closed on Abu Hafs' position and shot him.

Husayn escaped al-Marjah Square (his report does not describe how), but he knew the operation had been a disaster. If the Mukhabarat managed to interrogate Abu Hafs, it was impossible to know what he might reveal; the Syrian regime had very well-practiced torturers. In his report, Husayn was contrite about the failure. "My mistake from the beginning was that we should have withdrawn, and I did not take my weapon with me."[2]

It is easy to second-guess Husayn's decision to trust the Libyan when he suggested they meet in al-Marjah Square at the last minute. On the other hand, Husayn understood the risks involved in smuggling fighters through Syria into Iraq. The Syrian government often tolerated the jihadi smugglers; other times it cracked down. Always, spies were everywhere. Key nodes of the network regularly vanished. Abdallah al-Faranci, who held Belgian and Moroccan citizenship, had recently disappeared; the Mukhabarat had raided Umar al-Salmani's guesthouse; and Husayn suspected that Abu Yasir was secretly undermining Abu Ghadiyah, the organization's most important coordinator in Syria.

Despite the busted operation in al-Marjah Square, Husayn's commitment to the movement did not waver. They were involved in a historic project and he had no time to focus on the past. He had near-term responsibilities; most importantly, to get to Mecca where he would meet with brothers from Lebanon and Gaza.

It was August 2007, and Husayn was no ordinary smuggler. He was a soldier of the Islamic State.

Abu Hamzah al-Muhajir was named emir of al-Qaeda in Iraq on June 12, 2006, only three days after Zarqawi was killed.[3] It was a new role for the Egyptian jihadi, who had built his reputation as a bomb-maker.[4]

At first glance, Abu Hamzah's ascension to the leadership of AQI seemed like it would please al-Qaeda. Abu Hamzah had arrived in Baghdad in 2002 and had grown up in the Egyptian Islamic Jihad, Ayman al-Zawahiri's original terrorist organization. But some jihadis who knew Abu Hamzah were immediately concerned about the appointment. Harun Fadil, al-Qaeda's representative in East Africa (and a strong ally of Sayf al-Adl), was one. Fadil had worked with Abu Hamzah in Afghanistan and believed him to be a "patient and pious brother" but suggested he was more of an operator than a strategist and "does not like being an emir."[5] There were other problems as well. "From the moment Brother Hamzah was chosen as emir in Iraq," Fadil wrote, "I understood that the strategy would change, and some strictness would appear. . . . Specifically, I mean the Egyptian ideology of not accepting other people's views."[6] Fadil worried that Abu Hamzah would be even more intransigent than Zarqawi.

The dual questions hanging over Zarqawi's successor were whether he would align AQI more closely with al-Qaeda's central leadership and whether he could strengthen AQI's relationship with Iraq's Sunni tribes. The new emir had deep ties with al-Qaeda and Zawahiri, but he was also an ideological hard-liner more disposed to executing attacks than delicate politics. He was not well positioned to manage Iraq's intricate tribal relationships.

Abu Hamzah released his first major policy statement on September 7, 2006, nearly two months after he was appointed emir.[7] He clumsily tried to walk a fine line between Zarqawi-esque sectarianism, respect for al-Qaeda's leadership, and a blunt desire to continue Zarqawi's campaign to sort "true" Muslims from Sunni "apostates." He ended with a call to arms: over the ensuing fifteen days, every member of AQI was to kill an American soldier, and every Sunni in Iraq was to kill a Shia.[8] Those that did not would reveal their true colors.

Abu Hamzah was in no position to demand anything of Iraq's Sunnis writ large, but he was in a race against time. His public statements omitted a long-standing pillar of AQI's strategy, which was to kill Sunni leaders who opposed the polarization strategy in Iraq. Many of these Sunni leaders, enraged by AQI's attacks, its provocation of the Shia, and its efforts to take over smuggling routes and other illicit enterprises they had long controlled, increasingly rejected the group.[9]

In September 2006, a group of Sunni tribal leaders convened in Ramadi to declare their collective opposition to AQI and the Mujahidin Shura
Council.[10] Many had originally supported the Iraqi insurgency, but they
had more recently been negotiating with American forces about getting
weapons directly from the United States.[11] This new coalition quickly became known as the Awakening.[12]

The Islamic State of Iraq (ISI) was born into this hostile environment on
October 15, 2006.[13] Its mission was dramatically different from either AQI
or the Mujahidin Shura Council: the ISI was meant to govern both territory and people. In 2005 Zawahiri urged Zarqawi to establish an "emirate"
to forestall conflict among Sunnis, and before his death in 2006 Zarqawi
expressed his intent to declare a state. Their public support for the idea
was likely part of Abu Hamzah's rationale for declaring the ISI.[14]

The emir of this new jihadi state was not Abu Hamzah but a man totally
unknown to al-Qaeda's leadership: Abu Umar al-Baghdadi. The ISI later
explained that Abu Umar had been selected by a committee of senior leaders in Iraq, but there is no way he could have been designated without Abu
Hamzah's direct approval. Harun Fadil remarked that Abu Hamzah never
wanted to be an emir, so perhaps it was in character to choose another
man for that role. But Abu Umar had another qualification: Zarqawi's Shariah Committee had specified in 2005 that any future caliph should descend from the Prophet Muhammad's tribe of Quraysh. Abu Umar fit that
description; Abu Hamzah did not.

Most importantly, both the final decision to establish the ISI and Abu
Umar's selection occurred without al-Qaeda's input. To this day, al-Qaeda's
leadership resents the slight.

Abu Umar al-Baghdadi was born Hamid Dawud Muhammad Khalil
al-Zawi in al-Zawiyah, a neighborhood of Hadithah, a city in Anbar Province. He was from a prominent family, attended the police academy in
Baghdad, and ultimately served as an officer in Saddam Hussein's national
police. According to jihadi biographies, he was fired for espousing "extremist" views and returned to Hadithah to work as a handyman and serve
as the Imam at a small mosque.[15] Baghdadi trained with small jihadi
groups in Anbar even before the U.S. invasion; he joined Zarqawi's group
after meeting with Abu Anas al-Shami and another of Zarqawi's senior

aides, Abu Muhammad al-Lubnani, in 2003.[16] Abu Umar went on to serve as Zarqawi's governor in Diyala Province and then, in 2006, was appointed emir of the ISI and, implicitly, caliph-in-waiting.[17]

Zarqawi was dead and Zawahiri distant when the ISI was declared, but both had earlier conceived of the ISI as an interim step toward reestablishing a caliphate.[18] In the West, the ISI was seen as just another rebranded AQI, like the Mujahidin Shura Council.[19] In fact, however, it immediately set out to build a scalable bureaucratic framework that would eventually define the Islamic State during the Syrian civil war. Specifically, the ISI:

- Named a cabinet, including Ministries of Agriculture and Marine Wealth, Oil, and Health;
- Executed small-scale public works projects, like irrigation canals;
- Managed health and safety regulations, including setting speed limits on roads;
- Created an internal bureaucracy for political and military administration;
- Called on "Muslim brothers around the world, especially those neighboring our dear state" to emigrate, and promised to "provide them with benefits and expertise";[20]
- Enforced strict financial accounting procedures;
- Completely rebranded all of its propaganda;
- Enforced rigorous pay scales and cared for the family of deceased fighters;
- And recruited members with a range of administrative and scientific backgrounds, not just military experience.[21]

In other words, many of the affectations of a "state" that drew global attention when the Islamic State burst onto the global scene in 2014 were originally developed in 2006.[22]

Perhaps the most telling indicator of the ISI's institutional and strategic importance is the controversy it caused among Sunni militants in Iraq and jihadis around the globe. Even the group's critics—and there were many—considered the declaration a seminal event. The critiques fell into three categories: that the ISI was not powerful enough to govern and therefore should not have been declared; that its leadership—specifically Abu Umar al-Baghdadi—did not have the requisite reputation, experience, or support to lead an Islamic state; and that the ISI was attacking other Sunni militants in Iraq and therefore was illegitimate.[23]

Abu Hamzah and Abu Umar anticipated these criticisms and attempted to deflect them even in the announcement establishing the ISI.[24] Most powerfully, they compared the ISI to the Prophet Muhammad's original emirate in Medina. The Prophet's state, they argued, originally did not control a large territory and faced massive opposition from both internal and external enemies; yet no Muslim would consider it illegitimate. The ISI, they claimed, imposed "control over many areas, which have an area equal to the size of the first state of Medina."[25] The rhetorical trick was obvious: to doubt the legitimacy of the ISI was to doubt the Prophet himself.

The ISI published its version of *The Federalist Papers* later in 2006. *Informing the People about the Islamic State of Iraq* defended the new "government" from its critics and set out, in ninety pages, the key principles on which it was founded, including the state's responsibilities to its citizens and processes for leadership succession.[26] It described a flexible feudal organization built on regional leaders swearing allegiance to the emir, who would take power through one of three processes: a consensus of wise men, appointment by the previous emir, or—if needed—via force. The book also made the state's priorities clear: imposing Islamic law would take precedence over providing services to the population because "improving their conditions is less important than the condition of their religion."[27]

Critically, *Informing the People* rejected the notion that the ISI must defend a specific, static territory in order to be legitimate. Although controlling *some* territory was necessary, the ISI was conceived as a flexible entity with validity based on collective allegiance to its leader, rather than a fixed set of borders.[28] It also argued, ominously, that "the state of war is a natural state in the life of the Islamic state, whether in the beginning of its development, before, or after."[29]

When the ISI was initially declared, it did not preclude the existence of other jihadi networks in Iraq. But three weeks after the ISI was founded,

Abu Hamzah officially dissolved AQI and the Mujahidin Shura Council and announced "the integration of all the formations that we have established, including the Mujahidin Shura Council . . . under the authority of the Islamic State of Iraq." According to the erstwhile emir of AQI, this meant "putting at [Abu Umar al-Baghdadi's] disposal and direct orders 12,000 fighters, who constitute the army of al-Qaeda . . . as well as more than 10,000 others who are still not fully prepared."[30]

For many jihadis, Abu Hamzah's announcement represented a turning point in the history of jihad. Writing on Muhammad Khalil al-Hakaymah's *Promise Keepers* website, Yaman Mukhaddab, a prominent jihadi theorist and pundit, tied the announcement directly to *The Management of Savagery* and alluded to the seven-stage master plan: "By exploiting open combat, al-Qaeda removes the individual's third option: it will expose his hatred and hypocrisy and force him to reveal unbelief by joining the enemy's camp; or he will become a mujahid, in which case [al-Qaeda] will instruct him lovingly, correcting his beliefs, cleansing it of pollution, and . . . will train him in combat and destroying the enemy."[31] According to Mukhaddab, al-Qaeda's master plan to establish "a caliphate" in order "to restore sovereignty on earth to God, liberate enslaved Muslims . . . and protect Muslims' religion, life, honor, and wealth," had moved to the next stage.[32]

Mukhaddab clearly had Sayf al-Adl's master plan in mind. His statement was titled *Al-Qaeda Between the Last Stage and the One Announced by al-Muhajir,* and it suggested that the ISI's progress should be measured according to the plan's conceptual milestones rather than its specific timeline. Indeed, this is probably the best way to think about the master plan—not as a schedule, but a set of interim strategic goals to achieve in pursuit of a grand world revolution.

Mukhaddab seems not to have understood or cared that al-Qaeda's most senior leadership was not consulted on the declaration of the ISI. He certainly did not guess that the ISI's establishment would eventually lead to full-scale intra-jihadi civil war.[33]

If Mukhaddab had looked more closely, he might have seen that the outlines of that future conflict were already coming into focus. In early 2007, Sunni militants in Iraq angrily chastised al-Qaeda's leaders for the ISI's missteps. Refusing to acknowledge the group's new name, they declared that al-Qaeda would be held "responsible in front of God for blessing the work done by the al-Qaeda in Iraq organization without disavowing the scandals that are committed in your name."[34]

Such criticism must have stung al-Qaeda's leadership, much of which was already furious with Zarqawi before his death. "After all," they must have thought, "we have been trying."

Coup?

At 4:30 in the afternoon on October 16, 2006, the phone in the Anti-Smuggling and Organized Crime Directorate of the Gaziantep police station began to ring. The caller did not provide a name, and the official Turkish record of the phone call indicates that the police did not determine whether the caller was male or female. Whoever the anonymous caller was, however, they were well informed. He or she explained that several Iranian nationals were traveling from Gaziantep to Kilis, the Turkish city an hour south of Gaziantep and just north of the Syrian border. The Iranians were using forged passports, claimed the caller, and were traveling in a vehicle with the license plate 79 M 0064.[35]

Gaziantep is no stranger to odd travelers. It is a major transportation center with a population of 1.5 million and serves as a natural jumping-off point for traders and smugglers moving to and from Syria. After the Syrian civil war began in 2011, Gaziantep became a hub for all manner of men and women drawn to catastrophes—foreign jihadis, spies, journalists, and aid workers. For many jihadis traveling to join the Islamic State, Gaziantep is the last stop before they enter the "caliphate."

On October 16, 2006, however, the "caliphate" did not exist; indeed, the ISI had been announced, to minimal fanfare, only a day before. There were fewer foreigners in town than in 2016, but one had just attracted a lot of attention.

Based on the anonymous tip, the Anti-Smuggling and Organized Crime Directorate sprang into action. The police established a checkpoint at the University Boulevard intersection, at the southeast corner of Gaziantep University, and they soon intercepted a vehicle with the license plate 79 M 0064. They seized three adults—two men and a woman—and four children. The leader of the group was one of the adult males, who introduced himself as an Iranian named Muhammet Reza Reanjbar Rezaei, which matched the name on the Iranian passport he provided.[36]

The Directorate of Foreigners in the Gaziantep police department found the passport highly suspect. A Turkish entry stamp dated November 1, 2005, matched computerized entry records, but there was no exit stamp. Moreover, there were no computer records matching three other entry and exit stamps in the passport.[37] Whoever provided the mysterious tip to the Gaziantep police department was on to something.

The man calling himself Muhammet was given a lawyer and deposed at 11:00 p.m. on the same day he was captured. After some discussion about his passport's inconsistencies, and in an apparent effort to be cooperative, the man offered that his name was not actually Muhammet; it was Abdulrahman bin Yar Muhammad. Moreover, he was not Iranian. He had been born in Takhar, Afghanistan, and lived in Kabul with his wife and four children. Because of the "bad political and economic situation" in Afghanistan, the man now called Abdulrahman wanted to "go to a country where [he could] get a better job, to get a better education for [his] children, and to have a better life."[38] He was a refugee, he said, and ultimately hoped to take his family to Europe. He was arrested while on his way to Syria, where he planned "to do some sightseeing" during the holy month of Ramadan before moving on to the family's ultimate destination.

Abdulrahman was apologetic about the forged passport. He had purchased it for $500 from criminals in Iran, who promised that it would make his travel into Turkey easier. He said he had crossed into Turkey four days earlier and, after a brief respite in the lakeside town of Van, had arrived in Gaziantep the morning he was arrested. His wife, "Sonia," interviewed separately, told the same story.[39]

Abdulrahman was adamant that he did not want to return to Afghanistan. He requested asylum in Turkey; if that was not an option, he asked that his family should be sent to Pakistan.

Neither Abdulrahman nor the local police who arrested him knew that a different set of Turkish authorities knew quite a bit more about him than simply the license plate of the vehicle he was using in Gaziantep. Turkish intelligence had been tracking a cell phone carried by one of two Turkish al-

Qaeda operatives, Mehmet Yilmaz and Mehmet Resit-Isik, who had crossed into Iran to help Abdulrahman and his family across the border.[40] The intelligence officers knew that Yilmaz was a longtime al-Qaeda operative who had fought in Afghanistan in 2001 and allegedly supported the 2003 Istanbul bombers.[41] They knew that the two men had facilitated Abdulrahman's travel to Gaziantep, and they knew that another al-Qaeda operative, Mehmet Polat, had met the family and was to help them cross the border into Syria. Polat had been driving the vehicle the Gaziantep police stopped.[42]

Most importantly, they knew that the name of the man arrested in Gaziantep was neither Muhammet Reza Reanjbar Rezaei nor Abdulrahman bin Yar Muhammad.

He was Abd al-Hadi al-Iraqi: the Kurdish-born former Iraqi army officer who chafed when Abu Mus'ab al-Suri tried to poach his recruits in Kabul, and eventually became al-Qaeda's commander for all of Afghanistan. He was not a refugee en route to Europe: he was on his way to Iraq.[43]

In January 2006, al-Qaeda's Iraq committee explained to Ansar al-Sunnah that a man they knew well was on his way to resolve the problems with Zarqawi.[44] Indeed they did. In late 2003, Abd al-Hadi had politely asked Zarqawi whether he should personally travel to Iraq. At the time, Zarqawi said "no." In the wake of the disastrous Amman hotel bombings in November 2005, Zarqawi was not offered a veto.

In mid-2005, Ayman al-Zawahiri's letter to Zarqawi suggested AQI would be better off if led by an Iraqi. Zarqawi responded eventually by appointing an Iraqi head of the MSC in January 2006. But it is possible that Zawahiri was not thinking of just *any* Iraqi; he may have been thinking of a *particular* Iraqi: Abd al-Hadi.

Whatever Zawahiri's intent, Abd al-Hadi was one of al-Qaeda's top-tier leaders and, as an Iraqi, had credentials and connections that even Zarqawi could not match.

Abd al-Hadi's journey seems to have gone relatively smoothly, but it was slow. Al-Qaeda's note to Ansar al-Sunnah suggesting Abd al-Hadi was en route was dated January 29, 2006, but the United States Military Commission charge sheet against Abd al-Hadi indicates that he "began to travel to Iraq . . . in or about June 2006."[45] Abd al-Hadi did not actually arrive in Turkey until October, at which point Zarqawi had been dead for four months.

There are several possible explanations for this muddled timeline, including the logistics of getting out of South Asia or a long layover in Iran to engage al-Qaeda's leadership there.

It is also possible that al-Qaeda's January 2006 note referred to someone other than Abd al-Hadi, but this seems unlikely. As an Iraqi, Abd al-Hadi was a natural choice for the mission and he had indicated an interest in journeying to Iraq years earlier. Moreover, as an ethnic Kurd it would make sense that al-Qaeda's leaders would reference a familiarity between him and the predominately Kurdish leadership of Ansar al-Sunnah.

When Abd al-Hadi crossed into Turkey, the intelligence authorities were extraordinarily well-prepared. It suggests that they were tipped to Abd al-Hadi's travel far in advance, either by sources in Iran or the United States. According to the Turkish journalist Rusen Cakir, the CIA was deeply involved in the surveillance of Abd al-Hadi, and its operatives urged that he be arrested and deported to Iraq immediately after he crossed into Turkey. According to this story, Turkish officials explained that they could not arrest him arbitrarily and that they had no extradition treaty with Iraq. Turkish authorities did, however, surreptitiously stop the bus Abd al-Hadi took from Van to Gaziantep to confirm he was on board.[46]

The anonymous tip-off to the local police department reporting a forged passport may have been a mechanism to circumvent opposition to seizing Abd al-Hadi. Indeed, it is easy to imagine the CIA officials' angst as Abd al-Hadi waited in the Yozgat refugee camp while Turkey considered his asylum request.[47]

The CIA officials need not have worried too much. Although Abd al-Hadi's lawyer, Osman Karahan, was experienced in jihadi cases and in good standing with the Turkish judicial authorities, he lacked credibility. Two years earlier, Karahan was barred from representing Luai Sakka, the Syrian who was Zarqawi's first recruit at the camp in Herat, when Karahan himself was charged with supporting al-Qaeda.[48] The charges against Karahan were dropped, but his voice was not the most influential in Turkish courts. Eventually, Abd al-Hadi's request for asylum was denied.[49]

At 2:00 a.m. on October 31, 2006, Abd al-Hadi was ushered onto Turkish Airlines flight 706 from Istanbul to Kabul. When the plane landed, the

CIA was waiting for him.[50] So ended al-Qaeda's boldest attempt to assert direct control over the jihadi insurgency in Iraq.

It remains unclear exactly what Abd al-Hadi aimed to do in Iraq. Bin Laden wrote to Ansar al-Sunnah about its senior emissary while Zarqawi still lived, but Abd al-Hadi did not cross into Turkey until months after Zarqawi's death. Was his original mission to seize control of AQI from Zarqawi? Was he there simply to provide advice to AQI's leadership?

It seems deeply unlikely that either Zarqawi or Abu Hamzah would have relinquished authority, even to someone so senior as Abd al-Hadi. Perhaps Abd al-Hadi aimed to build an al-Qaeda affiliate out of Ansar al-Sunnah, which abided al-Qaeda far more than Zarqawi. Or maybe Abd al-Hadi aimed to negotiate integration between AQI and Ansar al-Sunnah? Abd al-Hadi's arrival might even have splintered the ISI and led to the sort of open warfare between jihadis that emerged years later in Syria between the Islamic State and the al-Qaeda affiliate Jabhat al-Nusrah.

Abd al-Hadi's route toward Iraq tells its own story. He did not try to cross directly into Iraq from either Iran or Turkey, but added at least two risky border crossings and detoured across hundreds of miles of Turkish territory. His itinerary suggests al-Qaeda trusted its networks in Turkey and Syria. Indeed, the strength of this connection foreshadowed the primary route of the greatest jihadi migration in history, which has occurred during the Syrian civil war.

But in the wake of Abd al-Hadi's arrest, at least some of al-Qaeda's Turkish network collapsed. The facilitators Mehmet Yilmaz and Mehmet Resit-Isik traveled to Iraq, where they became known as the "Turki Brothers" and were killed by U.S. troops on June 23, 2007.[51] Mehmet Polat, Abd al-Hadi's driver in Gaziantep, assumed leadership over the Turkish al-Qaeda network in Gaziantep. He had worked with Yilmaz for years, even testifying in 2002 that the two had traveled together across Iran for training in Afghanistan.[52] But Polat's reign was short; in January 2008, Gaziantep police killed him, his son, and two other men in a shootout.[53]

Abd al-Hadi remains confined at the military prison in Guantanamo Bay, awaiting trial.

Even the lawyers do not survive this story. In August 2012, Osman Kara-han, the lawyer who filed Abd al-Hadi's asylum petition, was killed in Aleppo fighting with the Syrian opposition.[54] For those watching closely, it was an early indication that many of the foreign recruits joining the fight in Syria had deep jihadi ties.

Muslim Blood Is the Red Line

Al-Qaeda's best chance to control the ISI fizzled when Abd al-Hadi was arrested one day after the new "Islamic State" was declared. But the ISI was about to face other challenges. The U.S. strategy to increase troops in Iraq and embed them more deeply in Iraqi neighborhoods—the "Surge"— encouraged Sunnis dissatisfied with the ISI to rebel against the jihadis and, in some cases, to engage the Iraqi political process. By early 2007 this uprising—the "Awakening"—was reshaping the Iraqi insurgency. Militant groups that had previously organized to maximize military effectiveness be-gan to splinter, and new coalitions emerged, built on shared political ideas.

The most important new coalition to confront the ISI was a collection of Iraqi Islamists known as the Jihad and Reform Front (JRF).[55] The JRF's component groups were self-declared salafis, many of which had a legacy in Saddam Hussein's military. Several had cooperated closely with the ISI previously. Nonetheless, the JRF was wary of the ISI's absolutism and fo-cused on reforming Iraq rather than reshaping the entire Middle East. Some of the JRF partners were even willing to engage the Iraqi political process, a controversial position that eventually doomed the coalition.[56] But in 2007, the JRF emerged as the ISI's most visceral enemy, in part because the groups had similar ideological perspectives.

The militant restructuring that gave rise to the JRF was often localized and personality-driven, but two broad shifts were critical. The first was the dissolution of Ansar al-Sunnah, a group that al-Qaeda engaged regularly and was the ISI's closest ideological partner in Iraq. The second was the formal splintering of Iraq's Ba'athist opposition.

Ansar al-Sunnah and the Zarqawiists always had a complex relationship. Ansar al-Sunnah's predecessor, Ansar al-Islam, hosted Zarqawi prior to the United States' invasion of Iraq, but Zarqawi distrusted the organization, and Ansar al-Sunnah was wary of subsuming itself in AQI. After the ISI was declared however, Abu Umar and Abu Hamzah renewed their call for Ansar al-Sunnah to swear allegiance. Al-Qaeda had long supported unity between Ansar al-Sunnah and the Islamic State's predecessors, and they continued to do so in early 2007. Al-Qaeda's leadership did not understand, however, that ISI leaders were increasingly disavowing the al-Qaeda leadership and that the ISI's wanton killing was alienating Ansar al-Sunnah.

At the same time, Ansar al-Sunnah was wrestling with internal conflicts. It was an amalgamated organization composed of a primarily Kurdish faction led by Abu Abdallah al-Shafi'i and a largely Arab faction that organized under Abu Wa'el, the Arab jihadi that the Bush Administration erroneously cited as evidence that Saddam was linked to al-Qaeda. The Bush Administration's claims were overstated, but it was true that Abu Wa'el was not fully aligned ideologically or politically with the rest of Ansar al-Sunnah. In early 2007, he walked out of an American prison in Iraq, and proceeded to tear Ansar al-Sunnah apart. In the process, he established himself as one of the ISI's most hated enemies in Iraq.

Zarqawi had hoped that sectarian war would compel Sunnis in Iraq to rally under his leadership, but the announcement of the ISI had the opposite effect. Ten days before the ISI was established, a competing salafi group called the Islamic Army of Iraq declared publicly that "[t]he Muslim blood is the red line" and hinted darkly at future conflict with the Zarqawiists.[57] In a publicly released speech, one insurgent described the ISI's history in terms unfamiliar to its supporters:

> [AQI] did not do anything wrong at the beginning . . . then the group suddenly, and oddly, began . . . to liquidate scholars of Shariah and others. This was followed by attacks on everyday Sunnis living their lives; they planted bombs in front of homes, schools, and hospitals, and under electric generators without considering the importance of [these facilities] for society. . . . They went too far on the issue of *Al-Tatarrus* [killing of Muslims as collateral damage], exceeding all limits.[58]

In January 2007 similar complaints emerged online from the Ansar al-Sunnah Shariah Commission (Shariah Commission), the faction of Ansar al-Sunnah led by Abu Wa'el. Their core complaint was the ISI's tendency to accuse "the Muslim who disputes with you of being a nonbeliever, and to regard blood feud (killing) him as lawful."[59] The message was startling, both because of its content and because it had been posted in a relatively public environment. Although the forum was password protected, other senior jihadi leaders would certainly be able to see it.

Abu Wa'el and the Shariah Commission were increasingly at odds with the rest of Ansar al-Sunnah, but they agreed on the ISI's crimes. Over the first three months of 2007, however, al-Shafi'i looked for a way to reconcile with the ISI. He and Abu Hamzah exchanged numerous letters in an effort to resolve their differences.[60] In a dispute that foreshadowed the conflict between ISIS and al-Qaeda's Syrian allies in 2014, al-Shafi'i demanded a panel of shariah experts to mediate their dispute, but the ISI saw itself as the highest Islamic authority and would not agree. In late March, Abu Hamzah drafted a handwritten note (which he considered a sign of respect) to al-Shafi'i apologizing for any wrongdoing, but rejecting impartial mediation. The ISI was a true state, he explained, and urged al-Shafi'i to "come over and let us be united against the others," which may have been a reference to the growing split between al-Shafi'i and Abu Wa'el.[61]

Al-Shafi'i was unsatisfied with Abu Hamzah's apologies, so his deputy emir reached out directly to al-Qaeda's Atiyah abd al-Rahman for help. He complained that the ISI had declared any Sunni insurgent working outside the "state" to be an apostate. Moreover, he explained, multiple people in the ISI "at the leadership level [claim] to be an independent state and to not have ties with al-Qaeda and the Sheikh (bin Laden)."[62]

The accusation concerned Atiyah deeply. Ansar al-Sunnah was led by credible jihadis, many of whom had fought and trained in Afghanistan; over the previous eighteen months the group had sent emissaries to meet with al-Qaeda's leadership. It was hard to believe the ISI would really consider itself independent of al-Qaeda, but Ansar al-Sunnah's testimony was credible.

On March 15, 2007, Atiyah elevated the complaint to Mustafa Abu Yazid, al-Qaeda's operations chief in Pakistan. "[The ISI claims] that if [other insurgents] carry out work without authorization from the ISI," he wrote, "[the ISI] will consider them sinful and deserving punishment."[63] Nonetheless, Atiyah continued to express confidence in the ISI's leadership, largely because Abu Hamzah himself told a much more positive story. Atiyah attached a recent letter from Abu Hamzah to illustrate his point.

Two weeks later, however, Atiyah's confidence was wavering. In another note to Abu Yazid, he lamented, "[T]he brothers [in Iraq are] making political gaffes," which "give our enemies and rivals an opportunity to exploit [the people]."[64] He was particularly concerned by a recent public speech from Abu Umar al-Baghdadi that suggested "they are extremists." Even worse, Atiyah complained, Abu Hamzah and Abu Umar had stopped communicating.

Despite his private reservations, Atiyah aimed to project confidence to Ansar al-Sunnah. On April 5, 2007, he downplayed the group's complaints. "These are strange stories," he argued. "[They] are unfounded and unreliable and they contradict what we are already certain of."[65] Although Atiyah privately fretted about Abu Hamzah's lack of communication, he assured Ansar al-Sunnah that "we are in continuous contact with [the ISI's leadership] . . . and we know their religion, knowledge, morals, and level of piousness."[66] Lastly, he reassured al-Qaeda's second-closest ally in Iraq that the ISI remained accountable to al-Qaeda's leadership. "Abu 'Umar and Abu Hamzah and their military and legal committees," he declared, "continue to send us with pleasure their letters of allegiance and loyalty."[67] If those letters exist, as of this writing they are not public.

Atiyah backed the ISI's leadership, but his response to Ansar al-Sunnah belied ignorance about Abu Umar and Abu Hamzah's increasing isolation in Iraq. He lamely assured Ansar al-Sunnah that any abuses by the ISI have been "the action of some of the junior officers in specific sectors."[68] That was probably partly true to an extent, but the ISI's internal discord was no defense. After all, Ansar al-Sunnah had its own problems.

On April 9, 2007, Abu Wa'el publicly renounced Ansar al-Sunnah and declared that the Shariah Commission was an independent organization.[69] It was a dramatic shift for Abu Wa'el. He had spent the previous two years in prison, but unlike so many other militants in Iraq, he did not radicalize there.[70] Instead, Abu Wa'el emerged ready to directly challenge the ISI. His enemies asserted that he had cut a deal with the United States while in prison; Abu Wa'el conceded that the United States had proposed a "truce," but that he rejected the idea.[71]

Regardless, Abu Wa'el founded the Jihad and Reform Front with the leaders of the Islamic Army of Iraq (IAI) and the Mujahidin Army. The IAI was the largest of these groups and was composed mostly of religiously minded former Iraqi army officers. The Mujahidin Army was grounded in Iraq's pre-invasion salafi community. Its shariah official, Muhammad Hardan, was particularly despised by the ISI. Not only had Hardan fought in Afghanistan, but he had also once taught Abu Bakr al-Baghdadi, who in future years would become Caliph Ibrahim, leader of the Islamic State.[72] Hardan's connections to international jihadis suggested other relationships as well: the IAI and, by default, the JRF were widely believed to receive financial support from Saudi Arabia.[73]

The JRF never renounced violence against the United States, but the front's opposition to the ISI suggests some odd relationships. Abu Wa'el, a man touted by the Bush Administration as a critical link between Saddam Hussein's regime and al-Qaeda prior to the invasion of Iraq, walked out of a U.S.-run prison in Iraq to become one of the ISI's most hated enemies.[74] If nothing else, Abu Wa'el was a first order opportunist.

Pressure was mounting on the ISI. In response, on April 17, 2007, Abu Umar gave a speech that remains one of the group's most famous public statements. His rallying cry that day has sustained the Islamic State's supporters ever since:

> The State of Islam will remain. It will remain because it has been built on the bodies of martyrs and has been irrigated by their blood. Preparations for going to heaven have been made in it. [The State] will remain because God's commitment to its success is clear. . . . It will remain because the leaders who have sacrificed their blood are honest and so are the soldiers who have committed so much. God will reward them. [The State] is the land of the mujahidin, and the haven of the oppressed.[75]

Abu Umar closed by drawing on the outsider *gharib* ethos that Zarqawi had embraced years earlier. Criticism of the ISI, Abu Umar explained, was actually evidence of its impending victory. The Islamic State "will remain because infidels of all stripes collude against us, and every coward with some new religious innovation defames and maligns [it], and therefore we became certain that the goal and our path towards it are correct."[76]

While Abu Umar tried to rally the ISI supporters with a public speech, Abu Hamzah aimed to exploit Ansar al-Sunnah's split to win over the factions that remained loyal to al-Shafi'i. On April 30, 2007, perhaps as a result of pressure from al-Qaeda central, he drafted an extraordinarily deferential note to al-Shafi'i with the ISI's best unification offer. Abu Hamzah apologized for past mistakes and even promised al-Shafi'i he would "carry your shoes on my head and kiss them a thousand times."[77] Most importantly, however, he offered al-Shafi'i a powerful role in the ISI if Ansar al-Sunnah agreed to swear allegiance. Like a politician trading ministerial positions to build a governing coalition in a parliamentary democracy, Abu Hamzah offered al-Shafi'i control over "the most important issues . . . which are the war and the justice."[78] Indeed, this was likely a literal offer for ministerial positions in the ISI, which had a minister of war and minister of shariah.

But there was a condition. If al-Shafi'i joined the ISI, he had to accept its commitment to building an Islamic State and respect the authority of Abu Umar. "The only request we have," Abu Hamzah explained, is "for you not to touch the scheme of work for the Islamic state by law and the Emir."[79]

If al-Shafi'i had accepted, this would have dramatically reshaped the history of the Islamic State, effectively unifying the jihadi community in Iraq under Abu Umar and giving al-Shafi'i control over the Islamic State's most important ministries. Ultimately, al-Shafi'i did not accept the offer. Ansar al-Sunnah remained independent of the ISI, and maintained its separate arrangement with al-Qaeda.

Ansar al-Sunnah was not the only Iraqi political movement in upheaval in early 2007. Saddam Hussein was executed on December 30, 2006, after being tried and convicted in an Iraqi court. But grainy video of his execution was punctuated by sectarian catcalls by Shia militiamen. For many Sunni Iraqis, the killing felt like vigilantism rather than justice.

Saddam's execution set off a raging controversy within the dissident Iraqi Ba'ath Party over who would be its next leader. The most obvious successor was Izzat al-Douri, who had organized the Iraqi army's defense of Baghdad during the U.S. invasion and led the "Faith Campaign" to Islamize Iraqi society prior to the U.S. invasion. He was the King of Hearts in the U.S. "deck of cards" identifying senior Iraqi leaders to be captured. He also had a bureaucratic advantage. As Saddam's deputy in the Ba'ath Party, he became interim leader when Saddam was killed.

But al-Douri was a controversial figure. He was imperious, implacably opposed to anything less than a total return to power, and suspicious of foreign governments. His intransigence left space for a challenger, in the form of Mohamed Yunis al-Ahmed, known as MYA among the U.S. Delta Force operators pursuing him. MYA was also a former general in Saddam's army who played a central role in organizing the early Sunni insurgency in Iraq.[80]

When Saddam was killed, al-Douri and MYA competed for control of the Ba'ath Party. Although al-Douri was technically Saddam's second-in-command, Saddam reportedly coordinated directly with MYA to manage the early insurgency, and MYA claimed the former Iraqi leader had named him as the successor.[81] The debate between al-Douri and MYA had policy consequences. Al-Douri opposed any compromise with the elected, Shia-led government in Baghdad, but MYA was open to negotiation and potentially a peace agreement.[82] He also was based in Damascus and had built a strong relationship with the Syrian regime.

The United States had mechanisms to engage with MYA, but various entreaties fell on deaf ears. In 2004, a joint U.S.-Iraqi raid captured MYA's son Ahmed, who showed intelligence agents how to communicate with his father. With United States personnel watching, Ahmed called his father, hoping to broker a discussion. MYA's response could not be misinterpreted. "Die like a man," he told his son, and hung up.[83]

Subsequent efforts to engage MYA—his phone number and address in Syria were reportedly known by U.S. officials—were rejected as well.[84]

In January 2007, MYA convened an extraordinary meeting of the Iraqi Ba'ath Party. They gathered openly in Aleppo, Syria, clearly with the support of the Assad regime, and voted to expel al-Douri from the party. Al-Douri promptly responded that the meeting was moot because, as Saddam's deputy, he had already banished MYA and his supporters from the party.[85] True or not, al-Douri's reliance on this technicality showed his political weakness.

The Ba'ath split was notable for its adolescent bickering about bureaucratic procedure, but the outcome was important nonetheless. Whereas al-Douri remained committed to violent opposition, MYA showed some willingness to engage the Iraqi government.[86]

Al-Douri responded to the upheaval by calling for unity among Iraq's insurgents, urging groups to come together in a "front" that would include multiple militant networks.[87] His traditional antipathy to Iran took on an increasingly sectarian tone in early 2007, which rankled Ba'athists who valued the party's secular ideology.[88] On January 4, 2007, a video attributed to al-Douri loyalists sounded suspiciously like the ISI when it declared war on "every follower of Moqtada al-Sadr and al-Hakim," two key Shia leaders.[89] The statement also asked that supporters online distribute the message on websites traditionally affiliated with both the Ba'ath Party (Basrah.net) and those used by jihadi groups (Hanin, Hesbah, Ekhlass).

But despite the sectarian rhetoric, al-Douri's followers did not adopt Zarqawiism or join the ISI en masse. Rather, they coalesced in the Jaysh Rijal al-Tariq al-Naqshabandi (JRTN) movement, which espoused a Sufi religious identity and Iraqi nationalism.[90]

As 2007 stretched on and the ISI suffered defeat after defeat on the battlefield, Iraq's insurgent groups fractured and reorganized again and again. MYA's Ba'athists increasingly engaged the political process, but al-Douri's followers did not. Neither fully embraced the ISI, although al-Douri came closer to it. In future years when sectarian politics reenergized the Sunni insurgency in Iraq, it would be al-Douri who found uncomfortable accommodation with jihadis.

Shia dominance over the Iraqi government and the Awakening shaped Iraqi politics at a macro level in 2007. Less visibly, the split in Ansar al-Sunnah and among the Ba'athists shaped internal jihadi insurgent politics—effectively the constituency that the ISI aimed to monopolize. The splits were not altogether positive for the ISI, but they reveal that the militant Sunni opposition in Iraq was hopelessly divided. For the ISI, this meant two things: they would be unable to dominate Sunnis as a whole, but factions of the Sunni opposition remained susceptible to their influence.

When Atiyah blamed rogue junior officers for the ISI's excessive violence, he was actually on to something. The ISI was not just failing to manage its external relationships; the group was also unraveling internally. One highly critical internal memo described some of the bureaucratic challenges. Local ISI organizations were top-heavy, naming an "emir" in charge of useless bureaucratic sections (an "Emir of Tents," joked one internal critic), and had developed a "garrisoning attitude" in which local leaders stockpiled materiel and personnel rather than employing them in operations against American or Iraqi forces.[91] This was "Second Fallujah and al-Qa'im" thinking, a reference to American victories over jihadi strongholds in late 2004 and 2005.[92] The ISI's local leaders were building their own fiefdoms at the expense of the organization's larger goals.

The "garrisoning" exacerbated growing tension between local jihadis and foreign fighters. The foreigners risked everything to travel to Iraq in order to fight or die, but they were often a battlefield liability. Most had no military training, and those who volunteered as suicide bombers longed to hit grand strategic targets rather than the more common objectives of police checkpoints and tribal meetings. Often the foreigners would refuse to follow operational security measures, and most spoke an Arabic dialect that marked them as non-Iraqi. Many had been "influenced by the media and propaganda" and did not even realize that Iraq was a predominately Shia country.[93] Local emirs, rightly or wrongly, were often more operationally cautious than the foreigners, which was very frustrating for the newcomers.

The ISI's failure to effectively utilize its human resources was central to its unraveling, which is why in 2007 al-Qaeda's leadership urged Abu Umar and Abu Hamzah to establish a special bureaucratic unit to "look for hidden capabilities among the brothers that have joined the Islamic State of Iraq and to activate them."[94]

Abu Muhjan al-Masri was the type of man al-Qaeda's leaders hoped the ISI would find. An Egyptian national with Italian citizenship, Abu Muhjan arrived in Iraq in early 2006. Six foot two inches tall, he was an athlete who enjoyed weightlifting and was a computer specialist in Italy. He spoke several languages; his favorite weapon was the Soviet-built PK-C machine gun, which he would carry on training runs; and most importantly, he had good connections with counterfeiters outside Iraq. He arrived with a sample $100 bill to prove the value of his connections.[95]

Abu Muhjan's local emir, failing to recognize the value of this unique asset, decided that his local cell was not in need of money and did not refer

Abu Muhjan to his superiors. Even worse, the emir did not have a strong operational plan in place. Rather than engage in strikes, Abu Muhjan trained with other foreign fighters for several months but only participated in a single attack. Frustrated, he decided to leave Iraq and hoped to join the Lebanese jihadi group Fatah al-Islam.[96]

Abu Muhjan was a dangerous man. He spoke English, Italian, and Arabic and held a European passport. It is easy to imagine him returning to Europe to conduct attacks, raise funds, or serve in a logistical role. Fortunately, it was not to be. After months of languishing, Abu Muhjan got his wish for martyrdom on November 7, 2006, at the hands of a Special Operations raid outside al-Qa'im.

Abu Muhjan's story is banal, but it illustrates one of the ISI's most important weaknesses: ineffective local leaders. Part of the problem was a lack of internal management skills, but the ISI also faced a very difficult oversight problem. With American forces stalking them, every communication introduced new levels of risk. Senior leaders had to balance the benefits of checking in on their underlings against the risk that such efforts would reveal them to hostile intelligence services.[97]

Despite these challenges, the ISI did have established communication procedures. Because it considered electronic and telephonic communication especially risky, the ISI relied on a "postal system" to physically deliver encrypted thumb drives between commanders on predetermined dates, and emissaries to meet or execute dead drops with reports and directives.[98] The system was good enough that the ISI imposed strict accounting and record keeping procedures on its regional and local commanders.[99]

By mid-2007, however, even this postal service was increasingly strained by Special Operations raids, defections, and American forces embedding in Sunni neighborhoods.[100] The inability to communicate sometimes contributed directly to the ISI's strategic missteps.

On April 5, 2007, the IAI accused Abu Umar of "transgressing Islamic Law" by "threatening some members of the [IAI] with death if they do not swear allegiance . . . permitting [the] kill[ing of] a group of Muslims . . . accusing people of unbelief and apostasy," prohibiting satellite television, and forcing women to wear the *niqab* (full veil over the face).[101] Only four days later, Abu Wa'el split from Ansar al-Sunnah and allied with the IAI.

Abu Umar aimed to avoid a direct confrontation with the IAI, but he would not get his wish.[102]

On May 13, 2007, all hell broke loose in Baghdad. How the fight began is disputed, but at the end, twelve members of the newly formed JRF were dead. The JRF claimed the ISI ambushed its fighters, but the local ISI commander reported to his superiors that his troops were defending a local shariah judge.[103] Other reports from inside the ISI suggest that this was simply a convenient story. Amplifying the confusion, many of the dead were from the al-Rabbi tribe, which included numerous former Saddam supporters that the ISI believed had recently begun cooperating with U.S. forces.[104]

Fighting between the JRF and the ISI exploded in other areas of Baghdad as well. A total of 726 bodies went unidentified in May 2007 in Baghdad, many of them concentrated in the western neighborhood of Amiriyah, where the ISI and JRF fought toe-to-toe.[105] The fighting in Amiriyah began when the ISI killed a local IAI commander, and the IAI retaliated by killing several ISI fighters and then refused to return their bodies for cleaning and burial.

A commander from Muhammad Hardan's Mujahidin Army tried to mediate between the two groups, but there was hardly room for compromise. The ISI's local commander demanded the bodies back within thirty minutes but was told it would take two days. Rather than seek direction from his political leadership, the local commander took matters into his own hands.[106]

"We, in Baghdad, are aware of the true nature of the Islamic Army and its leadership," the Baghdad commander wrote to his superiors on May 31, 2007. "We, in Baghdad, wish to show the blessed Emirate that we understand the Islamic religious law policy of our state in dealing with the other groups."[107]

But after another day of fighting fellow Sunnis on the streets of Baghdad, the commander acknowledged that he did not actually understand the ISI's policy in "dealing with the other groups." "I would like to request from you the big picture of dealing with the Islamic Army," he wrote; "I want a quick response . . . what is the guidance from the leadership about this issue?"[108]

Abu Umar's office responded to the inquiry on June 2, 2007, but not through the ISI's postal service, which apparently could not move quickly or reliably enough in a crisis. Instead, Abu Umar released a statement publicly—via physical pamphlets and online—ordering ISI fighters to stay home, promising to engage the IAI's most senior leaders, and urging local leaders to "suppress their rage and fury, despite any provocations."[109]

The IAI went public as well, and via a much larger forum. On June 1, 2007, the group's official spokesman alleged on Al Jazeera that the ISI had been extremely belligerent "since the announcement of their alleged state."[110]

Jihad and Reform Front elements were not communicating only with Al Jazeera producers. Days later, the coalition sent a note to Osama bin Laden and Ayman al-Zawahiri explaining that the al-Qaeda leaders had one "last chance to remedy the Jihad breakdown that is about to take place in Iraq." They tried to impress on al-Qaeda's leadership that "there are calamities taking place now that are much more severe than those of the past."[111]

Meanwhile, the ISI continued to raise the stakes. In addition to picking new fights, it was also using dangerous new tactics, such as rudimentary chemical weapons.[112] The ISI would load chlorine into truck and car bombs in an effort to enhance the bombs' impact. Such attacks were deadly because of the bombs, but the heat of the explosion destroyed most of the chlorine.[113]

The ISI's attacks on a small sect known as Yazidis were much more successful. After a campaign that a U.S. official called "ethnic cleansing," the ISI conducted a coordinated bombing of Yazidi villages in northern Iraq that killed more than 500 people.[114] It was the single most deadly attack of the Iraq war.

Despite its battlefield victory against the JRF in Amiriyah and its tactical "successes" with chlorine bombs and against the Yazidis, by early summer 2007 the ISI was losing the war in Iraq. Local commanders were behaving erratically and at odds with the group's political leadership. The logistics network providing new materiel, including for the chlorine attacks, was breaking down. Internal communications were failing, and new recruits were often criminals and thugs rather than dedicated jihadis.[115] As a matter of desperation and philosophy—after all, participation in jihad was believed to absolve previous sins—the ISI kept its door open to them.

Increasingly, the ISI's violence was reactionary and vengeful, not purposeful. In years past, al-Qaeda's leaders had warned Zarqawi about excessive violence, but in 2007 thoughtful ISI commanders suggested that the group's problems "would not have happened if Sheikh Abu Mus'ab were still alive."[116] Zarqawi embraced bloodshed, but he also ran a reasonably tight ship and understood tribal politics. The ISI's problem in 2007 was not Abu Umar and Abu Hamzah wantonly picking fights with other militants, though they certainly did not shy from sectarian attacks or killing "apostates." But on the whole, these leaders tried to limit the growing violence with other Iraqi militants in 2007. They simply failed to do so. The "splurge in blood" lamented by the IAI was only sometimes top-down policy; often it was "driven by young men" acting on their own, "uncontrolled by any Islamic law restraints."[117]

Abu Umar and Abu Hamzah faced the great challenge of managing an organization that exalted Zarqawist chaos, but required extraordinary discipline and precision to be successful. Zarqawiism's populism, which encouraged the ISI to embrace new recruits no matter how poorly prepared they were and encouraged decentralization to local leaders, was ill-suited to the political tightrope the ISI needed to walk in Iraq. During Zarqawi's reign, a forceful leader and a coherent organization bent those violent instincts into a bloody strategy. But in 2007 the ideology escaped its organizational shackles. Abu Umar and Abu Hamzah's inexperience played into that failure, but so did the U.S. campaign to destroy the leaders and communication mechanisms that held the ISI together operationally. The pressure of that campaign unleashed the ISI's most dangerous enemy: its own ideological demons.[118]

Allegiance or Disavowal?

In public, al-Qaeda strongly backed the ISI in early 2007, despite its deteriorating relations with other Iraqi militants. But the nature of their relationship at an operational level was ambiguous. Abu Hamzah declared in October 2006 that AQI was dissolved into the ISI and ceased to exist, but al-Qaeda continued to offer guidance as if the new group operated under its direction. In 2014, when the Islamic State and al-Qaeda split angrily and irrefutably, much of their disagreement centered on the relationship years earlier. The Islamic State held that it had been independent since the declaration of the ISI in 2006, whereas al-Qaeda held that the group had always secretly sworn allegiance to al-Qaeda.

A secret agreement is not implausible. Al-Qaeda actively promoted its allies and affiliates to brand themselves as independent actors during this period, including Fatah al-Islam in Lebanon and al-Shaabab in Somalia. In most cases, distinct branding aimed to allow local jihadi groups to avoid being conflated with the global group, but in the ISI's case al-Qaeda might have wanted to avoid being tarnished by the group's extraordinary violence.

After all, there were still distinct links between the two groups. In early 2007, al-Qaeda sent Mehmet Yilmaz and Mehmet Resit-Isik—the Turkish facilitators of Abd al-Hadi's journey toward Iraq—into northern Iraq. The "Turki brothers" did not survive long, but their work building the so-called Kurdistan Brigades is notable because it is the only group that publicly indicated it was both an element of the ISI and swore direct allegiance to bin Laden and al-Qaeda.[119]

In March 2007, a statement from the Kurdistan Brigades was included in a longer ISI propaganda video highlighting the group's operations. "The Kurdistan Brigades, as a division of the al-Qaeda organization, are on the path of loyalty and allegiance, which we pledged to our Emir, Osama bin Laden," they explained. "With God's help and strength we are at the service of our brothers in the Islamic State of Iraq and we promise and pledge allegiance to Sheikh Abu Umar al-Baghdadi."[120]

It was no foregone conclusion that swearing allegiance to both leaders was feasible. But justifying this sort of arrangement was one of al-Qaeda's key goals. After Abu Hamzah announced AQI was being dissolved, Atiyah Abd al-Rahman argued explicitly that this sort of arrangement was possible:

> There are two possible ways for an organization or group to enter into the state: either by the organization's disbanding and dissolving completely into the state, which is the most complete way, or by the organization entering into the state with its organizational personality. In the latter case, it remains an organization within the state. This is possible, and our brothers are considering it and whether or not it is appropriate, because it differs from case to case.[121]

At the time, Atiyah was probably hopeful that AQI would retain some public affiliation with al-Qaeda, which did not happen. But the Kurdistan Brigades example indicates that the ISI and al-Qaeda did experiment with this kind of structure.

The complexity of these relationships may help explain the ultimate dispute between the Islamic State and al-Qaeda. It suggests that some elements of the ISI might have formally aligned themselves with al-Qaeda, while the political institution as a whole remained distinct. This might explain how, in 2013, al-Qaeda supporters would insist that the ISI had secretly sworn allegiance to al-Qaeda whereas backers of the Islamic State rejected that proposition.

After Abd al-Hadi was captured in Turkey, the primary interlocutor between al-Qaeda and the ISI was Khalid Mashadani, the ISI's media emir. Mashadani was an old-line jihadi and one of the most senior Iraqis in the ISI; he had been involved in the insurgency as part of Ansar al-Sunnah since the U.S. invasion but defected to the ISI in 2005.[122] American troops captured Mashadani on July 4, 2007. Under interrogation, he offered a series of revelations that would shape the American understanding of the ISI for years. In what a longtime U.S. intelligence analyst called "a brilliant display of counterintelligence," Mashadani told U.S. interrogators that Abu Umar, the ISI's emir, was fictitious and that the group still took direct guidance from al-Qaeda.[123]

American intelligence analysts undoubtedly parsed the apparent revelation about Abu Umar in various ways, but it quickly informed the United States' military's public position on the ISI. Jihadis considered the ISI an authentic, if initially unsuccessful, attempt to govern and the nucleus of a potential caliphate. But an American spokesman at the time said, "[T]he Islamic State of Iraq is a front organization that masks the foreign influence and leadership within al-Qaeda in Iraq in an attempt to put an Iraqi face on the leadership of al-Qaeda in Iraq."[124]

If Mashadani's story was fabricated, the U.S. was not the only one being lied to; after all, al-Qaeda's senior leaders were about to receive the same information about Abu Umar.

Abu Sulayman al-Utaybi was born in Saudi Arabia in 1980. He studied at the prestigious Islamic University of Imam Muhammad bin al-Sa'ud in

Riyadh but abandoned his studies in 2006 and joined AQI.[125] Allegedly a favorite of Zarqawi's, in March 2007 he was made the ISI's chief shariah judge, just as the group faced controversy with other Iraqi militants.[126] Yet despite this meteoric rise, Abu Sulayman had deep reservations about the ISI leadership.[127]

Abu Sulayman's discontent did not stay secret for long; he was removed from his post as chief shariah judge in August 2007. The ISI's only explanation was that the "decision accords with a commitment to applying God's law, especially regarding theft, fornication, sorcery, prophesizing, blood and financial matters, and the worship of idols and tombs instead of God."[128]

Shortly thereafter, Abu Sulayman began a journey to take his grievances directly to al-Qaeda's leadership in Pakistan—after first sending a letter detailing his accusations. These ranged from the prosaic ("Mayors and emirs say they only provide accurate news to the state, but they only report the good news") to the eschatological (Abu Hamzah only declared the ISI because he believed that the apocalypse would occur within a year).[129]

Abu Sulayman's most biting charge was that the ISI was fundamentally fraudulent. He alleged that Abu Hamzah, in his rush to establish the ISI on an apocalyptic timeline, had invented Abu Umar. If the individual selected to play that role did not pan out, Abu Hamzah would simply find a new figurehead. It was a startling accusation, and it accorded neatly with what Mashadani had told U.S. interrogators.

It is not clear when the United States first learned of Abu Sulayman's accusations (if a digital copy of his letter was intercepted in 2007, the United States would likely not have released it to preserve their intelligence methods), but American forces did release a version captured in late 2008. Regardless, Abu Sulayman seemed to confirm that Abu Umar was indeed just a front man and that the ISI was a rebranded version of AQI rather than the embodiment of a new jihadi ambition to build a state and govern.

But Mashadani seems to have been lying, and Abu Sulayman—intentionally or because he had been misled—was also not telling the truth. Abu Umar was real and, though unknown to al-Qaeda's leadership, had been negotiating salafi circles in Iraq for more than a decade. By the time he was killed in 2010, the former appliance repairman was considered by the ISI's followers to be the future caliph.

It is impossible to know whether Abu Sulyaman's concerns were genuine, exaggerated, or manipulated by an intelligence service. Al-Qaeda's leadership considered all three possibilities.[130] On November 16, 2007, a senior al-Qaeda leader, believed by U.S. intelligence officials to be Sayf al-Adl, drafted a note to al-Qaeda's leadership warning that he had received a message from a "delegate" that was "of suspicious accuracy." Al-Adl urged an investigation into the accusations, explaining that such critics often "have no shame in allowing the apostate state intelligence to lead them. . . . There is a real threat against the establishment of the Islamic Emirate . . . and you need to be careful."[131]

While there is no proof that the letter referred to Abu Sulayman (as opposed to another "delegate"), al-Qaeda's leadership almost immediately followed up on Abu Sulayman's charges. Three days after receiving al-Adl's note, al-Qaeda's leaders drafted a letter to Abu Umar and Abu Hamzah explaining that Abu Sulayman was about to arrive in Pakistan and asking why he had been dismissed.[132] They did not get a response, which perhaps reflected the ISI's intransigence but might simply have been a function of Mashadani's arrest.

Unsure how seriously to take Abu Sulayman's charges, al-Qaeda's leaders wrote another letter to Abu Hamzah on January 25, 2008. They detailed Abu Sulayman's accusations and requested a swift reply, especially regarding "the most important thing and the biggest danger—if true—[which] is the existence of the corrupt influential men who have become leaders in the [Islamic] State."[133] The letter goes on to query Abu Hamzah about his views on the return of the Mahdi, a figure prophesized to lead Muslims during the apocalypse. By asking the question, al-Qaeda's leaders indicated that they thought Abu Sulayman's accusations about Abu Hamzah's apocalyptic outlook were, at minimum, worth looking into.

They got no response.

The third letter from al-Qaeda's leadership, dated March 8, 2008, was signed by Ayman al-Zawahiri and addressed to Abu Umar rather than Abu Hamzah. Clearly designed to be nonconfrontational, it urged the ISI to maximize its human resources by creating a database of jihadis under its command, and offhandedly requested an answer to the previous queries regarding Abu Sulayman.[134]

All three letters were included as appendices in a fourth note, dated March 10, 2008, addressed to Abu Hamzah. This letter explained that the entire al-Qaeda leadership group was aware of the Abu Sulayman controversy, but it reassured him that they were still simply investigating the claims. "Details are required and setting the record straight on all accounts," the letter read. Abu Sulayman "may have mixed truth and falsehood, and so it is necessary to provide details and to give whoever is in the right his due in word, judgment and action."[135]

There is no record that they ever got a response.

Unlike the earlier letters, however, there is firm evidence that the fourth letter arrived in Iraq, but Abu Hamzah or Abu Umar may never have seen it. What is clear is that the letter and its three appendices were captured in September 2008 when coalition forces killed the ISI's new information minister in Baghdad.[136]

Communication problems had undermined al-Qaeda's relationship with its partners in Iraq since Hassan Ghul's arrest in 2004. The most dramatic effort to resolve that challenge, sending Abd al-Hadi to Iraq, had failed. So, on March 5, 2008, the same week that the last two notes to Abu Hamzah and Abu Umar were written, al-Qaeda's second-in-command, Ayman al-Zawahiri, informed bin Laden that he was considering sending another senior-level emissary to Iraq. The ISI's leadership would not respond to al-Qaeda's letters, and al-Qaeda's information was simply not good enough to make informed decisions.

Zawahiri thought Atiyah, the man that chastened Zarqawi after the Amman hotel bombings, would be perfect, but Zawahiri was loath to send a highly valued colleague on such a dangerous mission. Zawahiri considered sending Abu Sulayman back to Iraq, but this was problematic for obvious reasons—"we have no information about him"—and not-so-obvious reasons: Abu Sulayman was proving untrustworthy in South Asia. He had abandoned a first tasking with al-Qaeda, he communicated with unknown contacts in Saudi Arabia, his agents took unauthorized photographs of U.S. airstrikes in Pakistan, and he had begun consorting with a rival jihadi organization.[137] Zawahiri did not trust him.

Abu Sulayman's campaign to discredit Abu Hamzah and Abu Umar with al-Qaeda's leadership fizzled. Only months after Zawahiri's note to bin Laden was published, al-Qaeda central announced that Abu Sulayman was dead, apparently killed by U.S. forces in Afghanistan's Paktika Province.[138]

It is difficult to know what to make of Abu Sulayman's claims except that al-Qaeda's leadership did not take them at face value and neither should anyone else. At least one claim—that Abu Umar was a made-up person—was demonstrably false. On the other hand, there is ample evidence that the ISI's leaders failed to recognize how quickly other Iraqi militants were shifting against them, and that local ISI commanders were acting independently—and counterproductively—from the ISI's leadership. Abu Sulayman was wrong about Abu Umar, but he understood ISI's political situation better than its own emir.

That is why it is difficult to know what to make of Abu Sulayman's claim that Abu Hamzah rushed to establish the ISI because he thought the world would end within a year. On the one hand, Abu Hamzah said nothing of the sort when he celebrated the state's founding and immediately blessed projects to create a state-like institutional structure. The minister of agriculture and marine wealth was named only months after the ISI was established, which seems discordant if the group's leaders truly believed the world would end within twelve months. On the other hand, both Abu Hamzah and Abu Umar often referenced a final judgment day and sometimes framed their analysis of current events within the prophetical "Signs of the Hour," which according to Islamic prophecy indicates that the final battle between good and evil is imminent.[139]

By 2014, the original eschatological question was largely forgotten, as was the dispute over whether Abu Umar was real.[140] But al-Qaeda did allege that the ISI's leaders had sworn a secret pledge of allegiance to al-Qaeda during this period. As an American al-Qaeda member put it in 2015:

> After Sheikh Abu Mus'ab's martyrdom in 2006, leadership of his group was transferred to Sheikh Abu Hamza al-Muhajir (may Allah have mercy on him), a former member of the Egyptian Jihad Group, who soon announced (without consulting al-Qa'eda's central command) the dissolution of the group and the formation of what was known as the Islamic State of Iraq under the leadership of Sheikh Abu 'Umar al-Baghdadi (may Allah have mercy on him), which in turn declared its allegiance to al-Qa'eda's

central command, except that this time the *bay'at* (pledge) was kept secret at the request of the brothers in Iraq.[141]

Ayman al-Zawahiri made the same assertion in May 2014, citing earlier correspondence that he claimed indicated that the ISI's leaders had sworn allegiance. The letters he produced indicate that al-Qaeda believed it was still in charge, but Zawahiri never produced the actual text of a secret pledge of allegiance, leaving some uncertainty.[142]

Paradoxically, the best evidence of close political coordination between the ISI and al-Qaeda is their public alignment on the ultimate dissolution of AQI. By late 2007, Sunni militants in Iraq had reached out to Osama bin Laden at least three times to complain about the ISI, including one note to "strongly reproach" al-Qaeda for not doing something about the organization's attacks on other Sunnis.[143] Al-Qaeda, the JRF wrote in 2007, was accountable for the murderous attacks of AQI "that are committed in your name."[144]

Shortly thereafter, secret pledge of allegiance or not, the ISI and al-Qaeda both publicly renounced their integration. In December 2007, Abu Umar flatly declared, "The Emir of al-Qaeda [in Iraq], al-Muhajir, publicly pledged allegiance to this humble servant. The organization was officially dissolved in favor of the state of Islam, the Islamic State of Iraq."[145] Two weeks later, al-Qaeda's second-in-command, Ayman al-Zawahiri, seconded that sentiment. "There is nothing today in Iraq named 'al-Qaeda,'" he explained. "[I]nstead the Qaeda Organization in Mesopotamia merged, by the grace of God, with other Jihadi groups in the Islamic State of Iraq, which is a legitimate emirate based on a proper legal methodology."[146]

The closely coordinated messages suggest some agreement between the ISI and al-Qaeda, but al-Qaeda's repeated queries about Abu Sulayman indicate that the ISI continued to ignore al-Qaeda throughout this period. It did not consult al-Qaeda on the declaration of the ISI, nor on the choice of an emir. The ISI's leaders did not even respond to al-Qaeda's queries about Abu Sulayman. Whether or not Abu Umar secretly pledged allegiance to bin Laden, the ISI operated independently from the moment it was declared in 2006.

Bin Laden was clearly unsatisfied by his relationship with the ISI. In private letters, he indicated to aides that he still had rightful authority over the ISI but was frustrated by their intransigence and independence.[147] Other al-Qaeda leaders were similarly angry. In 2011, an American member of al-Qaeda had enough of the ISI's disinterest and wrote to bin Laden that al-Qaeda:

> [S]hould declare the cutoff of its organizational ties with [the Islamic State of Iraq]. The relations between al-Qaeda and the [Islamic State of Iraq] have been practically cut off for a number of years. The decision to declare the State was taken without consultation from al-Qaeda leadership. Their improvised decision has caused a split in the Mujahidin ranks and their supporters inside and outside Iraq. What is left between al-Qaeda and the [Islamic State of Iraq], but the link of faith and Islam, which urges us to submit advice and apply the rule propagating virtue and preventing vice, and the support of good deeds?[148]

It was a good question.

Foreign Policy

The ISI lost ground in Iraq throughout 2007, but it gained market share online and its network outside the country continued to grow. The ISI's propaganda was produced by a dedicated media unit called the Al-Furqan Media Establishment and distributed by the al-Qaeda-affiliated al-Fajr Media Network to a shifting group of jihadi web forums. Al-Furqan's output ranged from simple videos of attacks on American or Iraqi forces to professionally produced documentaries exploring the daily life of foreign fighters and showing ISI fighters parading through Iraqi cities.

Other Iraqi militant groups also had media production units, but they were generally less active. Iraqi groups with a nationalist bent were focused on their local constituencies. The ISI, by contrast, depended on foreign fighters for its operational capability and aspired to jurisdiction over Muslims everywhere. Not surprisingly, it spent more time and energy trying to communicate digitally with a constituency outside Iraq.

That focus paid off when fights among militants inside Iraq spilled into cyberspace. The Islamic Army of Iraq filmed its own propaganda and distributed it primarily through the al-Boraq Islamic Forum, an outlet that hosted information from a range of Iraqi militant groups from 2005 through 2007. But whereas the IAI could slug it out with the ISI on the streets of Baghdad, it could not stand up to the jihadi group in cyberspace. When the IAI disavowed the ISI in 2007, the original al-Boraq Islamic Forum sided with the ISI.[149] The episode foreshadowed events to come: the ISI would suffer major setbacks in Iraq but maintain a potent global influence via digital media.

The ISI's online presence differed from al-Qaeda's as well. Both groups emphasized brand control, but al-Qaeda was obsessed with it. The ISI, meanwhile, experimented with early crowd-sourcing concepts. Freelance video producers would push content to the administrators of leading web forums, who would coordinate with al-Fajr and al-Furqan to determine when and how to distribute it.[150] This was far from the free-wheeling social media environment to come in later years, but it was years ahead of al-Qaeda's highly centralized approach.

The ISI's digital media had three basic purposes: to recruit new foreign fighters, to bind disparate jihadi groups into a common movement, and ultimately to elevate the ISI into a global institution that could be considered a true Islamic State.

Between 2003 and 2011, 4,000 to 5,000 foreign fighters traveled to Iraq, most to fight with the ISI and its predecessors.[151] Many of their identities were discovered in September 2007, when American Special Operations troops raided a desert camp outside the small northern Iraqi city of Sinjar. They picked up loose papers, computers, and thumb drives containing 595 unique personnel records for fighters that arrived in Iraq between August 2006 and August 2007.[152] These records revealed a highly structured on-boarding procedure for incoming fighters, who were asked questions familiar to any job applicant: name, contact information, next of kin, employment history, educational background, and special skills.[153] Fighters were also asked about their journeys to Iraq, their method of meeting a jihadi "travel agent" who could connect them to the right networks, and the Syrian smugglers who facilitated their travel.

The Sinjar records suggested that the Internet was relatively inconsequential for jihadi mobilization prior to 2007. Of the 152 fighters who described how they first engaged formal jihadi networks, only six mentioned the Internet. The vast majority relied on friends, family, or known radicals in their home countries.[154] A plurality came from Saudi Arabia, but there were a striking number from the eastern Libyan cities of Benghazi and Darnah. These towns had been jihadi hotbeds for years and would be central to the growth of the Islamic State affiliate in Libya after dictator Muammar Qaddafi was overthrown in 2011.[155]

The vast majority of the fighters listed in the Sinjar records were men between the ages of eighteen and thirty. Many had some college education. "Student" was the most commonly listed occupation. A large percentage traveled with friends or relations to Iraq.

The Sinjar records also suggested that the Syrian regime, at minimum, tolerated the flow of foreign fighters. Most incoming recruits flew to Damascus before connecting with human smugglers who would usher them across the border into Iraq. Fighters from Algeria, Tunisia, and Morocco, on the other hand, often traveled through ground networks in Europe before entering Syria through Turkey, just as Abd al-Hadi hoped to in 2006.[156] These fighters were trailblazers for the massive influx of foreigners who joined ISIS after the Syrian civil war began in 2011.

After arriving in Syria, recruits usually traveled to Dayr al-Zawr, a city in the eastern Syrian desert. Dayr al-Zawr offered easy access to a southerly route toward Iraq through al-Qa'im and a northern route toward Sinjar and Mosul. Most recruits took the southern route until early 2006, when the 3rd Armored Cavalry Regiment, led by Colonel H. R. McMaster, wrested al-Qa'im from AQI's control.[157] After that, recruits began taking the northern route.

The Syrian smugglers ranged from hardcore jihadis to criminal networks looking for profit. The ISI was not the only Iraqi militant group with ties in Syria; a range of other militants, including secular Ba'athists, various Islamists, and even the ISI's rivals in the Jihad and Reform Front, also found refuge there. In such a chaotic environment, Syria's policy toward the foreign fighters is difficult to parse. The regime both facilitated and cracked down on jihadi smuggling networks, sometimes almost simultaneously.

Husayn, the smuggler almost caught by the Syrian Mukhabarat in al-Marjah Square while attempting to collect a group of Libyans, worked for one of the most important smuggling networks. It was led by Abu Ghadiyah, a former aide of Abu Mus'ab al-Zarqawi.[158] Little is known about Abu Ghadiyah; he was memorialized as a jihadi diehard, and memos written by his assistants indicate that he was integrally involved in a wide range of operations linking the ISI to other jihadi groups around the world.[159] A 2008 State Department memo concluded that his "network continues to operate with the knowledge of the Syrian government."[160] Abu Ghadiyah operated out of Zabadani, on the outskirts of Damascus, with his two brothers, and despite occasional crackdowns like the raid that almost netted Husayn, he functioned relatively openly and faced little government interference.

Abu Ghadiyah's ties to Syrian intelligence sometimes generated animosity on jihadi websites. A commentator on the al-Fallujah website claimed that jihadis in Iraq "wanted him to stand trial for alleged links to Syrian intelligence and for stealing from the incoming brothers."[161] Indeed, the ISI did worry about theft from its recruits; every newcomer was queried about his treatment by smugglers in Syria, including how much money the smuggler demanded and whether it was taken by force. The ISI wanted to identify which smuggling networks were most reliable.

But the Sinjar data suggests that Abu Ghadiyah—referred to in the personnel records as "Abu Abdallah"—took less money from recruits than other smugglers.[162] Whatever Abu Ghadiyah's precise relationship with the Syrian regime, he did not prey on the incoming fighters.[163]

Abu Ghadiyah's apparent accommodation with the Syrian regime does not imply they shared strategic goals. Rather, Syria aimed to swiftly move potentially dangerous men into Iraq, both to promote domestic stability and to keep the United States pinned down in Iraq.[164]

Yet even as Syrian President Bashar al-Assad tried to manage the jihadi networks criss-crossing his territory, the ISI—with Abu Ghadiyah's help—was building an operational network that stretched across the entire Levant. In 2007 it was not focused on attacking the Syrian regime, but that time would come.

On January 15, 2008, an olive-green Honda Civic was parked across the street from Farid Kamel's tannery in the northern Beirut suburb of al-Karantina. Farid's father had opened the business in 1968, but it was forced to close in 1975 by raging civil war. In 1993, after the fighting stopped, Farid reopened the family business and thrived for fifteen years. But now the tannery faced a new threat: the Honda Civic, which had been stolen five months earlier and outfitted with a unique after-market feature—a forty-five-pound bomb.[165]

The bomb was detonated by remote control on a cloudless afternoon, just as a U.S. Embassy SUV was passing. The vehicle was badly damaged, its Lebanese driver injured, and three passersby were killed.[166] Farid Kamel's tannery was destroyed.

Although the attack was never formally claimed, suspicion immediately fell on Fatah al-Islam, a Lebanese jihadi group with deep ties to both the ISI and al-Qaeda. Indeed, an ISI internal memo dated July 7, 2007—six months before the bombing—referred to potential strikes against U.S. targets in Lebanon. "The Lebanese have a plan to attack the U.S. embassy in Beirut, and it is a beautiful plan," wrote the author, who appears to have been Abu Ghadiyah or someone in his network.[167] They may have had a "beautiful" tactical plan, but the perpetrators did not know how to claim credit for the attack. "The thing that halted their effort was; what next?" wrote the letter's author. "In whose name will the operation be claimed? They have chosen the name of the organization but are awaiting your approval."[168] It is not clear who, exactly, was the letter's intended recipient.

Al-Qaeda's Ayman al-Zawahiri later acknowledged the complexities of framing terrorist attacks in Lebanon. He claimed that al-Qaeda purposely ignored Fatah al-Islam's activities there because the group was trying to establish local credibility.[169]

Fatah al-Islam's position was complicated for another reason as well: like Abu Ghadiyah, the group had deep ties to Syria's intelligence services. Syria's support for Shia militants like Lebanese Hizballah and Palestinian Islamists like Hamas is well known, but Syria also backed salafi-jihadi organizations in Lebanon for decades.[170] Despite deep ideological differences with jihadis, successive Syrian regimes supported them in order to weaken Palestinian nationalist movements. Despite its animosity with Israel, the Syrian regime aimed to keep the Palestinian movement in Lebanon divided and weak—and jihadis were excellent for creating divisions.[171] The danger, of course, was that the jihadis sometimes bit the hand that fed them.

Shakir al-Absi, the founder and emir of Fatah al-Islam, was a career militant. Born in 1955 at the Ayn Sultan refugee camp, near the West Bank city of Jericho, al-Absi first joined the Palestinian Liberation Organization during its exile in Tunisia. Yasser Arafat sent him to Muammar Qaddafi's Libya, where he learned to fly Soviet-built MIG-23's and reportedly flew combat missions over Chad.[172] In 1980 al-Absi visited his brother, who was in medical school in Cuba, before heading to Nicaragua, ostensibly to support the Sandinistas. After Israel invaded Lebanon in 1982, he returned to Lebanon and fought in the Bekaa Valley. Eventually, he settled in Damascus.[173]

While in Damascus, al-Absi began working with Fatah al-Intifadah, a small Palestinian Islamist organization sponsored by the Syrian government that fought both Israel and other Palestinian groups. Al-Absi was sentenced to death in Jordan—alongside Zarqawi—for supporting the assassination of USAID Administrator Laurence Foley in 2002. The Syrian government deported some of the accused to Jordan for trial but held onto al-Absi, who was in Syrian custody at the time, allegedly for planning attacks inside Syria.

But in 2005 Syria released al-Absi, and he returned to Lebanon, ostensibly to continue working with Fatah al-Intifadah. His shariah advisor later acknowledged that he cut a deal with the Syrian government in order to gain his release, but claimed al-Absi always intended to double-cross the Assad regime. Rather than truly collaborate with the "apostate" Syrians, the advisor said, al-Absi "utilized the organization [Fatah al-Intifadah] that belonged to Syria to bring young men with forged identities into Syria in the name of the Intifadah organization" in order to bolster an independent, anti-Syrian jihadi organization eventually called Fatah al-Islam.[174] This account aimed to protect al-Absi's reputation, so the details may be off, but the general thrust rings true. There was no love lost between the Syrian regime and the jihadis, but Assad aimed to manipulate jihadi networks to his own advantage and al-Absi aimed to do the same to Syria.[175]

Fatah al-Islam announced its presence on November 26, 2006, in the Nahr al-Barid refugee camp near the northern Lebanese city of Tripoli.

Fatah al-Islam's recruits were diverse. Of the fifty-nine members indicted by the Lebanese government in September 2007, twenty-two were

Syrian and eleven were Tunisian. There were five Saudis and seven Palestinians (most of whom had been living in Lebanese refugee camps)[176] as
well as recruits from Jordan, Egypt, Oman, Yemen, and Algeria. Only
three were Lebanese.[177] Despite these numbers, some in al-Qaeda's leadership believed that Fatah al-Islam was the most "Levantine" jihadi group
operating in Lebanon—and potentially a good ally as a result. In March 2007,
Atiyah abd al-Rahman wrote to a superior in Pakistan that "the Tripoli
group . . . are the best . . . and I prefer them. They are people of the region
and not immigrants."[178]

Unsurprisingly, many of Fatah al-Islam's foreign fighters arrived via the
same logistical networks used by the ISI, even arriving in Damascus before moving west into Lebanon.[179] Some initially planned to operate in Iraq
but changed their mind. Given this logistics network, it is no surprise that
Fatah al-Islam saw the entire Levant as its area of operations. It is also unsurprising that Abu Ghadiyah, a Damascus-based logistician, had insight
into Fatah al-Islam's operational planning.

The collaboration between the ISI and Fatah al-Islam was extensive.
When a Fatah al-Islam fighter was diagnosed with leukemia, the ISI
funded his treatment.[180] Some Fatah al-Islam fighters traveled to Iraq, and
the group memorialized at least two fighters who "fell on the Syrian-Iraqi
border," far from the group's core operational area in Lebanon.[181]

Fatah al-Islam was not the only Lebanese jihadi outfit deeply integrated
with the ISI. It followed in the footsteps of Asbat al-Ansar and Jund al-
Sham, both based south of Nahr al-Barid in the Ayn al-Hilweh refugee
camp, and both of which hosted and trained fighters before dispatching
them to Iraq.[182] The ISI sent fighters toward Lebanon as well, often for
medical treatment or recuperation, making them fill out what amounted
to exit visas before beginning their journeys.[183]

One of the ISI fighters who made his way to Lebanon was Abu Muhammad al-Jawlani, a Syrian who joined Zarqawi's group in 2003. After Zarqawi's death in 2006, Jawlani left Iraq to support Jund al-Sham, the
Lebanon-based militant group that intended to wage war across the entire
Levant and had the same name as Zarqawi's original jihadi group near
Herat, Afghanistan.[184] On September 12, 2006, around the time Jawlani
arrived, Jund al-Sham was accused by the Syrian government of an attack

on the U.S. Embassy in Damascus in which three attackers attempted to throw improvised grenades over the wall into the embassy compound.[185] It was an awkward, indecisive beginning, but the war for Greater Syria was on.

The ISI never integrated with its Lebanese partners, but their operational networks overlapped, especially inside Syria. The Syrian Mukhabarat's role in all this is difficult to discern. Syria sponsored Fatah al-Islam's predecessor and ignored some ISI logistics networks inside Syria, which suggests they facilitated the cooperation. On the other hand, Jund al-Sham also had ties to the ISI and conducted attacks inside Syria. Meanwhile, the Mukhabarat intermittently cracked down on jihadis, including those they sometimes tolerated. All of the jihadi groups legitimately despised the Syrian regime even if they sometimes cooperated with it.

It is possible that the Assad government conducted false flag attacks to deflect attention from its engagement with jihadis. But, it is just as likely that the various jihadi groups cooperated with the Syrian regime and then stabbed it in the back. These are not mutually exclusive.

Moreover, the jihadis did not fully agree with one another. Despite their operational links, Fatah al-Islam never adopted Zarqawiism's ideological exclusivity or abided the ISI's direct leadership. The group respected Abu Umar's claim to be "Commander of the Faithful," but it looked to al-Qaeda to develop an operational plan for revolution in the Levant. "We ask the *international* al-Qaeda organization to develop a strategic plan for al-Sham and to send a commander to lead the men here," Fatah al-Islam's Shariah official explained in August 2007. "If al-Qaeda announces a plan for al-Sham (Greater Syria), we will renew our oath to al-Qaeda."[186]

Fatah al-Islam saw itself as part of a broader jihadi rebellion in the Levant. Although it never mentioned the seven-stage master plan, its emergence and grand strategy were consistent with the plan's third stage, which focused on building jihadi organizations in the Levant and confronting Israel. As Fatah al-Islam's Shariah leader explained in 2007:

The brothers' . . . purpose involved all of al-Sham; yes, all of al-Sham. . . . The concept was to build an Islamic Emirate in Tripoli (Northern Lebanon) to instigate the fight against the Jews and to support our brothers in Mesopotamia and to rally oppressed people . . . in Lebanon . . . and to rally the people in Syria, because the [Syrian] Ba'ath Party, through its authority, made the people fear their own power. When all of this happens, the Syrian Ba'ath Party will be in deep trouble because the mujahidin will surround it on both flanks: from Lebanon and Iraq. This was the plan and the belief upon which Fatah al-Islam was founded.[187]

Considering Fatah al-Islam's rejection of its Syrian benefactors, it was not surprising when the Lebanese government with Syrian backing, cracked down on the group in June 2007. In a three-month assault on the group's stronghold in Nahr al-Barid, dozens of fighters were killed or captured.[188] The only Lebanese jihadi group to offer Fatah al-Islam direct support was Jund al-Sham, which established roadblocks and conducted low-level strikes on Lebanese troops.

This is the context for the Mukhabarat's sting operation against Husayn and Abu Hafs in al-Marjah Square. It was August 2007, in the midst of the Syrian government's crackdown on remnants of Fatah al-Islam.[189]

Shakir al-Absi escaped the crackdown on Nahr al-Barid and fled into Syria, where his activities are largely unknown.[190] After losing its safe haven, Fatah al-Islam embraced terrorism, staging a series of attacks on the Lebanese military.[191] The group also claimed to have expanded its operations into the Gaza Strip and the West Bank. It joined calls from the ISI and al-Qaeda accusing the Palestinian groups Fatah and Hamas of failing to adequately attack Israel.[192]

Fatah al-Islam's expansion into Gaza was always more talk than action, but jihadi activism was growing in the Palestinian Territories. After Husayn tried to collect the four Libyans in al-Marjah Square, he planned a get-to-know-you meeting with the deputy emir of the Gaza-based jihadi group Jaysh al-Islam during a pilgrimage to Mecca. "We can understand their needs," Husayn wrote, "and they can send a message to the Sheikh," or "ask for [financial] help or pledge allegiance."[193] There is no evidence that Jaysh al-Islam made such a pledge, but Husayn's activism was again consistent with the third stage of al-Adl's master plan.

The nascent jihadi groups operating in the Palestinian Territories considered the existing Palestinian movements, including the Muslim Brotherhood-affiliated Hamas, to be collaborators with Israel. In February

2008, the ISI's emir excoriated Hamas and urged its military wing to join the jihadi-salafi movement. Among Hamas' reputed crimes were "joining the political process under a secular Constitution," offering "respect [for] international resolutions adopted by the United Nations," asserting "that they will not seek to Islamize society," recognizing "Israel by recognizing the Palestinian Authority," showing "excessive hostility to jihadi salafism," and "joining in a strange alliance with apostate regimes," especially "the Nusayri [Alawite] Syrian regime that has tormented Sunni Muslims in Lebanon."[194]

Meanwhile, al-Qaeda aimed to take Fatah al-Islam up on its offer to follow a leader from the international al-Qaeda movement. In November 2008, Kuwaiti authorities arrested a counterfeiting expert who, under interrogation, claimed to have helped several of Kuwait's most important jihadis to slip the country. The two most important were Muhsin al-Fadhli, who went on to be a key player for al-Qaeda's logistics operation in Iran, and Abu Talhah al-Kuwaiti.[195] Abu Talhah was a longtime al-Qaeda operative, and he is particularly interesting because of his career in the Levant.[196] After a failed attempt to traverse Damascus in 2007 (he was captured and deported to Kuwait), Abu Talhah fled Kuwait again, this time heading to Iran. He eventually arrived in Beirut from Athens in May 2009, but Lebanese authorities soon arrested him at a hotel in downtown Beirut.[197]

Lebanese prosecutors later fingered Abu Talhah as a key leader in a new effort to build an official al-Qaeda presence in Lebanon.[198] The emir of the new group was to be Abu Hammam al-Suri, the Syrian fighter who swore allegiance to Osama bin Laden in 1998 with a handshake in Afghanistan.[199] In 2009, Abu Talhah and Abu Hammam would pay for that allegiance to al-Qaeda with a sentence in Lebanon's infamous Roumiyeh prison.

Abu Talhah and Abu Hammam were first assigned to Ward B, a mixing bowl of Lebanon's competing underworlds: drug addicts and smugglers next to counterfeiters, jihadists, and would-be militants of various persuasions. Abu Talhah was dismayed by what he considered the moral depravity around him, though he also met "brave, upstanding brothers who had seen combat."[200] He befriended these fighters and "discovered their moral fiber and unwavering commitment to their ideology."[201] Just as the imprisoned jihadis in Iraq were building the future Islamic State in the American Camp Bucca prison, Lebanese jihadis were making similar connections in Roumiyeh. And, just as in Iraq, the walls of Roumiyeh prison would not hold Abu Talhah or Abu Hammam for long.

The ISI's tentacles allegedly reached further afield than the Levant. On June 29, 2007, police in London found two parked Mercedes near the Tiger Tiger nightclub packed with propane tanks, nails, and gasoline. The car bombs were to be detonated remotely via a cell phone by Bilal Abdulla and Kafeel Ahmed. Abdulla had previously been under surveillance by Britain's MI5, likely because of a series of trips he made to Baghdad in the years before the attack. Although raised in the United Kingdom, Abdulla had gone to medical school in Iraq, graduating in 2003.[202] He started a program in the United Kingdom that would get him a British medical license in 2004 and two years later was working with the National Health Service. In 2006 he again visited Iraq, just as violence was skyrocketing. According to his family, Abdulla returned to Britain deeply dispirited by the destruction in Baghdad and angry at the British government's part in the city's demolition.[203]

A technical glitch prevented the propane bombs in London from detonating, so Abdulla and Ahmed raced north from London, where they detonated a hastily constructed propane bomb in front of the Glasgow airport. Both were subsequently arrested, though Ahmed was badly burned by the explosion and died of his self-inflicted wounds. No one else was injured in the attacks.[204]

Intelligence agencies in the U.K. and United States found evidence linking Abdulla and Ahmed to the ISI, but none of it was introduced in court. The two men reportedly had cell phone numbers on their phones that were used by ISI fighters, and Abdulla's computer included a letter addressed to the "soldiers of the Islamic State of Iraq" that said, "God knows that the days I spent with you were the best and most rewarding days of my life."[205]

The public evidence does not definitively indicate that Bilal Abdulla was working for the ISI, though it strongly suggests the Iraqi group inspired him. "This event," an American intelligence official explained, "is best viewed as AQI-related, rather than AQI-directed."[206]

That conclusion seems reasonable, although there is one important dissenter: Abu Hamzah al-Muhajir, the ISI's minister of war. In 2008 he claimed that the "doctor's plot" was the ISI's doing and threatened more strikes in the West:

> The Crusade fights us in our home. Should we not fight in its home? Every country that has taken aggression against Iraq . . . [is] a legitimate target. Our right to respond does not subside because time passes. We have carried out numerous operations outside Iraq, notably the recent attack in Britain, including the small strike against the airport. The rest [of the attack] failed because one of the brothers made a mistake a few days beforehand. . . . But we advise the leaders of Britain, America, and Australia about what is coming. God has enabled us to prepare in ways that they will not be able to respond to or uncover.[207]

Abu Hamzah claimed responsibility for the Glasgow attack more than a year after it occurred, and just as Bilal Abdulla's terrorism trial was kicking off in London. He was certainly grandstanding; whether he was overstating the ISI's connection is another question.

After all, there were other hints of an ISI network in Europe.

In August 2007, two months after the London-Glasgow plot was executed, the Syrian ISI operative Husayn described a European network run by Abu Abdallah al-Baljiki ("the Belgian"):

> As for the operations in Europe, I have some [communication] lines. I even have someone that can take over and complete the work of Abu-'Abdallah al-Baljiki. Additionally, there is another person who works with me in gathering the funds over there. There are many brothers over there who want to work, however, over here, where you are, or over there in Europe, if Abu-Qaswarah [the ISI's emir in Mosul and chief of external operations] wants to give me the addresses, I will call them.[208]

It is not clear who Abu Abdallah al-Baljiki was, whether he was based in Europe or the Middle East, or even whether Husayn's reference to "operations in Europe" meant offensive strikes or fundraising and recruiting. But it is clear that the ISI had logistical networks in Europe and considered attacks there valuable enough to take responsibility for them and promise more. Abu Hamzah may have overstated the ISI's role in Glasgow, but the commonly held notion that the Islamic State only became interested in Europe after the Syrian civil war began is false. Indeed, the London-Glasgow attack, which was conducted by disconnected but Islamic State-inspired fighters, foreshadowed many of the attacks committed in the Islamic State's name after the caliphate was declared in 2014.

Retreat to Mosul

When the ISI was formed in October 2006, Abu Hamzah claimed it had more than 20,000 soldiers.[209] By early the following year, the group had a highly organized bureaucracy to delegate authority and responsibility throughout the organization. At the highest level was the formal cabinet, which provided national-level leadership, produced propaganda, and led the military effort. The overall organization was divided into "sectors," which were subdivided into districts, each led by a "district emir" who originally had six direct reports: emirs for medicine, propaganda, shariah, administration, security, and the military.[210]

The districts were primarily responsible for their own fundraising; a 2007 list of funding sources for a district in Anbar revealed that the organization controlled cement and chemical companies, banks, and a gas station. It was also taxing the population and charging fees for municipal services like water, sewers, and electricity.[211] A third revenue source was "booty"—money appropriated from enemy forces.[212]

Fundraising was critical because the ISI's districts had sprawling budgets. District emirs approved spending on automobiles, boats, explosives of various kinds, and bribes, often for the purpose of springing fighters from prison.[213] The largest expense category, by far, was fighters' salaries. These varied somewhat based on location and role, but fighters in Anbar were allocated 60,000 Iraqi dinars per month as a base salary, and an additional 30,000 per dependent (which included wives, parents, unmarried daughters and sisters, and sons and brothers younger than fifteen). Fighters were also allocated a housing allowance, set at the median rate for each area, to be distributed at the discretion of the local emir.[214]

Partly because they controlled much of their own funding, district emirs had tremendous authority and negotiated with one another for resources. For example, when fighters shifted from one district to another, they required a memo from one emir to the next.[215]

The ISI also took seriously its commitment to its fighters' families. The organization made extensive life insurance payments to the families of fighters who were killed. This undoubtedly maintained positive relations with tribes contributing personnel to the cause but was ultimately controversial internally because of the expense.[216]

These ISI districts also provided basic governance. The "general emirate" delegated most authority to local emirs but set policy broadly, including proscribing sleeping after dawn prayers and limiting the speed limit inside villages to 50 kilometers per hour and on public highways to 120 kilometers per hour.[217] The sector and district emirs expanded on these principles as they saw fit. In Ramadi, the ISI stole garbage trucks, apparently in order to provide municipal services more efficiently.[218]

The ISI's administrative procedures, however, were no defense against the political winds in Iraq. On October 15, 2007, exactly one year after the ISI was declared, one sector emir lamented his decline in fortunes. "There were almost 600 fighters in our Sector before the Tribes changed course 360 degrees under the influence of the so-called Islamic Army (Deserter of Jihad)," he complained. "Many of our fighters quit and some of them joined the deserters . . . and as a result of that the number of fighters dropped down to 20 or less."[219]

Despite—or, perhaps, because of—its increasingly formal bureaucracy, the ISI's first year was a disaster.

The ISI's leadership tried to learn from its early setbacks. At the end of September 2007, Abu Hamzah released dual guidance documents, one for soldiers and the other for emirs. These instructions included tactical guidance (ISI soldiers were not to travel more than three to a car or to have three or more people sleep without a guard at night), but the basic purpose was to encourage soldiers and emirs to work well with each other, to remain humble, and to respect the population they aimed to govern.[220]

"Don't authorize your brothers to kill or take as a prisoner [someone] who will split their unity [with the population]," Abu Hamzah wrote to the ISI's emirs, "even if it [is] permitted from a [particular] point of view." Essentially renouncing much of the ISI's behavior over the preceding year, Abu Hamzah explained that "unity . . . in the time of war is an outweighing interest and nothing is equal to it."[221]

If Abu Hamzah was hoping to coax better behavior out of his troops, it did not work. Overall violence in Iraq peaked in June 2007 and then declined dramatically. But this was not because of a kinder, gentler ISI. Rather, the organization was contracting as its fighters defected or were killed. Natural selection, not smarter doctrine, is the primary explanation for the ISI's more focused strategy after 2007.[222]

But the ISI's setbacks were not uniform. The Surge and Awakening were highly successful in Anbar Province, Baghdad, and provinces near Baghdad. But further north, in Ninawa Province and particularly the city of Mosul, the ISI still flourished.

Mosul was a useful redoubt for a couple of reasons. First, it was a key ISI logistics hub, particularly for foreign fighters, funds, and weapons entering the country through Syria.[223] Regrouping in Mosul shortened those supply lines.[224] Second, the city had a small but prominent Christian population, which made for easy scapegoats.[225] Third, Mosul's population was divided between Arabs and Kurds, and the ISI could capitalize on ethnic tension between the two groups to build a base of support.[226] Fourth, because Mosul was far from the Shia-dominated regions of southern Iraq, it simply was not the Iraqi government's top priority.

Mosul was not a total safe haven. American Special Operations forces bounced from one jihadi camp to another in raids that disrupted the ISI's ability to organize. But United States' conventional forces, which did the hard work of securing local populations, remained concentrated further south. Without the direct presence of American troops, some local factions decided it was safer to accommodate the ISI rather than challenge it.

The impact was profound. As Major General John Perkins explained in 2009, "For [the Islamic State of Iraq] to win, they have to take Baghdad. To survive, they have to hold on to Mosul."[227] In a nutshell, that is exactly what they did.

The man that ran the ISI's operation in Mosul had many names, but he is best known as Abu Qaswarah. Born in Morocco, he gained Swedish citizenship in the 1980s, married a Swedish woman, and had five children while becoming a leading figure at the Brandbergen Mosque in Stockholm, one of the most important centers of jihadi radicalization in Europe during the 1990s.[228] After stints in Afghanistan, he ultimately moved to Iraq and became the emir of Mosul and head of the group's external operations in June 2007.[229]

Abu Qaswarah was killed on October 5, 2008, in a gunfight with U.S. Special Operations troops. He detonated a suicide vest, which tore his own body apart but did not prevent the Special Operations team from collecting critical intelligence, including a slew of accounting and organizational documents that reveal how the ISI in Mosul was organized in late 2008.[230]

The documents demonstrate that although the ISI was in the midst of a dramatic setback at the hands of U.S., Iraqi, and tribal forces, it still had a formal bureaucracy, had aggressively taken root in and around Mosul as an underground movement, and was still laying the political groundwork for a state. Critically, its organizational structure was highly federated and cellular—district-level units were built to be self-sustaining—which made destroying the group extremely difficult. The ISI had the cellular structure of a traditional terrorist group, but a common bureaucratic language that would allow it to institutionalize quickly in the future.

By late 2008, the ISI was divided into thirty sectors across Iraq, each now led by an overall emir who commanded a triumvirate of direct reports: a shariah emir, a military emir, and a media emir.[231] The emirs for medicine, administration, and security were gone,[232] reflecting the group's increasingly modest operations.

In 2015, observers were dismayed by the Islamic State's effort to rename territories it controlled in Syria and Iraq, but this was an old tactic. In 2008, the ISI assigned a new name to every geographic unit it controlled as a stark way to distinguish its political vision from the secular administration of Ba'athist Iraq. Most of the new names honored dead jihadis; Mosul, for example, was "Mahmud al-Zanki," after Zarqawi's hero, the Crusader-era Kurdish commander Nur al-Din Zanki.[233]

The documents reveal great weakness across some of the ISI's provinces, and sophisticated and successful efforts to build deep ties in others. One document lamented the group's setbacks in the city of Tal Afar and complained that the Kurdish Peshmerga militia was keeping the ISI out of Zamzar and Rabiah, cities along the Syrian border just north of the group's primary road from Mosul into Syria.

But the ISI thrived around Mosul City. The group inserted operatives into every village and neighborhood in the area to map the physical and human geography, and then identified localized tactics to infiltrate each. It identified Turkmen speakers for specialized outreach to Turkmen communities and offered religious training courses as outreach tools. One report crowed that the first religious class in the city of Badush, just northwest of Mosul, attracted "sixty children and thirty young men."[234] The ISI also carefully selected tribal leaders for outreach, rated their financial well-being, and offered gifts of clothing, religious books, and toys for children to build rapport in a new community.

During this period, ISI sectors were responsible for their own fundraising, outreach, and operational planning. The top-level ISI organization was sustained by revenue from the sectors, not the other way around. Sectors were required to give 20 percent of their revenue to the central organization, and these funds were usually accounted in U.S. dollars rather than Iraqi dinars. In some cases, payments were made in gold.[235] The ISI's fundraising and operational model was reminiscent of a cellular terrorist organization, even as it established the political edifice of a nascent state. The hybrid organizational model cut two ways. On the one hand, the ISI was not well-positioned to govern consistently, even though that was clearly its long-term goal. On the other hand, the cellular organization offered tremendous resilience because if one sector was eliminated, the others could operate independently. In short, the ISI was built to do just what Abu Umar had decreed in April 2007: "to remain."

Just weeks after Abu Qaswarah was killed in October 2008, his counterpart in Syria, Abu Ghadiyah, was shot dead by U.S. Special Operations troops at a farmhouse outside of Albu Kamal, Syria.[236] It was the first time American troops engaged the Islamic State on Syrian territory, but it would not be the last.

The strike came as the Syrian government was increasingly worried about jihadis operating in its midst—and may have been countenanced beforehand by the Syrian regime.[237] The United States was actively courting Syria's cooperation against the foreign fighter networks on its territory. Dell Dailey, a Special Operations legend turned the U.S. State Department's coordinator for counterterrorism, traveled repeatedly to Damascus in 2008, even bringing along copies of academic reports based on the cache of ISI personnel documents known as the Sinjar Records.[238]

Events closer to home likely had an impact as well. On September 29, 2008, a nearly 450-pound car bomb exploded near the headquarters of the Palestine Branch of Syrian intelligence in Damascus, killing seventeen people.[239] Few details are available about the bombing, but Syria accused Fatah al-Islam of the strike and paraded ten of its members, including Shakir al-Absi's daughter, on television in a mass confession.[240] She claimed the suicide bomber was Saudi, but some observers suspected that the bomb was a Syrian false flag intended to deflect Western criticism of Syria's government for failing to crack down on foreign fighters crossing Syria into Iraq.[241]

False flag or not, the Syrian government's patience with its former jihadi partners was wearing thin. The following month, U.S. troops killed Abu Ghadiyah on Syrian territory amid rumors that the regime in Damascus had blessed the strike. And in December, Fatah al-Islam announced that al-Absi, its emir, had been killed in an ambush by Syrian troops.[242]

In April 2009, the phone rang at a man's home in Tunisia. The man, identified in court documents only as the brother of "Fighter 2," picked up and was surprised to hear a voice claiming to be from Iraq and asking whether the Tunisian was related to "Fighter 2," whose real name is not identified. The brother was surprised, because the man called Fighter 2 had told his family that he was working in Libya. To the contrary, the mysterious caller explained to the shocked brother that Fighter 2 was "martyred two days ago in combat in Mosul." He repeated this statement three times and then exclaimed, "May God witness what I say. God is Great. You will not be re-ceiving any more calls."[243]

The caller did not explain how Fighter 2 died, but federal investigators in the United States noted that days earlier a suicide truck bomb killed seven people at a police station in Mosul, Iraq.[244]

The following week, one of Fighter 2's compatriots drove a large dump truck toward United States' Forward Operating Base Marez, adjacent to the Mosul airfield. The truck, carrying 2,000 pounds of explosives, blew up fifty yards from the base's front gate, killing five Americans and two Iraqis. Seventy people were injured and the bomb reportedly left a crater sixty feet deep.[245]

According to federal prosecutors in the United States, the attack would not have been possible without an Iraqi refugee named Faruq Khalil Muhammad 'Isa, who, without ever leaving Canada, allegedly coordinated a network of facilitators in Syria and Iraq to arrange for the Tunisians to ar-rive in Iraq. Using clumsy code words (he explained to a compatriot, "[W]hen I want to name the brothers, I say the farmers—because they plant metal and harvest metal and flesh"), he served as travel agent for North African fighters traversing the underground road through Syria to Iraq.[246]

The Tunisians who attacked FOB Marez arrived in Iraq as the foreign fighter network in Syria was pushing more fighters through. After bottom-ing out at about five fighters a month arriving in Iraq, the number had re-bounded to around twenty.[247] This burst of activity was partly a function of new facilitators running things in Syria after Abu Ghadiyah's death, but al-Qaeda networks that had been disrupted after the arrest of Abd al-Hadi were improving in Turkey as well.[248] This development was particularly exciting to al-Qaeda's leadership. In August 2009, Atiyah wrote to bin Laden with the good news, but he notably saw Turkey as useful because of its proximity to Europe, not Iraq. "There is some improvement now," he wrote. "Soon we shall have an office in Turkey for the external work. . . . We have planned for this branch to fill in a huge gap and it would be an advance point towards Europe."[249]

In Syria, however, American diplomacy was shifting into high gear. Senior State Department and National Security Council representatives made repeated trips to Damascus in early 2009—and that outreach paid dividends.[250] Shortly after the attack on FOB Marez, Muhammad 'Isa's network in Syria began to wither. One facilitator in Syria called Muhammad 'Isa to complain, "[T]he government is trying to infiltrate through to us" and "that is why the door is closed to volunteers."[251] Days later, another facilitator reported that the first had been arrested near Mosul on April 21, 2009. A month later, it got worse. "Do you remember Facilitator 1, the friend of Facilitator 2 from Syria?" asked the bearer of bad news. "They had him arrested."

The ISI's own strategists had long recognized that too many foreign fighters created more problems than they solved—and moved to restrict the flow only to suicide bombers.[252] The Syrian government, after years of brazenly leaving the door open for foreign fighters, was closing it. For the moment, Assad was still able to manage the jihadi demons he helped create.

Stage Three of the master plan's timeline—the Stage of Reawakening— turned out to be a stage of setbacks for the ISI. Despite the propitious beginning—declaring an Islamic State—the group grew weaker rather than stronger. Nonetheless, it made several important advances, including building a political framework in Iraq and inspiring a new wave of jihadi activism in primarily Palestinian communities in Lebanon and Gaza. The first blows of the fight against the group's sometime partner in Damascus had been struck.

The Stage of Reawakening also marked the beginning of the ISI's break from al-Qaeda. The master plan was Sayf al-Adl's grandiose attempt to develop a unified strategic vision for al-Qaeda and the Zarqawiists. And, on the surface at least, this alliance remained, although the two groups agreed that AQI had been dissolved. Al-Qaeda had publicly endorsed the establishment of the ISI.

But the outlines of future conflict were set: al-Qaeda had attempted to challenge Zarqawi by sending Abd al-Hadi to Iraq, and failed. The ISI had introduced apocalyptic visions directly into its ideology and now followed an Iraqi leadership unaccountable to al-Qaeda. It fought openly with Ansar al-Sunnah, another close al-Qaeda ally. The master plan envisioned a resurrected caliphate within a broadly unified jihadi movement. The first part of that goal remained front and center for the ISI, but the latter was increasingly a fantasy.

Even some of the men that had shaped Zarqawi's original vision for jihad in Iraq were changing their tune.

Muhammad Khalil al-Hakaymah, reputed to be the pseudonymous author of *The Management of Savagery*, released a new strategic vision just a month before the declaration of the ISI. In *Towards a New Strategy*, Hakaymah emphasized strikes against military targets, urged commanders to avoid "cruel methods of fighting" such as beheading, and reminded them that "this conflict is a long-term one that could extend for a generation or more." Commanders should therefore build strong relationships with a wide range of Muslims, not try to separate "true" Muslims from apostates.[253] If Hakaymah was indeed the author of *The Management of Savagery*, then his vision had shifted significantly. The war in Iraq inspired immense soul-searching among the American national security elite; ironically, the excesses of Zarqawi and his successors inspired a similar process among leading jihadis.

Hakaymah's intellectual shift paralleled an organizational one. In November 2006 he appeared side-by-side in a video with al-Qaeda's second-in-command, Ayman al-Zawahiri, and formally swore allegiance to al-Qaeda. Hakaymah, who had been in Iran since he fled there in 2002, was now ensconced in the mountains along the Afghanistan-Pakistan border.

Hakaymah focused primarily on resurrecting al-Qaeda's operations in Egypt, but in late 2007 he aimed to redeem some of the ISI's mistakes in Iraq. Despite the risks revealed by Abd al-Hadi's capture, Zawahiri told bin Laden that Hakaymah "insisted on going [to Iraq] by any method, and he did not listen to any advice."[254] Despite that determination and Hakaymah's unusually productive relationship with the Iranian regime, Zawahiri reported that, "he was obliged to come back after he was forced." Damascus was restricting the road through Syria, and Tehran was doing the same in Iran.

In the wake of Abd al-Hadi's capture, Hakaymah tried to reach Iraq across Iran and Zawahiri mulled sending Atiyah abd al-Rahman on a similar mission. In the end, neither made it. Despite Zarqawi's death and the

ISI's humbling setbacks, al-Qaeda remained unable to shape events directly in Iraq.

Hakaymah learned the hard way that Pakistan was not necessarily any safer than Iraq. In October 2008, near the Pakistani town of Mir Ali, a drone-fired Hellfire missile eviscerated Hakaymah's car, killing him.

The jihadis might have had a seven-stage master plan, but Stage Three was a step backward, not forward. And, as Hakaymah learned, just surviving more than one or two was growing increasingly difficult.

4

The Stage of Recuperation
(2010–2013)

[This stage] will focus on overthrowing regimes by means of direct and fierce clashes . . . the raisons d'etre of these regimes will cease to exist. When the regimes gradually disintegrate, Al-Qaeda and the Islamic jihad trend will grow relentlessly.

Fuad Husayn, *Zarqawi . . . The Second Generation of al-Qaeda*

Mosul to Baghdad

In the aftermath of the American attack, there was only the detritus of a future insurgency: dozens of bloody mattresses, boxes of Nike and Adidas running shoes, shredded tents, and black scars running across the desert sand. Not far away, seventy-eight fresh graves contained the bodies of men from many countries, Iraq, Syria, Jordan, and France among them.[1] The American Apache helicopters that swept down on a jihadi training camp north of the western Iraqi city of Rawah in June 2003 were devastating.

But the assault left some survivors, among them a former Iraqi army officer known to his friends as Abu Ubayda.[2] Despite having more interest in smuggling than in Shariah, Abu Ubayda coordinated the foreign fighter training in Anbar Province for Zarqawi until 2005.[3] After the Rawah raid, the task of regenerating the eviscerated logistics network fell to him.

Abu Ubayda scoured Anbar Province and Baghdad for disaffected young men willing to fight the Americans. He did not have an ideological litmus test. He just wanted fighters.

Among his lieutenants was a twenty-eight-year-old Baghdad resident named Manaf abd al-Rahim al-Rawi. Al-Rawi was born in 1975 in Moscow, where his father, an Iraqi army officer, studied engineering. The family returned to Iraq before the Iran-Iraq war began in 1980, and after her husband was killed in the fighting, al-Rawi's mother was left alone to raise five sons. Al-Rawi never stood out as a student, but his family was reasonably connected in Saddam's Iraq: a well-networked uncle arranged for him to do his compulsory national service in the Ministry of Housing rather than the military.[4]

After being recruited by Abu Ubayda in late 2003, al-Rawi became a critical aide to one of Zarqawi's closest assistants, Abu Muhammad al-Lubnani. Lubnani was ethnically Kurdish, raised in Lebanon, and lived much of his life in Denmark. He was believed to have close ties to Mullah Krekar, the Kurdish leader of Ansar al-Islam, who had been based in Norway.[5] In 2003, Lubnani returned to Lebanon, where his friends and relations became some of the first Lebanese recruits to Zarqawi's cause in Iraq.[6] By the time al-Rawi met him, Lubnani was one of Zarqawi's most important advisors. Al-Rawi became his driver.

In that role, al-Rawi was not part of the jihadi inner circle, but he was adjacent to it. While serving as Lubnani's aide, he met the glitterati of Iraq's first jihadi generation, including Abu Hamzah al-Muhajir, Zarqawi's successor who would go on to found the ISI and serve as its minister of war.

Such connections would become critically important later in al-Rawi's career, especially after a long, unintentional break. He was arrested in early 2004 and spent the next three and a half years in the American prisons of Abu Ghraib and Camp Bucca. By the time he was released, in November 2007, most of al-Rawi's jihadi contacts were dead.

He reconnected with jihadis through a fellow prisoner from Camp Bucca who was known to have direct ties to the current leadership of the ISI.[7] This friend referred al-Rawi to the ISI's emir in Baghdad, a cantankerous sixty-year-old who clashed with other members of the group.[8] By

2009 he had been removed, and al-Rawi assumed command of the ISI's operation in Baghdad.

He took charge as the ISI was suffering massive setbacks across Iraq, but the terrorist network inside Baghdad was still effective. In that respect, 2009 in Baghdad looked something like 2003; the jihadis could not control territory, but they maintained underground networks and could mount devastating strikes.

On August 19, 2009, six years to the day after the UN Headquarters bombing organized by Thamir Mubarak, a series of truck bombs targeting the Finance and Foreign Ministries killed nearly 100 people.[9] More than 10 percent of Iraq's diplomatic corps was killed or injured in the attack. And it was just the beginning.[10]

Two months later, on October 25, 2009, a similar series of bombs killed 132 people near the Justice Ministry and the Ministry of Municipalities and Public Works.[11] On December 8, 2009, four explosions killed 127 people near public institutions in Baghdad, including a bank that was temporarily housing employees from the previously damaged Finance Ministry.[12]

The ISI had suffered dramatic territorial and personnel losses to the Surge and Awakening, but was still capable of mounting a highly successful terrorist campaign in Iraq. In the three years after the Surge, 2008–2010, more than 200 people were killed per month by terrorism in Iraq. It was a dramatic decline from the unremitting violence of previous years, but it was still an extraordinarily high number, especially for a country of only 24 million people.[13] If people were killed at the same per capita rate in a population the size of the United States, more than 3,100 people would be killed per month. That is more people than were killed on 9/11.

The ISI's under-the-radar counterattack after the Surge also focused on eliminating leaders of the Awakening. Craig Whiteside, a retired Army Lieutenant Colonel who wrote his dissertation on the ISI's assassination campaign, counted at least 1,345 Awakening leaders assassinated from the beginning of 2009 until 2013.[14] That is on top of 528 "Sons of Iraq" members killed in 2008.[15] This was a classic application of terrorist tactics in an insurgency: provoke a draconian counterattack from the government, which alienates the population, while carefully eliminating hostile leaders from the community you hope to lead. Most of the dead were "shot singly or in pairs" and, with the exception of prominent Awakening leaders like Abdul Sattar Abu Risha—who hosted the first Awakening meetings in 2006—"most killings were barely noticed by the Iraqi government or in the media."[16]

The government in Baghdad was apoplectic at the attacks on its ministries. After the August 2009 bombings, Iraq withdrew its ambassador from Damascus and accused the Syrian regime of harboring militants. They pointed to "Ba'ath party loyalists for planning the bombing and Al Qaeda [Islamic State of Iraq] operatives for carrying it out."[17] Al-Rawi echoed the general thrust of this argument after his capture. Abu Hamzah gave the orders, he said, and the car and truck bombs were assembled in Baghdad proper, but the logistics for his attacks were based in Syria.[18] Suicide bombers "arrive from Syria with the intention of carrying out a suicide operation," al-Rawi explained, "he does not cross the border if he is not prepared."[19] The fertilizer used to make explosives was also shipped in from Syria.[20]

The Iraqi government was particularly concerned that the ISI was working with Izzat al-Douri, Saddam's former deputy who led the most intransigent wing of the former Ba'ath Party. Al-Douri and the ISI were not ideological allies, but al-Douri's networks in Syria seemed to remain functional after the ISI's had been weakened. The militant networks, both wounded, needed tactical alliances to piece together a logistics system capable of producing a military impact.

Most worryingly, some Iraqi politicians used the attacks to blame not just the ISI or Syria-based Iraqi Ba'athists, but Sunni Muslims in general—including "Saudi Arabia and Gulf States"—of supporting the attacks.[21] For some, the Baghdad bombings were not isolated terrorist actions; they were hallmarks of a sectarian war that had lulled in Iraq but was growing regionally. This was exactly how the ISI saw the world, and compelling others—even its enemies—to see the world in similar terms was no small victory.

The ISI's underground campaign to exploit sectarian tension in Iraq corresponded with a decline in the United States' ability to restrain Iraqi political entropy. The United States signed a Status of Forces Agreement (SOFA) with Iraq's government during the waning days of the Bush Administration (November 18, 2008) that constrained U.S. operations and required that "All the United States Forces shall withdraw from all Iraqi territory no later than December 31, 2011."[22] The agreement required that prisoners held by U.S. troops in Iraq be transferred to Iraqi custody, and it prohibited U.S. forces from detaining anyone without an Iraqi warrant. President Obama campaigned on a platform of even quicker withdrawal. He let that expedited timeline slip but did not press the Iraqi government to amend the existing SOFA. The United States withdrew in full by the end of 2011.[23]

The ISI was a product of the United States' invasion of Iraq, but an intense U.S. military campaign suppressed the group and bolstered productive political trends in Iraq. As U.S. troops withdrew, the ISI took full advantage. Now, Iraq would face the ISI, and its own dysfunction, largely on its own.

The high point of cohesive Iraqi politics came in the January 2009 provincial elections. Prime Minister Nouri al-Maliki's Dawa Party did very well in largely Shia provinces, which sidelined groups that were believed to be more tightly tied to Iran. Sunnis, including tribal leaders from the Awakening, participated in voting. The actual electoral process was generally violence-free.

The Iraqi political process was always perilous. Prior to the U.S. invasion, Saddam's dictatorship entrenched Sunni rule in Baghdad, but free elections inevitably brought political groups that represented Iraq's Shia majority to power. However, Iraq's political parties did not align neatly into homogenous sectarian groupings; various Shia parties disputed how to engage Iraq's Sunni-Arab and Kurdish minorities, divide revenue, and engage the United States and Iran. In early 2009, however, the political process seemed to be working.

Under the surface, however, the foundation remained fragile. Prime Minister Maliki was looking ahead to national elections in 2010, which he knew would require broader support among Iraq's Shia population. In those national elections, which occurred as ISI terrorism was increasingly returning to Baghdad, the populist Shia party loyal to Moqtada al-Sadr did better than expected. This threw Iraq's politics into crisis as the Shia leaders negotiated a new governing coalition. Ultimately, Maliki retained power, but the Shia political class was left more sectarian, and more accountable to Iran.

Another key problem was that the Awakening was never a sustainable framework. Sunnis had been enticed to join the Awakening by steady paychecks from the United States, the promise of peace, and a path back to political power.[24] But by late 2009 all three were disappearing. The Awakening was too vast for the Iraqi government to fund perpetually, and Prime Minister Maliki had no intention of regularizing Sunni militias that had attacked his government just years before.[25] The Iraqi government also targeted Sunni leaders that it deemed problematic, because of criminal activity, a drift back toward militancy, or both.[26]

Adel Mashadhani embodied the challenge. A local insurgent leader in eastern Baghdad, Mashadhani embraced U.S. troops and the Awakening in 2007. Working with the United States, he rooted the ISI out of the neighborhood but took the opportunity to empower his own smuggling and extortion enterprises. That tradeoff was good enough to satisfy American troops, who were focused on destroying the ISI, but it was a recipe for trouble over the long run. When U.S. troops left the neighborhood in 2009, Iraqi government troops cracked down. Mashadhani was arrested, accused of supporting terrorism, and ultimately sentenced to death.[27] Regardless of Mashadhani's culpability, episodes like this convinced many Sunnis that as the United States withdrew from Iraq, the Iraq government would target them. Some drifted back toward allegiance with the Sunni resistance, which was increasingly dominated by the ISI.

Prime Minister Maliki's crackdown on Sunni leaders who he said worked with the ISI was clumsy and often politically motivated, but it was not completely baseless. In 2009, the ISI infiltrated mainstream Sunni institutions and was even working directly with some senior Sunni politicians. An internal ISI document, dated August 7, 2009, and signed by a pseudonymous "Hatim," shows that the ISI was communicating directly with Faruq 'Abd al-Qadir, Iraq's minister of communications, and with Hajj Riyad, the chief of staff to the deputy prime minister—and using such connections both to bolster its political position and raise money.[28]

The ISI's schemes are common all over the world: politicians direct contracts to businesses linked to illicit organizations that put the deal together and prevent "disruptions." In this case, Hatim negotiated with the minister of communications to direct a large contract for a new post office in Mosul to 'Abd al-Latif al-Zibari, a prominent Arab leader in the city. The ISI took a percentage of the contract.

The alliance went deeper than the post office. Al-Zibari offered the ISI political cover in Mosul, while ISI fighters offered al-Zibari muscle in a long-standing feud with Kurdish leaders in the city. The ISI's ideology elevates creed over nationality or ethnicity, but when push came to shove it was happy to capitalize on ethnic tension to secure its organizational future.[29]

Allying with the al-Zibari clan brought other advantages for Hatim and the ISI. One of 'Abd al-Latif's nephews was Daldar al-Zibari, the deputy chief of Ninawa Province. According to Hatim, Daldar was "willing to cooperate with [the ISI] in any field."[30] There is no hard evidence such a deal was ever struck, but Daldar's public warnings about the potential for increased violence resonate differently when you understand he was negotiating with the ISI behind the scenes. "We are afraid the situation in Mosul will worsen," Daldar said ominously in early 2010, while publicly protesting the torture of Sunnis in an Iraqi prison. "The citizens who renounced violence will return to it as a reaction to what happened."[31]

In 2009, the same year that General John Perkins explained that the ISI only needed to hold on to Mosul in order to survive, General Raymond Odierno described the group's disposition there: "They do not control large portions of Nineveh or Mosul, but they do have enough influence—or they do have some freedom of movement where they're able to conduct some high-profile attacks inside of Nineveh Province and Mosul."[32] For all of the ISI's setbacks, it was meeting Perkins' standard for survival.

Manaf al-Rawi would meet a man named Abu Ja'far at Mr. Milk, a small grocery in western Baghdad. Abu Ja'far would bring messages from Abu Hamzah al-Muhajir or, in special cases, would escort suicide bombers to Baghdad after they crossed from Syria into Iraq.[33] When an alert Baghdad traffic cop arrested al-Rawi at a traffic checkpoint on March 11, 2010, the first move of Iraqi intelligence was to set up a sting operation for Abu Ja'far. "They allowed me to meet him but they surrounded the entire area," al-Rawi said later. "Then they arrested him."[34]

The information al-Rawi and Abu Ja'far provided led Iraqi and American counterterrorism forces to a safe house near Lake Tharthar, south of Saddam Hussein's hometown of Tikrit. When they raided the home, they killed not only Abu Hamzah but Abu Umar al-Baghdadi, the emir of the Islamic State of Iraq.[35]

That raid was just the beginning. American commandos had spent the past four years perfecting the process of exploiting intelligence quickly and bouncing to follow-on targets. The raid on Abu Umar and Abu Hamzah netted leadership rosters, accounting documents, and situation reports. It was an intelligence goldmine and the resulting attacks came in quick succession.[36] "Over the last 90 days or so," Odierno reported six weeks after Abu Hamzah and Abu Umar were killed, "we've either picked up or killed 34 out of the top 42 al-Qaeda in Iraq leaders."[37]

It was not just the ISI that was under pressure. On May 4, 2010, Abu Abdallah al-Shafi'i, emir of Ansar al-Islam (Ansar al-Sunnah returned to its original name after Abu Wa'el and the Shariah Commission defected) and erstwhile partner of the ISI, was arrested in Baghdad.[38]

These attacks coincided with dramatic disruptions of the ISI in other arenas. By late 2009, the United States believed that only five foreign fighters were entering Iraq a month, down from seventy per month three years earlier.[39] Moreover, according to U.S. commanders, the ISI had been severed from "mainstream al-Qaeda," and had "degenerated into an organization that has to try to fund itself inside Iraq."[40]

In short, Odierno explained, the ISI was "no longer a broad-based insurgency. . . . They are what I call a covert terrorist organization . . . who are attempting to . . . have the population lose confidence in the government. And so they are targeting very specific governmental facilities."[41]

American military leaders would often return to the same metrics to describe the ISI's decline: its leadership had been eviscerated, its numbers were massively reduced, the group was scrapping to meet its financial commitments, it focused on terrorism not territory, and its connection to al-Qaeda Central had been severed.

All of this was true, but these operational metrics did not tell the whole story. Despite the ISI's battlefield setbacks it was achieving its political aim: many Iraqis were losing "confidence in the government."

Moreover, the ISI was extremely resilient. The decentralized, cellular structure that it borrowed from more traditional terrorist organizations was paying off. Sector emirs acted autonomously, raised funds independently, and brought in their own recruits. Even if one sector organization was destroyed, the others could continue to function. Moreover, the ISI had been financially self-reliant for years; the central organization was funded by a 20 percent tax on its own sectors, not by al-Qaeda or foreign funders.

Lastly, many in the global jihadi community continued to see the ISI as a vehicle for the restoration of the caliphate. Even though the U.S. government continued to refer to the ISI as "al-Qaeda in Iraq," many jihadis saw it as a distinct entity with a different mission.

Some in al-Qaeda evidently saw things the same way, and hoped that Abu Hamzah and Abu Umar's deaths would be an opening to improve relations. In a memo to bin Laden, Atiyah suggested that the leaders' deaths were an "opportunity to renew efforts at unity [with the Islamic State of Iraq] and to find a new structure that combines everything."[42]

Abu Hamzah and Abu Umar are sometimes dismissed as weak leaders because the ISI suffered massive setbacks during their tenure. But they also faced the full focus of the world's greatest military and yet built a resilient organization that could lose 80 percent of its leadership and still function. They should not be underestimated; the contemporary Islamic State would not have been possible without them.

Indeed, glowing eulogies for the two dead leaders rolled in from across the globe. Jaysh al-Ummah released two statements from Jerusalem; the managers of al-Fajr, the jihadi media distribution network, released a rare statement in their own name; a group of salafis imprisoned in Morocco expressed condolences and pledged their continued commitment to the ISI as the kernel of the future caliphate.[43]

The most important eulogy came from Ayman al-Zawahiri, then second-in-command to Osama bin Laden. In a video statement alternately displaying imagery from the ISI and his own face, Zawahiri memorialized the leaders and reminded their followers that, "despite their wounds, their certainty of the return of the glorious caliphate grows." The video closed with a reference to the ISI's most famous declaration, from Abu Umar's April 2007 speech. It read: "The State of Islam Remains: We will live under Islam's shadow or die the death of the noble."[44]

The U.S. command in Iraq certainly recognized the ISI's continued commitment to the caliphate. The Islamic State of Iraq "want[s] to establish a caliphate in Iraq," explained General Odierno on the same day he celebrated attrition in the group's leadership. "That's a tall task for them now . . . but they still sustain that thought process. They continue to look around the world for safe havens and sanctuaries . . . I believe that they'll have a very difficult time in Iraq doing that. But they will certainly continue to try."[45]

He was right.

The Caliph

Ibrahim bin Awad bin Ibrahim al-Badri al-Radawi al-Husseini al-Samarra's full name reveals much about his background. He is from the Iraqi city of Samarra, home to the golden domed al-Askariyya mosque that Zarqawi bombed in February 2006.[46] He is from the Albu Badri tribe, just like Haitham al-Badri, the AQI commander and former Ba'athist who planned and organized the attack on the al-Askariyya mosque. And like Abu Umar al-Baghdadi, the first emir of the ISI, he is descended from the Prophet Muhammad's tribe of Quraysh, through Husayn, grandson of the prophet himself.[47]

Ibrahim's father was a prominent figure in the Albu Badri tribe and an imam at their local mosque. Although Ibrahim never joined the Ba'ath Party, two of his uncles worked in the security services, and a brother joined the army.[48] Ibrahim was born in 1971 and grew up studious. Despite his quiet demeanor, he was a resolute competitor on the soccer field and came to life in the mosque, where he began leading prayers as an adolescent. His high school transcript at the Samarra High School for Boys indicates that he excelled in math and geography and scored adequately in Arabic, history, and economics. His weakest subject was English.[49]

Ibrahim moved to Baghdad after high school, where he studied at the University of Baghdad and then enrolled to study Islamic History at a PhD program at Saddam University for Islamic Studies, an institution founded during Saddam's "Faith Campaign" to Islamize Iraqi society. Like acquaintances who knew him in Samarra, his Baghdad neighbors and former classmates describe a quiet man devoted to religious study rather than political leadership or radicalism. Yet he joined the Muslim Brotherhood while in graduate school and quickly migrated toward its radical fringe, which in Baghdad at the time was led by a veteran of the anti-Soviet jihad in Afghanistan named Muhammad Hardan.[50]

Like thousands of other young Iraqis, both religious and secular, Ibrahim went to Fallujah in 2004. American records indicate he was arrested by U.S. troops on February 4, 2004, apparently at the home of a friend,[51] and sent to Camp Bucca, the American prison where many of the ISI's future leaders already resided. Manaf al-Rawi was arrested in Fallujah at about the same time. So was Umar, the son of Zarqawi's erstwhile mentor Abu Muhammad al-Maqdisi, who later crowed to his father that, "Iraq's prisons have become the biggest university for education, as teachers from the entire world are assembling in these prisons."[52] Indeed, the American prison system in Iraq was a networking hub for jihadis—a place where meetings that would otherwise have been "impossibly dangerous" were doable.[53]

By the time he entered prison, Ibrahim bin Awad was already going by the name Abu Bakr al-Baghdadi, the pseudonym that would become globally famous when ISIS proclaimed him caliph in 2014. In 2004, his knowledge of Islam won immediate respect among Camp Bucca's jihadis, and his quiet demeanor gave him credibility with the American guards. His soccer skills left inmates joking that he was the next "Maradona" rather than the next caliph.[54] It was not long before Abu Bakr was mediating disputes and moving among different social and political networks in the prison.[55] By the time he was released from Camp Bucca, ten months after he entered it, Abu Bakr had built the relationships that would eventually put him at the center of the jihadi movement.

There is no direct record of Abu Bakr meeting al-Rawi in Camp Bucca, but after being released he seems to have gone to work with Abu Ubayda, the man that brought al-Rawi into Zarqawi's network. Abu Bakr also seems to have adopted the nickname "Abu Dua," which for years would be the appellation used by American intelligence analysts to identify him. Abu Bakr worked to coordinate propaganda and foreign fighter transit for various militant groups, including AQI and Muhammad Hardan's Mujahidin

Army, two organizations that later were visceral enemies.[56] Abu Bakr worked out of both Damascus and, seemingly, the Iraqi border city of al-Qa'im, which at the time was the primary port of entry for foreign fighters. In 2005, American troops there chased a man called "Abu Du'a," who was close to Abu Ubayda and coordinated foreign fighters. They even reported—apparently erroneously—that he had been killed.[57]

Abu Bakr grew more prominent as emir of the Shariah Committee for the Army of the Followers of the Sunnah and the Collective (APSC), a small, sectarian jihadi group based primarily in Diyala Province.[58] Diyala is relatively diverse, with large Sunni and Shia populations, and the APSC responded to that complexity with a deeply sectarian vision. The group's propaganda hailed attacks on Shia militias and claimed responsibility for capturing and executing Iranian Special Forces officers training Shia militants.[59]

The APSC was officially independent from AQI, but Zarqawi and bin Laden were its political and ideological touchstones. Prior to formally aligning with Zarqawi, the group apologized publicly to him for violating a prohibition on attacks against the Mahdi Army, a Shia militia led by Moqtada al-Sadr. They sheepishly explained that, "they started the fighting first."[60]

From the beginning, the APSC had a political and economic vision for state building and governance that tracks with Abu Bakr's future as caliph. The group's "General Plan," written in 2005, explained its vision for state building:

> The construction of economic and social entities through financial investment in the creation of commercial, service, social, and scientific institutions. For example: commercial businesses, Islamic financial companies, factories, agricultural lands, hospitals, schools, sports organizations and clubs, cultural centers, etc. It is in this way that we will be able to build a society specific to us; we are cognizant of the fact that our enemies have taken control of the world in this way.[61]

On January 29, 2006, a few months after the APSC began releasing propaganda online, the group announced that it would join AQI's Mujahidin Shura Council, which had been established two weeks earlier. Abu Bakr was now Zarqawi's official ally.

Some reports claim that Abu Bakr subsequently served as a messenger for Abu Umar.[62] This is plausible; Abu Bakr had a reputation for discretion and Abu Umar reportedly ran Diyala Province for AQI, the same region where the APSC was most active. Moreover, the safe house where Abu Umar and Abu Hamzah died was in Salahuddin Province, not too far from where Abu Bakr was born and raised.

But the documentary evidence suggests Abu Bakr was more than just a courier inside the ISI. An ISI roster dated October 14, 2008, lists "Abu Du'a" as the emir of Mosul, which suggests Abu Bakr may have followed Abu Qaswarah in that role. It suggests he was the governor of the ISI's most important and successful geographic region during the crucial moments when the group restructured to survive the onslaught from the U.S. Surge and the Iraqi Awakening.[63]

Jihadis often use the same nickname, so it is perilous to rely solely on a name in captured documents to outline a biography. Yet the preponderance of evidence suggests that Abu Bakr was extremely well positioned to follow Abu Umar as emir of the ISI. He had a PhD in Islamic Studies, had worked with foreign fighters from the earliest days of the Iraq insurgency, managed foreign fighter logistics and propaganda at various times, outlined a plan for state building in late 2005, and applied some of those principles while managing the ISI's all-important stronghold of Mosul at a critical moment in the group's history.

After he was appointed emir, Abu Bakr also had the benefit of a smart "counter counter-insurgency" manual entitled A Manual to Improve the Political Position of the Islamic State of Iraq, which was published in early 2010. It advocated a detailed plan to engage Iraqi nationalists, build underground networks, and conserve men and materiel for the right opportunities.[64] The document undoubtedly outlined Abu Bakr's future strategy, but it also codified the approach the ISI had employed in Mosul when Abu Bakr was apparently the emir there. From Abu Bakr's perspective, the manual probably looked less like a new strategy document and more like a record of lessons learned.

In the 2006 book Informing the People about the Islamic State of Iraq, the head of the ISI's Shariah Committee explained three acceptable processes for selecting or replacing an emir. First, "through the pledge of a group of authoritative Muslims." Second, through "assignment from an [emir] for an individual to succeed him, or through nominating a number of individuals, so that one of them may be selected as emir." Third, by "attaining supremacy by force when there is confusion in the absence of an [emir] and reluctance of authoritative Muslims to appoint one."[65] The last method, he wrote, is not preferred, but "sometimes it is needed," and when that is the case, "this method of one becoming an emir through conquest and supremacy is inevitably legal."[66]

Three weeks after Abu Umar and Abu Hamzah were killed, the ISI announced that Abu Bakr would be the new emir. The statement explained that the first method—the pledge of "authoritative Muslims"—had been used to select him. The ISI's Shura Council "met continuously with the State's ministers, governors, and senior thinkers" to select "Abu Bakr al-Baghdadi Al-Husayni al-Qurayshi" as emir and "Abu Abdullah al-Husayni al-Qurayshi" as deputy emir.[67] Al-Nasir Lidin Sulayman was named Abu Hamzah's replacement as the minister of war.

The ISI's explanation of Abu Bakr's selection aimed to deflect criticism that the process of replacing Abu Umar had taken too long. From al-Qaeda's perspective, however, the process went too quickly.[68] Before Abu Bakr was named, Atiyah tried to convince the ISI Shura Council to consult with Osama bin Laden on its choice of a new emir. "We believe it is best that [the Council] delay—as long as there is not an impediment or a strong preference," he explained, "until they send us suggested names and a report about each of them."[69] Another note to bin Laden indicates he also hoped that more deliberation would enable the ISI to improve relations with other jihadis in Iraq, such as Ansar al-Islam.[70]

Once again, however, al-Qaeda could not control events in Iraq. The ISI wrote back that it had already made a permanent selection, which did not sit well with bin Laden.[71] Clearly annoyed, he wrote to Atiyah asking for details about Abu Bakr and instructing him to prevent any other al-Qaeda affiliates from establishing "Islamic states."[72] Atiyah assured bin Laden that he would "request information . . . and get a clearer picture."[73]

But the controversy over Abu Bakr's selection did not dissipate. A year after Abu Bakr's initial selection, the ISI felt the need to publicly defend its selection process. "The new emir of believers was nominated smoothly," explained Abu Muhammad al-Adnani, an early Zarqawi recruit from Syria and the ISI's spokesman, "and without dispute."[74]

Anger over Abu Bakr's selection erupted again in 2014 as the long-simmering tensions between the ISI and al-Qaeda burst into public view. That April, a jihadi critical of the ISI claimed that a senior ISI member and former Iraqi officer named Haji Bakr had manipulated the selection process to ensure that Abu Bakr was chosen.[75] Weeks later, Ayman al-Zawahiri suggested that Abu Bakr's selection had been illegitimate because the ISI had sworn allegiance to al-Qaeda but rejected its instructions for selecting an emir.[76] Haji Bakr's central role in Abu Bakr's selection is plausible; he was a skilled manipulator who went on to be a trusted aide of the new emir.[77] But the idea that he was singularly important is suspect. It is based on the testimony of a pseudonymous defector whose other key claims are disputed.[78]

The ISI's leaders may indeed have secretly sworn allegiance to bin Laden, but this is unproven. As evidence, Zawahiri offered both internal correspondence from al-Qaeda leaders indicating they believed the ISI remained under their authority and letters from ISI officials to al-Qaeda using language that suggests they made a secret pledge. The most direct reference is attributed to an anonymous ISI representative, allegedly written in 2011, which reads in part, "[D]o we renew the pledge in public or in secret as it was done before?"[79]

The evidence is robust that al-Qaeda genuinely believed it was in charge, but showing that the ISI secretly pledged allegiance to bin Laden is more complicated. Zawahiri cites numerous letters from ISI figures to al-Qaeda that suggest an association—especially prior to Abu Bakr's selection as emir—but none actually contains a pledge of allegiance.[80] It is also possible that, like the Kurdistan Brigades in 2007, a sub-unit of the ISI pledged allegiance to al-Qaeda and this was interpreted as a bayah from the entire organization. After all, in the wake of the ISI's establishment, Atiyah argued publicly that such agreements were acceptable.

Whether the ISI's leaders pledged allegiance or not—the preponderance of circumstantial evidence suggests they did—action ultimately speaks louder than words. Al-Qaeda correspondence makes clear that the ISI's most important decisions—establishing itself, selecting an emir, selecting a second emir—were all made without al-Qaeda's input.[81] Regardless of what its leaders told bin Laden and Zawahiri, the ISI was *functionally* independent from the moment it was established.[82]

Still, the charge that an Iraqi cabal led by Haji Bakr elevated Abu Bakr to emir compelled the Islamic State to adjust its history of Abu Bakr's selection. The ISI initially claimed Abu Bakr was selected through consultation among the ISI Shura Council. But after the criticism in spring 2014, the head of ISIS Shura Council distributed a widely cited biography of Abu Bakr claiming that the preceding emir, Abu Umar, had actually chosen Abu Bakr personally.[83] This claim is not preposterous—it is plausible that Abu Bakr and Abu Umar were close—but it is probably false. First, ISIS was changing its version of history, and in a manner that conveniently countered contemporary critiques of the organization. Second, Abu Bakr was not named emir for weeks after Abu Umar's death, which suggests deliberation rather than coronation.

Regardless of the process, Abu Bakr had one critical credential: his family long claimed to descend from the Prophet Muhammad's tribe of Quraysh. The Islamic State had formally held that the caliph must be descended from Muhammad since August 2005.[84] Abu Umar claimed he was descended from Quraysh; Abu Bakr claimed to descend from Quraysh; Abu Bakr's deputy (Abu Abdullah al-Husayni al-Qurashi) claimed to be from Quraysh. When Abu Bakr is ultimately killed, the next "caliph" will surely claim to be from Quraysh as well.

The stories of Abu Bakr's selection, both hagiographic and critical, likely contain elements of truth. He was probably chosen via a messy deliberative process in which Haji Bakr was a key supporter. But Haji Bakr was no Ba'athist plant inside the ISI; he had worked with Zarqawi since shortly after the U.S. invasion and was imprisoned with jihadis for years. Haji Bakr represented a cadre of Iraqi officials who had embraced Saddam's increasingly Islamic definition of Iraqi Ba'athism in the 1990s and then was radicalized by years of proximity to the world's most virulent terrorists.

The allegation that Abu Bakr and Haji Bakr purged their internal enemies after assuming power in the ISI is reasonable as well. After all, the ISI aspired to build a state, but modern workplace protections were not on their list of priorities.

The Social Revolution

The ISI continued to project confidence to its supporters on a global level even as its position in Iraq weakened. The group's media effort is easily dismissed as propaganda, but the ISI's ability to maintain a consistent brand during a moment of weakness enabled it to quickly expand when the operational environment became more favorable. The consistency has enhanced its legitimacy ever since.

The ISI continued to use the al-Furqan Media Establishment to produce written, audio, and video propaganda, including long, sophisticated documentaries highlighting key strategic issues. The longer videos often wove together multiple interviews, video of battles, and animated infographics. Until 2011, this material was primarily distributed through jihadi web forums like Hesbah, Shmukh, Fallujah, Boraq, and Hanein. After a period of very little security in the first years after the invasion of Iraq, these websites generally required a user login and password, which users could obtain only through a reference from an existing user or by waiting for short open-enrollment periods. The sites contained forums for discussing propaganda, events on the battlefield, theology, hobbies, and political developments around the world.

As digital technology evolved, so did the ISI's methods. Honing the techniques developed by Irhabi 007 in 2004, site administrators would upload new propaganda to file-sharing sites and then post links to the new videos on jihadi web forums. As mobile technology, HD video cameras, and Internet bandwidth improved, the file formats became more diverse so video and audio productions were released in high-definition and formats optimized for mobile devices. Although jihadis are often portrayed as technological savants, the ISI was rarely particularly creative; it simply kept pace with technological innovation.

The jihadi web forums were optimized to empower users already interested in jihadism to interact with each other, but they were not particularly useful for engaging new audiences. Though gaining access to a forum was relatively simple, it still usually required navigating a registration process; at minimum, it meant visiting a website with the singular purpose of disseminating jihadi material. These sites were easy to find, but you did have to look for them.

Because these sites were dedicated to jihadi causes and often hosted on servers outside the United States or western Europe, the jihadi web forums were also easy targets for denial-of-service attacks. If a government attacked the *Hanein* web forum, collateral damage was limited; no one was using *Hanein* "innocently." This simplified Western policy choices; the wisdom of attacking jihadi sites or leaving them up was a matter of balancing the counterterrorism value of disrupting enemy communications versus gathering intelligence. Free speech was not a primary question.

In September and October of 2008, four of the five main jihadi websites disappeared, apparently in cyberattacks.[85] (The remaining site, Hesbah, was left functional and later reported to be controlled by the Saudi Arabian government.)[86] This temporary disruption compelled digital jihadis to search for more sustainable platforms online. Some looked to a new class of social media outlets, including YouTube and Facebook. By the end of 2008, ISI supporters had created YouTube channels for distributing content, including mirrored versions designed to be resilient if some were removed (for instance, there were sequential channels titled "anasadon1," "anasadon2," etc., a practice that jihadis eventually emulated on Twitter). "So long as the house slave [President Obama] tries to hide [our videos]," wrote a jihadi on a lesser jihadi web forum, "we will release them on the Crusaders' very own websites."[87] The era of jihadi social media was fluttering to life.

Using social media sites changed the calculation for counterterrorism professionals. The United States could easily attack a dedicated jihadi web forum hosted on a foreign server. Attacking YouTube was not nearly so simple. Nor did the government have the authority to compel social media companies to remove content it deemed objectionable. Counterintuitively, sharing digital infrastructure with the jihadis made their communications more difficult to control.

Because social media was a new phenomenon, jihadi thought leaders created explanatory documents for new users, which were often frank about the source of their inspiration: Western politicians. The author of one manual, *Al-Nusrah 3: Blogs*, wrote that "the importance of blogs was highlighted in the 2008 U.S. primary elections, between two Democrats, Hillary and the House Slave Barack Obama, as well as between the Democratic

and Republican parties."[88] Another instructional post in 2009 urged jihadis to read up on Internet security in a comprehensive book called the
Encyclopedia of Jihad; to study jihadi booklets on Tor, the encrypted Internet network widely used by civil libertarians and criminal networks; and
to read a detailed book on how to recruit new jihadis called *A Course in the
Art of Recruitment*.[89]

Despite these efforts, the ISI and other jihadis were not passionate early
adopters of social media. Most preferred the existing jihadi web forums,
despite the risk of takedown, and viewed social media as a useful supple-
ment and fallback. The forums' major advantage was control. Jihadis are
extremely brand conscious, and many feared false-flag propaganda released
in their name. They valued control over the jihadi web forums where supporters could interact free from outside criticism and off-message posts
could be removed by friendly site administrators.

Al-Qaeda Central was particularly committed to its brand. When Western journalists wanted to interview Osama bin Laden in 1997, al-Qaeda
almost canceled the engagement out of fear that the journalists would edit
out threats to the United States. After 9/11, al-Qaeda initially released propaganda through Al Jazeera but stopped when the network stopped broad-
casting its long screeds in their entirety. Al-Qaeda's drive for control led it
to create highly rehearsed (often very boring) propaganda videos dominated by elderly sheikhs talking into the camera. The jihadi web forums
were the final step in a rigid propaganda production system.

The ISI also had an impulse for brand control, but it was not as overwhelming. The ISI's Zarqawiist ethos was more populist on all levels—it
devolved ideological authority to lower-levels, decentralized fundraising
and recruitment, aimed to kill "apostates" even if they were laypeople, not
leaders—and it extended that instinct to its propaganda. The ISI's more
regular operations meant more video of violence that, in turn, was distributed in relatively raw form. Whereas al-Qaeda aimed to rally the Muslim
masses, the Zarqawiists in the ISI thought brutal violence would help them
sort "true" Muslims from apostates. The ISI did not hide from its killing
and, as a result, was less fearful of false-flag propaganda released in its name.

When Abu Bakr took over the ISI, the era of jihadi social media had not
yet fully arrived, but the technological shifts and vulnerability of jihadi

sites were reshaping how jihadis thought about digital infrastructure. Jihadi web forums were still preferred, but the mindset was shifting. When the *Shmukh* forum appeared in September 2008, it touted itself as the "best alternative to Google and YouTube."[90]

On December 17, 2010, a fruit vendor in Tunisia set himself on fire to protest police harassment and the lack of economic opportunity. Video of the ensuing protest went viral almost immediately—largely because of social media—and prompted protest movements across the Arab world. Revolution and civil war were in the air and on the Internet.

The Arab Spring led to revolutions in Tunisia, a revolution and counterrevolution in Egypt, and civil wars in Libya and Syria. Events in all four countries had a dramatic impact on the Islamic State. Syria and Libya—where initial protests centered in Darnah and Benghazi, both key feeders of foreign fighters to Iraq—are now two of the Islamic States' most important operational arenas. The Muslim Brotherhood's failure to govern effectively in Egypt reinforced the ISI's commitment to violent revolution. And Tunisia has emerged as a recruiting hotbed for the Islamic State, even as its revolution empowered a moderate Islamist movement to lead.[91]

In general, the Arab Spring revolutions have failed. Yet at their height, even al-Qaeda was enchanted by the opportunity to remove corrupt governments peacefully. After decades of arguing that peaceful protest against Arab regimes was pointless, al-Qaeda's second-in-command, Ayman al-Zawahiri, endorsed peaceful revolution, though he hinted darkly that failed revolutions would only empower jihadis.[92] A range of other senior jihadi ideologues also supported the peaceful revolutions.[93]

True to form, however, the ISI made no concessions to the notion of peaceful revolution. For the ISI, the political goal of a caliphate could not be achieved except through violence. On February 8, 2011, the ISI's Ministry of War explained to supporters in Egypt that "the market of jihad [has] opened and . . . no mature, able-bodied [male] has any excuse to stay behind."[94] For the ISI, peaceful, popular uprisings against old dictatorships were not a path to the caliphate, but they were moments of regime weakness to be exploited.

Spring in Syria

On January 16, 2011, the United States Embassy in Damascus distributed a press release announcing the arrival of its new ambassador, Robert Ford. He was the first ambassador to serve in Damascus since 2005, when the previous envoy was withdrawn over Syria's role in the assassination of former Lebanese President Rafik Hariri. This, however, was no rapprochement. The Syrian protest movement and the government's efforts to repress it crept to life digitally soon after Ford arrived. Protesters scrambled online to organize protests in early February, and the Syrian government responded by blocking Facebook, Twitter, and YouTube. Protests were delayed, but the government was fighting an uphill battle to suppress information; protesters accessed the platforms via proxy servers.[95]

When Syrian troops arrested fifteen school-age boys in early March for spray-painting "The people want to topple the regime"—a slogan from Egypt and Tunisia—on a wall in the southern city of Deraa, the early protest movement escalated into revolution.[96] Deraa erupted in outrage, and the boys' families took their dissent to protests in Damascus. When government snipers began firing on protesters, the prospect for peaceful revolution withered.

Jihadis across the globe, including in the ISI and al-Qaeda, watched developments in Syria with great interest. The master plan had noted Syria's suitability for jihadi revolution more than half a decade earlier. Regardless of whether that blueprint was applied directly in the intervening years, its strategic analysis that Syria was uniquely vulnerable to jihadi revolution was widely known.

The ISI first publicly mentioned the Syrian revolution on April 11, 2011, when a member of the group's Shura Council mentioned it at the end of a long recorded statement. "We have heard good news about the Muslim people in some Syrian cities starting to mobilize," he said. "The suffering of Muslims in Syria at the hands of this regime has been far worse than their brothers' suffering in any other Muslim country."[97] The comment seemed to have been added at the last minute, perhaps after the rest of the statement had been recorded. It did not offer a detailed vision for the ISI's future engagement in Syria, but it did state the group's general intent. "It

[is] incumbent on all Muslims," the statement said, "to support their brothers by all means."[98]

It was relatively innocuous language, but to the ISI, "support" meant only one thing.

Indeed, the ISI was extraordinarily well situated to capitalize on the instability in Syria. In a remarkable display of coordination, the ISI killed seventy-four people with bombs in thirteen Iraqi cities on August 15, 2011. United States Major General Jeffrey Buchanan blamed "al-Qaeda in Iraq" and estimated that the group had "between 800–1,000 members of all stripes, from financiers, to smugglers, to media people to fighters."[99] Despite the large-scale attacks in Iraq, Buchanan explained the group was dramatically weaker than it had been before the Surge and Awakening. Buchanan was indisputably correct; the ISI was much weaker than before the Surge. But it remained one of the strongest jihadi organizations in the world.

In the summer of 2011, whether the ISI appeared "weak" or "strong" depended entirely on the benchmark used to assess it. Its 1,000 or so fighters were far fewer than the 12,000 Abu Hamzah claimed when the ISI was declared in October 2006, but vastly more than the approximately 200 members al-Qaeda had on 9/11.[100] From 2008 to 2010, when Iraq was theoretically at its most peaceful, the country still had more terrorist attacks than either Afghanistan or Pakistan. Indeed, as 2010 ended, the number of attacks in Baghdad proper shot up, suggesting that the group was expanding from its safe haven near Mosul.[101]

The ISI had other strengths as well. It had deep logistical networks in Syria even before the uprising and was increasingly adept at breaking members out of Iraqi prisons, which were being transferred from American to Iraqi control. In July 2010, only days after U.S. commanders ceremonially transferred authority by passing a gigantic ceremonial skeleton key to Iraqi prison authorities, four senior ISI leaders were spirited out of the Camp Cropper prison. The Iraqi warden went missing at the same time.[102]

Over the next two years, the ISI bolstered its ranks with prison breaks in Basra, Baghdad, and Tikrit.[103] Abu Bakr formalized the ISI's effort to free prisoners by announcing a "Destroying the Walls" campaign in July 2012, but by then the effort had long been underway.

Even as the ISI stretched its muscles in Iraq, it closely eyed the growing instability in Syria. On August 20, 2011, the ISI celebrated the fifth anniversary of its establishment with a slick, hour-long video commemorating its victories, sacrifices, and setbacks. The video closed in truly Zarqawiist fashion: one man lambasted Islamic scholars who opposed jihad in Iraq, while another urged the Syrian uprising to continue until "the Islamic State is established in Syria."[104]

He might as well have announced: we are coming.

As the ISI laid the groundwork for war in Syria, al-Qaeda suffered a powerful setback. When the CIA interrogated Hassan Ghul, Abd al-Hadi al-Iraqi's courier to Zarqawi in 2004, he did not just reveal information about Zarqawi's strategy in Iraq; he also mentioned a Kuwaiti who served as a courier for Osama bin Laden. Eventually, that name helped the CIA identify a compound in Abbottabad, Pakistan, where bin Laden was hiding. On the night of May 2, 2011, a team of Navy Seals raided the compound, killed bin Laden, and scooped up as much computer equipment and paper as they could carry.[105] Just as the Levant was finally opening to a jihadi uprising, al-Qaeda was faced with the first leadership transition in its nearly twenty-five-year history.

The obvious choice to succeed bin Laden was Ayman al-Zawahiri, the Egyptian doctor who had been his second-in-command since Egyptian Islamic Jihad integrated with al-Qaeda in 2001. However, while al-Qaeda leaders debated a permanent replacement, Sayf al-Adl, creator of the seven-stage master plan, was named interim emir.[106] Al-Adl was still under house arrest in Iran, but this confinement was not overly onerous; he had communicated with Fuad Husayn in 2004 and was directly involved in al-Qaeda's decision making in 2007 and 2008.

Most interestingly, however, al-Adl was rumored in 2010 to have been released from Iran in exchange for an Iranian diplomat, per the strategy approved by Abd al-Hadi al-Iraqi in 2003.[107] The opaque story goes something like this. In November 2008, the Pakistani Taliban kidnapped the Iranian commercial attaché at the consulate in Peshawar, Pakistan. The attaché was a relatively junior diplomat, but the jihadis nonetheless demanded the release of al-Qaeda leaders inside Iran in exchange.[108] By 2010, rumors were rampant that al-Adl had been released, but the only hard evidence was that, after a long public silence, he was able to publish several relatively uninteresting essays online.[109] Rather than going free, it seems Al-Adl remained in Iran but was better positioned to speak publicly.

Other jihadi prisoners were released from Iran in 2010, however, including Suleiman Abu Ghaith, al-Qaeda's spokesman on 9/11; Abu Abdallah al-Muhajir, the Egyptian preacher that introduced many of Zarqawi's most violent ideological tendencies; and several members of Osama bin Laden's family.[110] Ghaith was arrested upon crossing into Turkey, sent to the United States for trial, and is currently serving a life sentence at the Supermax prison in Florence, Colorado.[111] Abu Abdallah traveled first to Turkey and then prepared to return to Egypt.[112]

Despite the rumors about al-Adl, al-Qaeda's leadership ultimately selected Zawahiri to succeed bin Laden.[113] He was the candidate most deeply embedded in al-Qaeda's internal organization, but he was also abrupt, old, and not well liked by other jihadis. Bin Laden had commanded universal respect and admiration among jihadis; Zawahiri did not.

Bin Laden's death made it easier for jihadi groups to challenge al-Qaeda's authority, and soon the ISI would do just that.

The Assad regime aimed to snuff out the growing popular rebellion in Syria with a mix of violence and conciliation. Troops used tear gas and live ammunition to suppress protests, but at the same time the regime moved to release political prisoners, including Kurdish opposition leaders, democracy activists, and Islamists, from prison.[114]

Critics of the Assad regime point to the fact that some of these prisoners went on to fight for jihadi groups as evidence that the Assad regime intended to radicalize its opposition in order to justify a brutal crackdown.[115] Indeed, some of the ISI's early Syrian supporters went free in these amnesties and in aggregate, the amnesties emboldened the opposition, especially the jihadis.[116] Moreover, it is simply fact that the Assad regime had historically bolstered jihadi groups, especially in Lebanon, as a way to keep its enemies divided. There is no doubt that the emergence of jihadi groups in Syria was eventually politically valuable to the regime.[117]

But the accusation that Assad's amnesties early in the Syrian uprising were intended to strengthen the ISI rings hollow. For starters, the amnesty programs were widely hailed as a conciliatory "good start," by human rights activists at the time, who were more focused on releasing opposition leaders held unjustly without trial than the possibility that some of them would contribute to jihadi mayhem in the future.[118] Additionally, the first amnesty was announced before protesters widely called for Assad's removal. Considering the timing, it seems more likely that Assad's primary goal was to head off a full-blown uprising than to strengthen its most extreme elements. Finally, Assad had previously used amnesty programs as a conciliatory gesture, including in 2000 shortly after he took power. Indeed, the tactic was common in the Middle East; after all, Zarqawi—the Godfather of the Islamic State—was freed from a Jordanian prison as part of an amnesty program.

Still, there is no doubt that the Syrian regime did try to pin the legitimate protest movement on jihadi groups, most notably Fatah al-Islam and Jund al-Sham.[119] These claims were exaggerated, but like all good propaganda, they were based in a truth: both groups had long wanted to extend violent jihad into Syria proper and were organizing to do just that in 2011. In March 2011, Fatah al-Islam had little functional organization in Syria, but it still declared that, "There is no solution . . . except for jihad . . . to lift injustice and establish the Shariah of God, as well as to liberate the Syria of Islam and all the lands of the Levant from the claws of non-belief and polytheism."[120]

Indeed, the future jihadis in Syria were bolstered not just from former residents of Syria's Sednaya prison, but also from Lebanon's Roumiyeh. In 2010, several leading Fatah al-Islam figures escaped the prison, leading to hand-wringing among Lebanese politicians. In August 2011, Abu Talhah al-Kuwaiti, who with Abu Hammam al-Suri tried to establish a Lebanese al-Qaeda cell, aimed to join them.[121] He later claimed total confidence in his escape plan because he had a vision of "a noble and virtuous" woman directing the escape.[122] Having received the woman's guidance, Abu Talhah was confident as he and several co-conspirators climbed down a rope made of knotted sheets and strolled toward the prison's visitor's gate.[123] Indeed, the guards did not come as Abu Talhah climbed, nor when he approached the visitor's gate and asked to be let out under the pretense that he wanted to "buy some things for my relatives in the prison."[124] It is hard to escape the conclusion that Abu Talhah's noble and virtuous woman was actually a corrupt and deeply ignoble prison guard.[125] It was not just Assad's amnesty that empowered jihadis in Syria; so too did the weakness of governing institutions across the region.

On August 18, 2011, President Obama declared that "the time has come for President Assad to step aside" in Syria.[126] Despite the restless jihadi groups eyeing Syria from Iraq and Lebanon, American policy was built around the legitimate Syrian protesters. Policymakers were wise not to accept Assad's claim that jihadis led the protests—they did not—but the American debate also failed to account adequately for the ISI and its allies. Whatever the just purpose of Syria's original protesters, rarely has there been a nascent conflict so perfectly constructed for an already powerful jihadi organization to exploit. The notion that the Syrian uprising would not be exploited by the ISI, with its 1,000 people based just across an indefensible border in Iraq, was fantasy grounded in an exaggerated sense of the ISI's weakness.

Nonetheless, as American rhetoric and sanctions against Assad escalated, the growing rebel movement grew more confident. Protesters responded especially well to Ambassador Robert Ford, who repeatedly met with opposition leaders, including a high-profile trip to Hama, the scene of a terrible massacre by the Syrian troops in 1982 that killed more than 20,000 people in a matter of days.[127] Ford's activism showed that Assad's effort to discredit the protesters by labeling them jihadis had failed, but it also showed how prescient al-Adl's master plan had been in 2005.

Al-Qaeda's strategy since 1998 had been to target the United States in order to sever the relationship between the United States and the regimes that it aimed to overthrow. Al-Adl recognized in 2005 that there was an exception to this rule in the Middle East: the regime of Bashar al-Assad in Syria. In 2011, he was proven right. Al-Adl's logic held—regimes backed by the United States could not be destroyed—but the United States' relationship with Syria was such that it would not back the regime anyway. As Fuad Husayn described al-Adl's thinking: "al-Qaeda believes that the reaction against the Syrian regime will deny it the ability to effectively control the situation domestically."[128]

In 2011, al-Adl must have looked toward Syria with a certain satisfaction. Much of what he predicted was coming to be. Conditions in Iraq had opened Syria for jihad, and the United States, as predicted, was undermining rather than supporting the regime there.

At the same time, al-Adl should have had significant doubts. As prescient as his analysis was, al-Adl did not predict the vast changes in the jihadi movement itself. The master plan was built for an al-Qaeda that unified the traditional bin Laden wing with the Zarqawiists. But in 2011, bin Laden was dead, the alliance was frayed, and it was the unpredictable Zarqawiists who were best prepared to exploit the Assad regime's weakness.

The Jihad Ordeal in Syria

Sayf al-Adl brokered Zarqawi's original agreement with al-Qaeda, hoping to build a jihadi army in the Levant and to minimize the threat Abu Mus'ab al-Suri posed to bin Laden in Afghanistan. He succeeded on both counts. Al-Suri, however, was far from forgotten. After 9/11, his influence rose even as he traveled a dark course through Pakistani, American, and Syrian prisons. He wrote prolifically before his arrest in Pakistan, and al-Qaeda even embraced elements of his vision for decentralized jihadi activism. In early 2011, as the ISI quietly stalked Syria, al-Suri languished in a Syrian prison, but his voice lingered in the digital ether, whispering lessons from failures of jihads past.

After the U.S. attack on Afghanistan, al-Suri fled to Pakistan, and in 2002 he spent time in Iran.[129] He was implicated on the fringes of terrorist attacks in both Madrid and London but primarily spent time writing.[130] He wrote, and wrote, and wrote, eventually releasing a 1,400-page opus called the *Call to Global Islamic Resistance*, which outlined a structure for global jihad that encouraged both formal jihadi organizations like al-Qaeda and independent cells to conduct small-scale strikes.

Pakistani police arrested al-Suri in November 2005 and eventually transferred him to U.S. custody. His next years are unclear, but his lawyer suggested he was incarcerated at a U.S. military base on the Indian Ocean island of Diego Garcia.[131] In 2009, al-Suri's lawyer reported that he had been transferred into Syrian custody.[132]

During this period, al-Suri's ideas proliferated dramatically. Even al-Qaeda, which was always extremely hierarchical, embraced al-Suri's notion of a network of radicalized individuals conducting small-scale terrorist attacks on their own volition. Indeed, an entire jihadi literature detailing tactics for aspiring lone wolves emerged, though al-Qaeda generally had little success spurring such operations.[133]

Anwar al-Awlaki was the exception. An American al-Qaeda propagandist living in Yemen, Awlaki successfully inspired numerous would-be jihadis in the West to conduct attacks on their own.[134] In English-language propaganda outlets, like *Inspire* magazine, Awlaki communicated directly to potential recruits living in the West in a colloquial English backed by his own personal story of radicalization in the United States. The Islamic State was taking notes.

Jihadis in Syria looked to some of al-Suri's earlier writing for guidance on tackling the Assad regime. After all, al-Suri wrote the definitive jihadi lessons-learned document from the Islamist uprising against Hafez al-Assad in the 1970s and 1980s. In *Lessons Learned from the Jihad Ordeal in Syria*, al-Suri argued that the mujahidin in the 1980s did not have a comprehensive strategy and were "spread among numerous organizations," leading to "friction, hatred, and partisan bickering."[135] This created "conflict between the faithful youth," which al-Suri argued damaged their prospects for victory more than the regime itself.

Many of the rebels framed their fight in sectarian terms, al-Suri explained, as a means of discrediting the Assad family and its Alawite supporters. (The Alawite creed has a unique theology but shares many tenets with Shia Islam.) Jihadis consider the Alawites apostates, but such name-calling, al-Suri wrote, was ultimately counterproductive because for most Syrians it obfuscated the rebels' political program.[136]

The rebels also failed to prepare for a protracted conflict. They did not adequately indoctrinate new recruits, which meant that after the first generation of fighters was killed, "the leadership [opened] the doors to anyone who was willing to join [so] the organization grew in quantity at the expense of quality."[137] The rebels also failed to mobilize all of Syrian society, especially the Kurds, and did not run an effective media campaign inside the country.

In general, al-Suri thought the rebels were far too dependent on foreign countries for support. He concluded that foreign supporters in Iraq, Jordan, Saudi Arabia, and the Gulf were "temporary allies with their own interests and agendas" and should never be trusted.[138] Future Syrian insurgents, he argued, should "not rely on outside sources for financing, weaponry, training, and support; they have to depend on themselves." Moreover, they should have a military capability outside Syria, both to attack regime targets and to deter other governments from supporting the Assad regime.[139]

Thirty years later, the mainstream Syrian rebels would repeat many of the same mistakes, which probably doomed their project to depose Assad. The ISI, however, was playing an entirely different game. It was less interested in getting rid of Assad than in carving out a plot of land on which to build a kernel of the caliphate.

Abu Muhammad al-Jawlani crossed into Syria from Iraq using a well-trod route for smuggling everything from sheep to electronics to human beings.[140] It was August 2011 and his mission from Abu Bakr al-Baghdadi was to operationalize the jihadi networks inside Syria. Jawlani was well prepared for the mission. He was Syrian, had joined Zarqawi's movement in Iraq before the fall of Saddam, and had fought in Fallujah. Jawlani was also familiar with the jihadi networks crisscrossing Syria. He left Iraq after Zarqawi's death in 2006 to work with Jund al-Sham, the small, radical Lebanese jihadi movement that was implicated in an attack on the U.S. Embassy in Damascus in 2006.

Jawlani returned to Iraq after his stint in Lebanon and, like many other jihadis, did a stint in the Camp Bucca prison, where he reportedly taught classical Arabic to other prisoners.[141] Released in 2008, he rejoined the ISI and reportedly served in the Mosul governorate, at about the time that Abu Bakr served as emir there. Mosul offered ample learning opportunities: the ISI there deftly infiltrated local communities, offered free religious training to build rapport with the population, and developed cooperative fundraising programs with key tribal leaders. Even before the Syrian civil war, the Mosul governorate of the ISI was effectively a transnational enterprise, with logistics and training functions housed inside Syria.[142]

During Jawlani's tenure in Mosul, the sector faced internal discord over the most prosaic of questions: money.[143] The ISI's organizational system required geographic sectors to send 20 percent of their general revenue to the central organization. The rest was to be spent locally. The dispute in Mosul centered on whether certain practices—extortion rackets, smuggling, "taxes" on local businesses, and scams to skim money from various Iraqi ministries—constituted plunder, which was supposed to be given to the central ISI in its entirety.[144] Predictably, the Mosul leadership concluded that such money was not plunder and thus could be used locally at their discretion.[145] Some of their underlings disagreed.

Local commanders also objected to orders to attack "financial targets"— banks, jewelry stores, and the like—to raise money. "You know very well that the guerilla warfare depends first on the populace base," one local commander wrote, "and [attacks on banks] increase the weakness of the populace base."[146] It is not clear if Jawlani or Abu Bakr was directly involved in this debate, but the fight foreshadowed coming struggles between them. When Jawlani's fight in Syria began, he prioritized building tight relationships with other Syrian militants and sought financial independence from the central ISI and Abu Bakr.

After entering Syria, Jawlani settled in Hasakah, not far from the Iraqi border. His first orders from Abu Bakr, according to two ISIS defectors, were to organize a terrorist attack in Turkey and assassinate key Sunni leaders in Syria who opposed the ISI.[147] Jawlani refused to do either.

First on the alleged ISI hit list was Muhammad Hardan, Abu Bakr's mentor before the U.S. invasion and co-founder of the Jihad and Reform Front (JRF), the ISI's hated enemy from the Awakening period in Iraq. Some of Jawlani's early advisors in Syria later claimed that such orders were not new; they had previously been ordered to assassinate other Iraqi militants living in Syria, including Abu Wa'el, once the reputed link between Saddam Hussein and al-Qaeda and another co-founder of the JRF.[148]

The story is credible. A handwritten ISI directive from 2007 or 2008 orders the assassination of leaders from the JRF[149] and mentions an "Abu Abd Allah," which may be a pseudonym of Mohammed Hardan.[150] Likewise, Abu Wa'el's name appeared ominously on a July 2010 jihadi list of Sunnis who had participated in the Iraqi political process.[151] Jawlani's future aides were ordered to kill Abu Wa'el in Damascus at about the same time.[152]

Abu Wa'el had certainly earned the ISI's ire. "The al-Qaeda [in Iraq] organization," he proclaimed disdainfully in December 2008, "which I would not hesitate to call the Islamic State of Iraq if I believed it were actually a state, has isolated itself from the rest of the mujahidin, so their jihad is illegitimate."[153]

Abu Bakr's reputed assassination campaign did not go as he planned. Abu Wa'el was not assassinated in 2010, and Jawlani, who had grown friendly with Hardan while imprisoned at Camp Bucca, did not attack him in 2011.[154] At the end of the day, Abu Bakr acted like a Zarqawiist: he aimed to purge the world of "apostates." Jawlani acted like a student of bin Laden: he aimed to ultimately win over other militants.

The fight underscored another difference between Jawlani and Baghdadi. Jawlani believed that the fight in Syria required a different strategy from the fight in Iraq, whereas Abu Bakr insisted that the ISI would be strongest if it leveraged its transnational reach. One reason the battle between these men eventually grew so severe is that, on this critical question, they were both right.

The Syrian civil war ratcheted up as 2011 wore on, but Syria's various revolutionaries were tremendously disorganized. Local coordination committees advocating a wide range of ideological and political positions organized militancy inside Syria, and various groups emerged outside the country in an effort to organize them. But the networks with international cachet generally had little credibility inside Syria.

There were structural reasons for the lack of organization as well. In previous uprisings, such as the anti-Soviet jihad in the 1980s, foreign intelligence services were key gatekeepers for funding and weapons.[155] But by 2011 the proliferation of communication technology enabled small militias to connect directly with both nation-state and private funders around the world, and Syria's accessible border enabled them to offer material support easily.[156] The result was that militant groups had no incentive to coalesce under a single command. This factionalism made the rebellion harder to defeat but also limited its ability to strike decisive blows.

The ISI saw an opportunity.

The ISI's underground campaign in Syria grew significantly more public on January 23, 2012. Jawlani was publicly declared the emir of Jabhat al-Nusrah (JaN), a new jihadi group "consisting of jihadists from the Levant who were in the arenas of jihad."[157] The announcement implied a link to Iraq but purposefully obscured JaN's connections to either the ISI or al-Qaeda.[158]

There were, however, hints of the ISI's influence in JaN's disdain for Iran's government, which the ISI had long seen as the real power behind Shia parties in Baghdad. "Any sane person can see Iran's support, side by side, for [the Syrian regime]," proclaimed the JaN in its first statement, "to spread Safavid ideology . . . and restore the Persian Empire. . . . The Levant is the lungs of Iran's extinct project."[159] JaN did not acknowledge the ISI's authority in 2012, but it framed its fight in similarly sectarian geopolitical terms.

Syria's demographics were a key reason that al-Adl thought it was prime ground for establishing the caliphate. Others in al-Qaeda agreed. One undated letter to bin Laden (which means it predates his death in May 2011) from a senior advisor explained that Iraq was "the last country to be thought of as a land of caliphate," presumably because the country was 60 percent Shia. Rather, it was best considered "an incubator for the great project." The unnamed al-Qaeda author endorsed the master plan's original finding that "the caliphate would be in 'Bilad al Sham' (Greater Syria)."[160] The note was also deeply critical of the ISI's extremism, but it illustrates that the geopolitical assessment of the master plan remained a point of agreement between the Zarqawiists and al-Qaeda's leadership.

The public announcement of the JaN was careful to obscure its ties to other jihadi groups, but the ISI was less circumspect. A week before JaN was announced, the ISI's spokesman Abu Muhammad al-Adnani suggested the group's geographic scope was expanding because a broader sectarian war was afoot. "We say to the sons and soldiers of the Islamic State of Iraq . . . you are a locked door in the Safavid's face. You protect the blood, honor, and treasures of Sunnis in Iraq, the Levant, and the [Arabian] Peninsula," he argued. "If this door is broken, Iraq, the Levant, and the Peninsula will cease to exist."[161]

Left unsaid was that many traditional Sunni leaders in Saudi Arabia and the Gulf viewed Iran, and its allies in Damascus and Baghdad, with similar trepidation. They did not support the ISI or JaN overtly, but their analysis of regional geopolitics overlapped significantly with the jihadis'.

Inside Syria, the mainstream rebel groups initially did not even acknowledge JaN's existence. In part because Assad tried to smear the entire rebel movement as led by jihadis, they dismissed early JaN attacks in Syria as false-flag operations run by Assad. The rebels' ambivalence toward JaN was misguided, but they were right to be paranoid; JaN was committing, and claiming, major attacks in Syria, including a February 2012 suicide bombing that rebel groups erroneously blamed on the Assad regime.[162] The rebels should have saved their conspiracies for May 2012, when an explosion in Damascus was later claimed in JaN's name on YouTube. The statement was later discredited as a fraud.[163]

Regime supporters used JaN attacks to besmirch all rebel factions in Syria, while rebel groups argued the false-flag episodes validated their position that Assad had created the jihadi threat to justify a murderous crackdown on the legitimate protest movement. In the end, the only real winner was JaN, which the Assad regime considered useful politically and mainstream rebels alternately ignored or praised when they conducted a successful attack.

The ugly reality is that both sides in the Syrian civil war initially thought the jihadis would help them prevail.

For its part, the false claim of responsibility on YouTube reinforced the jihadis' fear of social media in general. Far from wholeheartedly embracing social media early in the Syrian civil war, JaN explicitly disavowed the tools and recommitted itself to the jihadi web forums. "Media distributed by Jabhat al-Nusrah will be distributed through jihadist websites," the group explained, "which is not what occurred in this case."[164]

JaN's caution with social media was eventually a weakness, but it embraced other forms of propaganda. In February 2012, JaN profiled a distraught *niqab*-wearing woman who alleged that five men from the Syrian army broke into her home, killed her young son, and then tortured and raped her. It was reminiscent of early Zarqawi recruitment pitches from Iraq, which raised the specter of U.S. troops raping Iraqi women. In the 2012 video, a young Syrian jihadi makes the final pitch to potential recruits: "They raped her one after the other and killed her boy. No young man who follows my path can stand idly the suffering of that sister."[165]

But even recruiting frightened the increasingly paranoid JaN. "Not everyone who comes to you anonymously without someone vouching for them, yet with heroic experience, is someone . . . with an honorable record," wrote an anonymous advisor. "The intelligence service will not hesitate to sacrifice a few soldiers to get one into the group's command . . . so be cautious, cautious, cautious."[166] JaN followed this advice, requiring new recruits to receive *tazkiyya*, an assurance of reliability, from commanders before they were allowed into the organization.[167]

JaN's paranoia—both in terms of propaganda and recruiting—was reminiscent of al-Qaeda, which tightly controlled its media presence and always aimed to be a small, elite organization. JaN also emulated al-Qaeda in its effort to build alliances with a wide range of other militant networks. In mid-2012 an Islamist coalition called Ahrar al-Sham emerged in northwestern Syria.[168] Ahrar al-Sham was a truly big tent organization with salafi hard-liners, Muslim Brothers, and nationalists. Moreover, it had deep connections to foreign backers in Turkey and Qatar. Despite such ties, however, JaN engaged the new movement aggressively, even accepting members that belonged to both groups.[169]

Such alignments foretold the schisms to come between jihadis in Syria. JaN was following the al-Qaeda playbook; it was a relatively small, elite organization with extensive links to a wide range of militants of differing ideological predilections. This approach differed from the Zarqawiists in the ISI, who demanded ideological uniformity, but aimed to build a broad, populist organization.

The difference between these approaches was quickly coming to a head. The master plan had been designed for an alliance between the Zarqawiists and the bin Ladenists, but the days of that coalition were numbered.

The Islamic State of Iraq and al-Sham

The nationalist and Islamist rebels arrayed against Assad initially ignored JaN, but they were quickly impressed by the group's operational effectiveness.[170] Many of Syria's insurgents were amateur rebels, and they were no match for JaN's experienced jihadis. By mid-2012, the rebels' foreign backers tacitly supported JaN as well. Money and weapons from Turkey, Saudi Arabia, Qatar, and Kuwait flowed into Syria.[171] The assistance was ostensibly for nationalist rebels in the Free Syrian Army or Islamists in Ahrar al-Sham, but JaN inevitably benefitted.

American policymakers finally stepped in when JaN looked to join a coalition of mainstream Islamist groups called the Supreme Joint Military Council. The U.S. State Department maintains a list of groups that are officially considered Foreign Terrorist Organizations (FTO). In December 2012, the United States officially adjusted the existing designation of "al-Qaeda in Iraq" to include "Jabhat al-Nusrah" as a pseudonym.[172]

Although JaN was clearly a jihadi group with links to al-Qaeda and the ISI, many people were not happy about the move. Salim Idris, the military council's leader, responded that it "would not exclude anyone" and asserted that "there are no such things as extremist forces" in Syria.[173] If only the west engaged with JaN directly, he argued, it would discover that "not all who wear beards long are terrorists."[174] A Facebook page for supporters of the rebellion in Syria announced, "No to American Involvement [in Syria]—We are all Jabhat al-Nusrah."[175] The page received more than 20,000 "likes."[176] Even some American analysts opposed designating the ISI's representative in Syria a terrorist organization. "I'm not saying they aren't a terrorist group. But given the circumstances and given their cooperation with the opposition as a whole, designating them now would be disastrous," argued Elizabeth O'Bagy, then an influential analyst with the Institute for the Study of War in Washington, D.C.[177]

The dispute over JaN revealed a fundamental disconnect among would-be allies. Syrian rebels and their backers prioritized destroying the Assad regime (and weakening its Iranian backers) and were willing to empower jihadis in order to do so. The United States, meanwhile, did not have clear priorities in Syria. President Obama called for Assad to step down and had demurred from designating JaN for nearly a year, but the United States ultimately would not empower a jihadi group tied to the ISI and al-Qaeda.[178]

The confusion regarding JaN's status is precisely why neither the ISI nor al-Qaeda publicly claimed ties to the group. Al-Qaeda in particular had long recognized that its brand was toxic, and it encouraged affiliates to use distinct nomenclature. It is hard to imagine that Syria's more moderate rebels could have embraced JaN had the group been called "al-Qaeda in Syria" or "the Islamic State of Iraq's Syria Province." The jihadis' strategy of ambiguity had paid major dividends.

But that was about to change.

When the United States declared that JaN was a pseudonym for "al-Qaeda in Iraq," the group's functional and terminological independence became less valuable to the ISI. Meanwhile, the operational distinction between two groups was disintegrating. In early March 2013, forty-eight Syrian troops fleeing rebels crossed into Iraq's Anbar Province and were killed by the ISI.[179] The Iraqi government blamed JaN, but the ISI claimed credit, saying the Syrians fled into Iraq because of "blessed operations to cleanse [Syria] of the abomination of the filthy Nusayris," a derogatory reference to Alawites.[180] In short, the ISI was no longer obfuscating its role in Syria.

This operational and rhetorical shift was accompanied by a move to reassert control over Jawlani. This was bound to be controversial and, in retrospect, it is clear that Abu Bakr understood this might precipitate a confrontation with al-Qaeda. After years of relying on al-Qaeda's al-Fajr Media Center to distribute propaganda, in February 2013 the ISI announced it would distribute via other jihadi outlets as well—the Yaqin Media Center and the Global Islamic Media Front.[181] It also announced the creation of a new media production wing—al-I'tisam—that would handle propaganda for the ISI's governorates. In short, the ISI was ensuring its media could operate independently from al-Qaeda.

Al-I'tisam's first video, released in early March 2013, confirmed the ISI's cross-border intentions. It included old footage of Zarqawi spliced together with video from Iraq's Anbar Province and JaN. A voiceover says that JaN and the ISI are "the groups that uphold Islam best, in theory and practice."[182] It was not yet official, but Abu Bakr clearly intended to reunite the ISI and JaN.

This ambition did not sit well with Jawlani. According to @wikibaghdadi, a self-described jihadi insider on Twitter, Abu Bakr ordered Jawlani to attack nationalist Syrian rebels; when he refused, the ISI's Emir declared that if Jawlani did not comply, JaN would be "disbanded and a new entity created."[183] @wikibaghdadi's claims are uncorroborated, but they make sense. Abu Bakr and the ISI believed they were accountable only to God; from their perspective, Jawlani and JaN aspired to be accountable to a Syrian rebel council as well.

Jawlani did not reply to Abu Bakr's ultimatum, so on April 9, 2013, the ISI leader announced JaN's dissolution. In a terse audio statement, he recounted the group's history from Zarqawi forward, and then got to the point:

> We deputized al-Jawlani, who is one of our soldiers, along with a group of our people. We sent them from Iraq to the Levant to engage our cells there. We put plans in place for them; we built the operational policy; and we gave them half the money we collected. . . . We announce the abolition of both names, the Islamic State of Iraq and Jabhat al-Nusrah, and we merge them under one name: the Islamic State in Iraq and al-Sham (ISIS).[184]

Jawlani rejected the merger immediately. "The banner of [Jabhat al-Nusrah] will remain," he declared the following day, "although we are proud of the banner of the [Islamic State of Iraq], those who upheld it, and those brothers who sacrificed their blood under its flag."[185] The ISI had played a major role in establishing JaN, Jawlani acknowledged, but it did not command the group.

Most explosively, Jawlani explained that he had sworn allegiance to al-Qaeda's Ayman al-Zawahiri, not to Abu Bakr. The implication was twofold. First, that he stood on equal ground with Abu Bakr; and, second, that the ISI was still accountable to al-Qaeda. It was a direct shot at the ISI narrative that it had separated formally from al-Qaeda in October 2006.

This debate over authority within the jihadi movement had simmered for years as the ISI implied allegiance to al-Qaeda but operated independently. Now that pot was boiling over. The old question of whether the ISI was independent or a subsidiary of al-Qaeda was finally coming to a head.[186]

Zawahiri tried to de-escalate the conflict, but he asserted his own authority over the ISI. He reached out privately to Abu Bakr on April 11, 2013, and when Abu Bakr did not respond, tried again on May 5. Zawahiri complained that the ISI had "disobeyed" a "directive from an Emir" and treated him as no more than a "wise man" engaged to adjudicate between two rivals.[187] Unfortunately for Zawahiri, there was no misunderstanding. Whether or not Abu Bakr and the ISI secretly swore allegiance to bin Laden or Zawahiri in the years after 2006, by 2013 that is exactly how Abu Bakr thought of Zawahiri.

On June 9, after getting no response from Abu Bakr, Zawahiri announced his position on ISIS. He praised Abu Bakr and Jawlani for their sacrifices and reprimanded both for allowing the dispute to become public. Then, believing he had authority to resolve the dispute, declared his decision: "the Islamic State of Iraq and al-Sham shall be revoked."[188] Abu Bakr's authority would be limited to Iraq; Jawlani would lead JaN in Syria. Both groups would be directly accountable to al-Qaeda Central.

In order to prevent local crises from boiling over, Zawahiri also appointed a local representative in Syria who could speak for him. The choice brought al-Qaeda's relationship with the Zarqawiists full circle. Zawahiri's representative was Abu Khaled al-Suri, the old ally of Abu Mus'ab al-Suri that al-Qaeda arranged to leave Afghanistan in 1999 when his wife grew ill.[189] Abu Khaled was arrested alongside al-Suri in Pakistan and eventually transferred to Syrian custody, which released him during one of the 2011 amnesties.[190] Despite the suggestion by Abu Hafs in 1999 that Abu Khaled had "abandoned" al-Suri, he never renounced his long-time friend. Rather, it was al-Qaeda whose perspective shifted. When Zawahiri named Abu Khaled to manage Zarqawi's intellectual and organizational offspring in Syria, he effectively aimed to rectify the mistake al-Qaeda made fifteen years earlier when it embraced Zarqawi.

Not surprisingly, Jawlani gleefully applauded Zawahiri's message. Not only did it affirm his independence from Abu Bakr, but Abu Khaled was a leader in Ahrar al-Sham. His appointment as Zawahiri's representative in Syria effectively endorsed Jawlani's strategy to engage the group.[191] Indeed, Abu Khaled's appointment embodied the strategic opportunity facing savvy jihadis in Syria. Virtually every party to the conflict empowered Abu Khaled in one way or another: the Assad regime released him from prison; a leading opposition group elevated him into a leadership role; key Assad opponents in Turkey and Qatar backed that opposition group; and al-Qaeda's emir embraced him.

Unsurprisingly, Abu Bakr rejected Zawahiri's proclamation separating the ISI from JaN. In April 2007, when the ISI was widely pilloried as illegitimate, the first ISI emir, Abu Umar, famously declared that the ISI would "remain because it has been built on the bodies of martyrs and been irrigated by their blood." Now Abu Bakr recalled similar rhetoric to draw a line in the sand:

> The Islamic State of Iraq and the Levant will remain as long as we are alive. It will remain. We will not bargain over it and we will not relinquish it until it achieves victory or falls over our dead bodies. It is a state that was introduced by Abu Mus'ab al-Zarqawi. It is a state that has its soil mixed with the blood of Abu Umar al-Baghdadi and Abu Hamzah al-Muhajir. It will not withdraw from any spot it has reached. . . . We crossed the borders that the malignant hands drew among the Muslim countries to restrict our movement and to confine us. God willing, we will remove [those borders].[192]

Abu Bakr accused Zawahiri of accepting the legitimacy of the Syrian-Iraqi border, which was a product of British and French colonialism in the Middle East. Abu Muhammad al-Adnani, ISIS spokesman, sharpened the response further. Not only would ISIS "remain," but the command to separate the ISI and JaN represented "a great sin," made by a "judge" with little knowledge of the situation.[193] The medium was part of ISIS message. Adnani's statement was not released through al-Qaeda's al-Fajr Media Network. Contrary to JaN's disavowal of social media only a year earlier, Adnani's statement was pushed directly to YouTube. Unlike JaN, ISIS was not afraid of social media.

Rejecting criticism made far from the battlefield was classic Zarqawi-ism. In this case, however, it was only possible because Zawahiri was now al-Qaeda's emir. It is hard to imagine that bin Laden would ever have been treated so roughly.

Zawahiri answered ISIS in a private letter on September 4, 2013. He castigated the group's intransigence and mustered legalistic arguments to assert his authority as an "emir" rather than a "judge."[194] Right or wrong, such arguments were doomed.[195] ISIS was fundamentally Zarqawiist: power and authority flowed from engagement on the battlefield—and Zawahiri was in hiding, far away. Abu Hamzah had not asked al-Qaeda's permission when he declared the ISI in 2006 and Abu Bakr was selected emir without al-Qaeda's input. Why would he defer to al-Qaeda now?

Even as the split between ISIS and al-Qaeda deepened, however, Zawahiri was still trying to rebuild productive relations. As a symbol of good faith, he noted in a letter to Abu Bakr that an old al-Qaeda tactic had borne fruit again. "Our brothers in Yemen," he explained, "have been able to take an Iranian hostage. We would like you to send us a list with the names of the imprisoned sisters . . . and the names of the brothers who have been sentenced to death in Iraq, in order that we include them in the negotiations if they ever ensue."[196] Zawahiri had lost nearly all of his leverage over ISIS, but he knew the group was deeply committed to freeing its prisoners, hundreds of whom still languished in Iraq and Iran.

In the midst of an epic confrontation between ISIS and al-Qaeda, this was a significant peace offering and it demonstrated that Zawahiri still had cards to play. But it was too little, too late.

Abu Bakr had other relationships in Syria besides Jawlani—and as JaN and ISIS split he scrambled to recruit as many jihadis as he could. In Aleppo, brothers 'Amr al-Absi and Firas al-Absi led a small group called the Mujahidin Shura Council. Both were veterans of the jihad in Iraq, and Firas reportedly met Zarqawi in Afghanistan in the late 1990s.[197] Firas had been jailed in 2007 during Syria's crackdown on jihadis but was released in Assad's 2011 amnesty program.[198] The al-Absi brothers were particularly adept at integrating early foreign fighters into Syria, and had their greatest victory capturing the Bab al-Hawa border crossing with Turkey. The al-Absi brothers also embodied Syria's contentious rebel politics; Firas was killed in a dispute with more nationalist fighters associated with the Free Syrian Army.[199]

Many of the early foreign fighters linked to the al-Absi brothers operated under the command of Abu Omar al-Shishani, an ethnic Chechen born in Georgia's Pankisi Gorge.[200] Like the al-Absi brothers, al-Shishani was technically independent of both JaN and the ISI, but he had significant ties with both. After the Mujahidin Shura Council helped JaN capture the last major Syrian army outpost west of Aleppo, it operated an independent training camp on the facility, even though JaN controlled overall access.[201]

As the relationship between JaN and ISIS broke down, Abu Bakr shifted his command into Syria. To make this work, he dispatched Haji Bakr, the former Iraqi army officer and senior aide, to negotiate with 'Amr al-Absi (Firas had already been killed) and al-Shishani.[202] Shortly thereafter, al-Absi swore allegiance to ISIS; after some cajoling, al-Shishani did as well.[203] These networks were particularly valuable because they welcomed many of the foreign fighters arriving in Syria. In May 2012, only about 100 salafis and up to 400 total foreigners were fighting in Syria. By the end of 2013, the International Centre for the Study of Radicalisation suggested there might be 11,000.[204] The numbers would only go up from there.

Abu Bakr's move into Syria culminated with the seizure of the city of Raqqah. JaN and Ahrar al-Sham originally captured the city from Assad in March 2013, but they quickly lost control as jihadis defected to the newly formed ISIS. On May 14, 2013, daylight executions broadcast via video made Raqqah's new reality apparent to the world.[205] Soon, Raqqah would be considered the capital of the Islamic State.

ISIS strategy differed from that of other rebels in Syria. Most focused on destroying the Assad regime, but ISIS prioritized control over Sunni-dominated eastern Syria, the region the regime valued least. Assad was focused on securing an arc of territory from Damascus to the Mediterranean coast along the border with Lebanon. Not only did this include much of the country's population, but the majority of the Alawites and Sunni elites that formed the base of his support.

Assad focused his military attention on the rebel groups that challenged him most directly—and ISIS, for the time being, was not one of them. Moreover, because ISIS goal was building a caliphate, it fought against both Syrian troops and other rebel groups in the areas it aimed to control. The result is that ISIS and the Assad regime—despite their ideological hostility and occasional clashes—were de facto operational partners.[206]

When the Assad regime did feel threatened, it acted with extraordinary brutality. In the morning darkness of August 21, 2013, the Syrian army fired surface-to-surface missiles armed with sarin gas into the Damascus suburb of Ghouta. More than 1,300 people died horribly of suffocation as sarin paralyzed the muscles in their lungs.[207] The attack seemed reckless. President Obama had declared that the use or transfer of Syria's chemical weapons was a "red line" that might result in U.S. military strikes, and United Nations weapons inspectors were actually in Syria at the time to investigate allegations of an earlier chemical strike.[208] But despite the "red line," Obama chose not to take military action, though the United States did sponsor a United Nations program to remove Syria's chemical weapons.

Still, this was the kind of war ISIS relished; one with no good guys and no more red lines.

The discord between JaN and ISIS was anathema to the vision articulated in the master plan, but real-world events still aligned with the master plan's timeline. Bin Laden believed that resurrecting The Caliphate would require decades, if not centuries, because of the need to sever the United States' relationship with "apostate" regimes. But al-Adl had seen an opportunity in the Levant because Syria's demographics favored Sunni revolution, and geopolitics ensured the United States would not prop up Assad. That vision had come to pass.

In the bloody mess of intra-jihadi warfare in mid-2013, it was easy to see the jihadi movement as a swirl of chaos without any clear direction. Perhaps that was true; there is no evidence that ISIS leaders were checking their progress against al-Adl's master plan. But there was another important truth as well: the master plan predicted that The Caliphate would be reestablished in Syria between 2013 and 2016, and on that most important prediction, it was right on target.

The Caliphate was imminent.

5

The Stage of Declaring the State
(2013–2016)

The Western fist in the Arab world will loosen. . . . The rising unity
of Europe will not continue . . . future events will favor the global
Islamic jihadist trend such that it will be able to declare an Islamic
state—a Caliphate.

Fuad Husayn, *Zarqawi . . . The Second Generation of al-Qaeda*

Fitna

The civil war was raging in Syria—hundreds of thousands were dead
and millions displaced—but it was across the border in Iraq where ISIS
captured a city of 300,000 people. Fallujah, only fifty miles from Baghdad
and straddling a key route from Iraq's heartland to the Syrian border, fell
into ISIS hands on January 4, 2014. The symbolism of the conquest was
even more important than the geography. Zarqawi had first endeared himself to Osama bin Laden by temporarily holding Fallujah a decade earlier.
In November 2004, nearly one hundred Americans died retaking the city
from him. In 2014, however, there were no U.S. Marines to retake Fallujah. That responsibility would fall to the Iraqi army.

This army was a far weaker fighting force than its numbers suggested.
Troops were undisciplined and poorly led. Billions of dollars of equipment
provided by the United States over the previous decade had not been maintained.[1] Sophisticated weapons systems had fallen into disrepair, and the

army often did not have replacement parts or sufficient ammunition to sustain a long-term campaign.[2] Some of these shortages were not the fault of anyone in Iraq; a bloated American bureaucracy for selling weapons could not keep pace with the operational requirements. Six weeks after Fallujah fell, Iraqi Prime Minister Nouri al-Maliki turned to Iran to buy weapons on a more expedited timeline.[3]

Still, whatever its material limitations, the army's political challenges were worse. There was deep distrust between enlisted soldiers and an officer corps swollen by politically motivated appointments.[4] The most effective units of the Iraqi army were Shia-dominated, but many Sunnis in Iraq believed them to be sectarian hit squads.

Many Sunni tribal and political leaders considered the Iraqi army more dangerous than ISIS. Harith al-Dari, a Sunni religious leader long despised by ISIS for supporting Iraqi elections, declared the prime minister "an evil, sectarian man."[5] Likewise, the most senior Sunni cleric in Iraq called the Iraqi army's nascent campaign against ISIS "genocide" against Sunnis in general.[6] Sunni antipathy to Baghdad had grown so great that the Sunni insurgent groups that had gone dormant or folded into the Awakening had begun to reemerge. Some of ISIS old enemies reasserted themselves as anti-government militants. The Islamic Army of Iraq, Ansar al-Sunnah, and the Mujahidin Army had united in the Jihad and Reform Front (JRF) to fight the ISI in 2007, but all claimed to participate in Fallujah's capture in 2014. Ansar al-Islam, Zarqawi's first friends in Iraq, looked dead in 2010 when its longtime Emir Abu Abdallah al-Shafi'i was captured, but in 2014 the remnants rose in support of ISIS in Fallujah and Mosul. Most eventually swore allegiance to Abu Bakr.[7] The old Sunni insurgency was back.

These groups eventually relearned that cooperation with ISIS was fruitless, but in early 2014 their frustration with the Iraqi government made supporting the jihadis an attractive option. As jihadism researcher Ayman Jawad al-Tamimi later put it, "The main reason for coordination was undoubtedly hope on the part of these groups that they could carve out their own spheres of influence without being subjugated by [ISIS]. But quite predictably, the opposite of what they expected took place."[8]

ISIS territorial progress in early 2014 was modest. It controlled large swaths of Fallujah and parts of Ramadi, a city of 800,000 people between

Fallujah and Baghdad. But the shift in political geography was more dramatic. ISIS growth in Anbar Province emboldened Sunnis resentful of the Baghdad government. Many disapproved of ISIS political program but had come to see the map of Iraq in starkly sectarian terms.

Zarqawi's old strategy of sectarian polarization was finally paying off.

Back in the United States, the public conversation about ISIS was very different. Three days after Fallujah fell, President Obama spoke with the *New Yorker's* David Remnick, who pushed Obama about the recent jihadi surge, arguing that "the flag of Al Qaeda is now flying in Falluja, in Iraq, and among various rebel factions in Syria; Al Qaeda has asserted a presence in parts of Africa, too."[9] Obama responded with some of the more regrettable lines of his presidency:

> I think the analogy we use around here sometimes, and I think is accurate, is if a JV team puts on Lakers uniforms, that doesn't make them Kobe Bryant. I think there is a distinction between the capacity and reach of a bin Laden and a network that is actively planning major terrorist plots against the homeland versus jihadists who are engaged in various local power struggles and disputes, often sectarian. . . . But let's just keep in mind, Fallujah is a profoundly conservative Sunni city in a country that, independent of anything we do, is deeply divided along sectarian lines. And how we think about terrorism has to be defined and specific enough that it doesn't lead us to think that any horrible actions that take place around the world that are motivated in part by an extremist Islamic ideology is a direct threat to us or something that we have to wade into.[10]

In many ways, Obama's misunderstanding was a function of 9/11. The scope and horror of that attack had created a perception in the United States that the threat from jihadi groups was roughly analogous to the threat of an attack on the homeland or U.S. institutions abroad. Few foreign policy thinkers—it was not just Obama—recognized the danger jihadi groups posed to U.S. geopolitical interests or that a super-empowered ISIS was likely to eventually support terrorism against the United States. As a result, the jihadi threat to the United States was still understood primarily as a function of al-Qaeda; so long as ISIS was primarily focused on the Middle East, it was considered a second-tier danger.[11]

Obama was not the only man to make a mistake during the infamous "JV" interview. Remnick, by erroneously citing "the flag of al-Qaeda" flying in Fallujah, failed to distinguish between al-Qaeda and its erstwhile affiliate, ISIS.[12] This misstep may seem minor, but it is indicative of a failure by leading foreign policy voices to recognize that ISIS was a fundamentally different kind of organization, with distinct goals. And, as a result, it posed a different sort of threat.

The U.S. State Department keeps an official list of Foreign Terrorist Organizations. When 2014 began, ISIS was not on it. The list still referred to "al-Qaeda in Iraq"; Jabhat al-Nusrah was included as a pseudonym for that organization in December 2012. Publicly, the military and intelligence communities used "al-Qaeda in Iraq" as well. One reason for this continuity is that "al-Qaeda in Iraq" was familiar terminology. The Arabic names of different militant groups and terrorists could confuse policymakers, so there was value in using recognized terminology. That is likely why Remnick used the name.

But there was another reason for maintaining the fiction that ISIS was "al-Qaeda in Iraq": the dysfunction of the United States Congress.

Since 2001, the United States' war on jihadis had been waged under an authorization to use military force (AUMF) against al-Qaeda and the Taliban, passed in 2001, and an AUMF against Iraq in 2003. The 2001 authorization was much broader because it allowed the military to target al-Qaeda and its affiliates anywhere in the world. But if ISIS was not actually part of al-Qaeda, would the 2001 AUMF still apply? Would Congress have to pass another authorization to enable military action against ISIS?

The Obama Administration argued that it had the authority to wage war on ISIS under the 2001 AUMF, but requested that the Republican-controlled Congress pass a new AUMF anyway. Instead, Congressional leaders refused to debate and vote on the issue, which would have required Members to take a definitive stand on a deeply contentious issue. Both hawks and doves were reticent to take a vote: hawks did not want to be seen as advocating an Iraq-like invasion in the Middle East and doves were wary about opposing a resolution focused on the destruction of ISIS. Regardless of the reasoning, Congress' unwillingness to address an ISIS-focused AUMF was

an abdication of political leadership on a critical national security question. Whatever the legal merits of basing the war against ISIS on the AUMF
built for al-Qaeda, it was factually and politically tenuous.

Some legal continuity in the face of changing terrorist group names
makes sense. In 2006, when "al-Qaeda in Iraq" was dissolved into the ISI,
it did not make sense to immediately require a new AUMF. After all, the
ISI maintained relations with al-Qaeda and allegedly pledged allegiance
secretly. It would be self-defeating to allow a terrorist group to avoid attack
simply by changing its name. But by 2014, viewing ISIS as part of al-Qaeda
was nonsensical: ISIS had claimed independence for eight years and had
been publicly feuding with Zawahiri for more than a year. Moreover, ISIS
was in a shooting war with JaN, a self-declared al-Qaeda affiliate.

The first rule of Prussian military theorist Carl von Clausewitz is to
"establish . . . what kind of war you are embarking on," which includes understanding the nature of your enemy.[13] Critics of President Obama, including in Congress, complained that he refused to refer to the threat from
al-Qaeda and ISIS as "radical Islam." But the real problem was not an unwillingness to use indistinct terminology like "radical Islam," but an inability to understand the unique and specific threat that ISIS posed. The
political conversation focused on how ISIS had erupted suddenly from the
Syrian civil war; in fact, it was the legacy of a war in Iraq that never should
have been, and that went unfinished.

The U.S. policy community did not understand ISIS, and Congress preferred to misunderstand the threat so that it would not be compelled to
debate the difficult question of whether or not to authorize force against
it. This constitutes an intelligence failure at a policy level: politicians, policymakers, journalists, academics, and think tankers all share the responsibility. Even those that saw hints of the ISIS resurgence are culpable for not
shouting loudly enough that ISIS posed a novel threat, and was on the
march.[14]

To the contrary, the Mujahidin Army knew exactly where ISIS came
from. The group's emir, Muhammad Hardan, had taught Abu Bakr al-
Baghdadi prior to the U.S. invasion, but the Mujahidin Army eventually
helped found the JRF and fought the ISI. So in January 2014, when the

Mujahidin Army's Shura Council attacked ISIS theological roots, they did not pretend it had emerged suddenly in the wake of the Syrian civil war.[15] Rather, the Mujahidin Army reacted directly to *Informing the People About the Islamic State of Iraq*, the ISI's "Federalist Papers" that outlined the structure, obligations, and processes of ISI government. *Informing the People* was originally released in 2006, but in 2014, the Mujahidin Army recognized it was the blueprint for ISIS governance—and so they attacked it.

Washington still called ISIS "AQI," but the group's closest and bitterest enemies knew they were facing a "state" already eight years old.

Of course, ISIS had far more success in 2014 than the ISI did in 2006. Chaos in Syria expanded the battlefield dramatically and offered far better demographics than Iraq—approximately 60 percent of Iraqis are Arab Shia, about the same that are Arab Sunni in Syria. Moreover, many people—in Iraq and around the world—considered the fight against the Assad regime legitimate, which facilitated huge flows of foreign fighters, money, and materiel to the battlefield. The fear Iraqi Sunnis felt for Baghdad overshadowed memories of ISI crimes and blunted an immediate "Awakening-like" uprising. Moreover, many of the Awakening's key leaders had been quietly assassinated by the ISI since the movement's heyday. Lastly, in 2007 there were 150,000 American troops in Iraq; in 2014 the number was closer to 1000.

Still, some Sunnis did reject ISIS in both Syria and Iraq. "The conspiracy [in Syria] is the same as the conspiracy in Iraq," declared Abu Muhammad al-Adnani, ISIS spokesman. "The conspiracy of the civil state and the nationalist project, the conspiracy of the Awakening Councils. We know this conspiracy and its ways. Yesterday in Iraq there was the . . . Islamic Army [of Iraq], the Mujahidin Army, and other factions and groups. And here today, they are confronting us in the Levant, with the same supporters and financiers. They even have the very same names!"[16]

ISIS did not reflect on the Awakening and endeavor to engage intransigent tribal groups more productively. In some cases, ISIS learned not to negotiate with tribes at all. This brutality was best illustrated in October 2014, near Ramadi, when ISIS massacred hundreds of members of the

Albu Nimr tribe, a grouping that had opposed the jihadi movement since the Awakening in 2007.[17]

ISIS was also increasingly at war with other jihadis. In September 2013, ISIS fighters killed JaN's emir in Raqqah, which by then was effectively the ISIS capital. Sa'd al-Hadrami was a Raqqah tribal leader who joined JaN before the split with ISIS. He briefly supported Abu Bakr after the separation, but backed JaN when Zawahiri announced it represented al-Qaeda in Syria. Furious about the betrayal and concerned that al-Hadrami might have coordinated with secular militants, ISIS killed him.[18] It acknowledged the murder in January 2014.[19]

JaN was apoplectic. "How is it possible that [al-Hadrami] could go so quickly from being a senior Emir in your ranks to an apostate collaborator?" asked JaN in a furious public announcement. "And then you preach about pious temperament. . . . The strong among you in Raqqah run around without accountability or responsibility, up to your ankles in injustice and sacrosanct [Muslim] blood."[20]

The fight compelled Zawahiri's representative in Syria, Abu Khaled, to intervene. He did not feign evenhandedness. "The devil lies in wait for humankind in every conceivable place," he wrote, "and he lies in wait for the mujahidin, so that they fall into the traps of extremism and the killing of Muslims."[21] Abu Khaled saw no path to repentance for ISIS. In an audio statement distributed online, he urged Zawahiri to "denounce" ISIS and "wash your hands of them and their acts."[22]

On February 3, 2014, Zawahiri took this advice. "The al-Qaeda group announces that it has no connection with the group called ISIS. . . . [ISIS] is not an affiliate of al-Qaeda and has no organizational relationship," he declared. "Al-Qaeda is not responsible for ISIS actions."[23] It was the sort of renunciation that Iraqi opponents of ISIS had been calling for since 2007.

Abu Khaled argued that a coalition of Islamist groups led by Ahrar al-Sham was the true nucleus of an Islamic State in Syria. This diverse coalition ranged from hardcore salafis to Muslim Brotherhood factions and de facto nationalists. Abu Khaled represented Ahrar al-Sham's radical wing, but American allies Turkey and Qatar continued to support the group. They pointed to its Muslim Brotherhood roots, which were more inclusive than jihadi ideas. The United States government did not share its allies' sanguine approach toward Ahrar al-Sham or Abu Khaled. Although the United States refrained from listing Ahrar al-Sham as a Foreign Terrorist Organization, the U.S. imposed sanctions on several of the group's prominent supporters, including a Qatari with close ties to the royal family.[24]

ISIS, of course, saw Abu Khaled as an enemy as well, so, in typical fashion, they killed him with a suicide bomber.[25] ISIS did not claim the assassination, but rumors swirled among jihadis that ISIS warned Abu Khaled privately that it had five suicide bombers targeting him.[26]

Jawlani's eulogy for Abu Khaled completed the split between ISIS and al-Qaeda. He remembered Abu Khaled as "a man who belonged to all mujahidin" and "who sought to solve problems, not create conflicts."[27] Then he leveled an ultimatum that echoed Ansar al-Sunnah's challenge to the ISI seven years earlier: either ISIS would commit to arbitration by authorized scholars, or there would be all-out war, not just in Syria, but, "even in Iraq."[28]

Jawlani's public ultimatum terrified senior figures in the jihadi movement. ISIS extremism was widely recognized, but an overt, intra-jihadi war could only be destructive. Even Abu Muhammad al-Maqdisi, who had clashed with Zarqawi a decade earlier and subsequently denounced ISIS, asked Jawlani to retract the ultimatum.[29]

Of course, just as the ISI had rejected arbitration when Ansar al-Sunnah demanded it in 2007, ISIS did the same in 2014. Their reasoning was simple; as a true Islamic State, there was no higher legal authority to adjudicate disputes. The buck stopped with Abu Bakr. Jawlani surely knew ISIS would never agree to arbitration by religious scholars, but it was his soldiers being killed in Syria. ISIS had responded to disagreement with blood and JaN would do the same.

Thirty years earlier, Abu Khaled's longtime friend Abu Mus'ab al-Suri concluded that conflict among rebel factions was the key reason the uprising against Bashar al-Assad's father had been crushed in the early 1980s.[30] Just before his death, Abu Khaled foresaw a similar future:

> The biggest beneficiary of infighting is the Assad regime . . . fighting and confining factions into corners, declaring Muslims apostates and deeming

their blood and wealth permissible [to take] will leave them with one option, which is to defend themselves. This results in weakening the rebellion, advancing the regime . . . animosity among the mujahidin, and the
loss of popular support.[31]

ISIS hard-line stance might have Zarqawi smiling from the grave; but it
also had Bashar al-Assad—very much alive—smiling from a palace in
Damascus.

Managing Savagery

Even after Abu Khaled's assassination, some in JaN tried to build productive operational relationships with ISIS in order to better combat the
Syrian army. Abu Hammam al-Suri, who swore allegiance to bin Laden
with a handshake in 1998, was one.[32] He arrived in Syria after being released from Lebanon's Roumiyeh prison, and quickly stepped in to run
JaN's military operations.[33]

Abu Hammam had little time to learn on the job. In early 2014, the
most intense battle of the Syrian war unfolded around Aleppo, where numerous rebel factions faced off against the Syrian army and ISIS advanced
on the city from the east. JaN had allied with the rebels, and Abu Hammam hoped to negotiate a ceasefire with ISIS that would allow the opposition to repel attacks from the Syrian army. It did not go well.

The first challenge was finding an ISIS counterpart with the authority to
make such a deal. This was no small task. Mid-level commanders were
unconcerned about the fighting among rebel groups, and Abu Hammam
was quickly exasperated. "How could you remove [ISIS brigades] from
their defensive position" against the Syrian army, he demanded of an ISIS
commander, "in order to fight the Free Syrian Army? If the [Syrian] Army
comes . . . they will rape, pillage, and kill everybody including ISIS members." But in Abu Hammam's retelling, the commander only shrugged and
said, "Let them come."[34]

Frustrated, Abu Hammam asked another ISIS commander why his
fighters attacked Islamists who were fighting the Syrian regime. "The attackers were probably foreigners," explained the ISIS leader. "They do not

understand or speak Arabic, and at night we did not see the banner" marking which faction was present. Foreign fighters had been making similar mistakes on the Islamic State's behalf since at least 2006, and the commander offered no apology. "What was done," he told Abu Hammam, "cannot be undone."[35]

Eventually Abu Hammam contacted Abu Ali al-Anbari, a former Iraqi military officer whom Abu Bakr deputized to manage all ISIS affairs in Syria. Not a modest man, Abu Ali made clear that he could cut a deal. "I am a decision maker," he said to Abu Hammam. "My decision is effective on everyone in ISIS, even [Abu Bakr] al-Baghdadi himself."[36]

But Abu Ali was not interested in a ceasefire either. From his perspective, the other Syrian rebels were just newer versions of the Awakening in Iraq rather than true jihadis. "He always repeated phrases like 'these awakenings, these apostates; we will exterminate everyone who carries arms against us,'" Abu Hammam recounted.[37] Most Western observers thought the ISI lost Iraq in 2007 by alienating Sunnis with its harsh violence, but Abu Ali concluded the opposite. The lesson he drew was that the ISI had clumsily tried to accommodate local demands, which then grew more expansive. And he remembered that Sunni Iraqi rebels had eventually allied with the United States and the Shia-led Iraqi government. He feared a similar realignment in Syria and vowed not to collaborate with groups he did not trust.

The negotiation with Abu Ali at a dead end, Abu Hammam tried one last ISIS contact: Abu Omar al-Shishani, ISIS General Military Commander.[38] Abu Hammam initially found al-Shishani reasonable, but the comity soon disintegrated. Abu Hammam broadcast images of a mutually agreed ceasefire, but the document, as he put it, "was not worth its ink."[39] The day after it was signed, ISIS fighters attacked one rebel-controlled neighborhood south of Aleppo and sent a car bomb to another. It is not clear if Abu Omar reneged on the agreement or if other factions in ISIS torpedoed it.

In the end, Abu Hammam seemed more confused than angry about ISIS intransigence. "I do not know who the decision maker in ISIS is," he said, echoing complaints from Iraqi insurgents about the ISI in 2006. "We could not find a responsible official in ISIS who would seek a ceasefire to spare the blood of Muslims."[40]

Despite his long history with al-Qaeda, Abu Hammam did not really understand the people he was dealing with.

In Raqqah, a modest city of 200,000 people that served as ISIS capital, the group's extremism was plain. Prior to the Syrian civil war, Raqqah was relatively unimportant to the ISI's Syrian logistical effort supporting operations in Iraq. But in revolutionary Syria, it was valuable. Perched along the Euphrates River, Raqqah is a 90-minute drive south of the Turkish border and sits near a highway intersection leading toward the critical Iraqi border crossings in the north, near Mosul, and in the south, near al-Qa'im. The highway west runs directly to Aleppo, Syria's second-largest city and its most hotly contested battlefield. After ISIS seized Raqqah from JaN, the city became a proving ground for its version of governance.

Informing the People About the Islamic State of Iraq lists nine obligations of "Islamic" governance. Most of these focus on judicial processes, security, and taxation, but they also include social support for the needy.[41]

The most important obligation is enforcing *hudud*, mandatory punishments for crimes believed to violate divine intent. The range of prohibited behavior includes adultery, homosexuality, witchcraft, consuming alcohol or drugs, and robbery. Among the mandatory punishments for such crimes are stoning, crucifixion, amputation, and flogging.

Informing the People explained how the *hudud* were applied in a 2006 case of adultery:

> The *hudud* were postponed until she gave birth and her partner, who was unmarried, confessed his sin. . . . The Imam leading Friday prayers spoke to the worshipers of the nobleness of carrying out *hudud*. . . . Then, the people surrounded the man and carried out the punishment against him, praise be to God. Numerous sorcerers were also hunted and killed.[42]

In typical Zarqawiist fashion, *Informing the People* anticipated the international backlash that enforcing *hudud* would bring—and embraced that criticism as a test of faith and commitment to the Islamic State's goals:

> Those whose minds are polluted by the poison of modern paganism, and whose hearts are pierced by arrows of westernization, think that the *hudud*

are barbaric, backward, and a reason for the international community to be angry. . . . This test reveals the mettle of men. That is why the scholars made it necessary for the Caliph to forcefully impose the *hudud* without fear of anyone. The cowards who tremble in fear of the international community accusing them of barbarism or human rights violations; those cowards should never be entrusted with the Shariah of God or the interests of their nation.[43]

Brutality, in ISIS view, is both inherent to a divinely inspired legal code and a tool to sort "true" Muslims from apostates. Zarqawi was long dead by the time ISIS captured Raqqah, but the *gharib* ethos he embraced still informed its jihad.

As ISIS territory expanded, local governors developed regulations to operationalize the *hudud*. A late-2013 document in Aleppo extolled the virtue of crucifixion for punishing "highwaymen" and other thieves.[44] The directive was included in a compilation of *hudud* subsequently released in Aleppo in March 2014.[45] Both ISIS supporters and their enemies began to tweet images of crucifixions in Raqqah and Aleppo in the spring of 2014.[46] As *Informing the People* predicted, the international media reacted with horror.[47] For ISIS, however, that approbation was something to celebrate, not fear.

ISIS is not the only polity in the Middle East to apply a version of the *hudud*. Saudi Arabia also applies corporal punishment, including whipping and beheading for a range of crimes, including drug offenses.[48] Saudi judicial processes are more regularized than ISIS and presumably require higher standards of evidence for convictions. The primary difference, however, is that Saudi Arabia generally conceals its most brutal punishments from the outside world, whereas ISIS celebrates them.

Assad Teausant Bigolsmurf

"Assadthelion" liked social media, amateurish religious pronouncements, and bold political statements. In June 2013 an anonymous stranger online asked which "foreign country" he disliked most. Assadthelion did not mince words. "I live in it."[49]

A month later, another anonymous questioner asked Assadthelion where he wanted to "go for fighting." His response was the same as thousands of other young men all over the world. "I want to go fight in Syria."[50] Assad-thelion's unflinching talk inspired another, more direct question. "Are you a terrorist?" This time his response was evasive and jumbled. "Lol as if I would tell the truth about That haha wow and no I'm not."[51]

Assadthelion was communicating via Ask.fm, a social network mostly unknown to Americans over twenty years old, but with hundreds of millions of users globally and a growing cadre of young American adherents. In 2013, Ask.fm was gaining a reputation among jihadis because it allowed users to ask questions anonymously and enabled respondents to use obvious pseudonyms like "Assadthelion."

Assadthelion was not actually concealing his identity very well. His profile included a photograph of his real-world self and accurately listed his hometown as Lodi, California. Moreover, he was active on other social media outlets, where his online handle—"Assad Teausant bigolsmurf"—offered even more hints to his real-world identity.

Assadthelion posted a range of disconcerting material online, most of it seemingly empty braggadocio. But on August 5, 2013, he seemed to get a bit more operational, posting a message that read, "Anyone know where I can get the 'lone Mujahid pocket book'?"[52] It was accompanied by the hashtag "#alqaeda#jihadist#jihad#islamicpride#muslim#mashallah#islam#allah#AllahuAkbar#thelonemujahid."[53]

The *Lone Mujahid Pocketbook* was published in March 2013 by al-Qaeda's affiliate in Yemen, known as al-Qaeda in the Arabian Peninsula (AQAP), which was best known in the West for producing slick, colloquial propaganda in English. The group's most famous propagandist was Anwar al-Awlaki, who directed the production of *Inspire*, an English-language magazine that urged would-be jihadis to operationalize on their own. He was killed by a U.S. drone strike in September 2011, but his legacy lived on.[54] As the complaint against Teausant put it, the *Lone Mujahid Pocketbook* was a "how-to guide for becoming a lone wolf terrorist . . . and includes articles like: 'Torching Parked Vehicles,' 'Bomb Making,' 'Remote Control Detonation' . . . it is, in essence, a compilation of [articles from] previous issues of *Inspire* magazine."[55]

It did not take long for federal investigators to discover that Assadthelion's real-world name was Nicholas Teausant and that he was a college student living in Lodi, California. Teausant had a convert's zeal for Islam and sometimes expressed it online, including in a YouTube video in which he waggled a finger at viewers while proclaiming that Islam prohibits smoking because it is tantamount to suicide.[56] He was a dedicated video game fanatic and followed dozens of YouTube channels, ranging from conservative Muslim preachers and "Faces of Death" videos to the British singer Adele.[57]

Teausant was in school, but his life was drifting. He tried to join the U.S. Army National Guard, but was dismissed because he did not have the appropriate academic credits. He had a young daughter and believed that he had arranged for his mother to care for her if he "disappeared." He also believed his mother to be *kafir*—a nonbeliever—and despite claiming to love her, said he would kill her if she were to "jeopardize something that [he] had going."[58] After his arrest, Teausant was treated for schizophrenia.[59]

Teausant's digital antics attracted the FBI's attention, which introduced an informant to discuss his intentions.[60] He toyed with various ideas, including an attack in the United States, but eventually allegedly planned to travel to Syria. He journeyed first to the state of Washington, where he allegedly planned to cross the border into Canada, and from there would fly to Turkey and then head to Syria. But not far from the Canadian border, on the night of March 16, 2014, federal agents stopped the bus carrying Teausant and arrested him.[61]

Teausant seemed not to fully understand how much trouble he was in, but suggested that he had been entrapped. If he had not met the FBI informant, he explained, "I probably would be at home playing Battlefield 4," a video game.[62] Instead, he was repatriated to California and charged with attempting to provide material support to a terrorist organization.

The material support charge is commonly used in American terrorism prosecutions, but it is somewhat strange. A person may be charged with "material support" only if the State Department has designated as a Foreign Terrorist Organization the group he or she aims to support. In March 2014, Teausant was charged with material support to "al-Qaeda in Iraq."

But that was problematic. The ISI officially dissolved AQI in 2006, and senior al-Qaeda leaders publicly acknowledged the dissolution in 2007.

Although the groups maintained a secret relationship of some kind, ISIS rejected al-Qaeda's leadership more forcefully in 2013 and al-Qaeda definitively disavowed all connection to ISIS in February 2014.[63] In short, by March 2014 when Teausant was charged with providing "al-Qaeda in Iraq" material support, there was no such thing.

The State Department added the "Islamic State of Iraq," as a pseudonym of "al-Qaeda in Iraq" in January 2012 and "Jabhat al-Nusrah" was added in December 2012.[64] The official designation did not mention the "Islamic State of Iraq and al-Sham" nomenclature, which had been adopted in early 2013. This meant that when Teausant was charged, the United States government legally considered the "Islamic State of Iraq" and "Jabhat al-Nusrah"—two organizations functionally at war with one another on the ground in Syria—as pseudonyms for a single organization: "al-Qaeda in Iraq."

Although the U.S. government did not legally distinguish between ISIS and al-Qaeda, Nicholas Teausant did. He was adamant that he wanted to join ISIS, not JaN, the al-Qaeda affiliate, because he believed it was taking money from Qatar and Turkey. "It didn't make a whole lot of sense to me," he explained, ". . . fighting for a group that's getting paid by the people they're trying to fight."[65] The State Department's list of Foreign Terrorist Organizations, long out of touch with the shifting reality in Iraq and Syria, was now creating farce. Nicholas Teausant was being charged with trying to support an organization—al-Qaeda—when he explicitly rejected that group and was trying to join its enemies.

To its credit, the State Department recognized the problem. On May 14, 2014, more than a year after JaN and ISIS began fighting openly, the State Department revised its terrorism designations to bring official U.S. policy in line with reality. It amended "the designation of al-Qaeda in Iraq (AQI) as a Foreign Terrorist Organization (FTO) . . . to add Islamic State of Iraq and the Levant (ISIS) as its primary name and remove all aliases associated with al-Nusrah Front (ANF)." Additionally, the Department of State announced the designation of ANF as an FTO.[66]

The Teausant paradox—charging a man with attempting to join a terrorist group he explicitly said he did not want to join—was not terribly damaging in the end. The State Department updated its designation, and the case against Teausant moved forward. In late 2015, he pled guilty and was subsequently sentenced to twelve years in prison.[67]

The Teausant case was a harbinger of things to come. Many more ISIS-related prosecutions, and plots, in the United States revealed suspects and perpetrators that had been inspired by Anwar al-Awlaki, but switched their allegiance from al-Qaeda to ISIS during the Syrian civil war. Likewise, FBI sting operations emerged as the federal government's most reliable tool for generating terrorism convictions.

Perhaps most importantly, however, the Teausant case highlighted the State Department's belated designation of ISIS as an official Foreign Terrorist Organization. Even as American citizens were mobilizing to fight for ISIS, the group remained a second-tier problem in Washington. That was dangerous, because ISIS was about to pull off its biggest trick yet.

The State

"What is your name?" the ISI fighter asks from just outside the camera's view.

"My name is Hasan Muhammad Ali."

Captions at the screen bottom indicate that Ali is an agent of a spy network working for the Iraqi government in northern Iraq. The logo of the al-Furqan Media Establishment, the propaganda house created when the ISI was founded in 2006, hovers in the top-left corner.

"When were you recruited?" the voice asks from off-screen.

"In July 2011. I advise everyone watching to avoid my path and to listen to the Islamic State."

"What do you think your destiny is?" asks the voice.

"My destiny," says Ali without emotion, "is to be beheaded."

He was wrong. This time, ISIS enforcers shot their blindfolded victim in the back of the head.

Ali's murder was captured in an ISI production called the *Clanging of the Swords—Part 1*, which was released in June 2012. It was the first in a series of four videos illustrating the Islamic State's newfound strength. The imagery in these videos includes Iraqi soldiers shot point-blank, grainy night-vision footage of raids on Iraqi checkpoints, captured soldiers begging for their lives in vain, and declarations of commitment from venerated Islamic State leaders, ranging from Abu Bakr al-Baghdadi all the way back to Zarqawi. The message of the *Clanging of the Swords* series was clear: the ISI would hunt down and kill members of the Iraqi security forces and Sunni collaborators, but members of the police and Awakening who "repent" would be welcomed back into the Islamic State.[68]

The fourth installment of the *Clanging of the Swords* is now infamous— the most visceral scene shows an Iraqi official beheaded in his bedroom— because it was released in May 2014, just prior to ISIS' most important military victory.[69] When it was released, ISIS already controlled significant territory in Iraq and Syria so journalists and analysts were watching. But the *Clanging of the Swords* narrative did not change much over four installments and two years. The only real difference is that in 2014 the international media was paying attention.

On the ground in Iraq, soldiers and policemen long knew their fate if captured by the Islamic State; if they were lucky, like Hasan Muhammad Ali, they would be shot in the back of the head. In 2014, however, what Iraqi soldiers and policemen did not know was even more important: when ISIS came for them, whether at night in their bedroom or on a battle line outside Mosul, who among their fellow soldiers had taken ISIS offer "to repent?" Who among their fellow soldiers were spies? And, who among their fellows would stand and fight?

It turns out, many of them would not.

The attacks occurred nationwide. In Baghdad, car bombs killed fifty-two people. In Ramadi, gunmen raided Anbar University, briefly taking students hostage before retreating.[70] Near Mosul, ISIS Iraq commander, a captain in the Iraqi Presidential Guard during the days of Saddam and then a close ally of Zarqawi, detonated a suicide vest while surrounded by Iraqi troops. Documents captured in his safe house revealed what the Iraqi command already feared: the ISIS offensive was coming. It was June 7, 2014, and Iraq was about to be changed forever.

The Iraqi commanders in Mosul knew an ISIS offensive was imminent. ISIS already controlled large blocks of territory in both Syria and Iraq. In

Anbar Province, ISIS controlled major sections of Fallujah, Ramadi, and a series of smaller towns running up the Euphrates River to the Syrian border. ISIS controlled much of the Syria-Iraq border and the Syria-Turkey border as well. In Syria's north, its fighters could travel safely all the way to Aleppo in the west and to the Iraqi border across from Mosul in the east. Moreover, ISIS had deep roots in Mosul. Its predecessors had operated there consistently since 2003. Mosul was ISIS strongest redoubt during the Surge and Awakening. Mosul was a safe haven for ISIS, long before it was conquered.

Iraqi commanders knew that an attack in Mosul was coming, and they also knew they were woefully unprepared. On paper, the Iraqi army had 25,000 soldiers in Mosul, but the real number was closer to 10,000. The 6th Brigade of Iraq's 3rd Army Division listed 2,500 troops in Mosul but actually had only 500, and they were short of ammunition.[71] Many soldiers had been shifted closer to Baghdad in Anbar Province, where ISIS had already captured Fallujah and threatened Ramadi. Other fighters on the docket were "ghost soldiers," who were in the books but never showed up to train or fight. They often split their salary with a unit's commanding officers.

ISIS strikes in Baghdad, Ramadi, and elsewhere were clearly intended to keep Iraq's military occupied in multiple areas. When ISIS Baghdad command released a statement claiming responsibility for five car bombs, it explained that the attacks were a "Raid to Avenge Our People in Mosul."[72]

ISIS did not actually fight its way into Mosul. As experienced ISIS fighters from Syria advanced from the east, sleeper cells rose up from within the city itself. The result was chaos, and despite a vast numerical advantage over ISIS fighters, the Iraqi army collapsed. Only days after the first ISIS elements began their fight in Mosul, the entire city west of the Tigris River was under their control.[73]

The fall of Mosul was the most significant operational success for any jihadi group since 9/11. Before its fall, Mosul was a vibrant city of nearly two million people with ancient Muslim and Christian communities, straddling Iraq's most important ethnic division between Arabs and Kurds. Decades earlier, one of Zarqawi's spiritual mentors had grown disillusioned in Mosul because girls and boys went to school together. The city embodied Iraq's extraordinary diversity, history, and potential. In June 2014 it became ISIS crown jewel.

ISIS broadcast video of cheering crowds welcoming its fighters into Mosul, along with the punishments meted out to those deemed collaborators with the Iraqi government.[74] The executions were standard ISIS fare, but instead of isolated assassinations before a desert backdrop, these killings occurred in busy traffic circles or on top of high-rise buildings. ISIS also began to advertise its crackdown on "deviancy" in the city.[75] As it had done in Syria, the group released a list of banned activities and began a campaign to destroy churches, Shia mosques, and shrines deemed un-Islamic.[76] Its propaganda avoided mention of the nearly 500,000 Iraqis who fled when it seized control.[77]

ISIS benefitted in other ways from the capture of Mosul. The fleeing Iraqi army left behind weapons, ammunition, Humvees, tanks, even helicopters.[78] The United States had provided much of this equipment to the Iraqi army, and it was quickly distributed to ISIS units throughout Iraq and Syria.

The fall of Mosul was also a windfall for ISIS treasury. Even before taking over, the group was earning $12 million per month in Mosul running mafia-style protection rackets.[79] After it conquered the city, such schemes were rebranded as taxation. Conquest also created opportunities to seize money and goods. ISIS exact proceeds are unknown (some claimed that up to $430 million was stolen from banks), but the group allowed many bank branches to continue functioning and used these institutions to move money across the international banking system.[80]

Capturing Mosul also reset the larger battlefield. With the Iraqi army in full retreat, ISIS charged down the Tigris River valley, capturing Saddam Hussein's hometown of Tikrit and surrounding an Iraqi air force facility known as Camp Speicher. Its fighters rounded up terrified Iraqi soldiers fleeing Camp Speicher with promises of free transport to Baghdad. Video released by ISIS shows what actually happened next. The captured soldiers huddled together in shallow depressions in the earth while ISIS fighters massacred them with automatic weapons. By some estimates, 1,700 people were slaughtered.

One survivor interviewed by Tim Arango of the *New York Times* fell forward into the mass grave and lay among his comrades' bodies for hours before beginning a harrowing journey to Baghdad. At least one ISIS fighter noticed that he was still alive, but did not kill him. It was not mercy. "Let him suffer," another ISIS militant urged. "He's an infidel Shia. Let him suffer. Let him bleed."[81]

ISIS military success owed much to cooperation from Sunni militants who had once rejected the ISI as part of the Awakening. In 2007, Muhammad Dabash, an early founder of the Islamic Army of Iraq, helped create the anti-ISI Jihad and Reform Front. In the wake of Mosul's capture, he signaled that times had changed. "We are not allied with anyone," he explained to reporters from the London-based daily *Asharq al-Awsat*. "Each side has their own policy, but when the two interests met with a common enemy attacking us both, we decided to point our weapons against this government together."[82]

Dabash was bullish about the return of Sunni control in Iraq, and in denial about ISIS future role. "In two days, tribal revolutionaries will control Anbar," he declared on June 23, 2014. Despite the social regulations ISIS was already imposing in Mosul, Dabash claimed that ISIS had "handed control of the city over to the other factions."[83]

ISIS new partnerships were driven in part by improved relations with the infamous Ba'athist commander Izzat al-Douri.[84] A powerful figure in Iraq's insurgency since day one, al-Douri soured on the ISI during the Awakening but strongly praised ISIS in July 2014. "God's blessings be upon the armies and factions of the revolution . . . and at the forefront of all these groups come the heroes and knights of al-Qaeda and the Islamic State. I send them a special greeting because I admire, respect and take pride in them."[85]

Like ISIS, al-Douri believed the Shia-led government in Baghdad was controlled by Iran, and he considered "the Safavids" his most dangerous enemy. But despite this agreement, al-Douri remained an Iraqi nationalist and hoped that appeals to Iraqi nationalism would trump sectarianism. "We call on the jihadist factions to rise above religious, sectarian, tribal, or regional divisions and to keep in mind that the heroic people [Shia] in southern and central [Iraq] confronted the fierce storm of [Ayatollah Ruhol-lah] Khomeini in the 1980s."[86]

Some Western analysts wondered whether Ba'athists had effectively co-opted ISIS. They pointed to al-Douri's praise for ISIS and the role of former Iraqi military officers, like Haji Bakr, in elevating Abu Bakr to ISIS leader-ship in 2010. Some analysts argued that the ISIS complex bureaucracy was evidence of Ba'athist influence.[87]

But this analysis was too clever. Not only did the ISI have sophisticated bureaucracy years before the Syrian civil war—or Abu Bakr's elevation to Emir—but al-Qaeda had built one decades earlier.[88] It is indisputable that many former Iraqi officers rose to prominent roles in ISIS, but it is not particularly surprising that an organization primarily based in Iraq for a decade would eventually incorporate many Iraqis.[89] The suggestion that the group's ideological or political outlook changed significantly as a result is unfounded.

After all, most of the former Iraqi officers inside ISIS had embraced ji-hadi thought for more than a decade by the time Mosul fell. Indeed, ISIS dedicated the attack to the former Iraqi officer, and ISIS commander, who detonated a suicide vest rather than be captured just days before the strike. After the Mosul victory, ISIS spokesman Abu Muhammad al-Adnani de-scribed his history:

> Abu Abd al-Rahman al-Bilawi al-Anbari . . . was one of the first people to join the jihad against the crusaders in Mesopotamia. Compared with all the Ansar [Iraqi jihadists], he is one of their best veterans, as for "al-Tawhed wa'l-Jihad," he was one of its founders. And with respect to the Islamic State, a pillar of its military command. . . . By his side was Abu Mus'ab al-Zarqawi. It was the encounter of the best Ansar with the best Muhajir [for-eign fighter], their friendship lasted three years during which he was imbued with [Zarqawi's] doctrine and became his right arm until his cap-ture by the crusaders.[90]

The proof, ultimately, is in the pudding. Despite the bravado of Ba'athists like al-Douri or Nationalist Islamists like Muhammad Dabash, ISIS col-lected the political benefits of the 2014 Sunni revolution in Iraq. Tribal groups did not seize control of Anbar "in two days." Instead, ISIS began to purge Ba'athists and tribal operatives in Mosul and Anbar.[91] The Iraqi militias that collaborated in the capture of Mosul and Anbar quickly learned a critical lesson: if you legitimize or empower ISIS, they will stab you in the back.

The victory in 2014 ultimately belonged to ISIS alone.

When Hani al-Sibai, a London-based jihadi cheerleader, saw that ISIS had conquered Mosul, he worried the group had even grander aspirations. Since the ISI's establishment in 2006, the group had referred to its emir as the "Commander of the Faithful," a title that positioned him not simply as emir of an Islamic State but potentially as a caliph, the leader of a transnational caliphate. When Mosul fell, ISIS propaganda began to emphasize the title, which Sibai understood to mean that ISIS planned to declare The Caliphate. Such a claim, he fretted, would be "explosive."[92]

Since the Prophet Muhammad's death, various dynastic caliphates have operated in the Muslim world, each led by a caliph who held both spiritual and political authority. The last widely acknowledged caliphate was embodied in the Ottoman Empire, whose sultans claimed the "Caliph" title for nearly 600 years. But the Turkish state that replaced the Ottoman Empire after World War I was envisioned as nationalist and secular, and it disavowed the Ottomans' religious underpinnings in 1924.

Eighty years later, the master plan predicted that the combined forces of al-Qaeda and Zarqawi would reestablish The Caliphate on Syrian territory between 2013 and 2016.[93] By the time ISIS was ready to make good on that scheme, the alliance between the Zarqawiists and al-Qaeda had dissolved, and their commitment to al-Adl's plan was tenuous.

Nonetheless, ISIS was right on schedule.

Abu Muhammad al-Adnani had recorded many audio statements since becoming the ISI's official spokesman, but nothing quite like the one he released on June 29, 2014, the first day of the holy month of Ramadan.[94] He began, as jihadis often do, by comparing contemporary events to the Prophet Muhammad's life. Like many Islamists before him, al-Adnani explained that the present was a period of *jahilliya*—ignorance—just like the period before Muhammad received his revelations from God. Just as

Muhammad needed to build a state to impose God's law, so too did "true" Muslims today. And critically, that law must be offered globally, not just in the territory already controlled by ISIS. The time had come, he argued, to reestablish The Caliphate:

> The flag of the Islamic State, the flag of monotheism waves here. Its shade stretches from Aleppo to Diyala. . . . All of the *hudud* [mandatory punishments] are implemented. . . . The people of the State travel for trade and otherwise, secure that their lives and wealth are safe. Governors and judges have been appointed. . . . Taxes and alms from believers and non-believers are collected. Courts resolve disputes and complaints. Evil has been removed. People are educated in the mosques. . . . The last issue is the obligation that Muslims must not abandon. It is a forgotten obligation. Muslims have not tasted honor since they forgot this obligation. This dream lives in the heart of every Muslim; it informs the heart of every monotheist. It is the caliphate. It is the caliphate—the abandoned obligation.[95]

Al-Adnani moved on to the two remaining questions: who would be the Caliph? And, how far did The Caliphate's authority extend?

> The Islamic State, represented by its people of wisdom and authority . . . pledge allegiance to the Sheikh, the mujahid, the scholar who practices what he preaches, the worshipper, the leader, the warrior, the reviver, descendant from the Prophet's family, slave of God, Ibrahim bin Awwad bin Ibrahim bin Ibrahim bin 'Ali bin Muhammad al-Husayni al-Qurayshi by lineage, al-Samarra by birth and upbringing, al-Baghdadi by residence and scholarship. He has accepted the *bayah*. Thus, he is the imam and Caliph for Muslims everywhere. Accordingly, the "Iraq and Levant" qualification in the Islamic State's name is henceforth removed from all official communications, and the official name is the "Islamic State."[96]

Every Muslim, including in other jihadi groups, was expected to swear allegiance to the new Caliph:

> We want to clarify for Muslims that the Caliphate has been declared and it is incumbent on all Muslims to pledge allegiance to Caliph Ibrahim [Abu Bakr al-Baghdadi] and support him. All emirates, groups, states, and

organizations are null when the Caliphate arrives with soldiers in their area.[97]

The new caliphate had a well-considered roll-out strategy. Two days after al-Adnani's declaration, Abu Bakr spoke himself. After the fall of the previous caliphate, he said:

[T]he disbelievers were able to weaken and humiliate the Muslims. . . . They achieved this by conquering [Muslim] lands, placing treacherous agents to rule Muslims with an iron fist, and spreading sparkling and deceptive slogans like: civilization, peace, co-existence, freedom, democracy, secularism, Ba'athism, nationalism, and patriotism. . . . Today—by God's will—you have a state and Caliphate that will regain your dignity, strength, rights, and supremacy. This is a state where Arab and non-Arab, white man and black man, easterner and westerner are all brothers. It is a Caliphate to unite the Caucasian, Indian, Chinese, Levantine, Iraqi, Yemeni, Egyptian, North African, American, French, German, and Australian.[98]

The most dramatic moment of ISIS caliphate roll-out came on July 4, 2014, when Abu Bakr climbed to the minbar (pulpit) at Mosul's Nur al-Din mosque to lead Friday prayers. His sermon addressed a deep tension in the caliphate's creation. The group was built and sustained in its hardest moments by Zarqawi's populist ideology, which empowered soldiers and lay preachers to disavow religious and political hierarchies, and to reject religious leaders that avoided jihad. But now the Islamic State was building a global state and doing its best to confer absolute religious and political authority in the Caliph. The fundamentally antiestablishment movement was trying to institutionalize itself.[99]

"I have been appointed your leader," Abu Bakr told his listeners, "but I am not the best among you. I am no better than you." His authority, he explained, was drawn not from his position or his knowledge but from his actions. "If you see that I am right, then support me. . . . However, if you see that I am wrong, advise and guide me. Obey me as long as I obey God. But if I do not obey God, do not obey me."[100]

Abu Bakr knew that the Islamic State's confrontation with other jihadis was not over. Muslim scholars, both mainstream and jihadi, denounced

The Caliphate wholesale. Saudi Arabi's leading mufti called ISIS "evil and a scourge" a day before the Grand Imam of al-Azhar University in Cairo—the most influential intellectual home for Sunni religious scholarship—lamented the group's "inhuman crimes."[101] These denunciations were echoed by Yusuf al-Qaradawi, a Muslim Brotherhood–aligned preacher with massive reach via an Al Jazeera show. In 2013 he had accelerated the rebellion in Syria by declaring jihad against the Assad regime to be a personal obligation for all Muslims.[102] But he called the new caliphate "void," adding that, "simply announcing a caliphate is not enough to establish a caliphate."[103]

Most jihadi scholars had also condemned the ISI in 2006, and the substance of the critiques was largely the same.[104] Then, however, al-Qaeda's leadership publicly rallied behind the ISI, but in 2014 they sided with the critics.

Not surprisingly, Zarqawi's old mentor, Abu Muhammad al-Maqdisi, was deeply critical as well.[105] "Will this Caliphate be a sanctuary for every Muslim?" he asked. "Or will this creation take up a sword against Muslims who oppose it?"[106] He then answered his own question, calling the Islamic State "deviant" and questioning the validity of any group that "threatened to shoot the heads of their Muslim opponents."[107]

Many older jihadi scholars echoed Maqdisi's criticisms, but a younger generation of theologians was more divided—and the Islamic State opportunistically championed their praise.[108] The most prominent of these scholars was a young Bahraini named Turki bin 'Ali, who ultimately joined the Islamic State and led its shariah ministry.[109] Bin 'Ali emerged as a forceful champion for the Islamic State, combining religious knowledge with the "manliness" and battlefield proximity that Zarqawi had once sought in his religious advisors.

By declaring a caliphate, the Islamic State was not just declaring war on the West or "apostate" governments; it was effectively renouncing the legitimacy and utility of political Islamist movements—including jihadis—as they had existed since the 1920s. The Muslim Brotherhood was founded in 1928 as a response to the Ottoman Caliphate's demise; the Islamic State argued implicitly that its raison d'être had been eliminated. The Wahhabi movement tied itself to the Saud family for institutional support; the Islamic

State presented itself as the only legitimate institutional protector of Islam. The Islamic State was threatening even jihadi groups outside of its core operational areas; it effectively declared their agendas moot without Abu Bakr's consent and support. The Islamic State was not just stretching ideological expectations of a caliphate and girding for war with the West, it was challenging the authority of every Islamist or jihadi leader on the planet.

The last element of the caliphate's rollout hit the Internet the same day as the video of Abu Bakr in the Nur al-Din mosque in Mosul. The first issue of a glossy, English-language magazine called *Dabiq* celebrated the "Return of the Khilifah." One of its features, "In the Words of the Enemy," quoted Western analysts explaining that ISIS was "a de facto state."[110] It was clever, but subtly suggested ISIS weakness. The group claimed to need no external legitimization, yet it still sought affirmation by selectively quoting Western researchers.

The first issue of *Dabiq* focused on one key theme: *hijrah*, or emigration to the new caliphate, which Abu Bakr declared "obligatory."[111] ISIS framed this call in religious terms, but Abu Bakr's speech belied more practical considerations: He wanted emigrants with specific skills. "We make a special call," he said, "to scholars, legal experts and judges, as well as people with military, administrative, mechanical expertise, along with medical doctors and engineers of all specializations."[112] Polemics aside, the Islamic State faced the daunting challenge of governing the territory it now controlled.

The declaration of a caliphate in 2014 was a stunning fulfillment of the master plan's most important prediction, precisely on schedule, almost a decade after the plan was scoped. But declaring the caliphate was not the culmination of the master plan. Two more stages were to follow, and the Islamic State still had many enemies to fight.

League of the Righteous

Abdul had been to the Baghdad Garage in the Iraqi city of Amarah before. This time his commander had personally selected him for a specialized training course. Trainees with passports would cross the border legally, but Abdul and others without documentation would move more quietly.

They boarded a minibus at the Baghdad Garage and drove east, exiting a few miles before the invisible border running through the maze of marshes where the Tigris and Euphrates rivers shake hands. The marshes were an ancient barrier to those that did not know them well, but to the experienced they offered food, shelter, and covert paths between Iraq and Iran.

Abdul and the others were ushered into a rowboat, and the men guiding it knew exactly where they were going. Soon Abdul disembarked in Iran, where another minibus stood waiting for them.[113]

Abdul completed his training course (subjects ranged from marksmanship to counterintelligence tradecraft) after three weeks, but several classmates dropped out after being forced to visit a shrine of Grand Ayatollah Ruhollah Khomeini, the leader of the Islamic Revolution in Iran.[114] Although Abdul and his fellow trainees were all Shia Muslims, they were also Iraqis who remembered the brutal Iran-Iraq war in the 1980s. The Iraqi militiamen valued the Iranian training, but many resented the Persian trainers, who looked down on Arab Iraqis. Perhaps because of this tension, those who passed the course did not stay in Iran for long.

Abdul's journey occurred in late 2007 or early 2008, when the ISI was moving fighters through Syria, often with the tacit acquiescence of the Syrian regime. The ISI was not the only group that the Syrian regime had empowered. Abdul and his fellow trainees were not members of the ISI; they were Shia militiamen, and after their training stint in Iran, they headed to Syria and Lebanon. In 2007, they were training to kill American soldiers in Iraq, but a few years later they would emerge as some of the Islamic State's most dangerous enemies.

Landing in Damascus under the cover of darkness, Abdul and his fellow Iraqis were ushered into Chevrolet Suburbans and driven from the airport west toward Lebanon. They switched vehicles twice to shake surveillance and threaded a circuitous route through the mountains. Abdul tried to peek out the curtained windows, hoping to see the terrain and to catch a glimpse of the trainers from Lebanese Hizballah. He was excited. Hizballah offered several advantages over the Iranians. They were Arab and had the experience of fighting Israel's Western-style military.

Abdul was a member of Asaib al-Haq (AAH: The League of the Righteous), one of several Shia militant groups fighting U.S. forces in Iraq.

AAH was led by Qays Khazali, whose close relationship with the Qods Force of the Iranian Revolutionary Guard Corps (IRGC) ensured that the group received more advanced training than other militias.

This training was evident on January 20, 2007, when a group of AAH fighters snuck onto a base near Karbala, Iraq, killed one soldier on site and kidnapped four others, all of whom were eventually executed. American Special Operations Forces eventually captured Qays, along with his brother and a man named Ali Musa Daqduq. After pretending to be mute, Daqduq eventually revealed that he had been a member of Lebanese Hizballah since 1983. Hizballah was not just training Iraqi fighters like Abdul; it advised them directly on the ground in Iraq.[115]

Years later, the same coalition of Iranian advisors, Iraqi militants, and Lebanese Hizballah are still working together. But instead of targeting American troops in Iraq, they fight for the Assad regime in Syria and operate as shock troops against the Islamic State in Iraq.

These Shia militias create powerful dilemmas for the United States as it fights the Islamic State. On the one hand, the militias are an effective ground force in an area with few other options.[116] On the other hand, they were killing Americans only a few years ago; they regularly commit atrocities against the Sunni community in Iraq; and they are aligned with Iraqi politicians who favor Iranian influence in Baghdad.

If the United States were to put significant troops in Iraq to target the Islamic State, AAH and its allies would likely resume their attacks against Americans.

The Shia militants fighting ISIS in Syria and Iraq have roots in the Dawah movement, an Islamic revivalist organization founded in 1958 by students and scholars at the Shia seminary in Najaf, Iraq.[117] The ruling Ba'ath Party suppressed Dawah—closing its schools in Baghdad, banning its publications, expelling hundreds of non-Iraqis from the Najaf seminary,[118] and passing a law requiring Shia seminary students to serve in the Iraqi military.[119] That law was not enforced until 1976, when Saddam Hussein became general secretary of the Iraqi military. The result was a diaspora of Dawah alumni across the Middle East. Most avoided politics, but some embraced political and militant activism.[120]

Many Dawah activists supported the Iranian revolution, which culminated in 1979 with the declaration of the Islamic Republic of Iran. Saddam Hussein, who became Iraq's president the same year, was unwilling to risk a similar uprising among Iraq's majority Shia population. He had Dawah's leader, Grand Ayatollah Muhammad Baqir al-Sadr, arrested and killed. Sadr's death caused Dawah to splinter. Most groups remained peaceful, but some embraced militancy and sought support from the new Islamic Republic in Iran.

Saddam did not limit his war on Dawah to Iraq. He assassinated its activists across the region, especially in Lebanon, where many members of Dawah would play key roles in the formation of Hizballah.[121] After Hizballah was founded, in 1982, it often collaborated with Dawah militants in a shell organization called Islamic Jihad.[122] Indeed, many of the terrorist attacks Americans associate with Hizballah, including the attacks on the U.S. and French embassies and the Marine Barracks in Lebanon, were originally claimed in the name of Islamic Jihad.[123]

The massacre in Lebanon was not the last "Islamic Jihad" attack on the United States and France. Less than two months later, a truck carrying butane gas canisters exploded at the front gate of the U.S. Embassy in Kuwait. Other vehicle-borne bombs targeted the French Embassy, Kuwait's international airport, and water and oil facilities.[124] Six Kuwaitis were killed, and an annex of the U.S. Embassy was destroyed.[125]

Kuwaiti authorities rounded up many of the attackers, including two Kuwaitis and several Lebanese members who played critical logistical roles. However, because of the large number of Iraqis implicated in the plot, the group became known as the "Dawah 17."[126] Two of the men involved in the Kuwait attack would go on to have extraordinary militant careers.

Mustafa Badreddine was the brother-in-law of legendary Hizballah terrorist Imad Mugniyah, who led the group's external operations wing for twenty years. Badreddine remained in Kuwaiti custody until 1990, when he escaped during the chaos of Iraq's invasion of Kuwait[127] and rejoined Hizballah. He was implicated in the assassination of former Lebanese President Rafik Hariri in 2005.[128] In 2008, after Imad Mugniyah was assassinated in Damascus, Badredinne assumed leadership of Hizballah's external operations, which included support to Iraqi militias and the Assad regime.[129] Taking over for Mugniyah must have been daunting.[130] Until he was killed in Syria in May 2016, it is easy to imagine that Badreddine took some comfort knowing he was working with an old compatriot.[131]

Abu Mahdi al-Muhandis was a driver during the 1983 Kuwait attack, and he escaped the Kuwaiti dragnet.[132] Although an Iraqi citizen, he fled Kuwait to Iran and joined the Badr Corps, a military unit composed of Iraqi exiles.[133] Sentenced to death in Kuwait for his role in the attack, he rose through the Badr Corps to ultimately manage Iran's support for underground Iraqi militants fighting Saddam after the Iran-Iraq war ended in 1988. In that role, he worked closely with Hadi al-Amiri, head of the Badr Corps, and Qassem Soleimani, head of the Qods Force, Iran's external special operations unit, which was responsible for supporting the Iraqi rebels. Muhandis, al-Amiri, and Soleimani have remained a key triad of Iranian influence in Iraq ever since.

Iran was eager to see Saddam deposed and did not oppose the U.S. invasion of Iraq, but in the wake of the regime's fall it sponsored militant groups and politicians to bolster its own political influence.[134] Even U.S. forces valued Iranian involvement. In 2004, the United States flew Muhandis—who had spent decades as an international fugitive for attacking a U.S. embassy—into Najaf to negotiate with a young cleric named Moqtada al-Sadr, who was leading a chaotic Shia insurrection.[135] Such comity did not last. When relations between the United States and Iran soured, Muhandis returned to his traditional role as Soleimani's most trusted Iraqi militant. Al-Amiri, meanwhile, entered Iraqi politics and became the Iraqi minister of transportation in 2006.

The Iranian-backed militias burst to the forefront in Iraq after Zarqawi bombed the al-Askariyya Mosque in Samarra in February 2006, but they operated long before the U.S. invasion. The groups varied in tactics, organization, and dedication to Iran, but they were all tied to the Badr Corps in one way or another.[136] None were perfect proxies for Iran, but all were levers that Soleimani and the Qods Force could pull when the time was right.

The Badr Corps was extraordinarily well organized in Iraq. In 2010, it had nearly 2,000 fighters in Baghdad alone and professionally organized units across Iraq dedicated to a range of specialized tasks that included combat engineering, administration, communications, headquarters units, and mobilization of popular forces.[137] Its fighters drew salaries of between $85 and $225 dollars per month, depending on rank, paid by Iran.[138] A roster of 325 Badr fighters in Diyala Province included, for each one, his full name in Arabic, a battlefield nickname, and an Iranian name. One hundred fifty had been on Iran's payroll since the 1980s, 115 since the 1990s, and only ten enlisted during the 2000s, all prior to the U.S. invasion of Iraq.[139]

By the time the United States invaded the Badr Corps was aging, but it was experienced. Iran had literally been paying some of its soldiers' bills for thirty years.

When the Islamic State complained about Iranian influence in Iraq they were not all wrong.

At the end of the Bush Administration, the United States signed a Status of Forces Agreement (SOFA) with Iraq. Among other requirements, it obliged the United States to transfer all of its prisoners into Iraqi control. Many ISIS leaders were transferred, as were Shia militia leaders, including Qays Khazali.[140] Iraqi Prime Minister Maliki quickly embraced Khazali, however. Not only could he help the prime minister shore up support among militia members, but Khazali feuded with Moqtada al-Sadr, who was a much larger political threat to Maliki. Despite Khazali's role in kidnapping and murdering Americans, the prime minister of Iraq effectively rehabilitated him politically. As an advisor to Maliki said, "Qais al-Khazali has a problem with the Americans. He doesn't have a problem with us."[141]

Even as the United States shifted militia leaders into Iraqi custody, it moved to blacklist others. On July 2, 2009, the State Department listed Muhandis as a Specially Designated global terrorist, citing both his support for terrorism in Iraq and the 1983 attack on the U.S. Embassy in Kuwait.[142] It was quite a shift from 2004, when American helicopters had carried him into Najaf.

The United States also tried to maintain control over Ali Musa Daqduq, the Lebanese Hizballah operative captured in Iraq.[143] But the SOFA required the United States to transfer Daqduq to Iraqi custody; it did so in December 2011, only days before the final withdrawal from Iraq. The United

States subsequently charged Daqduq in a military tribunal similar to those used for prisoners at Guantanamo Bay, but the Iraqi government would not return him to American custody. It released him less than a year later.[144]

Iraqi militias eventually repaid Hizballah's support in Iraq by fighting in Syria.[145] Hundreds of Shia militants from Iraq, Iran, and Afghanistan have fought under Hizballah commanders in support of the Assad regime,[146] ignoring the Syrian-Iraqi border as easily as the Islamic State does. The spiritual guide of Khazali's AAH explained the fight in Syria in terms that mirrored ISIS. "The battle in Syria is not to defend the shrine of Sayida Zeynab [a Shia shrine in Damascus] but a battle of infidels against Islam, and Islam should be defended."[147]

That battle returned to Iraq when the Islamic State seized Mosul and drove south. The threat compelled Iraq's most senior Shia religious leader, Grand Ayatollah Ali al-Sistani, to bless militia groups—which were institutionalized as Popular Mobilization Forces—as bulwarks against the Islamic State.[148] Although some Popular Mobilization Forces were Sunni militias, most were rebranded versions of Shia militias that had existed for years. Indeed, Sistani's endorsement for the militias was reminiscent of his calls for militias to defend Shia shrines after the 2006 bombing of the al-Askariyya shrine in Samarra.

Unsurprisingly, the same old triad of Soleimani, al-Amiri, and Muhandis—who had managed Iranian-backed militia activity in Iraq since the 1980s—coordinated the militias.

The Shia militias did strengthen Iraqi defenses against the Islamic State, but they also complicated the political relationship between the United States and the Iraqi government—and therefore complicated the fight against the Islamic State. After all, Maliki himself had spent decades in Iran while exiled from Iraq; by endorsing the Shia militias—which were responsible for numerous war crimes of their own[149]—he seemed to undermine the notion that Iraq's government could serve its entire population and not operate with sectarian favoritism. That perception, whether justified or not, played directly into Islamic State propaganda. The United States eventually made Maliki's departure a condition of direct military assistance against the Islamic State.

In September 2014, Haider al-Abadi replaced Maliki as prime minister, and U.S. warplanes began to bomb Islamic State positions in Saddam Hussein's hometown of Tikrit. But Abadi's political position was—and is—perilous. If he were to favor the United States too much, or publicly endorse a robust U.S. military presence in Iraq, he risks an Iranian-backed coup.

Those militias were a double-edged sword; they offered key ground forces when the Iraqi army was in chaos, but complicated the United States' ability to confront the Islamic State directly. The relationship between U.S. forces and the Shia militias has remained guarded. The United States said it would not directly coordinate with Popular Mobilization Forces, but as American planes bombed Islamic State positions in Tikrit, al-Amiri and Muhandis rallied troops on the edge of the city.[150] The Islamic State has produced some very strange bedfellows.

The Shia militias eventually recaptured Tikrit for Iraq, beginning a very slow process of retaking ground from the Islamic State's newly declared "caliphate." But that victory only confirmed the policy conundrum for the United States. Just who would benefit most from the Islamic State's defeat?

6

The Stage of Absolute Confrontation
(2016–2018)

The stage of absolute confrontation will begin immediately after the
Islamic State is established. The world will be split into two camps:
the camp of faith and the camp of atheism. . . . When the conflict
begins, falsehood will perish.

Fuad Husayn, *Zarqawi . . . The Second Generation of al-Qaeda*

Caliphate

In April 2007, Abu Umar al-Baghdadi declared that the ISI "would remain."[1] Dogged tenacity defined the Islamic State's strategy for the next
seven years. But in mid-2014, shortly after the capture of Mosul and declaration of the caliphate, Abu Bakr al-Baghdadi opted for a more aggressive
tone. The fifth issue of the Islamic State's magazine *Dabiq* carried on its
cover the group's new slogan: "Remaining and Expanding."[2]

That issue of *Dabiq* was dedicated largely to pledges of allegiance given
to Abu Bakr by jihadis operating in Algeria, Libya, the Sinai Peninsula,
Saudi Arabia, and Yemen. Those commitments, *Dabiq* argued, reflected the
caliphate's transformation from a regional movement in Iraq and Syria
into a transnational entity with various regional *wilayat* (provinces). Only a
few of these new provinces actually provided significant military capability, but their collective pledges reinforced the Islamic State's claim to global
political authority.

According to al-Adl's master plan, establishing the caliphate was to be followed immediately by the Stage of Absolute Confrontation between the "forces of faith and the forces of global atheism." There is no evidence that Abu Bakr intentionally followed this blueprint when he expanded the Islamic State to include affiliate "provinces," but his approach reflected the strategy regardless. He even echoed the master plan's language in December 2015 when he celebrated the strength and breadth of the coalition arrayed against the Islamic State. Unlike the mere "crusader campaigns" the infidels had mounted in the past, the contemporary fight was different:

O Muslims, the battle today isn't just a Crusade, it's a full fledged war between the nations of Kufr against the nations of Islam; never in the history of our Ummah has the whole world gathered against it in a single battle like today, and every Muslim is included in this war.[3]

This, effectively, is what al-Adl had meant by "absolute confrontation."

The Islamic State's leaders believed that these uniquely high stakes required jihadi groups to evolve. This was a different kind of war, and it demanded a jihad led by a single caliphate, not the hodgepodge of jihadi groups that had existed previously. Prior to 9/11, al-Qaeda maneuvered to lead the jihadi movement, but the Islamic State's claim to authority was on another level entirely. Al-Qaeda aimed to lead a coalition of jihadi groups; it did not want to pull them all into a single political structure. The Islamic State did.

Al-Qaeda's effort to lead the jihadi community generated a backlash among other jihadis, so too has the Islamic State's assertion of authority. Ironically, the Islamic State's supposed war against the West has more often been a war against other Muslims.

Despite its failure to unite the jihadi movement and tendency to kill Muslims, the Islamic State has been bolstered by the largest international flow of jihadis in history. A year after the caliphate was declared approximately 30,000 foreign fighters had come to Syria and Iraq, mostly to join the Islamic State. These fighters hailed from more than eighty countries and included thousands of Western passport holders.[4] This was more than three times the number of foreign mujahidin that traveled to Afghanistan to fight the Soviets during the 1980s, an experience that defined jihadism for a decade afterward. The Soviet jihad has remained seminal for al-Qaeda, but the Islamic State is unencumbered by focus on that history; it focuses instead on writing its own, primarily in Syria and Iraq.

A key lesson from the anti-Soviet jihad was that many foreign fighters would commit to violence after they left the core battlefield. After a few initial probing attacks in Europe, the Islamic State formally declared its intent to attack abroad shortly after the caliphate was declared, in September 2014.[5] Islamic State spokesman Abu Muhammad al-Adnani called for the group's supporters in the West to "kill a disbelieving American or European— especially the spiteful and filthy French—or an Australian, or a Canadian, or any other disbeliever from the disbelievers waging war." In typically Zarqawiist fashion, he urged supporters not to wait for a ruling from religious scholars but to "kill the disbeliever whether he is civilian or military."[6]

Al-Adl's master plan foreshadowed this shift. After the caliphate was established, the Stage of Absolute Confrontation was to conclude with a shift toward international terrorism, in which infidels "would learn the meaning of real terrorism . . . that would terrify the enemy and make them think a thousand times before attacking Muslims."[7]

Adnani and his boss Abu Bakr may not have based their decisions on al-Adl's master plan, but they had something similar in mind.

Enforcing *hudud* is the foundation of Islamic State authority, but its governance does not stop there. At its grandest moment, the Islamic State governed approximately six million people in Iraq and Syria, spread across a territory roughly the size of Great Britain. Managing such an expanse requires complex bureaucracies. Although *The Management of Savagery* is most famous for its discussion of "savagery," the portions on "management" contain insights as well. "We must make use of books on the subject of Administration," it explains, "especially the management studies and theories which have been recently published, since they are consonant with the nature of modern societies."[8] Jihadi utopia might be a divine vision, but running it was a practical endeavor.

The Islamic State learned from other Western practices as well. After watching the governance disaster in Iraq after the United States evicted

Ba'athists from the bureaucracy in 2003, the Islamic State aimed to maintain existing bureaucratic infrastructure when it conquered new territory.
Teachers, trash collectors, and others providing key services returned to their
jobs after being vetted, though they received new policy guidance. (Many of
these employees continued to be paid by the Iraqi and Syrian governments.)[9]
Teachers, for example, had to follow new education guidelines that emphasized Islamic history, military training, and "useful science" such as chemis-
try and engineering. "Un-Islamic" topics such as evolution were banned.[10]

Moreover, the Islamic State drew on its earlier work building geographic
divisions, constructing resilient bureaucracies, and fundraising. Long before the Islamic State declared the caliphate, the ISI had "ministries" led
by cabinet officers managing everything from war to agriculture.[11] Before
the Islamic State established governorates, the ISI was also divided into
sectors subdivided into districts, each assigned an overall emir, and deputy emirs to manage critical functions. Contemporary Islamic State governorates have more emirs, which reflect the broader array of services they
provide, but these roles have always been flexible. After the ISI suffered
operational setbacks in 2007, it reduced the number of emirs assigned to
each sector from six to three.[12] The framework can expand and contract.

The ISI's governance was less comprehensive than the Islamic State's,
but it was meaningful. The ISI ran educational programs for children, set
speed limits, collected garbage, established guidelines for prayers and public behavior, paid fighters and cared for their next of kin, adjudicated disputes, and embarked on public works projects to win supporters.[13] Its
fundraising, largely organized at the sector level, combined taxation and
extortion, smuggling operations, and management of state-owned enterprises ranging from gas stations to concrete plants and agricultural lands.
ISI provinces carefully tracked both revenue and expenditures and passed
20 percent of their income to the national-level ISI, which redistributed
the funds as needed.

The Islamic State's bureaucracy is organized today much as the ISI's
was in 2006, with a few fundamental changes. Most importantly, the Islamic State provides a wider range of services, so it has increased the number and scope of cabinet ministries (In mid-2016, Islamic state propaganda
suggested it had fourteen bureaucratic divisions). In certain areas, it also

controls territory much more securely than the ISI did, which means it has established more overt mechanisms for direct engagement with the population, including permanent offices, industrial and commercial sites, media kiosks, social events, and regularly scheduled public punishments.[14]

The Islamic State's most significant structural bureaucratic shift since declaring the caliphate is the embrace of *wilayat* above the sector level as a mechanism for managing the group's increasingly broad geographic reach. The second is the development of advisory councils reporting directly to the Emir on issues of critical importance, including military strategy.

But neither this innovation nor others reflect an ideological or political evolution in the organization since 2006; they are simply operational adjustments for a different environment. The goal remains the same, and the fundamental structure of government and bureaucracy remain the same. The real difference is that the ISI faced a much more hostile operational environment than the Islamic State—and so it was denied the ability to establish organizational roots at the scale seen after the Syrian civil war.

The Islamic State's relatively permissive operating environment is a double-edged sword, however. The ISI could always blame its failings on U.S. military pressure, after all there were 150,000 U.S. troops in Iraq when the ISI was crushed. If the Islamic State suffers similar setbacks, it is likely to attempt such excuses again. But this time around, the argument will be much more difficult to make; despite U.S. and international pressure, there are far fewer troops arrayed against the Islamic State. The Islamic State has many enemies, but no easy bogeyman to blame.

There is one key exception to the Islamic State's relative ideological consistency. It is arcane, but it is critical. The Islamic State has moderated the Zarqawiist notion that Muslims ignorant of a religious obligation must be excommunicated and killed. Zarqawi had adopted the idea from Abu Abdallah al-Muhajir in Afghanistan prior to 9/11, but the idea encouraged internal factionalization. This was useful for undermining social structures in Iraq, but is dangerous to a governing institution like the Islamic State.[15] After all, the principle implied that every ideological disagreement, even between Islamic State supporters, could escalate into intramural bloodshed.

Even resolving this problem was dangerous. Islamic State Shariah advisor Turki Bin 'Ali championed the shift, but not everyone in the Islamic

State agreed, which led Abu Bakr to order a crackdown on the few hard-liners that rejected this mild form of "moderation." History repeating itself; the Taliban had eventually grown weary of Abu Abdallah's provocations in Afghanistan and disbanded the training camp where he preached. In doing so, they pushed him right into the arms of Zarqawi.[16] The Islamic State was far more radical than the Taliban, but the prerogatives of governance created a logic that even the Islamic State acknowledged—and now it was the descendants of Zarqawi cracking down on the hard-liners in their midst.

The risk of governance failure is why bin Laden opposed jihadi efforts to establish states. He worried the movement did not have the requisite skills to be effective and thought the United States would be able to destroy any territorially bound entity. After the ISI's establishment, bin Laden suppressed moves by al-Qaeda affiliates in Somalia and Yemen to establish "states."[17] "We should stress the importance of timing in establishing the Islamic State," he wrote to one of his close aides. "The establishment of the state begins with exhausting [the United States] . . . that overthrew the Islamic Emirate in Afghanistan and Iraq despite the fact this power was depleted. We should keep in mind that this main power still has the capacity to lay siege on any Islamic State."[18]

The actual Islamic State suffers the limitations bin Laden identified, but it benefits from the weakness of surrounding governments and the United States' reluctance to reengage in a major military operation in the Middle East. Like the ISI before it, the Islamic State also endeavors to attract recruits with specialized administrative, engineering, and medical skills.[19] It runs schools and develops curriculum (its first textbooks were borrowed from Saudi Arabia); it provides military, physical, and ideological training for incoming foreign fighters; it proudly touts inexpensive healthcare; and it celebrates wealth redistribution to the needy.[20] The Islamic State organizes street cleaning and municipal building programs and has a department to provide marriage licenses, administer mosques, and enforce religious codes around dress and commerce.[21]

Ultimately, however, the Islamic State's first priority has always been imposing *hudud*, not providing services. There is no reason to think that priority has shifted since it was formalized in *Informing the People About the Islamic State of Iraq* in 2006. And if the Islamic State loses its ability to provide a broad range of services, it will fall back on what it prioritizes most: imposing its draconian vision of Islamic Law.

Like all governments, the Islamic State must raise money. Unfortunately, it has experience doing just that. In 2008, the ISI's Ninawa Province raised nearly $1 million a month through extortion, protection rackets, and local businesses, which is a significant amount considering how weak the organization was at the time. But the Islamic State has more recently made that look like pocket change. In early 2014, the Islamic State was earning $12 million a month in Mosul alone through similar schemes.[22]

Under the caliphate, the extortion programs and protection rackets favored by the ISI have reemerged as "taxation" and state-authorized property. An accounting document for the Islamic State's Dayr al-Zawr governorate inside Syria shows that the largest revenue source, almost 45 percent, was "confiscations," whereas oil, gas, and electricity production and sales accounted for just over 30 percent. About 24 percent came from taxation.[23]

The Islamic State's reliance on large-scale industrial enterprises has centralized some of its fundraising, but much of the group's money is still collected at the local level and then flows up toward the center. This decentralized structure is a hallmark of terrorist organizations, and it suggests that the Islamic State will remain resilient even if it loses significant territory. This structure helped ensure the ISI's resilience after its decline in 2007; the financial and operational independence of Islamic State sectors suggests local organizations will be able to function even if the organization as a whole is badly damaged.

The bottom-up model also makes estimating the Islamic State's overall revenue very difficult, a problem that no doubt plagues both Western intelligence agencies and the Islamic State's internal auditors. The best estimates suggest that in late 2015, the group earned about $80 million per month, or close to $1 billion annually. (Islamic State supporters claim annual revenue of $2 billion, of which they say 99 percent goes to managing the state rather than "war efforts.")[24] Whatever the precise amount, revenue comes through four primary vectors:[25]

- Looting and booty. Like the ISI before it, the Islamic State seizes money and property from its defeated enemies. The most famous seizure was a reported $430 million captured from the Mosul Central Bank when the city fell in 2014, but smaller offensives offer similar opportunities to "nationalize" property. The U.S. Treasury estimated in December 2015 that the Islamic State had looted between $500 million and $1 billion from Iraqi banks.[26]

- Taxation. The Islamic State requires its Muslim "citizens" to pay *zakat*, which amounts to 2.5% tax on their personal and corporate capital annually.[27] Although there is ample evidence that so-called "People of the Book" are often killed in the Islamic State, the Islamic State also imposes the *jizya*, a specialized tax for Christians and Jews. According to Islamic State propaganda, the *jizya* is a graduated income tax of $178 annually for the poor and $875 for the wealthy.[28] The Islamic State also taxes the salaries paid by the Iraqi and Syrian governments to workers in Islamic State territory. According to some reports, the Iraqi government alone sent $130 million every month to employees living in territory controlled by the Islamic State, which reportedly skimmed off 30 to 50 percent.[29]

- State-owned enterprises. The Islamic State has nationalized a host of businesses, including most of Syria's oil wells, as well as agricultural fields, food production, and retail outlets.[30] Some of these industries, like oil, offer revenue opportunities at several points on the value chain: extraction, refining, distribution, and trade. The oil industry has also undergirded trade with neighboring countries, even as the Islamic State has attacked those states. Capitalizing on the same underground networks that Saddam used to smuggle oil under a UN embargo, the Islamic State trades with the Kurds, Turkey, and businesses in Damascus and Baghdad.[31] According to U.S. sources, it has made more than $500 million from such trade and as much as $40 million per month.[32] The Islamic State also generates revenue from electricity production and distribution, and telephone services.[33]

- Criminal scams. Many of the extortion scams employed by the ISI in previous years have now been regularized into "taxation" schemes; nonetheless, the group still uses blatantly criminal activity to fundraise. The Islamic State famously ransoms kidnapping victims and regulates the exploitation and sale of antiquities looted from historical sites in Iraq and Syria.[34] In general, however, the revenue from these operations is small compared to the attention they receive in Western media. The Islamic State also uses Iraqi financial institutions to fraudulently exchange Iraqi dinars for U.S. dollars. It is not clear how much money the Islamic State has generated through these scams, but such "white-collar" crime is almost certainly more lucrative than ransoms or antiquities sales, which have gained far more public attention.[35]

Considered as a terrorist group, the Islamic State appears spectacularly wealthy. As a point of comparison, al-Qaeda had fewer than 200 members on 9/11 and an annual budget of about $30 million. The Islamic State has tens of thousands of employees and accepts responsibility to provide a host of government services to six million people on a budget of about $1 billion.[36]

But if you compare the Islamic State to functional governments, it appears much weaker. Massachusetts, for instance, has a similar population to the Islamic State (6.7 million), and its 2015 budget was $36 billion.[37]

It is easy to think of the Islamic State's fundraising progression from the ISI as a shift in type—from terrorism and organized crime to pseudo-statehood—but sociologists and political scientists have long noted that these concepts are not so different.[38] The Columbia University sociologist Charles Tilly famously argued that taxation by a state reflects the same basic concept as an organized crime "protection racket."[39] The major difference is that one is considered politically legitimate while the other is not. According to Tilly, the racketeer both creates a threat and offers protection against it. State builders, he argues, do the same. A state aims to monopolize the use of violence within its borders and requires citizens to contribute or face sanctions.

Tilly, writing in the 1980s, was thinking about revolutionary France in the 18th century, not the Islamic State, but his analysis should give pause to anyone who sees the Islamic State's demise as a foregone conclusion.[40]

After declaring a caliphate, the Islamic State existed in a murky classification netherworld—neither purely a terrorist group nor a "real" state. Tilly might have called the ambiguity downright traditional, but it confounded Western policymakers used to applying one set of rules to states and another to terrorist organizations. Even as Western policy struggled to keep up, however, Islamic State supporters from around the world, including Western countries, were quick to make clear that they were not worried. For them, the Islamic State was utopia.

For recruiting foreign fighters, the appearance of governance is almost as important as actual governance. This is why the Islamic State expends tremendous effort promoting its utopian promise, even drawing specious comparisons between social services provided in the Islamic State to those offered in Europe or the United States.

The most obvious fabrication is the currency. The Islamic State rejects the legitimacy of any currency not backed by gold (the master plan considers currencies not backed by gold a "Jewish conspiracy").[41] In the months after the caliphate was declared, the Islamic State established its own money, "based on the intrinsic values of gold and silver," to replace Iraqi dinars, Syrian pounds, and U.S. dollars.[42] In practice, however, the Islamic State's currency is rarely used even within its borders, and most transactions still occur in U.S., Iraqi, and Syrian denominations. This monetary policy is an apt metaphor for Islamic State governance as a whole: it looks more coherent and better implemented on the Internet than in Raqqah or Mosul.

There are exceptions to this rule, but they tend to be limited and closely tied to the Islamic State's recruiting priorities. The Islamic State advertises itself as a sexual utopia for frustrated young men with few marriage prospects. It recruits women to marry male recruits and advertises this to male recruits. It also permits the rape and sexual enslavement of non-Muslim women. After capturing Mosul, the Islamic State released guidelines—clarified in a formal *fatwa*—delineating rules for sex slaves, including procedures for capture, standards for intercourse, and instructions for reselling slaves.[43] Victims later reported that Islamic State fighters would pray before raping them, apparently in the belief that such abuse could lead to conversion.[44]

In a rare display of shame, however, some in the Islamic State seem to recognize that sexual slavery is bad for its image in certain circles. Its Aleppo Province released guidelines prohibiting the posting of pictures of sex slaves on social media.[45]

Of course, the Islamic State advertises many other cruelties, including throwing homosexuals off buildings and utilizing child soldiers. Such brutalities have grown more ubiquitous, but they are not new. In 2008, Abu Hamzah assured supporters that the ISI "does not accept children who have not reached puberty as soldiers," which probably was little consolation to a fast-maturing eleven year old.[46] And jihadis have long abused homosexuals; in Afghanistan, Sayf al-Adl once described his method for determining whether a new recruit was a "sodomite," and therefore considered a security risk: "Take an egg and place it in his anal cavity. If it goes in all the way, he is a sodomite; if it does not, he is good."[47] Al-Adl might not have advocated murder as punishment, but judging by the extraordinary fear he engendered in his prisoners, he would not have shied from torture.

The Islamic State released a video of American journalist James Foley being beheaded on August 14, 2014. It was calculated, brutal, and in substance little different from dozens of decapitations the group committed previously. Many followed Zarqawi's script for beheading the American businessman Nicholas Berg in 2004. Like Berg, more recent Islamic State victims are often shown wearing orange jumpsuits reminiscent of Guantanamo Bay uniforms and being prompted to denounce the West before being killed. Foley's murder followed this well-trod script, but his killing was particularly impactful. It came shortly after the establishment of the "caliphate" and President Obama's declaration that the United States would begin targeted airstrikes against the Islamic State. Moreover, video of Foley's murder was just a click away on social media, and it seemed to encapsulate the emerging confrontation between the world's only superpower and world's most important jihadi group.

"ISIS speaks for no religion," Obama charged the day that video of Foley's killing went public. "Their victims are overwhelmingly Muslim, and no faith teaches people to massacre innocents. . . . ISIS has no ideology of any value to human beings. Their ideology is bankrupt."[48]

Obama's condemnation was unlikely to dissuade Islamic State support-ers, though he was correct that the Islamic State's ideology and brutality are anathema to most people, including Muslims. Concern that Zarqawi's excessive violence would discredit al-Qaeda prompted Zawahiri to call on Zarqawi to stop his decapitation campaign in 2005. More recently, the world's most prominent Muslim theologians denounced the group, and polls in Muslim majority countries reveal the Islamic State is widely de-spised. Even most jihadi scholars reject the Islamic State.[49]

But the Islamic State's ideology is not quite as bankrupt as Obama im-plied because the group does not intend to appeal to Muslims broadly. The Islamic State, like its godfather Zarqawi, endeavors to sort "true Muslims" from "apostates" rather than win over all Muslims. In 2015, an Islamic State fighter channeled Zarqawi's *gharib* (stranger) ethos when he explained: "[W]hen I sit and think about [the Muslims] who hate us . . . it brings tears to my eyes. . . . But I always find comfort in that through Islamic history those who were on truth were hated."[50]

This was Zarqawiism in a nutshell. The Islamic State claims authority over all Muslims, but it defines that community much more narrowly than most people, including President Obama or al-Qaeda. The Islamic State softened its stance on laypeople that do not abide its vision of Islam, but it still wants to kill as apostates many of the same people that al-Qaeda con-siders lapsed Muslims who should be reformed and recruited. A "softer" Islamic State remains extremely hardline.

It is a mistake, however, to imagine that the Islamic State only appeals to recruits through violence. Despite the Islamic State's brutality, much of its messaging focuses on positive themes of governance, justice, and belong-ing. A comprehensive analysis by the Quilliam Foundation, a British anti-extremist think tank, identified five other major themes:

- Mercy toward captured people;
- Victimhood of Muslims at the hands of the West or apostates;
- Embrace of war as a defining feature of the Islamic State;
- The sense of belonging found by Islamic State recruits;
- The utopianism of the Islamic State's project to build a society based on divine law.[51]

These themes are less likely to make the evening news in the West, but they are critical to the Islamic State's communication strategy—which aims to portray both brutality and a positive, utopian vision. Recruits join the Islamic State believing they can make the world a better place. Bruce Hoffman famously noted that terrorists see themselves as altruists. The Islamic State is no different.[52]

The Islamic State can combine these messages because its propaganda machine is extremely prolific. At its peak, the Islamic State released three videos a day, along with fifteen photographic reports and numerous radio bulletins in multiple languages.[53] These reports are produced across the group's *wilayat*, though the majority focus on Iraq and Syria.[54] The production of this propaganda is highly organized. The Islamic State has several centralized media production and distribution units and specialized teams working for its regional commands.[55] Media officials are paid better than fighters, and videographers receive daily assignments from superiors who control production and editing.[56]

The content of the Islamic State's propaganda is much like its predecessors', but it has drawn far more attention from the global media. Political and media professionals sort media into "paid media" (advertisements), "owned media" (content on a blog or website), and "earned media" (engagement through third-party outlets and events the media deems worthy of covering on their own).[57] Political campaigns often try to generate advertisements ("paid media") so compelling that they become earned media, garnering free replay by news broadcasters. With a combination of slick video production, brutality (some of it directed at journalists), and accessibility, the Islamic State plays the same game.

Accessibility is critical. Most Islamic State propaganda is produced in Arabic, but English-language content tends to get far more attention in the international press—and it should be thought of as an effort to generate earned media. In other words, it is often constructed so that journalists will cover the content and amplify the Islamic State's message.[58] For the Islamic State, this also means making propaganda easier to access. As digital advertisers have long known, small differences matter to maximize content accessibility online.[59] Since 2005, jihadi propaganda has never been more than a few clicks away on a jihadi web forum, but there is a dramatic difference between placing Arabic-language propaganda on a dedicated jihadi website and English-language propaganda on a general-use platform like Twitter. Jihadis now have near-universal access to the journalists they hope will amplify their message.

The Islamic State's ideology has encouraged its embrace of social media, but the process did not happen overnight. After all, JaN rejected YouTube in 2012 after someone (probably the Syrian regime) falsely claimed an attack in its name.[60] But after its estrangement from JaN and al-Qaeda, the Islamic State has proved more sanguine about the disorder of social media. While JaN and al-Qaeda hoped to control the news cycle with carefully crafted propaganda, the Islamic State recognized that in a digital world, the only constant was change and "control" was a chimera.

Message content matters as well. Both JaN and al-Qaeda have much more nuanced political positions than the Islamic State, which incentivizes message discipline and control. In contrast, the Islamic State takes very blunt positions and embraces brutality so extreme that it is hard to imagine a false-flag attack that would discredit the group any more than the actions it claims directly.

Indeed, the Islamic State has blitzed key social media outlets. A comprehensive study of the Islamic State's Twitter operation in 2014 estimated the group controlled 46,000 accounts, most of which were computer-controlled "bots" that simply amplified the reach of existing content.[61] In February 2016, Twitter announced that since mid-2015 it had suspended more than 125,000 accounts for supporting terrorism, most of them "related to ISIS."[62]

The Islamic State's digital propaganda gets a lot of attention, but the link between propaganda and recruitment is complex. Recruitment is not a simple process of exposure to radical images or messages online. Indeed, a 2014 study found that only 13 percent of German jihadis were radicalized solely online, though a study of thirty-two plots associated with the Islamic State showed that the Internet played a radicalizing role in almost half (fifteen cases).[63] The continued importance of human networks probably explains why radicalization patterns vary so much from country to country. In the United States, approximately 250 people attempted to join the Islamic State by the end of 2015, fewer than half the number from Belgium, which has a fraction of the population.[64] Moreover, even with the vast reach of its propaganda on social media, the majority of Islamic State recruits have come from the Middle East or North Africa, including 2,500 from Jordan and as many as 3,000 from Tunisia.[65] By late 2015, more than 30,000 people had traveled to Syria or Iraq to join the Islamic State.[66]

Studying these fighters is difficult for a range of reasons, but initial reports suggest that motivations vary significantly. A study of forty-nine fighters in Syria showed that Western recruits tended to be "identity seekers" looking for "the structure, rules, and perspective that come from belonging to a group."[67] Fighters from Muslim majority countries, on the other hand, tended to be "thrill seekers" looking to complete "an arduous task . . . [survive] a harrowing adventure . . . [or] engage in action while enjoying a certain level of impunity."[68] As a Belgian Islamic State recruit put it, "Every person has his own reason. . . . For example, one might not feel at home anymore in his home country. The other one might have a criminal life and he's being harassed 24/7. The other one might have family over there."[69] These varied motivations make it hard to draw broad conclusions about recruitment processes.

The jihadis themselves understand that radicalization is highly individualized. In 2009, a jihadi theorist calling himself Abu 'Amr al-Qaedi published a handbook titled *A Course in the Art of Recruitment,* which focused on methods for recruiting jihadis in countries with strong law enforcement and intelligence services.[70] The book describes a five-stage process premised on building a tight personal relationship with a recruit—who is often selected for his or her lack of religious knowledge. *A Course in the Art of Recruitment* urges recruiters to avoid religious recruits because they have existing notions about Islam, whereas jihadis hope to define "Islam" singularly as militant activism.

Interestingly, the methods described in *A Course in the Art of Recruitment* are transferable to social media platforms that allow direct one-on-one interaction. For example, the book emphasizes sending birthday cards, encouraging a recruit to read selected religious texts, demanding recruits reject mainstream Muslim organizations, and slowly building a community around the notion of violent jihad.[71] *A Course in the Art of Recruitment* does not emphasize high-quality propaganda, though plenty of that content existed in 2009 when it was written. Instead, it argues that a recruiter should watch propaganda with a recruit in order to build a human connection. Propaganda is not expected to radicalize people on their own. The Islamic State has recruited so many people that there are clearly various methods at play, but for many of the jihadi-curious, publicly available propaganda is probably not as important as personal relationships built offline or on private messaging services.

The Islamic State's recruitment efforts are aided as well by its natural colloquialism in multiple languages and its diverse stable of members. The archetypal Islamic State communicator was Anwar al-Awlaki, the American-born imam of Yemeni descent who worked with al-Qaeda's affiliate in Yemen.[72] Mixing colloquial English, religious expertise, and his personal story of radicalization in the United States (the ostensibly devout preacher failed to mention that he left the United States after the FBI stumbled on his prostitution habit), Awlaki encouraged young English-speaking Muslims to join the jihad. With another American al-Qaeda member, he also founded and managed al-Qaeda in the Arabian Peninsula's (AQAP) English-language magazine, *Inspire*.

The United States killed Awlaki with a drone-fired Hellfire missile in September 2011, but his legacy includes several terrorist plots and a dramatic increase in Western al-Qaeda recruits. He has even had a hand in Islamic State violence. Years after his death, Awlaki's words inspired Assadthelion to join the Islamic State. Likewise, a couple that claimed allegiance to the Islamic State while killing fourteen people in San Bernardino, California, in December 2015 was allegedly drawn to violence by Awlaki years before the Islamic State was declared.[73]

The Islamic State's seminal English-language magazine, *Dabiq*, is an effort to replicate *Inspire*'s success. Named for a town in Northern Syria where the Islamic State believes the final apocalyptic battle between good and evil will occur, *Dabiq* borrows heavily from *Inspire*'s editorial and visual style. Its glossy pictures, compelling graphics, and varied articles make for easy page-turning. *Dabiq*, however, is even more an official organ of the Islamic State than *Inspire* was for al-Qaeda. *Inspire* was a niche publication tailored to promote militancy to a Western audience; *Dabiq* is a core tool for all sorts of Islamic State communications.

The difference is subtle but important. Students of a foreign language often say that they have gained fluency when they stop translating in their heads and start to dream in the new language. With the exception of Awlaki, al-Qaeda has always translated from Arabic in its head; the Islamic State dreams in several languages, including English.[74]

The Islamic State's battlefield success and familiarity with English have helped *Dabiq* capture much of *Inspire*'s market share—and that has been reflected in the changing patterns of Western terrorism. In 2009, during Awlaki's heyday, there were just over forty jihadi-related investigations in the United States. That number declined to thirty-seven in 2010 and then, when Awlaki was killed, dropped to fewer than twenty in 2012 and 2013. But the numbers shot up after the Islamic State declared a caliphate and began to release *Dabiq*. In 2015 there were nearly sixty jihadi-related terrorism cases in the United States, the vast majority involving recruits trying to go to Syria.[75]

Not all jihadis arrive in Syria looking to join the Islamic State; some are agnostic about the organization they aim to join and simply want to fight the Assad regime. The Islamic State attracts many of these people with its open organizational culture, especially compared to JaN, its chief jihadi competitor. JaN collaborates better with other militant groups than the Islamic State, but, like al-Qaeda, it is deeply paranoid. As a result, JaN vigorously vets recruits, including requiring a recommendation letter from a trusted source.[76] The Islamic State, despite its antipathy to other militant groups, embraces individual recruits. As Peter Neumann, Director of the International Center for the Study of Radicalisation, put it, "If you're a Muslim, you're already part of the Caliphate. So even if you're too fat, or too old to be a fighter, we'll find something else for you to do. You have a right to emigrate."[77]

Of course, it is easy to overstate the rush of foreign fighters to the Islamic State. Although Syria and Iraq have attracted an unprecedented number of foreign fighters, that remains a tiny fraction of the world's Muslim population. There are 1.6 billion Muslims in the world; about 30,000 have joined the Islamic State. Indeed, the Islamic State has far more Muslims who are running away from the Islamic State than are running to it. Nearly 10 million Syrians have been displaced from their homes and 4.7 million have fled the country.[78]

The Islamic State banks on its reputation as an emergent government, but by any normal standard, it has never been anything other than a failing state.

Despite these weaknesses, the Islamic State has been able to expand. It does this in two ways: by accumulating pledges of allegiance from other jihadi groups, and by capturing adjacent territory. It announced its first group of *wilayat* in November 2014—in Algeria, Libya, the Sinai Peninsula, Saudi Arabia, and Yemen—and has subsequently accepted pledges of allegiance from jihadis in Nigeria, Afghanistan, and the Caucasus. In mid 2016, it claimed thirty-five official *wilayat* and less formal relationships with even more jihadi groups. Most of these pledges come from disaffected factions of existing jihadi groups, including al-Qaeda affiliates in Algeria and Yemen, and breakaway Taliban factions along the Afghanistan-Pakistan border.

The Libyan and Sinai Islamic State *wilayat*—both operating in countries where longtime dictators were upended by Arab Spring protests—are particularly worrisome because of their extensive ties to the Islamic State's core group in Iraq and Syria. In the Sinai, the *wilayat* was built out of a preexisting jihadi group called Ansar Bayt al-Maqdis, which itself capitalized on networks from an old Zarqawi ally, the Abdallah Azzam Brigades. After swearing allegiance to the Islamic State, it progressed quickly from small-scale bombings to complex attacks on well-defended military and police installations.[79] The group has suffered setbacks from Egyptian security forces, but increasingly intends to conduct urban bombings in Cairo and cross-border attacks into the Israeli-controlled Gaza Strip.[80]

Northeastern Libya, meanwhile, has had an active jihadi movement since the 1980s and was one of the key sources of suicide bombers for AQI and the ISI during the U.S. occupation of Iraq.[81] Some of those jihadis mobilized as part of the popular uprising against Muammar Qaddafi in 2010 and rallied behind the Islamic State in the civil war that followed Qaddafi's collapse.

The *wilayat* in Libya is particularly worrisome because veterans of the fight in Syria arrived to administer the Libyan *wilayat* in early 2015. Shortly thereafter, the group publicly massacred groups of captured Christians and began public beheadings in the group's Libyan capital of Sirte.[82] Some reports even suggest that the Islamic State's former commander for all of Iraq arrived there in late 2015, which would indicate that Libya is central to the Islamic State's future plans. This sort of commitment to an "affiliate" is unprecedented for a jihadi group. It suggests that Islamic State leaders genuinely see Libya as an arena for governance like Iraq and Syria, and a launchpad for expansion across Africa.

The Islamic State's *wilayat* in Afghanistan is politically important even though it is operationally weaker than the Sinai and Libyan affiliates. The *wilayat* is led by a former member of the Pakistani Taliban who lost his bid to lead the network and subsequently defected to the Islamic State.[83] Establishing a foothold in South Asia was a direct challenge to Mullah Omar, longtime emir of the Afghan Taliban and, by extension, al-Qaeda, which had been pledged to Mullah Omar since before 9/11. Al-Qaeda renewed that pledge in July 2014 as part of its broader rebuttal to the Islamic State's declaration of a caliphate.[84] It was important for al-Qaeda not simply to reject Abu Bakr but to show that there were alternative leaders of the jihadi movement.

Unfortunately for al-Qaeda, it had pledged allegiance to a ghost. Mullah Omar died of natural causes in early 2013, but the Taliban maintained an elaborate ruse that he was still alive, complete with statements in his name.[85] Al-Qaeda was not informed. The inevitable reckoning came in the summer of 2015 when the Taliban ruefully acknowledged that Mullah Omar had been dead for years. Al-Qaeda found itself committed to a dead man.[86]

Mullah Omar's death capped a distinctive era in the modern history of jihadi movements. As the Taliban's leader, he governed what many jihadis in the 1990s considered to be the only true Islamic State. And he sheltered not only al-Qaeda but numerous other jihadi groups pursuing revolution around the globe. But Mullah Omar and the Taliban always had critics, and some of them were deeply influential on the evolution of Zarqawiism, which has become the defining ethos of the Islamic State.

The Taliban's jihadi critics in Afghanistan were diverse, but many concentrated at the Khalden training camp near Jalalabad. These fighters disavowed Afghan cultural practices and tolerance of diversity in Islamic thought. One of the most prominent of these thinkers was Abu Abdallah al-Muhajir, who was deeply influential on Zarqawi and was invited to teach at his camp in Herat. It was al-Muhajir who eventually defined Zarqawi's embrace of violence, and fostered his willingness to use it against other Muslims. Although al-Muhajir and Zarqawi were both compelled to fall in line behind Mullah Omar after 9/11, his death would have pleased them both, primarily because Abu Bakr now claimed to lead a polity that would have made them much happier than the Taliban did.

On a global level, the Islamic State has been able to swipe aside al-Qaeda's moral and institutional authority within the jihadi movement. On a local level, however, the Islamic State still has not mastered governance and tribal politics. Militarily, it is vastly over-extended. So even as the caliphate was "expanding" in 2015, it found that "remaining" in Syria and Iraq was getting more and more difficult.

The Forces of Faith and the Forces of Atheism

The Islamic State's headlong rush down the Tigris River valley after capturing Mosul in 2014 never allowed it to defend stable borders. The Islamic State overreached militarily, and its battlefield successes subsequently began to unwind. Iranian-backed militias reinforced the Iraqi army; Russia inserted troops in Syria to bolster the Assad regime; Turkey eventually began to better control its border with Syria; the United States escalated a bombing campaign, trained Kurdish, Iraqi, and Syrian forces, and even began occasional Special Operations raids against Islamic State targets. The silver lining for the Islamic State was that these parties were deeply divided themselves, but this was ultimately little solace. The jihadi group was powerful by the standards of a terrorist group, but it was no match militarily for the forces arrayed against it. By early 2016, the Islamic State still controlled a vast territory, but it was steadily shrinking.

The divided anti-Islamic State coalition did not prevent the state from suffering territorial losses, but it did threaten decisive strategic blows against the group. In Syria, Assad and his backers in Tehran and Moscow aimed to fight the Islamic State, but focused most of their energy on rebels more immediately threatening to the regime. Likewise, other rebel groups eventually learned that the Islamic State would target them as apostates, but the groups still prioritized the fight against Assad until they had no other choice. The rebels' backers in Saudi Arabia, Qatar, and Turkey made a similar calculation, at least until late 2015, giving lip service to the fight against the Islamic State but putting most of their energy into undermining the Assad regime and, in Turkey's case, making sure that Syrian Kurdish rebels do not grow too strong.

In Iraq, the problems were similar. The central government focused on defeating the Islamic State, but the army was ineffective when unsupported by U.S. firepower. The most capable fighters in Iraq are Iranian-backed militias that only a few years ago were actively killing Americans. Iraq's Kurdish parties, which have ruled an autonomous region in Iraq since 1990, fight the Islamic State, but their primary focus is defending borders that both Baghdad and Ankara reject. Some of the Kurdish groups even collaborate with the Kurdistan Workers Party (PKK), which the United States has designated a Foreign Terrorist Organization and is responsible for killing hundreds of Turkish civilians in recent decades.

The Islamic State is vastly outgunned and vulnerable to military pressure. By the end of 2015, it had lost approximately 30 percent of the territory it controlled a year earlier. That trend will continue. Yet, the offensive against the Islamic State moves slowly because of the fractured coalition facing off against it. The master plan prophesied that during the Stage of Absolute Confrontation, The Caliphate would fight a global coalition of "atheists." In reality, the cracks in that coalition are the biggest reason for the Islamic State's success.

Stages Six and Seven of the master plan are deeply connected. The former focuses on the political conflict between the forces of "faith" and those of "atheism"; the latter describes the military conflict, most importantly a campaign of "real terrorism," that "will horrify the enemy and force them to think very hard about whether to attack Muslims or attempt to violate their rights."[87]

In September 2014, the Islamic State's spokesman, Abu Muhammad al-Adnani, called for Muslims around the world—including in the West—to commit terrorist attacks. "If you cannot find an IED or a gun, then find a disbelieving American, Frenchman, or one of their allies," al-Adnani urged.

"Smash his head with a rock, or slaughter him with a knife, or hit him with a car, or throw him from some high place, or choke him, or poison him." It was the most forceful call for terrorism against the West by the Islamic State or any of its predecessors—and it signaled clearly that the Islamic State was not just building a proto-state, it was in the global terrorism business as well.[88]

Al-Adnani was concerned that some supporters would be loath to kill without a ruling from a religious scholar blessing their target, so he reminded followers of Zarqawiism's core teaching on targeting. Rejecting most just-war theory and jihadi thinking, al-Adnani argued that instead of trying to identify who was a legitimate target, jihadis should assume that everyone is a target, and instead endeavor to avoid killing the narrow classes of people that were exceptions. Echoing Zarqawi in 2005, al-Adnani explained that "the only thing that makes blood illegal to spill is Islam or a covenant. Blood becomes legal to spill through disbelief."[89]

Al-Adnani's threat was particularly worrisome across the Middle East, North Africa, and in Europe, which had seen thousands of young Muslim men (and some women) journey to Syria and Iraq to fight. The concern was that some of them would use their Western passports or increasingly large refugee flows out of Syria to enter Europe and kill. Concern about this so-called "bleedout" predated the Syrian civil war; European security services had similar fears about the war in Iraq. But far fewer Western Muslims journeyed to Iraq, and the vast majority of foreign fighters then were used as suicide bombers or were killed relatively quickly.

In 2007, Abu Muhjan al-Masri filled out an intake form when he joined the ISI, but the group failed to identify that his computer skills, Italian passport, and ties to criminal networks in Europe might make him more useful there.[90] Eight years later, a fighter named Reda Hame filled out a very similar intake form, but Islamic State representatives quickly identified that his computer skills and French passport made him more useful outside of Syria than in it.[91] Unlike Abu Muhjan al-Masri, when Hame arrived he was referred to a specialized organization focused on international terrorism.

The increased threat to Europe was a function of three new developments. First, the vast increase in foreign fighter numbers. Second, the Islamic State prioritized foreign terrorism more so than its predecessor the

ISI. Third, in 2015 the Islamic State controlled a vast safe haven that allowed the operational space to identify operatives like Hame; in 2007, the ISI was much more embattled, and its leaders were often focused narrowly on survival, not strategy.

Even before al-Adnani's September 2014 declaration of war on the West, Islamic State–inspired fighters were killing in Europe. In May 2014, a French jihadi walked into the Jewish Museum in Brussels and killed four people with an AK-47. He had previously been an ISIS jailer in Syria; one former prisoner later remembered him bragging about raping a woman and beheading her baby.[92]

Larger, more sophisticated plots were in the works as well. On January 7, 2015, two attackers shot up the Paris office of a French satirical magazine, *Charlie Hebdo*, whose editor was included on a 2013 hit list by AQAP.[93] A third terrorist took hostages at a Kosher grocery two days later, killing four.[94] Two of the attackers had trained in Yemen with AQAP years earlier; one claimed allegiance to the Islamic State. For all the fighting between the Islamic State and al-Qaeda, the groups' foot soldiers were joining forces in the West to kill.

It was a disrupted attack, however, that truly marked the beginning of organized Islamic State terrorism against the West. On January 15, 2015, Belgian police raided a house in the town of Verviers, killing two men and taking another into custody. Inside, they found automatic weapons, chemical precursors for a powerful explosive called TATP, and police uniforms that suggested the group intended to infiltrate an official site.[95] All three men had fought with the Islamic State in Syria. Most worryingly, they remained in contact with an Islamic State operative named Abdelhamid Abaaoud.

Abaaoud was a miniature Zarqawi, raised in Belgium. A third-generation Belgian from a family of Moroccan immigrants, Abaaoud slipped into a life of petty crime as an adolescent. He was admitted to a prestigious Catholic school but ultimately expelled for behavioral issues. After several years in and out of prison, Abaaoud's life of criminal insignificance changed dramatically in 2012. He became one of dozens of young Belgians—many with similar criminal histories—to join the fight in Syria. He fell in with the Islamic State and was selected by al-Adnani to manage a network of jihadis preparing attacks in Europe.[96]

Abaaoud was particularly proud of his ability to sneak across borders. In 2013, he returned to Belgium to entice his thirteen-year-old brother to Syria, and then came back a year later to direct the Verviers cell.[97] Although the Verviers cell was disrupted, Abaaoud escaped, and the escapade revealed that the Islamic State was not simply calling for lone-wolf terrorism in the West; it was actively directing plots.[98]

Back in Syria, Abaaoud reported to al-Adnani, who led the Islamic State's external operations wing.[99] "Paris before Rome and before Al Andalus [Spain]," al-Adnani explained in March 2015, "after which we will . . . destroy your White House, Big Ben, and the Eiffel tower." But that was just the beginning. "We want Kabul, Karachi, Chechnya, Qom, Riyadh, and Tehran. We want Baghdad, Damascus, Jerusalem, Cairo, Sanaa, Doha, Abu Dhabi, and Amman. Muslims will reclaim sovereignty and lead everywhere."[100] But al-Adnani was not actually speaking for Muslims across the globe; he was declaring war on them. The Islamic State aimed to govern Muslim societies globally, and it aimed to fight both Western powers and Muslim-majority countries in order to do so.

The Islamic State's intent to strike the West was plain after the Verviers raid, but its reason for doing so was less obvious. On the one hand, the Islamic State champions the prophecy of an apocalyptic battle near the Syrian town of Dabiq; some analysts concluded its attacks in the West intended to lure the West into deeper involvement in the Syrian war. When the Islamic State executed American Peter Kassig, his murderer declared, "Here we are, burying the first American crusader in Dabiq, eagerly awaiting the rest of your armies." Indeed, every edition of the Islamic State's English-language magazine begins with a quote from Zarqawi alluding to the apocalyptic prophecy: "The spark has been lit here in Iraq, and its heat will continue to intensify—by Allah's permission—until it burns the crusader armies in Dabiq."[101]

On the other hand, Islamic State leaders must be aware that the United States and Europe outclass them militarily; they experienced it firsthand during the Surge in Iraq. Likewise, they have almost certainly read Abu Mus'ab al-Suri's history of jihad in Syria, which advocated "military deterrence capabilities on the outside" of Syria in any future uprising.[102] The Islamic State's predecessors have been interested in territorial control since Fallujah in 2004; to essentialize them as primarily interested in the apocalypse ignores the group's history and investment in administration and bureaucracy. In this reading, the Islamic State's attacks in Europe aim to deter Western countries from fighting in Syria and Iraq. Deterrence was certainly why the master plan urged "real terrorism." The master plan reasoned that major strikes would "terrify the enemy and make them think a thousand times before attacking Muslims."[103]

Al-Adnani laughed at Western efforts to parse the Islamic State's intentions. "You have realized the threat of the Islamic State, but you have not become aware of the cure," he taunted in September 2014. "If you fight it, it becomes stronger and tougher. If you leave it alone, it grows and expands."[104]

As 2015 wore on, however, virtually no one was leaving the Islamic State alone. Iraqi forces, backed by U.S. airstrikes, recaptured several cities, including Ramadi, a city of 800,000 people that serves as the capital of Anbar Province. Kurdish forces cut key Islamic State supply lines, and the Russian air force began operations to bolster the Syrian government. By June 2016, Iraqi troops and their militia allies were fighting their way into Fallujah, one of the most symbolically important cities controlled by the "caliphate."

All of these efforts weakened the Islamic State, and prompted President Obama to tout the success of his policy. "Our goal has been first to contain, and we have contained them," he said on November 12, 2015. "They have not gained ground in Iraq. And in Syria, they'll come in, they'll leave."[105] This statement was accurate, but its scope was limited. Obama was talking about the Islamic State's posture on the ground in Iraq and Syria, not its growing strength in North Africa or its external operations.

But defining and characterizing progress against a hybrid entity like the Islamic State is perilous.

Even as Obama spoke, the Islamic State was in the midst of a terrorist campaign against the breadth of its enemies. On October 31, 2015, a chartered Russian jet that had taken off from the Egyptian resort town of Sharm el-Sheikh exploded in midair over the Sinai Peninsula. Two hundred twenty-four people were killed. Western intelligence agencies, citing intercepted Islamic State communications, concluded that the plane had been bombed, a finding Russia confirmed a week later.[106] According to the Islamic State, it had planned to smuggle a bomb onto a Western airliner in

Sharm el-Sheikh, but chose a Russian plane instead after Russian troops entered Syria on behalf of the Assad regime.[107]

Two weeks after the Sinai attack, two bombs exploded in a Shia neighborhood of Beirut. Forty-three people were killed.[108] The Islamic State and its predecessors had always considered Lebanon a part of Greater Syria and a gateway to Israel. Moreover, the neighborhood was a stronghold of Lebanese Hizballah, the Iranian-backed Shia militant movement that had fighters in Syria supporting the Assad regime. The Islamic State hated Hizballah's monopoly on access to Israel's northern border and hoped to provoke sectarian conflict in Lebanon, as it had done years earlier in Iraq.

However, the Islamic State was not done.

Abaaoud returned to Syria after the Verviers cell was disrupted, but he did not stay long. Over the next few months, he was linked to at least three jihadi plots in France, including one that was disrupted when young Americans subdued the attacker on a high-speed train.[109] In July 2015 Abaaoud was convicted in absentia in Belgium for his role in the Verviers cell and sentenced to twenty years in prison. Despite his growing notoriety, Abaaoud returned to Europe in 2015, where he transited Budapest and infiltrated the United Kingdom via ferry because there was less security at ports than airports or train stations.[110] For reasons not totally clear, Abaaoud met with contacts in London and Birmingham and took pictures of London landmarks.[111] He certainly seemed to be planning something.

Despite the interlude in the UK, Abaaoud decided to spend the autumn in Paris. On the evening of November 13, 2015, a day after Obama called the Islamic State "contained"—Abaaoud unleashed a scheme to turn the City of Lights into a battleground. Three teams of attackers struck almost simultaneously.[112] The first explosion was a suicide bombing near the Stade de France, where a soccer game was underway in front of a jammed stadium, after which shooters in a black SEAT car raked restaurant-goers with automatic weapons fire. Two more suicide attacks followed at the Stade de France; then at the Bataclan concert hall, attackers fired into the crowd at a rock concert. A French SWAT team eventually raided the Bataclan, but not before three attackers detonated explosive vests. By night's end, 130 people were mortally wounded.[113]

Abaaoud, the attackers' ringleader, lingered near the Bataclan during the attack but raced away in the black SEAT, no doubt hoping to kill again.[114] He was holed up with two compatriots in Saint Denis, just north of Paris, when French law enforcement found him. Five days after the Paris massacre, police raided the apartment, killing all three.[115]

The Islamic State claimed responsibility for Paris a day after the attack, giving a disturbingly accurate account of events. In January 2016, it released a video profiling seven of the Paris attackers, and showing them executing captives during their time in Syria.[116] Most worryingly, the Islamic State also threatened follow-up attacks.

Salah Abdeslam, an old friend and partner-in-crime of Abaaoud, fled Paris during the attack and eventually returned to Belgium.[117] After a massive search, he was captured in Brussels after a shootout with police.[118] What happened next revealed just how large Abaaoud and al-Adnani's European terrorist network had grown. Frightened that Abdeslam's arrest might doom their own plot, another terror cell in Brussels set off suicide bombs in the metro and at the airport, killing thirty-two people. The interconnected plots revealed a jihadi network of unprecedented scope inside Europe. The attacks would not be the Islamic State's last.

The Islamic State's European terrorism campaign in late 2015 and early 2016 has not clarified the group's broader strategic intent. On the one hand, the attack on the Russian Metrojet seemed to reflect a desire for revenge and an instinct for deterrence. Al-Suri would have approved of striking a hostile foreign power intervening against the group in Syria. The bombings in Beirut suggest a motive of sectarian hatred and intent to approach Israel. The coordinated strike in Paris was perhaps an effort at deterrence, but if so, it failed. France responded by increasing its military operations against the Islamic State in Syria. Perhaps the attacks were meant to draw France into the fight?

The unifying strategic theme, if there is one, is the continuation of Zarqawi's old strategy of polarization. The Islamic State claims a global scope, so it aims to foster a global confrontation to force Muslims the world over to reveal whether they are "true Muslims" or apostates deserving death. Such attacks also bolster the Islamic State's inflated sense of global importance, which is particularly important for recruitment as the group loses territory.

The Islamic State's terrorist campaign in the West also owes much to Anwar al-Awlaki, the AQAP propagandist that modernized jihadi propaganda to engage Western Muslims. Although Awlaki eschewed Zarqawi's brutality toward other Muslims, he hoped to inspire a backlash against Western Muslims that would compel them to radicalize. In a March 2010 recording, "A Message to the American People," he declared:

> Muslims of the West, take heed and learn from the lessons of history: There are ominous clouds gathering on your horizon. Yesterday America was a land of slavery, segregation, lynching and Ku Klux Klan and tomorrow it will be a land of religious discrimination and concentration camps. Don't be deceived by the promises of preserving your rights from a government that is right now killing your own brothers and sisters. Today, with the war between Muslims and the West escalating, you cannot count on the message of solidarity you may get from a civic group or a political party, or the word of support you hear from a kind neighbor or a nice co-worker. The West will eventually turn against its Muslim citizens![119]

Years later, the Islamic State picked up on Awlaki's theme, which was a version of the polarization strategy Zarqawi had employed in Iraq. "Muslims in the crusader countries will find themselves driven to abandon their homes for a place to live in the Khilāfah," declared the Islamic State in *Dabiq*, "as the crusaders increase persecution against Muslims living in Western lands so as to force them into a tolerable sect of apostasy in the name of 'Islam' before forcing them into blatant Christianity and democracy."[120]

The Islamic State's proposed solution was simple.

> Let every . . . muwahhid barred from hijrah [emigration to the Islamic State] purify himself of the branches of lesser hypocrisy that hold him back from performing jihād in his location. Let him record his will, renew his bay'ah, carry the Khilāfah banner, and strike the crusaders and their pagan and apostate allies wherever he can find them, even if he is alone.[121]

Al-Adnani taunted Westerners trying to discern whether the group chose terrorism to bait the West into invading Syria or to deter it from attacking. But there is a simpler explanation. The Islamic State conducts terrorist attacks globally because its leaders genuinely believe that they have global authority. And they genuinely aim to radicalize Muslims from Damascus to Detroit. They may not be motivated by the apocalypse, but they certainly want a Manichean showdown with what the master plan calls the "forces of atheism." The Islamic State conducts terrorist attacks globally because its fundamental purpose is global war. If it does not operationalize that identity, its reason-for-being evaporates.

There are numerous ironies in this approach. The master plan envisioned rallying 1.5 billion Muslims behind the new caliphate, but the Islamic State believes that many, perhaps most, of those people are apostates that deserve death. It is the Islamic State's most basic diversion from the master plan's core vision. Indeed, the Islamic State wages war on the West and on Muslims with the same intensity. It is a point Western politicians should remember before calling for discrimination against Muslims; in doing so, those would-be statesmen condemn the very people that the Islamic State hates, and fears, the most.

Caliph vs. Emir

The Islamic State's terrorism was not limited to Egypt, Lebanon, and France. In Saudi Arabia, Islamic State supporters bombed Shia mosques in an effort to inflame sectarian tensions, and new Islamic State recruits murdered family members that worked for the security services.[122] When Turkey, after ignoring the Islamic State's logistics on its territory for years, finally cracked down on Islamic State networks, the Islamic State struck at political rallies and tourist sites.[123] In the United States, jihadis once inspired by Awlaki swore allegiance to Abu Bakr during the attack in San Bernardino, California, that killed fourteen people.[124] In June 2016, an American citizen killed forty-nine people inside a gay nightclub in Orlando, Florida. During the attack, he pledged allegiance to Abu Bakr al-Baghdadi in a phone call to police and on his Facebook profile. In Bangladesh, militants assassinated liberal bloggers, massacred restaurant-goers, and credited the Islamic State.[125] In July, Islamic State supporters attacked the Istanbul airport and Nice, France, killing dozens. The Islamic State's campaign of terrorism was broader, and more deadly, than anything al-Qaeda had mounted since 9/11.

The Islamic State's rise frightened even old-line jihadis. After the Islamic State immolated Jordanian pilot Muath al-Kasasbeh in February 2015, Zarqawi's onetime mentor Abu Muhammad al-Maqdisi lamented his inability to negotiate for Kasasbeh's life. "They claim that slaughter is a prophetic norm," he later complained. "They understand conquest and victories only through slaughter."[126]

The Islamic State showed no respect for a man widely considered the most influential living jihadi scholar.[127] In *Dabiq*, the Islamic State showed no restraint:

> They ask the Muslims to follow those "scholars" who abandoned jihad in an era where jihad is fard ayn [obligatory on every individual]. . . . Is it not the obligation to hate these "scholars"? . . . [T]hose who abandon jihād are akin to the fornicators, the sodomites, and the drunkards, and yet the claimants of Islam request the mujāhidīn to blindly follow these sinful "scholars," those who prefer to sit in the shades of the tawāghīt [unjust rulers] and crusaders rather than perform jihād against the kuffār [infidels and apostates].[128]

At his death, many analysts held that Zarqawi had been an effective military commander but was not a true jihadi ideologue. A decade later, however, Zarqawiism is alive and dominating the global jihadi movement.

Al-Qaeda is not dead, however. It continues to plot attacks on the United States, and its affiliates spar with Islamic State fighters in Syria, Yemen, North Africa, and South Asia. The Islamic State's fight against al-Qaeda has led to splits among jihadi groups in many of these places. In *Dabiq*, the Islamic State denounced groups that inhabit a "gray zone" by embracing militancy but withholding allegiance to the new "caliph."[129] That rhetoric has fractured several militant networks when second-tier leaders have used pledges of allegiance to Abu Bakr to promote personal aspirations.[130]

The division and animosity between these groups may seem like a boon for counterterrorism, but research suggests that competitive terrorist organizations may actually prove more deadly to their enemies as they try to "outbid" one another in increasingly deadly attacks.[131] The fight between the Islamic State and al-Qaeda inhibits their ability to operate smoothly, but it probably does not reduce the risk of terrorism.

Despite these divisions, al-Qaeda and the Islamic State have found ways to cooperate in certain areas; the barriers are high, but it is not inconceivable that they find ways to accommodate one another again. After all, al-Qaeda tried to avoid disavowing the Islamic State when it clashed with JaN, and repeatedly tried to repair the rift afterward. Moreover, even as the groups argued in 2013, Zawahiri offered to help free Islamic State prisoners held in Iran and Iraq, using an Iranian diplomat named Nour Ahmad Nikbakht as trade bait. Zawahiri asked Abu Bakr to "send us a list with the names of the imprisoned sisters, including Hasna, the widow of Sheikh Abu Hamzah al-Muhajir, God bless his soul . . . and the names of the brothers who have been sentenced to death in Iraq, so that we can include them in the negotiations."[132]

This offer preceded the Islamic State and al-Qaeda's final split in 2014, but Zawahiri's willingness to deploy some of al-Qaeda's limited leverage over Iran to help the Islamic State was striking nonetheless. Even more remarkable is that two years later—after the Islamic State's formal divorce from al-Qaeda—there was indeed an al-Qaeda prisoner swap with Iran that included operatives close to the Islamic State.

Sometime in the first half of 2015, Iran reportedly released five jihadi captives, among them Sari Shihab and Khalid al-Aruri, both friends of Zarqawi's, who had been imprisoned in Iran since 2002.[133]

The most important man to be reported discharged, however, was Sayf al-Adl, the primary designer of the master plan and the man who originally negotiated the union between Zarqawi and Osama bin Laden.[134] His present location is unknown, but if anyone can resolve the differences between Abu Bakr and Zawahiri, it is al-Adl.[135]

Al-Qaeda's propaganda has hinted at al-Adl's potential release. In August 2015 he belatedly released a eulogy for Abu Khaled al-Suri, al-Qaeda's representative in Syria whose assassination finalized the split between the Islamic State and al-Qaeda. The ironies were thick. Al-Adl fondly recalled Abu Khaled training young jihadis in Afghanistan prior to 9/11, but slyly made no mention of al-Qaeda's effort to pry Abu Khaled away from Abu Mus'ab al-Suri at the time.[136]

The same month, al-Zawahiri released a series of public statements that simultaneously declared the Islamic State's caliphate to be illegitimate and held out the possibility of working with the group.[137] He seemed to be holding open the possibility of eventual reconciliation.

Al-Adl surfaced publicly at an auspicious moment. Much of the master plan he scribbled on yellow wax paper a decade earlier had come to pass. The Islamic State had declared a caliphate precisely on the timeline he sketched, and the Stage of Absolute Confrontation was proceeding largely as he outlined. Perhaps most powerfully, al-Adl's strategic rationale for focusing on Syria to pursue the caliphate had been validated.

Some of the master plan's other predictions were also dramatically realized, most notably that the United Kingdom would reject "the rising unity of Europe." The so-called "Brexit" vote to leave the European Union actualized much of that prediction. On the other hand, key elements of al-Adl's master plan remained unfulfilled. Jihadis had not succeeded in forcefully attacking Israel and the United States had not suffered economic collapse.

Most importantly, however, the seven-stage master plan was conceived for an alliance between the Zarqawiists and al-Qaeda that had collapsed in recrimination and gunfire. Before his death, bin Laden disavowed major parts of the plan as well—arguing essentially that the tension between the United States and Syria that made the Assad regime vulnerable to jihadi attack did not imply that jihadis would be capable of building a sustainable Islamic State on its corpse.

The greatest failing of al-Adl's master plan is that it was designed for a jihadi coalition that no longer existed.

7

The Stage of Final Victory
(2018–2020)

The enormous potential of the Islamic state—particularly because the Muslim population will amount to more than 1.5 billion—will terrify the enemy. . . . Israel will not be able to withstand [it]. . . . The world will learn the meaning of real terrorism. . . . Such terrorism will terrify the enemy and make them think a thousand times before attacking Muslims.

Fuad Husayn, *Zarqawi . . . The Second Generation of al-Qaeda*

Another Step Back

Sayf al-Adl's master plan predicted the timing and location of the caliphate's declaration a decade ahead of time. No other analysis of jihadi behavior has ever been so prescient. Yet, it remains unclear whether the master plan was simply an accurate forecast or an actual blueprint that guided jihadi action.

Regardless, the master plan's prediction of a jihadi final victory by 2020 is doomed. Al-Adl's vision was designed for al-Qaeda's relatively flexible ideological outlook, which accepted ideological differences (at least among jihadis). Instead it was Zarqawi's inimically violent, exclusionary, and anti-intellectual offspring that fulfilled the master plan's vision for a resurrected caliphate. Zarqawiism enabled the Islamic State to overcome overwhelming obstacles to achieve tremendous territorial gains, but it will also prevent the organization from achieving its goal of global domination. A Zarqawi-ist organization will never inspire a broad enough coalition to achieve a goal that ambitious.

That failure does not mean the Islamic State will be defeated or will cease to be a significant threat. To the contrary, the same elements of the Islamic State's ideology that limit its broad appeal will help it remain resilient. The Islamic State is likely to suffer dramatic territorial setbacks in the coming years, but it will maintain a potent ability to conduct terrorist attacks—and is likely to regenerate if conditions allow. The Islamic State is moving into its second decade since being declared in 2006. It was almost defeated in 2010, but it "remained." And despite the very real setbacks the Islamic State faces on the ground in Iraq and Syria, it will continue to do so.

The anti-Islamic State coalition must not assume that dramatic territo-rial and personnel losses mean the Islamic State is "defeated." The United States made this mistake once before—after the successes of the Surge and Awakening—but the Islamic State of Iraq proved capable of surviving, and regenerating. The fight against the Islamic State has been ongoing for more than a decade and it will take another decade, at least, to truly defeat the group. Some will argue that the Islamic State's declaration of a caliph-ate means its ideological appeal will dissipate if it loses territory. Do not believe it. If the past is prologue—and it usually is—the Islamic State will lose recruits as its battlefield position declines, but it will remain capable of unleashing terrorist attacks and continue to attract enough diehard sup-porters to be a terrible danger. The ISI was one of the world's most deadly terrorist groups even *after* the Surge and Awakening. Western leaders must be wary not to declare another premature, and pyrrhic, victory.

Whatever the Islamic State's fate, it has changed jihadism forever. By declaring The Caliphate resurrected today, it rejects both Western influence in the Islamic world and the incremental approach of most modern Is-lamist movements, including jihadis like al-Qaeda. The Islamic State rep-resents a younger, more absolute, and more populist generation of jihadi activism. This is partly a generational shift. If the previous jihadi cohort was united and catalyzed by the anti-Soviet jihad in Afghanistan—which Zarqawi barely touched—the Islamic State generation finds its spiritual and mythical center in Iraq and Syria.

The Islamic State's inability to achieve its goal of governing globally does not mean the United States and forces of civilization will achieve their own geopolitical goals. The fight against the Islamic State is a negative sum game. Even as it fails, the Islamic State will make the world much worse for everyone else. A core challenge for policymakers from Washington to Paris, Damascus, Baghdad, Riyadh, and Tehran is to actually define a collective positive vision for the Middle East. It is easy to denounce the Islamic State's dystopia, but the coalition arrayed against it has not offered a coherent alternative and is unlikely to do so.

In fact, the contradictions between U.S., Saudi, and Iranian conceptions of the future are lifeblood for the Islamic State. The Assad regime—which is responsible for more deaths than even the Islamic State—will never again dominate Syria as it once did, but it has survived the Syrian insurrection. The regime's persistence virtually offers the Islamic State a perfect grievance narrative that will help it remain politically viable even as it loses the ability to control territory. American policymakers often talk about winning the war of ideas, but real-world conditions will shape perceptions of the Islamic State more than any messaging campaign. To truly defeat the Islamic State it will require a positive, collective vision for the parts of the world where most Muslims live. Oppressive dictatorships may be able to suppress the Islamic State, but in a world of digital connection and vast access to weaponry, they will not defeat it entirely.

For the United States, the lack of a collective, positive, countervailing vision to the Islamic State is most evident in how far the goalposts have shifted, negatively, since al-Qaeda attacked two U.S. embassies in 1998. American policymakers then worried about how to defend U.S. interests from a covert terrorist group with fewer than 200 members. Today, al-Qaeda has franchises on three continents, and the Islamic State, even diminished, has rallied tens of thousands of recruits, simultaneously governed millions of people, attacked on five continents, and once legitimately controlled a territory the size of the United Kingdom. The ups and downs of the fight against the Islamic State should not obscure the fact that the scope of the fundamental problem has changed dramatically.

By its very nature, terrorism tends to be analyzed in terms of tactics. After attacks like the November 2015 strike in Paris or the Orlando shooting in June 2016, it is easy to overestimate the Islamic State's strength. After a successful raid on an al-Qaeda or Islamic State leader, it is easy to think that the forces of civilization are winning.

Step back a bit as President Obama did in November 2015 when he called the Islamic State "contained," and it is clear that the group is indeed generally on the defensive, especially in Iraq and Syria. The Islamic State is slowly losing territory and its ability to "govern" effectively. The Islamic State's ability to conduct terrorist attacks will persist even after it loses territory, but the territorial setbacks constitute major defeats nonetheless.

The problem is that if you step back just a bit more, and look at the jihadi movement as a whole since al-Qaeda declared war on the West in 1998, it is clear that the jihadis have made extraordinary gains. The Islamic State, even weakened, is more powerful than all of the jihadi groups in Afghanistan during the 1990s combined. The military campaign against the Islamic State is succeeding; the macro fight against the jihadi threat to civilization is not.

The growth of Zarqawiism is a key reason for the Islamic State's durability, and a central reason that the master plan's vision for a consolidated, globe-spanning caliphate will not come to pass. Combining the religious absolutism of Abu Muhammad al-Maqdisi with the raw violence of Abu Abdallah al-Muhajir and the street-savvy anti-elitism of Zarqawi himself, Zarqawiism is insular, irrevocably violent, and deeply resilient.

Zarqawiism is revolutionary, but it is not new. Many scholars point to Maqdisi as Zarqawi's most important intellectual influence, but this is wrong. Although Zarqawi adopted Maqdisi's hard-line stance against the religious establishment in Saudi Arabia, the elements that make Zarqawiism unique—the anti-elitism, the redefinition of the "true Muslim" community in extraordinarily exclusive terms, and the embrace of unremitting violence against everyone else—were developed more fully after Zarqawi left Maqdisi and traveled to Afghanistan in 1999. Indeed, Zarqawi's rejection of religious scholars far from the battlefield was developed of his fight with the elder jihadi.

It is tempting to ascribe Zarqawiism primarily to Zarqawi's upbringing on the streets of Zarqa, and it is true that his anti-intellectualism and support for the redemptive power of violence draws on that history. But Zarqawi—and Zarqawiism—came of age in the last six years of the Jordanian's life, in Afghanistan and Iraq. He attributed key concepts to al-Muhajir, who led an important jihadi school in Afghanistan during the 1990s and taught at his camp in Herat. It was al-Muhajir's writing that was distributed in Fallujah in 2004 and his book that was the first book printed by the Islamic State. Likewise, Abu Anas al-Shami was Zarqawi's first true spiritual advisor in Iraq, and the man who in his persona defined what Zarqawiists came to expect in a spiritual leader.

In the end, Zarqawiism is fundamentally a wartime ethos that exalts battlefield logic over all else. During his life, Zarqawi and his followers aimed to build a "state" as well as an army, but by prioritizing the wisdom of militants, not statesmen or scholars, Zarqawiism is a shaky basis for long-term governance. The Islamic State has tried to reverse the most entropy-enhancing elements of Zarqawiism—specifically by refuting the notion that any fighter may excommunicate another over essentially any ideological dispute. But that congenital demon is in the Islamic State's DNA; it was championed for Zarqawi by al-Qaeda in Iraq's Shariah Emir in 2005.

Indeed, it is hard to imagine a true globe-spanning Zarqawiist caliphate because the ideology encourages disavowing so many Muslims as apostates. Whereas al-Qaeda generally agrees with the Pew Foundation (and most other people) that there are about 1.6 billion Muslims in the world, the Islamic State considers most of these people to be apostates, worthy of death. It effectively imagines a much smaller *Umma* (global community of Muslims).[1] In the Islamic State's view, most of the 1.6 billion people that Pew considers Muslims are effectively well-disguised impostors. Al-Qaeda disavows many of those people as well, but it has always been open to political alliances with groups with which it disagrees, and it embraces the idea of calling many of those "lapsed" Muslims to its version of Islam. The Islamic State simply aims to kill them as apostates.

This constraint dooms the master plan's logic for achieving final victory. When Sayf al-Adl conceptualized a united jihadi movement supporting a renewed caliphate, he imagined rallying "1.5 billion" Muslims to "terrify the enemy" and achieve final victory. Although the Islamic State has attracted tens of thousands of recruits, it fundamentally rejects the idea of attracting 1.5 billion Muslims. To the mind of a Zarqawiist, most of those 1.5 billion are targets, not allies.

The Islamic State's basic definition of its constituency is directly at odds with the master plan's final stage.

If a terrorist group declares a state but no one pays attention, is it real?

The Islamic State celebrated its tenth anniversary in June 2016, but most Americans—including policymakers—imagine it emerged first during the Syrian civil war, which began in 2011. The Islamic State's perspective is obviously self-serving, but policymakers in the West and the Middle East should take it seriously, lest they unnecessarily repeat mistakes from the past.

The Islamic State was born of the U.S. invasion of Iraq in 2003, and it was given a lifeline by the United States' incomplete war in Iraq and withdrawal in 2010. Although declared in October 2006, the Islamic State's earliest incarnation was largely, but not completely, suppressed by 2009. United States policymakers treated the Islamic State of Iraq solely like an insurgent organization, not a hybrid entity. The ISI was initially conceived as a proto-state, but it quickly began to operate as a robust terrorist organization—and it both survived and thrived on that basis.

After the success of the Awakening and Surge, American commanders and policymakers celebrated the ISI's inability to control territory. This was undoubtedly a triumph, but largely overlooked in that victory was the group's continued existence as a distinct, and very powerful, terrorist organization. At its nadir in 2009 and 2010, the ISI remained one of the deadliest terrorist groups in the world and conducted a careful campaign of assassination to destroy its enemies. For all its failures, the ISI executed a strategy designed to remain viable and regenerate.

There is a lesson in this history for contemporary policymakers: the destruction of the Islamic State's political institution will not necessarily destroy its ability to operate as a terrorist group. And, just as importantly, that terrorist organization will readily be able to reassert itself as a "state" when conditions allow. How do we know? Because the Islamic State has done it before—when the Syrian civil war broke out.

Of course, the Islamic State's reach today is much broader than the ISI's was in the first decade of the 21st century. It suggests both that the Islamic

State's campaign of terrorism going forward will be more severe and far more widespread than the ISI's, which was limited to Iraq. It also suggests that the range of locales where the Islamic State might resurrect governance activities is broader. Beyond Syria and Iraq, which will remain deeply unstable even if the Islamic State loses all of its territory, the most prominent option today is in North Africa, specifically in Libya.

In a nutshell, the current incarnation of the Islamic State emerged from the remnants of the Islamic State of Iraq, which was devastated by the Awakening and the Surge from 2007–2010. But it was not defeated, and it regenerated stronger than it had been previously. The United States and the rest of the Islamic State's enemies are in the process of "defeating" the jihadi group once again. The big, long-term question is whether they will finish the job this time and, if not, how strong the Islamic State will be when it regenerates?

Some argue that the Islamic State's embrace of former Iraqi Ba'athists means that its ideological core has shifted or that it is now inimically tied to Iraq's geography. This is a mistake. Iraqi members of the Islamic State rose to leadership because they were better trained than foreign fighters and more likely to survive. But they have embraced Zarqawiism just as the group's other members. Every Islamic State recruit was someone else before they embraced Zarqawiism, which exalts the redemptive power of violence. It does not matter to Zarqawiists who a recruit was previously, only that they embrace the ideology today—and prove that commitment by embracing brutal violence. Zarqawi's early Iraqi and Syrian recruits now direct bombings in Europe and have redeployed to North Africa to guide operations. However their radicalization proceeded, today they are jihadis.

The Islamic State will not achieve "final victory," so the United States should focus on building a positive vision of its own—and encouraging stakeholders to get on board. It is of course true that the United States cannot, and should not, unilaterally impose a vision on the Middle East, but it needs to articulate one. Polemicists like to argue that the Islamic State has no affirmative vision of the future, but this is not true. They have one; it is just violent, bloody, and intolerant. Instead, it is the various countries and militants fighting the Islamic State that do not have a collective coherent vision. Key members of the coalition—Saudi Arabia and Iran—see each other as primary geopolitical enemies. Many countries continue to see the Assad regime as a larger threat than jihadis. The Assad regime and its backers in Moscow and Tehran still prioritize crushing the Syrian opposition rather than the Islamic State. The United States has not articulated a clear vision other than opposing the Islamic State.

The Islamic State can be suppressed by a fractured coalition, but it will not be defeated by one. That is why the current fight against the Islamic State is not a recipe for victory; it is a recipe for perpetual, low-level war.

This war is likely to play out across much of the world, though it will differ from region to region. In the Islamic State's heartland of Syria and northwestern Iraq, the outcome may look something like the border between Afghanistan and Pakistan, a poorly governed region that has housed militant groups—most notably al-Qaeda—for decades. The open deserts of Syria and Iraq offer less topographical security than the mountains of Afghanistan and Pakistan, but Western countries are far more accessible from Syria and Iraq, and the political situation is just as dysfunctional.

The situation is similarly worrisome elsewhere in the world. From North Africa to Southeast Asia, Islamic State *wilayah* will persist as relatively small organizations united and empowered by digital connection with similar groups around the globe. In Libya, the various Islamic State factions face weak states and vast spaces that militant networks have utilized for centuries. A strengthened military campaign against the Islamic State there is likely to limit its ability to hold territory, but is unlikely to destroy the group. Egypt will also remain receptive to jihadi insurrection, owing as much to a broader Islamist backlash against the government's authoritarianism as to the Islamic State itself. Likewise, the Islamic State is likely to redouble efforts to target Israel, as discussed in the master plan. A successful campaign of attacks on Israel is one of the few true gamechangers the Islamic State might produce.

The Internet will continue to be a critical lifeline for the Islamic State. Social media companies are increasingly adept at identifying and removing Islamic State content, but the Islamic State will retain a powerful digital media capability. Video is simply too easy to produce and publish to the web to expect that the Islamic State will not continue to utilize it. Denying the Islamic State a safe haven may undermine its ability to produce sophisticated media productions, but this is of secondary importance. In decline, the Islamic State's most important propaganda priority will be to demonstrate that it can still attack.

The scale of the Internet remains tremendously valuable for the Islamic State, especially if it is forced to adopt a more covert operational model. Irhabi 007's method of uploading a file to many web locations simultaneously remains a devilishly simple and useful technique to move data globally. Relying on this model will generate less media attention and limit the Islamic State's ability to generate a mass movement, but it will help sustain a core, embattled group. Whatever the relative benefits of encryption technology for modern society, these tools make defeating the Islamic State more difficult because they will allow covert networks built on physical and digital battlefields to remain in contact securely. The infrastructure of the Internet is better suited to sustain the Islamic State today than it was in 2010 when the group survived its first near-defeat.

The Islamic State's geographic reach and continued assertion that it leads all Muslims everywhere means that it is likely to continue to clash with al-Qaeda. Yet the fortune of these two organizations is likely to oscillate over time. The relative decline of the Islamic State does not mean the decline of jihadism generally, nor does it directly imply a decrease in the threat of terrorism in the West. Indeed, the competition between these two groups creates challenges for counterterrorism officials. The groups are similarly vulnerable to suppression via military strikes, but they also have distinct strengths and vulnerabilities.

The Islamic State, for example, defines ideological authority as a function of participation in violent jihad, so it is better situated than al-Qaeda to disregard criticism from mainstream religious leaders. Indeed, the Islamic State's entire ideological framework is built around the delegitimization of ideological leaders who preach accommodation from outside a battlefield. This approach limits the Islamic State's broad appeal, but it also insulates it from critics.

This has direct implications for how to criticize the Islamic State. Rather than promote scholarly voices, countries battling the Islamic State should promote defectors that speak from battlefield experience and highlight captured internal correspondence that reveals discord within the organization. American Special Operations have long embraced the notion of intelligence-driven operations, in which intelligence is quickly triaged to inform subsequent strikes. It must be more aggressive in transforming that raw intelligence data into information that can be distributed publicly to discredit the target. The Islamic State is a mess of backstabbing and internal dysfunction when its veil of secrecy and propaganda is removed. Intelligence analysts and scholars know this; the global public should as well.

Zarqawiism is a deeply antiestablishment ethos, which both makes it resilient and difficult to scale.[2] It is challenging to criticize the Islamic State in ways that its supporters find credible, but it is also difficult for the Islamic State's leaders to maintain their own authority over a sprawling enterprise. Although the Islamic State has tried to package ideological authority into the institution of the caliph and moderate its most destabilizing ideological precepts, the ideology is fundamentally prone to internal fractures because it has historically delegated tremendous ideological authority away from traditional leadership figures to anyone pulling a trigger.

Despite the Islamic State's efforts to formally reform these ideas, the group's organizational culture has been shaped by them. Al-Qaeda squabbled with other jihadi groups, but it has never faced the Islamic State's challenge because it defines itself as a small, elite movement and always emphasized top-down organizational control. Al-Qaeda has had plenty of internal dissenters over the years, but they tend to fall in line peacefully even when their views are overruled. Bolstered by Zarqawiist antiestablishment thinking, the Islamic State's internal dissenters are not so accommodating. That does not mean that the Islamic State is incapable of ideological compromise or tough choices in order to advance its strategic goals—only that doing so is likely to cause violent unrest internally.

Indeed, scale and scope is a key reason for the split between the Islamic State and al-Qaeda. Al-Qaeda's leadership was frustrated repeatedly by its inability to assert authority over Zarqawi and his successors from a distance, even when they were ostensibly accountable to al-Qaeda. That is why they spent so much time and effort trying to push senior jihadi leaders into Iraq, with minimal success. There was Abd al-Hadi's offer to join Zarqawi in 2003 and his ill-fated journey in 2006; Hakaymah and Atiyah abd al-Rahman endeavored to travel in 2007 and 2008, about the time that Abu Talhah and Abu Hammam were trying to build a formal al-Qaeda affiliate in Lebanon. The only two efforts that showed any success came from the "Turki Brothers," who arrived in northern Iraq from Turkey (but were killed shortly thereafter) and Issa al-Masri, who arrived in Syria from Pakistan in 2009. In the end, al-Qaeda learned that commanding an army from another time zone is much easier said than done.

One of the most controversial choices an Islamic State leader could make is to reconcile with al-Qaeda. This is unlikely, but it is possible. Although the groups have important differences, they have a history of compromise. Bin Laden understood Zarqawi's ideological extremism in 1999, but the threat from Abu Mus'ab al-Suri and the opportunity to build a powerful jihadi movement in the Levant trumped those concerns. Likewise, Zarqawi's extremism did not prevent him from engaging al-Qaeda, relying on Iran for logistical support, or temporarily allying with non-jihadi militants in Iraq. The Islamic State's recent unwillingness to compromise ideologically reflects its strong operational position as much as anything else. As the group weakens, its leadership may reassess that intransigence.[3] After all, Sayf al-Adl—the man that originally brokered Zarqawi's relationship with al-Qaeda—is now free from confinement. Might he repeat the trick?

Probably not. Aside from their strategic and ideological differences, the Islamic State and al-Qaeda now have deep visceral animosities. Blood has been shed on both sides, particularly in Syria. This goes beyond al-Qaeda's feuding with other jihadi groups; those disagreements never boiled into the sort of killing seen between the Islamic State and Jabhat al-Nusrah.

The Islamic State and al-Qaeda are most likely to reconcile if they are forced by strategic circumstance. As a practical matter, that probably means a dramatic contraction of the Islamic State's territory in Syria and Iraq and the death of one or more of the relevant key leaders, meaning Ayman al-Zawahiri from al-Qaeda, Abu Bakr al-Baghdadi from the Islamic State, or Abu Muhammad al-Jawlani from JaN. On a five-year time

frame, all of that is likely to happen, which is why the prospect of reconciliation should not be completely discounted.

The more likely outcome, however, is that the two groups will feud in-
definitely, with occasional defections from one side to the other.

This squabbling probably undermines the Islamic State's territorial aspirations—in Syria and elsewhere—but it may incentivize both groups to
increase their efforts to strike in the West as they try to assert themselves
as leaders of the global jihadi movement.[4] The distinction between the Islamic State and al-Qaeda matters within the jihadi movement, and it
should shape how counterterrorism professionals attack the groups, but it
matters little to the victims of terrorism whether a bomb was set by al-
Qaeda or the Islamic State.

Neither al-Qaeda nor the Islamic State is likely to attract the mass movement they would like. The Islamic State considers the majority of the
world's 1.6 billion Muslims apostates—and, unsurprisingly, the vast majority of those 1.6 billion want nothing to do with it. Al-Qaeda, despite an
image somewhat softened by contrast with the Islamic State, has still killed
far more Muslims than anyone else. Amid the understandable concern
about the tens of thousands of people rushing to join the Islamic State, it is
easy to forget that the vast majority of the millions of refugees running
away from it are Muslim. The Islamic State hopes some of these people will
adopt its ideology and violence; but it considers all that do not apostates.

That is why prejudicial policies directed at refugees and Muslims in
Western countries are counterproductive. Capitalizing on a strategy first
articulated by Anwar al-Awlaki, the Islamic State aims to use terrorism to
provoke Western policymakers into discriminating against Muslim citizens and refugees. The Islamic State hopes this will act as a political cen-
trifuge that will separate a violent fringe from the bulk of Muslims. It is
not so different from the strategy Zarqawi employed to provoke Shia militias in Iraq. Advocating discrimination against Muslims writ large does
not suggest a serious understanding of the Islamic State or jihadism in
general. The implication that Muslims generally agree with the Islamic
State fails to understand that the Islamic State disavows most Muslims—
and aims to kill them. Rejecting Muslim citizens or refugees under the

pretense that they are allied with the Islamic State demonstrates a basic failure to understand the Islamic State and what it believes.

Effectively, while trying to thwart the Islamic State, prejudicial Western policymakers do its bidding.

The Islamic State will not achieve its objective of a globe-spanning caliphate. There will be no "final victory." But the Islamic State will kill many, many people in the process of failing. Worse, neither the United States nor any of its partners have a clear countervailing vision to the Islamic State. This is not a recipe for the Islamic State's defeat, rather for messy stalemate against a diminished, but still very deadly, jihadi group.

The Islamic State operates like a nasty bacterial infection. The Surge and the Awakening almost killed it, but the remnants that survived emerged more resistant to the antibiotics of military force—and even more capable of recruiting widely. The Islamic State is likely to lose territory, leaders, and money. But it will effectively transform itself to operate like a terrorist group when necessary. It will continue attacks globally. And it will build digital networks of supporters. The Islamic State's most ambitious goals will never be achieved, no matter what the master plan predicted. But neither is it likely to be truly defeated without a massive, semi-permanent American intervention in the Middle East. And so, in the end, the Islamic State will not achieve "final victory" for the foreseeable future. It will, however, remain.

The 2005 "General Plan" of the Army of the Followers of the Sunna and Collective

This is the "General Plan" of Abu Bakr al-Baghdadi's first jihadi group in Iraq, as released on the group's website www.alsabeel.net. This version was translated from an archive of the site taken in 2005, before the group officially aligned with al-Qaeda in Iraq.

To all Muslims, specifically those who adhere to the path of the Quran and Sunna according to the understanding of those first generations of the Muslim community who cleaved in word and deed to the fixed ideas of the followers of the Sunna and the Collective. We mention that group specifically because they are the hope of the Muslim community and the light that guides us on the way.[1]

Our brothers in Iraq have been given the task by God of making their land a place of struggle and of building, so up now! Let us join together in union and unify our tools and goals in order to establish God's law on God's land.

God said: "He has prescribed for you that religion with which he charged Noah, and that which we revealed to you, and that with which we charged Abraham, and Moses, and Jesus. Perform the religion and become not disunited. He has laid down for you as religion that He charged Noah with, and that We have revealed to thee, and that We charged Abraham with, Moses and Jesus: 'Perform the religion, and scatter not regarding it.' That to which you call them is too painful for the idolaters. God chooses for himself whomsoever he wishes and guides to himself whomsoever turns to him" (Quran 42:13, al-Shūrā). As a general principle, this "religion" can only be performed in accordance with the path of the Quran and Sunna according to the understanding of the first generations of the Muslim community. God said: "Whomsoever breaks with the Messenger after the guidance has been made clear to him, and whomsoever follows a path other than the path of the believers, we will entrust him to that to which he has entrusted himself and we will roast him in hell; an evil destination" (Quran 4:115, al-Nisā').

With regard to detail, we have a number of practical thoughts that we have titled "The Central Plan for the Army of the Followers of the Sunna and the Collective," and this plan is built on three primary fulcrums from which the remaining details can be scientifically derived. The three fulcrums are:

1. The undertaking of the general and specific call [to Islam] in a comprehensive fashion, founded on the single practical principle of methodological seriousness (al-jiddīya wa-l-manhajīya) without immoderation or negligence, carried out through the purifiying and pedagogical speech of the scholars.

2. The construction of economic and social entities through financial investment in the creation of commercial, service, social, and scientific institutions. For example: commercial businesses, Islamic financial companies, factories, agricultural lands, hospitals, schools, sports organizations and clubs, cultural centers, etc. It is in this way that we will be able to build a society specific to us; we are cognizant of the fact that our enemies have taken control of the world in this way. Who among us who does not know the Zionist lobby, how they took control of immense funds with which they impose their deadly poison, and that America is nothing but a tool that they manipulate when and where they wish? All evil has fallen in on top of us, and this proves the Prophetic saying: "The nations will be about to fall on you like people devour a bowl of food" (Hadith). We therefore need to close ranks and gird ourselves for confrontation with the enemies of God. The Prophet said, "The believers are, in their mutual love, compassion, and sympathy, like the body. If one part of the body aches, the whole body shares its insomnia and fever" (Hadith). We contend that we must entrust our ambitions to this fulcrum; it is a long process but the rewards will be sweet and radiant.

3. The construction of a comprehensive armed forces, built on scientific principles and the fixed ideas of legal methodology, that will protect all Muslims together from the schemes and stratagems of our enemies, and attack the unbelievers and the apostates. We have, with the permission of God, formed a nucleus for this army that can be modified and evaluated as new factors emerge. We move forward behind the unity of our ranks, a unity that results from the methodology of the Quran and Sunna according to the understanding of the first generations of the Muslim community. We take very serious consideration of the role of the scholars who work to construct that methodology and we consider them to be the leadership of the Muslim community, the lights that guide the way, and the inheritors of the prophets. We have practical details with regard to the structure of this army and its specific prerogatives, and these will be published in the future in an unhurried fashion. . . .

We therefore ask for your advice and guidance in our undertaking, certain as we are that we are human beings who both err and succeed. As we always say, "We are a part of the whole," and we will not deviate from the path of the Muslim community, nor will we stray from the fixed ideas of the followers of the Sunna and the Collective. Should there be any excess or immoderation in this or that regard, then counsel us as your workforce.

O God! There is no easy thing but that you make it easier, and if you wish you can make sorrow easy.

O God! We ask you to make us sincere, true, firm, and sound in this entire matter. Make us and our Muslim community live in the Sunna and resurrect us with the followers of the Sunna. . . .

The conclusion of our call is to praise God the lord of the two worlds and may the prayers of God be upon Muhammad the trustworthy, and upon his family and his companions all together.

The Central Office of the Army of the Followers of the Sunna and the Collective.

NOTES

Prologue: The Kandahar Meeting

1. Attributed to Sayf al-Adl, published in Fuad Husayn, *Zarqawi . . . The Second Generation of al-Qaeda*, serialized in *Al-Quds al-Arabi*, May 13, 2005, to June 8, 2005.

2. Guido Steinberg, *German Jihad* (New York: Columbia University Press, 2013), 44–48, citing phone conversation given as evidence in Verdict in the Case Against Mohamed Ghassan Ali Saud Abu Dhess et al., Oberlandesgericht Düsseldorf, 2 StE, March 2006, 56–61.

3. "Treasury Designates Six al-Qaida Terrorists," U.S. Department of Treasury, https://www.treasury.gov/press-center/press-releases/Pages/js757.aspx, September 24, 2003.

4. The Taliban governor in Herat was Mullah Abdul Hanan Jihadwal. "Mullah Jihadwal Martyr Biography," Taliban Sources Project. This document was archived by Anand Gopal, Felix Kuehn, and Alex Stricht van Linschoten as part of the Taliban Sources Project, by far the preeminent effort to collect and categorize Taliban primary source material. Although the Taliban Sources Project is not yet public, Gopal was kind enough to provide a translation of this document to the author.

5. Abu Zubaydah, "Notebook 6: Abu Zubaydah Diary," Al Jazeera, November 7, 2013, 35. http://america.aljazeera.com/articles/abu-zubaydah-diaries.html.

6. Sayf al-Adl's history of the escape credits Zarqawi with leading the operation, whereas Taliban histories credit Gul Muhammad, nephew of the Taliban governor Mullah Jihadwal. Abu Zubaydah's diary supports the Taliban claim. The Taliban biography also said that Mullah Jihadwal and Zarqawi were personally close and that Zarqawi would send Jihadwal flattering letters from Iraq, addressed to "my father professor." Sayf al-Adl, "The al-Qaeda Organization Writes

a Letter to the Iraqi People," Jihadist Websites, March 5, 2003; "Mullah Jihad-wal Martyr Biography," Taliban Sources Project.

7. Abu Zubaydah, "Notebook 6: Abu Zubaydah Diary," 42–43.

8. There are three first-person retellings of the Kandahar meeting. Abu Jihad Khalil al-Hakaymah, *Journeys of a Jihadi*, Midad al-Suyuf, www.almedad.com (accessed March 16, 2006), al-Adl, "Chronicling the Rise of Abu Mus'ab al-Zarqawi," Abu Zubaydah, "Notebook 6: Abu Zubaydah Diary."

9. Abu Zubaydah, "Notebook 6: Abu Zubaydah Diary," 52.

10. It was not Zarqawi's last close call in Afghanistan. While traveling through a darkened Kandahar in December 2001, he was almost shot accidentally by a trigger-happy young Saudi jihadi named Muhammad al-Tamimi, who was on patrol for the Taliban. Al-Tamimi interview with *Al-Hayat*, reproduced at http://www.jammoul.net/forum/showthread.php?t=1628 (accessed April 30, 2012).

11. Abu Zubaydah, "Notebook 6: Abu Zubaydah Diary," 52–53.

Chapter One: The Awakening Stage

1. Mary Anne Weaver, "The Short, Violent Life of Abu Musab al-Zarqawi," *The Atlantic*, July 2006.

2. Joby Warrick, *The Black Flags: The Rise of ISIS* (New York: Doubleday, 2015), 51.

3. Fuad Husayn, *Zarqawi . . . The Second Generation of al-Qaeda*, serialized in *Al-Quds al-Arabi*, May 13, 2005, to June 8, 2005.

4. Zarqawi and his successors would ultimately go on to disavow Sayyaf, owing to his ultimate collaboration with the United States in the post-Taliban government. See, for example, "From Jihad to Fasad," *Dabiq* Vol. 11, 1436 Dhul-Qa'dah, 25.

5. A 1998 Human Rights Watch publication describes credible but uncorroborated reports of Sayyaf's Ittihad al-Islami putting imprisoned Hazara prisoners, who were Shia, in shipping containers and then lighting fires around the containers to cook the prisoners alive. See http://www.hrw.org/reports/pdfs/a/afghan/afreporo.pdf (accessed February 17, 2015).

6. Jarret Brachman, *Global Jihadism: Theory and Practice* (New York: Routledge, 2009), 114; See also Jeffrey Gettleman, "The Reach of War: A Profile in Terror; Zarqawi's Journey: From Dropout to Prisoner to an Insurgent Leader in Iraq," *The New York Times*, July 13, 2004; *United States of America vs. Usama bin Laden et al.*, "Transcript" (Testimony of Essam al-Ridi), February 14, 2001, https://cryptome.org/usa-v-ubl-05.htm (accessed February 2, 2016); *United States of America vs. Usama bin Laden et al.*, "Transcript" (Testimony of Wadih el-Hage), February 15, 2001, https://cryptome.org/usa-v-ubl-06.htm (accessed February 2, 2016).

7. See Mustafa Hamid and Leah Farrell, *The Arabs at War in Afghanistan* (London: Hurst Publishers, 2015), 183.

8. Weaver, "The Short, Violent Life of Abu Musab al-Zarqawi."

9. Ibid.

10. At the center of that group was Mohamad Elzahabi, an American citizen of Lebanese descent. See *Affidavit in USA vs. Mohamad Kamal Elzahabi*, 04MJ261JSM, June 25, 2004, http://www.investigativeproject.org/documents /case_docs/758.pdf (accessed August 1, 2015, via The Investigative Project on Terrorism); Brynjar Lia, *Architect of Global Jihad* 2014 (London: C. Hurst and Co. Publishers, 2007); Tine Gade, "Fatah al-Islam in Lebanon: Between Local and Global Jihad," *Norwegian Defence Research Establishment,* May 12, 2007; Abu Mus'ab al-Suri, *The Call to Global Islamic Resistance,* 2004, p. 784, https:// archive.org/details/The-call-for-a-global-Islamic-resistance (accessed June 3, 2016).

11. The setting of Zarqawi's first meeting with Maqdisi is disputed. The most commonly recounted story comes from Sayf al-Adl, al-Qaeda's Egyptian security chief. He claimed that his father-in-law Mustafa Hamid introduced Zarqawi and Maqdisi. But Hamid himself rejects this story. See Mustafa Hamid, "Dialogue with Leah Farrell," http://allthingscounterterrorism.com/archive /my-dialogue-with-abu-walid-al-masri/arabic-and-english-versions-of-abu -walids-answers-to-my-questions/english-trans-abu-walids-fifth-reponse/ (accessed December 1, 2015); and Sayf al-Adl, "Chronicling the Rise of Abu Mus'ab al-Zarqawi," in Husayn, "Al-Zarqawi: The Second Generation of al-Qa'ida."

12. Joas Wagemakers, *A Quietist Jihadi* (Cambridge: Cambridge University Press, 2012), 39.

13. Abu Sayf Muwahiid, "About the Author," foreword to *Democracy: A Religion!* by Abu Muhammad al-Maqdisi (Springvale South, Australia: Murqan Islamic Information Centre, 2012).

14. Maqdisi studied briefly in Sarajevo, at the University of Mosul in Iraq (where he was dismayed to find men and women studying in the same classrooms), and finally as an unofficial student auditing courses at the University of Medina, in Saudi Arabia. Wagemakers, *A Quietist Jihadi.*

15. This is perhaps not surprising considering that Maqdisi was influenced by Juhayman al-Utaybi, whose ill-fated occupation of Mecca's Grand Mosque in 1979 was predicated on disdain for the Saudi royal family. Bin Laden's family, in contrast, had helped end al-Utaybi's occupation when its construction company provided building schematics of a recent renovation of the Grand Mosque complex. Steve Coll, *The bin Ladens: An Arabian Family in the American Century* (New York: Penguin, 2009).

16. Wagemakers, *A Quietist Jihadi,* chap. 8; al-Maqdisi, *Democracy: A Religion!*

17. Husayn, "Al-Zarqawi: The Second Generation of al-Qa'ida."

18. Maysarah al-Gharib, "Secrets of History: From the Experiences of Abu Mus'ab al-Zarqawi, Part I," http://www.openforum.ws/vb, September 10, 2004.

19. Nibras Kazimi, "A Virulent Ideology in Mutation: Zarqawi Upstages Maqdisi," *Current Trends in Islamist Ideology 2005* 2:59–73.

20. Wagemakers, *A Quietist Jihadi,* chap. 8.

21. Husayn, "Al-Zarqawi: The Second Generation of al-Qa'ida."

22. Weaver, "The Short, Violent Life of Abu Musab al-Zarqawi."

23. Ibid.

24. Warrick, *The Black Flags,* 25–28.

25. Ibid.

26. Brian Whitaker, "Syria to Free 600 Political Prisoners," *The Guardian,* November 17, 2000.

27. Husayn, "Al-Zarqawi: The Second Generation of al-Qa'ida"; as a jihadi described the Jordanian government's procedures: "The situation in Jordan, the government is not opposing the travel after the death of [King] Hussein and everyone can travel without any objection. During my interrogation, I was told that, you should go to Afghanistan with all the other Islamists, because we want to get rid of you. I conveyed that to the brothers. . . . Every Jordanian is called by the Intelligence services upon his return." See Abd al-Hadi al-Iraqi (al-Ansari), Memo to Sayf al-Adl, November 8, 1998 (HADI-1-006278); "Letter to Hatim," undated, context suggests 1999 (HADI-1-018398—HADI-1-018416), *USA v. Abd al-Hadi al-Iraqi,* AE35.

28. Warrick, *The Black Flags.*

29. Steve Coll, *Ghost Wars* (New York: Penguin, 2004).

30. Thomas Hegghammer, "The Rise of Muslim Foreign Fighters," *International Security* 35, no. 3 (Winter 2010/2011): 53–94.

31. See Lawrence Wright, *The Looming Tower* (New York: Alfred A. Knopf, 2006), and Fawaz Gerges, *The Far Enemy* (Cambridge: Cambridge University Press, 2009).

32. Abu Mus'ab al-Suri, *The Call to Global Islamic Resistance.* See also Lia, *Architect of Global Jihad,* 2007, 347.

33. Alex Strick van Linschoten and Felix Kuehn, *An Enemy We Created: The Myth of the Taliban–al Qaeda Merger in Afghanistan* (Oxford: Oxford University Press, 2012), 173–179.

34. Lia, *Architect of Global Jihad,* 2007, 242–243.

35. Ibid.

36. Abd al-Hadi al-Iraqi, "Letter to Muntassir al-Zayyat," March 11, 2000 (HADI-1-018584), *USA v. Abd al-Hadi al-Iraqi,* AE35; Abu Hafs (al-Masri), "Letter to Abd al-Hadi al-Iraq," April 12, 1999 (HADI-1-008096-HADI-1008097), *USA v. Abd al-Hadi al-Iraqi,* AE40.

37. Peter Bergen, *Holy War Inc.: Inside the Secret World of Osama bin Laden* (New York: Free Press, 2002); Lia, *Architect of Jihad,* 165–170.

38. Alan Cullison, "Inside al-Qaeda's Hard Drive," *The Atlantic,* September 2004; Alan Cullison and Andrew Higgins, "A Once-Stormy Terror Alliance was Solidified by Cruise Missiles," *The Wall Street Journal,* August 2, 2002.

39. Abd al-Hadi al-Iraqi, "Notes from Abdul Hadi," April 2000 (Harmony Document AFGP-2002-000091).

40. Hamid and Farrell, *The Arabs at War in Afghanistan*, 257–258.

41. Abd al-Hadi's guesthouse was an early stop for many new recruits in Afghanistan, so he was alert to potential security threats, both from other jihadis and from hostile intelligence services. The concern about al-Suri poaching recruits seems to stem from a twenty-three-year-old Syrian recruit named Marwan Hadid. Hadid arrived in Afghanistan in late 1998 after being inspired by pirate jihadi radio broadcasts from northern Lebanon. During al-Qaeda's formal investigation of Hadid, he testified that he stumbled on a series of al-Suri recruiting pamphlets at the al-Qaeda guesthouse and later found himself seated next to the older Syrian during a training session at al-Faruq. Al-Suri explained that he was building his own independent training camp focused on "urban fighting" and invited Hadid to join him. But al-Suri also warned that he was controversial in Afghanistan. "He informed me that some people believe that he is a *takfiri*," Hadid explained to al-Qaeda investigators, using the term for a jihadi willing to excommunicate other Muslims. "However, he is not like that but he is somewhat extremist and does not respect the scholars." Testimony of Marwan Hadid (Basim Umar al-Sury), undated, but probably sometime in 1999 (HADI-1-018345—HADI-1-018347) AE35, Part 3.

42. Al-Qaeda's investigation into Hadid and several other men who arrived around the same time revealed more worrisome findings. Two Iraqi recruits had worked with Iraqi opposition leader Ahmed Chalabi, who led an unsuccessful uprising against Saddam Hussein in 1995 (and would later play a critical role spurring the U.S. invasion of Iraq in 2003), and the Jordanians admitted contact with the intelligence services, though they claimed such contact was unavoidable in Jordan. Other testimony indicated that Emirati intelligence agencies were closely monitoring al-Qaeda recruits. Memo from Abd al-Hadi al-Ansari to Sayf al-Adl, November 8, 1998 (HADI-1-006278); "Letter to Hatim" (HADI-1-018398—HADI-1-018416), undated, context suggests 1999; Hamid and Farrell, *The Arabs at War in Afghanistan*, 274.

43. Hamid and Farrell, *The Arabs at War in Afghanistan*, 274.

44. Abu Mus'ab al-Suri, "Letter to Abu Khabab," April 7, 1999 (Harmony Document AFGP-2002-001111).

45. Abu Hafs (al-Masri), "Letter to Abd al-Hadi al-Iraq," March 24–25, 1999 (HADI-1-008072—HADI-1-008068), *USA v. Abd al-Hadi al-Iraqi*, AE40.

46. Abu Hafs (al-Masri), "Letter to Abd al-Hadi al-Iraq," April 12–13, 1999 (HADI-1-008096—HADI-1-008097), *USA v. Abd al-Hadi al-Iraqi*, AE40.

47. See Guido Steinberg, *German Jihad* (New York: Columbia University Press, 2013) 110, and Lia *Architect of Global Jihad* (Oxford, UK: Oxford University Press 2009) p. 189–193.

48. See Guido Steinberg, *German Jihad: On the Internationalization of Islamist Terrorism* (New York: Columbia University Press, 2013), 110; and Lia, *Architect of Global Jihad*, 189–193.

49. Abu Hafs (al-Masri), "Letter to Abd al-Hadi al-Iraq," March 24–25, 1999 (HADI-1-008072—HADI-1-008068).

50. Ayman al-Zawahiri, "Letter to the Leaders of the Two Jihad Groups," May 23, 2013. For English translation, see http://s3.documentcloud.org/documents /710588/translation-of-ayman-al-zawahiris-letter.pdf (accessed December 1, 2015).

51. Al-Adl, "Chronicling the Rise of Abu Mus'ab al-Zarqawi."

52. Abu Hafs al-Masri mentions the need to coordinate with "Abu al-Walid"—a name used by Mustafa Hamid at the time—in both letters he sent to Abd al-Hadi al-Iraqi regarding the fight with Abu Mus'ab al-Suri. It is reasonable that Abu Hafs would coordinate with Abu Walid on this matter, a) because he was widely respected by the full range of Arab groups operating in Afghanistan, b) because he was Sayf al-Adl's father-in-law, and c) because he had known Abu Mus'ab al-Zarqawi since the late 1980s. See Abu Hafs (al-Masri) letter to Abd al-Hadi al-Iraqi, March 24–25, 1999 (HADI-1-008072—HADI-1-008068), AE40, Part 1; and Abu Hafs (al-Masri), letter to Abd al-Hadi al-Iraqi, April 12–13, 1999 (HADI-1-008096—HADI-1-008097), AE40, Part 1.

53. Stephen Kurkjian and Peter DeMarco, "FBI Proves 'Sleeper Cell' Possibility," *The Boston Globe*, June 27, 2004.

54. See Bernard Rougier, *Everyday Jihad: The Rise of Militant Islam among Palestinians in Lebanon* (Cambridge, MA: Harvard University Press, 2007), and *Affidavit in USA vs. Mohamad Kamal Elzahabi*.

55. Rougier, *Everyday Jihad*, 166.

56. Holger Stark, "Terror in Europe: Syrian Had Inside Knowledge of 9/11 and London Bombings," *Der Spiegel*, August 24, 2005.

57. Ahmad Kurayshan, "The GID Uncovers al-Qa'ida and Ansar al-Islam Group," *Al-Ra'y*, September 13, 2003.

58. Hamid Munsir, "Yemeni Investigators Leave for Jordan," *Al Ra'y al-Amm*, December 10, 2000.

59. Al-Adl, "Chronicling the Rise of Abu Mus'ab al-Zarqawi."

60. Ibid.; Coll, *The bin Ladens*.

61. Hamid and Farrell, *The Arabs at War in Afghanistan*, 257–258. Farrell notes on p. 258 that Zarqawi's radical ideological perspective and penchant hardly aligned him with al-Suri. Al-Suri championed the Taliban, whereas Zarqawi believed the Afghan movement was too tolerant of local tribal practices.

62. Ibid.

63. Ibid.

64. Al-Adl did not name his partner but described him as a student of the Egyptian sheikh Abd-al Akhir Hammad, himself a hard-liner with the Egyptian Islamic

Group, who argued that violent jihad was always appropriate and not just acceptable under strict conditions, as argued by some jihadis. Hakaymah, the Egyptian jihadi present when Zarqawi was almost killed by an American missile, was an acolyte of Sheikh Abd-al Akhir Hammad, even staying at Hammad's home in Yemen while the two worked together in the early 1990s. Years later, Hakaymah cited the "virtuous Sheikh" Abd al-Akhir to criticize Imam al-Sharif, the founder of Egyptian Islamic Jihad, who in 2004 renounced al-Qaeda from an Egyptian prison cell. But Hakaymah seems to have been in London when Zarqawi arrived in Afghanistan. Another possibility is Abu Abdallah al-Muhajir, the spiritual guide at Khaldan camp near Jalalabad. He was a leading hard-liner in Afghanistan and Egypt, and ultimately became one of Zarqawi's most important ideological influences. A third possibility is Abu Hamzah al-Muhajir, who followed Zarqawi as emir of al-Qaeda in Iraq. "Interview with the As-Sahab Media Establishment in 2006," quoted in *Retractions from Behind Bars* (At-Tibyan Publications, 2010). https://archive.org/details /RetractionsFromBehindBars-At-tibyn (accessed May 27, 2016).

65. Mary Anne Weaver cites "multiple sources" corroborating al-Adl's basic version of events, but she does not name those sources. Those sources may very well have been basing their judgment on al-Adl's original message. Weaver, "The Short, Violent Life of Abu Musab al-Zarqawi."

66. "Zamray" (Usama bin Laden), "Letter to Sheikh Mahmud (Atiyah abd al-Rahman), September 26, 2010," Bin Laden's Bookshelf. https://www.dni.gov /files/documents/ubl/english/Letter%20to%20Shaykh%20Mahmud%20 26%20September%202010.pdf .

67. Ibid.

68. Notes from Ali Soufan interview, November 12, 2003, https://www.archives.gov /declassification/iscap/pdf/2012-048-doc7.pdf (accessed March 20, 2016).

69. "Mullah Jihadwal Martyr Biography," Taliban Sources Project.

70. Zarqawi's mentor Abu Muhammad al-Maqdisi later asserted that Zarqawi's dispute with al-Qaeda was really about him (Maqdisi). According to Maqdisi's account, Zarqawi insisted on teaching the apostasy of the Saudi royal family at his camp in Herat, but bin Laden remained unwilling to excommunicate the al-Saud family. Yasir Abu Hilalah, "Interview with Abu Muhammad al-Maqdisi," Al Jazeera, July 5, 2005.

71. Weaver, "The Short, Violent Life of Abu Musab al-Zarqawi"; "Abu Musab al-Zarqawi: An Enduring Threat," CIA, April 7, 2003, 2, quoted in *9/11 Commission Report*.

72. Al-Adl, "Chronicling the Rise of Abu Mus'ab al-Zarqawi"; Weaver, "The Short, Violent Life of Abu Musab al-Zarqawi."

73. "Abu Mus'ab Letter to Abu Muhammad (likely Abu Muhammad al-Maqdisi)," undated (Harmony Document AFGP-2002-601693).

74. Steinberg, *German Jihad*, 121–123.

75. Ibid., 121.

76. Guido Steinberg and Philipp Holtmann, "The November 2003 Istanbul Bomb-ing," in *The Evolution of the Global Terrorist Threat,* ed. Bruce Hoffman and Fernando Reinares (New York: Columbia University Press, 2014). Sakka made a range of grandiose claims about his role in the al-Qaeda organization, raising questions about his reliability.

77. Al-Adl, "Chronicling the Rise of Abu Mus'ab al-Zarqawi."

78. "Testimony of Sheikh Farouq Abu Hammam al-Suri," Al-Baseera Media Pro-ductions, March 2014, https://pietervanostaeyen.wordpress.com/2014/03/ (accessed May 27, 2016).

79. Many jihadis also transited Damascus on their way to Afghanistan. Some flew from Damascus to Tehran before transiting to Afghanistan. See Department of Defense, Office for the Administrative Review of the Detention of Enemy Com-batants at U.S. Naval Base Guantanamo Bay, Cuba, *Unclassified Summary of Evidence for Administrative Review Board in the Case of Ald Mohammad al-Hala,* July 11, 2006; *Unclassified Summary of Evidence for Administrative Review Board in the Case of Ald Mohammad al-Bidna,* March 22, 2006; *Unclassified Summary of Evidence for Administrative Review Board in the Case of Jihad Ahmed Mustafa Deyab,* October 13, 2005.

80. "Taliban Threatens Retaliation if Iran Strikes," CNN, September 15, 1998, http://www.cnn.com/WORLD/meast/9809/15/iran.afghan.tensions.02/index .html (accessed March 9, 2015).

81. Chris Zambelis, "Egyptian Gama'a Islamiya Public Relations Campaign," *Jamestown Monitor* Vol. 3, no. 35, September 12, 2006.

82. Abu Mus'ab al-Suri, *The Call to Global Islamic Resistance.*

83. Abu Jihad Khalil al-Hakaymah, *Journeys of a Jihadi* (Midad al-Suyuf), formerly hosted at http://www.almedad.com (accessed March 16, 2006).

84. "World Islamic Front Statement," February 23, 1998, http://fas.org/irp/world /para/docs/980223-fatwa.htm (accessed May 27, 2016).

85. Hakaymah, *Journeys of a Jihadi.*

86. Ibid.

87. Hakaymah and his family were apparently accompanied by Osamah Hasan Ah-mad Muhammad Hasan, another EIG member. One of his sisters married Ayman al-Zawahiri, the current emir of al-Qaeda. See Hani al-Siba'I, "The Martyrdom of Osamah Hasan, Ayman al-Zawahiri's Brother-in-Law," al-Maqrizi Center for Historical Studies, April 18, 2011.

88. Hakaymah, *Journeys of a Jihadi.*

89. Ibid.

90. Many records of the Arabs fleeing Afghanistan to Iran imply that they traveled there directly; in fact, most jihadis went first to Quetta. Muhammad al-Tamimi, a Saudi al-Qaeda member, fled Kandahar with fifty-five other jihadis, including Abd al-Hadi Daghlas. Each member of the group paid $100 to Pakistani soldiers

guarding the border. Al-Tamimi claimed that he paid a smuggler $1,000 for passage to Iran. Muhammad al-Turayri, "Saudi al-Qaeda Member Relays His Experience of the September 11 Attack Alongside bin Laden," *Al-Hayah,* September 20, 2006.

91. Hakaymah, *Journeys of a Jihadi.*

92. Abu Jarir al-Shamali, "Al-Qa'ida in Waziristan," *Dabiq,* Vol 6, 1436 Rabi al-'Awwal.

93. Al-Adl was not arrested until April 23, 2003, shortly after a series of terrorist attacks in Saudi Arabia that he was accused of orchestrating. Brian T. McHugh, Michael Butsch, and Nehad Abu Suneima, "Statement of Sulayman Abu Ghaith," March 6, 2013, 415A-Ny-3016L6, 4L5A-NY-307616-302. Available: http://kronosadvisory.com/Kronos_US_v_Sulaiman_Abu_Ghayth_Statement .1.pdf.

94. Al-Adl, "Chronicling the Rise of Abu Mus'ab al-Zarqawi."

95. Ibid.

96. Muhammad al-Shafi'i, "Islamic Organization in London: Jordan Has Arrested Fundamentalists on Their Return from Chechnya and Is Holding a Syrian," *Al-Sharq al-Awsat,* July 10, 2000.

97. Muhammad Abu-Rumman and Hassan Abu Hanieh, *The 'Islamic Solution' in Jordan* (Amman: Friedrich Ebert Stufting, 2013), 341, http://library.fes.de/pdf -files/bueros/amman/10360.pdf (accessed May 27, 2016); Muhammad Abu-Rumman, "Power Struggle Shakes Jihadis in Jordan," *Al-Ghadd,* March 13, 2005; Abbas al-Badri, "Source in Talabani's Party Tells *Al-Sharq al-Awsat:* We Filmed the Funeral of the Four Jordanian Afghans," *Al-Sharq al-Awsat,* November 27, 2001.

98. Hilalah, "Interview with Abu Muhammad al-Maqdisi"; Abu Muhammad al-Maqdisi, *Al-Zarqawi: Support, Counsel, Suffering, Hopes,* September 2004, http://atc2005.blogspot.com/2006/06/al-zarqawi-second-generation-of-al .html (accessed May 27, 2016); see also Camil Tawil, "Arab Mujahidin in Iraq Are 2,000 and Continue to Increase; Their Leader Is al-Zarqawi and Their Banner Is al-Qa'ida," *Al-Hayah,* November 8, 2004.

99. Untitled video released by Ansar al-Sunnah, December 8, 2007; Rasim Rahhal, "'Jund al-Islam' Group in Kurdistan, Links with Iraq, bin Laden," *Al-Wasat,* October 8, 2001; Jonathan Schanzer, "Saddam's Ambassador to al-Qaeda," *The Weekly Standard* 9, no. 24 (March 1, 2004); 'Abd-al-Rahim Bin-'Abd-al-Razzaq al-Janku, "Testimony" (HADI-1-018560), *USA v. Abd al-Hadi al-Iraqi,* AE35.

100. Rahhal, "'Jund al-Islam' Group"; David Romano, "An Outline of Kurdish Islamist Groups in Iraq," The Jamestown Foundation Occasional Paper, September 2007 http://www.jamestown.org/uploads/media/Jamestown-Romano IraqiKurds_01.pdf; Muhammad Salah, "Official Confirms Existence of Afghan Arabs in Kurdistan," *Al-Hayah,* September 29, 2001; Zuhayr al-Dujayli,

"Al-Shafi'i Is the Alias of a Kurdish Figure Who Deposed Mullah Krikar and Used Machetes Against Own People," *Al-Qabas,* September 6, 2003. Drawings made by a jihadi volunteer in Afghanistan indicate that there was a "Kurds Camp" on the outskirts of the al-Faruq training camp north of Kabul. See al-Janku, "Testimony" (HADI-1-018560), AE35, Part 3.

101. Jund al-Islam website, http://www.geocities.com/kordestaan/jundalislameng-lish9.htm (site captured on December 1, 2001; accessed via the Wayback Machine on www.archive.org on May 3, 2015).

102. Brynjar Lia, "The Ansar al-Islam Group Revisited," paper presented at the "Islamism and European Security" Seminar on June 15–16, 2006.

103. Jund al-Islam website.

104. Scott Peterson, "The Rise and Fall of Ansar al-Islam," *The Christian Science Monitor,* October 16, 2003.

105. Secretary of State Colin Powell, in his United Nations presentation, referred to Abu Wa'el when discussing Ansar al-Islam: "Baghdad has an agent in the most senior levels of the radical organization, Ansar al-Islam, that controls this corner of Iraq. In 2000 this agent offered Al Qaida safe haven in the region." Colin Powell, "Remarks to the United Nations," February 5, 2003; "Death Industry: Interview with Sadiq Ja'far Abd-al-Hasan al-Shammari," *Al-Arabiyah,* April 18, 2014; Colin Powell, "Presentation to the United Nations Security Council," February 6, 2003, http://www.cnn.com/2003/US/02/05/sprj.irq.powell.transcript.09/index.html (accessed December 2, 2015).

106. Jean-Charles Brisard and Damien Martinez, *Zarqawi: The New Face of al-Qaeda* (New York: Other Press, 2005), 111.

107. Jonathan Schanzer, "Ansar al-Islam: Iraq's al-Qaeda Connection," *Washington Institute Policy Watch* no. 699, January 15, 2003.

108. Abu Hamzah al-Muhajir, "Letter to Ansar al-Sunnah," undated (Harmony Document NMEC-2007-636878), https://www.ctc.usma.edu/posts/letter-from-abu-hamza-to-ansar-al-sunnah-highlighting-divisions-original-language-2 (accessed December 2, 2015).

109. Brisard and Martinez, *Zarqawi,* 111.

110. Jund al-Islam website. Representation in the main text is slightly edited for clarity. Verbatim, text reads: "CLAİM 3- The claim of "the number of Jundel Islam is more than 1000 and they have all kind of military materials and 150.000$ that were sent from Osama Bin Laden. REPLY 3- There are more interesting claims than these E.g., Jundel Islam has relation with Iran, Iraq, Sheikh Osama bin Laden etc. . . . We wonder why they forgot the names of other contries and persons that are enemies of America."

111. Abu Wa'el has gone by several names, including Abd-al-Wahhab Bin-Muhammad al-Sultan and Saadun Qadi. "Ansar al-Islam: From the First Banner of Jihad to Enabling the Emirate in Iraq," Media Office of Ansar al-Islam, September 8, 2010; "Ansar al-Sunnah Group: Chronology, Call and Jihad," Media Office of the Ansar al-Sunnah Group, June 9, 2010.

112. Al-Shafi'i's official history of the period argued—self-servingly—that Abu Wa'el remained in Kurdistan only because his network in Baghdad was crushed by Iraq's intelligence agencies. CIA, *Iraqi Support for Terrorism*, September 2002, 20, quoted in Senate Select Committee on Intelligence, *Postwar Findings About Iraq's WMD Programs and Links to Terrorism and How They Compare with Prewar Assessments*, September 8, 2006, https://www.gpo.gov/fdsys/pkg/CRPT-109srpt331/pdf/CRPT-109srpt331.pdf; "Ansar al-Islam: From the First Banner"; Ansar al-Islam's position was reiterated by a senior member of Ansar al-Sunnah after his capture in 2014. See Sadiq Jafar Abd-al-Hasan al-Shammari's comments in "Death Industry."

113. Abu Abdallah al-Shaf'i, "Statement," Riyadh Fwaed Islamic Network, September 4, 2003; Lia, "The Ansar al-Islam Group Revisited."

114. "Interview with Ansar al-Islam Faction's 'Ousted' Leader Mullah Krekar," *Manama al-Wasat*, August 27, 2003; Abu Muhammad al-Shafii, "A Statement Attributed to Ansar al-Islam Announces the Dismissal of Mullah Krekar as Group Leader," *Al-Asharq al-Awsat*, August 23, 2003; Jund al-Islam website.

115. Iranian leaders hoped to trade jihadis to the United States for U.S.-based members of the Iranian opposition group Mujahidin e-Khalq (MEK). At the time, the MEK was a designated terrorist group in the United States, stemming from attacks on U.S. personnel during the 1979 revolution in Iran. The MEK was officially removed from the U.S. State Department's list of terrorist organizations on September 28, 2012.

116. al-Shamali, "Al-Qa'ida in Waziristan"; Warrick, *The Black Flags*.

117. "Jordan Hangs Two for Killing U.S. Diplomat," Reuters, March 12, 2006.

118. Souad Mekhennet and Michael Moss, "A New Face of Jihad Emerges in Lebanon," *The New York Times*, March 15, 2007.

119. Steinberg, *German Jihad*, 44–48.

120. Ibid., 44–48, citing Georg Bonisch, Dominik Cziesche, Georg Mascolo, and Holger Stark, "Ziele in Deutschland" (Targets in Germany), *Der Spiegel* 18 (2002): 95–96; Holger Stark, "Die Hunde horen Mit" (The dogs listen in), *Der Spiegel* 48 (2002): 46–47.

121. Steinberg, *German Jihad*, 44–48, citing "Phone conversation given as evidence in Verdict in the Case Against Mohamed Ghassan Ali Saud Abu Dhess (et al[.])," Oberlandesgericht Düsseldorf, 2 StE, March 2006: 56–61.

122. Shihadah Naji al-Kilani and Muhammad Ratib Qutayshat, "Jordanian Military Prosecutor Charges Dead Jordanians," September 19, 2003.

123. George Tenet, *At the Center of the Storm* (New York: Harper Perennial, 2007), 350–351; Lawrence Wright, "The Man Behind bin Laden," *The New Yorker*, September 16, 2002.

124. "Testimony of Sheikh Farouq Abu Hamam al-Suri," Al-Baseera Media Productions (undated).

125. Captured Iraqi Intelligence document ISGZ-2004-019920, http://www.dcox files.com/ISGZ-2004-019920.pdf (accessed March 12, 2015).

126. "Testimony of Sheikh Farouq Abu Hamam al-Suri," Al-Baseera Media Productions (undated).

127. Isaac Peltier, "Surrogate Warfare: The Role of U.S. Army Special Forces," School of Advanced Military Studies, May 26, 2005.

128. For a more detailed retelling, see Mike Perry, "Operation Viking Hammer," SOFREP, May 20, 2012, http://sofrep.com/7160/operation-viking-hammer /#!prettyPhoto (accessed May 5, 2015).

129. 'Abd al-Halim Adl (Sayf al-Adl), "Letter to Mukhtar (Khalid Sheikh Muhammad)," June 13, 2002, https://www.ctc.usma.edu/v2/wp-content/uploads/2013 /10/Al-Adl-Letter-Translation1.pdf.

130. Sayf al-Adl, "To Our Kinfolk in Iraq," quoted in Muhammad al-Shafii, "Al-Qaeda Military Official Advises Iraqis About Fighting Americans," *Al-Asharq al-Awsat,* March 9, 2003.

131. Senate Select Committee on Intelligence, "Committee Study on the Central Intelligence Agency's Detention and Interrogation Program," December 3, 2014, 374n2114.

Chapter Two: The Eye-Opening Stage

1. Thamir Mubarak was mentioned by Islamic State of Iraq emir Abu Umar al-Baghdadi as Thamir al-Rishawi in 2007. Abu Umar al-Baghdadi, "Lowly with the Believers, Mighty Against the Rejectionists," Al-Furqan Media Establishment, December 22, 2007.

2. Abu Anas al-Shami, "The Battle of the Parties in Fallujah," April 2004, https://archive.org/details/abu-anas-shami-book (accessed May 29, 2016).

3. "The Republishing of the Biographies of Eminent Martyrs in the AlQa'ida Organization in the Land of Two Rivers," Al-Sumud Media Brigade, November 9, 2005.

4. Yasir Abu Hilalah (Al Jazeera bureau chief in Amman), "Interview with Abu Muhammad al-Maqdisi," Al Jazeera, November 5, 2005.

5. Abu-Rumman and Abu Hanieh, *The 'Islamic Solution' in Jordan,* (Amman: Friedrich Ebert Stufting, 2013) 341, http://library.fes.de/pdf-files/bueros/amman /10360.pdf (accessed May 27, 2016).

6. The two best primary sources on al-Qaeda's disposition in Iran are Brian T. McHugh, Michael Butsch, and Nehad Abu Suneima, "Statement of Sulayman Abu Ghaith," March 6, 2013, 415A-Ny-3016L6, 4L5A-NY-307616-302, available: http://kronosadvisory.com/Kronos_US_v_Sulaiman_Abu_Ghayth_Statement.1 .pdf; and Abu-'Abd-al-Rahman Anas al-Subay'i, "Letter to Unknown Sheikh," October 13, 2010 ("Letter dtd 13 Oct 2010," Bin Laden's Bookshelf, https://www .dni.gov/index.php/resources/bin-laden-bookshelf).

7. Eventually, Abu Ghaith was offered email access to his family.

8. McHugh, Butsch, and Abu Suneima, "Statement of Sulayman Abu Ghaith."

9. Urs Gehriger, "Abu Mus'ab al-Zarqawi: From Green Man to Guru," *Die Weltwoch,* October 6, 2005.

10. A sample of these notes was included with Urs Gehriger's story in *Die Weltwoch.* That has since been taken down. I recovered the document via the Wayback Machine on www.archive.org. (accessed May 27, 2016).

11. Attributed to Sayf al-Adl, published in Fuad Husayn, *Zarqawi . . . The Second Generation of al-Qaeda,* serialized in *Al-Quds al-Arabi,* May 13, 2005 to June 8, 2005.

12. In 2004, al-Adl published a column on operational security measures in *Al-Battar Training Camp,* a magazine produced by al-Qaeda members based in Saudi Arabia. See, for example, Sayf al-Adl, "Rumors and Propaganda," *Al-Battar Training Camp* 8 (April 2004); Sayf al-Adl, "Search and Seizure," *Al-Battar Training Camp* 17 (September 2004); Sayf al-Adl, "Security and Intelligence," *Al-Battar Training Camp* 7 (March 2004); and Sayf al-Adl, "Safe Houses," *Al-Battar Training Camp* 14 (July 2004).

13. Email from Fuad Husayn to Brian Fishman, November 7, 2015.

14. Ibid.

15. For more, see William McCants, *The ISIS Apocalypse: The History, Strategy, and Doomsday Vision of the Islamic State* (New York: St. Martin's, 2015).

16. National Commission on Terrorist Attacks upon the United States, *9/11 Commission Report* (Washington, DC: Government Printing Office, 2004), 251.

17. Attributed to Sayf al-Adl, published in Fuad Husayn, *Zarqawi . . . The Second Generation of al-Qaeda,* serialized in *Al-Quds al-Arabi,* May 13, 2005 to June 8, 2005.

18. Email from Fuad Husayn to Brian Fishman, August 12, 2015.

19. Attributed to Sayf al-Adl, published in Fuad Husayn, *Zarqawi . . . The Second Generation of al-Qaeda,* serialized in *Al-Quds al-Arabi,* May 13, 2005 to June 8, 2005.

20. Ibid.

21. Ibid.

22. Ibid.

23. Ibid.

24. There are several notable exceptions. See Yassin Musharbash, "The Future of Terrorism: What al-Qaida Really Wants," *Der Spiegel,* August 12, 2005; Gehriger, "Abu Mus'ab al-Zarqawi"; Lawrence Wright, "The Master Plan," *The New Yorker,* September 11, 2006; Aaron Zelin, "Jihad 2020: Assessing al-Qaida's 20-Year Plan," *World Politics Review,* September 11, 2013.

25. Yaman Mukhaddab, "Al-Qaeda Between the Past Stage and the One Announced by al-Muhajir," Promise Keepers website, November 14, 2006.

26. Abu Bakr Naji (Muhammad Khalil al-Hakaymah), *The Management of Savagery,* 2003, released online, translated into English by William McCants via a grant from the John M. Olin Institute for Strategic Studies at Harvard

University, https://azelin.files.wordpress.com/2010/08/abu-bakr-naji-the-man
agement-of-savagery-the-most-critical-stage-through-which-the-umma-will
-pass.pdf.

27. Ibid.

28. See Sabil al-Rishad, "Facts on the Relationship Between al-Qaeda and Iran,"
https://www.youtube.com/watch?v=RHQLpR2dLts&sns=tw (accessed October 12, 2015). Imam al-Sharif knew Hakaymah personally and is a towering jihadi figure despite having renounced violence from an Egyptian prison cell in
2004. Even before al-Sharif outed Hakaymah as Naji, Hani Nasira, an Egyptian
expert on jihadi groups, made the same claim. He cites three reasons: First,
sources close to both al-Sharif and the family of Sheikh Omar Abdel-Rahman—
the Egyptian Islamic Group founder convicted of planning the 1993 bombing
of the World Trade Center in New York—asserted that Hakaymah was Naji.
Second, Naji's writing style is similar to Hakaymah's. Both are highly analyti-
cal, frequently refer to Western source material, and favor short, structured
chapters with many numbered lists. Moreover, as William McCants points out,
Naji uses turns of phrase that suggest he is from North Africa, like the Egyptian Hakaymah. Third, articles under Naji's name stopped appearing about the
same time that Hakaymah was killed. Hani Nasira email to Brian Fishman,
June 9, 2015, and Hani Nesira, "The Assad Regime and Jihad Management,"
Al-Arabiya Institute for Studies, May 26, 2014. See http://studies.alarabiya.net
/hot-issues (accessed May 5, 2015), available in English at http://estudies
.alarabiya.net/content/agassi-al-nusraassad-experience-jihadi-investment.
See also McCants, *The ISIS Apocalypse*, 82–84.

29. Many thanks to Craig Whiteside for making this point effectively and repeatedly.

30. Malcolm Nance, *The Terrorists of Iraq: Inside the Strategy and Tactics of the Iraq
Insurgency, 2003–2014*, 2nd ed. (New York: CRC Press, 2015), 57–90.

31. Ghaith Abdul-Ahad, "Outside Iraq but Deep in the Fight," *The Washington Post*,
June 8, 2005.

32. Amatzia Baram, *Saddam Husayn and Islam: 1968–2003; Ba'thi Iraq from Secularism to Faith* (Washington, DC: Johns Hopkins University Press, 2014),
251–253, 268–269.

33. Nance, *The Terrorists of Iraq*, 57–90.

34. Amatzia Baram, "Who Are the Insurgents?," *United States Institute of Peace Special Report 134* (April 2005); "Izzat al-Douri: ISIL's Friend and Foe," *Shafaq
News*, August 21, 2014.

35. Hafez describes this as the difference between "system integration" and "system transformation." See Mohammed Hafez, *Suicide Bombers in Iraq* (Washington, DC: United States Institute of Peace Press, 2007).

36. Joe Klein, "Saddam's Revenge," *Time*, September 18, 2005.

37. "Jordan Embassy Blast Inquiry," BBC, August 8, 2003, http://news.bbc.co.uk/2
/hi/middle_east/3134145.stm (accessed May 5, 2015).

38. *Report of the Independent Panel on Safety and Security of UN Personnel in Iraq,* October 20, 2003, http://www.un.org/News/dh/iraq/safety-security-un-personnel-iraq.pdf (accessed May 6, 2015).

39. Ibid., 15.

40. Ansar al-Islam officially expanded its area of operations from Kurdistan to all of Iraq in September 2003. See Camile Tawil, "Ansar al-Islam Expands Its Operations from Kurdistan to All of Iraq," *Al-Hayah,* September 5, 2003.

41. Jamie Tarabay, "UN Bombing May Have Been an Inside Job," Associated Press, August 23, 2003.

42. Michael Weiss and Hassan Hassan, *ISIS: Inside the Army of Terror* (New York: Simon and Schuster, 2014), quoting Derek Harvey, U.S. Army colonel and senior Iraq analyst from November 2004 to December 2005.

43. "Biographies of Eminent Martyrs, Part IV," Al-Furqan Media Establishment, November 5, 2005.

44. See, for example, Christopher Reuter, "The Terror Strategist: Secret Files Reveal the Structure of the Islamic State," *Der Spiegel,* April 18, 2015.

45. "Biographies of Eminent Martyrs, Part IV."

46. In 2015, the Islamic State denied that it was inspired by *The Management of Savagery,* though it acknowledged that Zarqawi, when he read it, said, "It is as if the author knows what I am planning." This may be revisionist thinking. The Islamic State writers criticized *The Management of Savagery* for advocating tolerance of cultural customs prohibited by the group's restrictive understanding of Islam. See "The Revival of Jihad in Bengal," *Dabiq,* Vol. 12, 1437, Safar editor's note 2, 39. Many thanks to Craig Whiteside for originally identifying this note.

47. Aaron Zelin, Evan Kohlmann, and Laith al-Khouri, "Convoy of Martyrs in the Levant," Flashpoint Partners, June 2013.

48. Scott McLeod and Bill Powell, "Zarqawi's Last Dinner Party," *Time,* June 20, 2006.

49. Hakim briefly returned to Iraq during the 1991 uprising against Saddam Hussein. See John Lee Anderson, *The Fall of Baghdad* (New York: Penguin Books, 2005).

50. "The Return of Shiite Leader Ayatollah Bakir al-Hakim," *PBS NewsHour,* May 12, 2003.

51. Ibid.

52. Abu Mus'ab al-Zarqawi, "Letter to Osama bin Laden," February 2004, http://2001-2009.state.gov/p/nea/rls/31694.htm. (accessed May 29, 2016).

53. Ibid.

54. Thanks to Craig Whiteside for his useful comments on this section.

55. "Iraqi Group Wants POWs Freed," Reuters, August 16, 2004, http://articles.latimes.com/2004/aug/16/world/fg-tehran16 (accessed May 29, 2016).

56. Abu Hamzah al-Muhajir, "Interview with the Minister of War of the Islamic State of Iraq," Al-Furqan Media Establishment, October 24, 2008.

57. Al-Duktur al-Islami, "Biography of Abu Mus'ab al-Zarqawi: The Leader of al-Qa'ida in the Land of Two Rivers," Jihadist Websites, May 1, 2005.

58. Abd al-Hadi also went by the name Nashwan 'Abd al-Razzaq 'Abd al-Baqi. See "Abd al-Hadi al-Iraq Charge Sheet," United States Military Commission, February 3, 2014, http://www.mc.mil/Portals/0/pdfs/alIraqi/Hadi%20Al%20 Iraqi%20Referred%20Charge%20Sheet.pdf (accessed June 30, 2015).

59. Senate Select Committee on Intelligence, "Committee Study on the Central Intelligence Agency's Detention and Interrogation Program," released December 3, 2014, 372 (footnote 2096).

60. " 'Shkin Letter' and Related Documents" (ADI-1-006519—HADI-1-006527), *USA v. Abd al-Hadi al-Iraqi,* AE43.

61. Senate Select Committee on Intelligence, "Detention and Interrogation Program," 374 (footnote 2114).

62. Ibid.

63. Ibid.; "Marwan Hadid Testimony" (HADI-1-018383, HADI-1-018576), *USA v. Abd al-Hadi al-Iraqi,* AE35.

64. Senate Select Committee on Intelligence, "Detention and Interrogation Program," 374 (footnote 2114).

65. Under interrogation, Ghul described four personal email accounts used by Zarqawi and explained a telephone code that the jihadi leader would use to verify his identity. See Senate Select Committee on Intelligence, "Detention and Interrogation Program," 401.

66. Ibid., 375 (footnote 2118).

67. Ibid.

68. Redacted Title Cable, January 2004, cited in ibid., 375 (footnote 2114).

69. The CIA seems to have been well attuned to such travel. One of the individuals Zarqawi requested was "Khatal al-Uzbeki," who seems to have been taken into CIA custody in 2004. See Senate Select Committee on Intelligence, "Detention and Interrogation Program," 374 (footnote 2114) and 460 (Appendix 2: CIA Detainees 2002–2008 #109 "Qattal al-Uzbeki").

70. Ibid. (footnote 2118).

71. Aram Roston, "Cloak and Drone: The Strange Story of an al-Qaeda Triple Agent," *Vocativ,* January 9, 2014.

72. Zarqawi, "Letter to Osama bin Laden." February 17, 2004.

73. "Jordanian Military Prosecutor Charges Dead Jordanians," Islamic Observation Center, September 19, 2003.

74. Yasir Abu Hilalah, "Interview with Abu Muhammad al-Maqdisi," Al Jazeera, November 5, 2005.

75. Will McCants, *The Militant Ideology Atlas* (West Point, NY: Combating Terrorism Center, 2006).

76. Abu Muhammad al-Maqdisi, "Fruits of Jihad: Individual or Group Action," Global Islamic Media Center, January 13, 2004.

77. Yasir Abu Hilalah, "Interview with Abu Muhammad al-Maqdisi," Al Jazeera, November 5, 2005.

78. Joas Wagemakers, *A Quietist Jihadi* (Cambridge: Cambridge University Press, 2012), 46.

79. Al-Maqdisi, "Fruits of Jihad."

80. Abu Muhammad al-Maqdisi, "Zarqawi: Support and Advice, Pain and Hope," *Minbar al Tawhed wa'al Jihad*, July–August 2004.

81. For an insightful and contemporary rundown on the debate between Zarqawi and Maqdisi, see Nibras Kazimi, "A Virulent Ideology in Mutation: Zarqawi Upstages Maqdisi," *Current Trends in Islamist Ideology 2005*, 2:59–73.

82. Abu Mus'ab al-Zarqawi, "Those Holding Firebrands," Al-Furqan Media Establishment, September 30, 2005.

83. Yasir Abu Hilalah (Al Jazeera bureau chief in Amman), "Interview with Abu Muhammad al-Maqdisi," Al Jazeera, November 5, 2005.

84. Al-Shami, "The Battle of the Parties in Fallujah," April 2004.

85. Abu Anas al-Shami's real name was Omar Yousef Juma'a. He was a Palestinian who was born in Jordan and studied under Maqdisi.

86. Robert Fisk, "Atrocities in Fallujah," *The Independent*, April 1, 2004.

87. Al-Shami, "The Battle of the Parties in Fallujah."

88. Ibid.

89. Tawil, "Ansar al-Islam Expands Its Operations."

90. Hani al-Sibai, "Has Iraq Become Fertile for Islamic Jihadist Movements?," Al-Maqrizi Center for Historical Studies, March 14, 2004; *Report of the Independent Panel on Safety and Security of UN Personnel in Iraq*.

91. Al-Islami, "Biography of Abu Mus'ab al-Zarqawi." The Mujahidin Shura Council formed in mid-2004 should not be confused with the group of the same name formed in January 2006. The latter group was inspired by the earlier collaborative but was a separate effort.

92. Abu Ismail al-Muhajir, "Biographies of Eminent Martyrs: The Scholar Abu Anas al-Shami," Al-Furqan Media Establishment, June 20, 2007.

93. Al-Shami, "The Battle of the Parties in Fallujah."

94. Ibid.

95. Rudwan Aqil, "The Birth of Jund al-Sham in Ayn al-Hilwah," *Al-Nahar*, June 26, 2004.

96. "Lebanon Part of Its Military Map; 'Jund al-Sham' Cell in Damascus: Training in Iraq and Priority for Syria," *Al-Safir*, June 13, 2005; Nir Rosen, "Al Qaeda in Lebanon," *Boston Review*, January 1, 2008.

97. "An Interview with the Jihadist Commander Salih bin-Abdallah al-Qar'awi," Al-Fajr Media Center, April 4, 2010.

98. "The Untold Story of al-Zarqawi's Wife," *Asharq al-Awsat*, May 11, 2013.

99. "Saudi Arabia's 85 Most Wanted Terrorists," Saudi Arabian Ministry of Interior, February 3, 2009.

100. Hakaymah's website, www.althabeton.co.nr, has not been functional since ca. 2008. Muhammad Khalil al-Hakaymah, *The History of Jihadi Movements in*

Egypt, Experiences and Events from 1946–2006, www.althabeton.co.nr. For marriage to Hakaymah's daughter, see "An Interview with the Jihadist Commander Salih bin-Abdallah al-Qar'awi."

101. See "The Declaration of Victory of the General Command of the Iraqi Islamic Resistance in the Battle of al-Fallujah, the Second Battle of Badr," Al-Basrah Net, January 23, 2005, quoted in Nance, *The Terrorists of Iraq*, 271–272.

102. Ibid.

103. Abu Mus'ab al-Zarqawi, "Political Fortress," Jihadist Websites, April 6, 2004, http://fas.org/irp/world/para/zarqawi040604.html (accessed May 29, 2016).

104. Ellen Knickermeyer, "Details Emerge in Alleged Army Rape, Killings," *The Washington Post*, July 3, 2006; Seymour Hersh, "Torture at Abu Ghraib," *The New Yorker*, May 10, 2004.

105. The most complete history of jihadi propaganda during this period is Jarret M. Brachman, *Global Jihadism: Theory and Practice* (New York: Routledge, 2008).

106. Robert Mueller, "Speech to the Council on Foreign Relations," New York City, September 28, 2007, http://www.cfr.org/terrorism/prepared-remarks-fbis -robert-mueller/p14323 (accessed May 29, 2016).

107. Hanna Rogan, "Al-Qaeda's Online Media Strategies: From Abu Reuter to Irhabi 007," Norwegian Defense Research Establishment, December 1, 2007.

108. Nadya Labi, "Jihad 2.0," *The Atlantic*, July/August 2006; Tsouli was arrested, and ultimately convicted, after an American counterterrorism researcher identified his location using his Internet Protocol address and passed it to British authorities. Gordon Corera, "Al-Qaeda's 007," *The Times* (London), January 16, 2008.

109. "Untitled" Vimeo, May 2014 (accessed November 10, 2015).

110. "Zarqawi Beheaded U.S. Man in Iraq," BBC News, May 13, 2004.

111. *Compilation of Statements by Abu Mus'ab al-Zarqawi and Tawhed w'al Jihad* (e-book), Global Islamic Media Front, October 17, 2004.

112. Ibid.

113. "This Is Turkish al-Qa'ida," *Istanbul Milliyet*, December 4, 2003.

114. Guido Steinberg and Philipp Holtmann, "The November 2003 Istanbul Bombing," in *The Evolution of the Global Terrorist Threat*, ed. Bruce Hoffman and Fernando Reinares (New York: Columbia University Press, 2014), 461–482; Kamil Elibol, "Bomber's Sponsor Spotted in Syria," *The Daily Star*, January 4, 2004; Chris Gourley and Jonathan Calvert, "Al-Qa'ida Kingpin: I Trained 9/11 Hijackers," *The Sunday Times*, November 25, 2007; Ian Cobain, "The Man Who Says He Sat in Judgment on Murdered Hostage Kenneth Bigley," *The Guardian*, April 20, 2006.

115. See Holger Stark, "Terror in Europe: Syrian Had Inside Knowledge of 9/11 and London Bombings," *Der Spiegel*, August 24, 2005; Levent Korkut and Aysegul Usta, "Present at Execution of Turkish Truck Driver in Iraq," *Hurriyet*, August 12, 2005.

116. Al-Islami, "Biography of Abu Mus'ab al-Zarqawi."

117. Abd al-Rahman al-Shamri, "A Lesson in Creed and Beheading the Infidel Arab," *Sawt al-Jihad* 23 (August 2004).

118. "Fatwah on Beheadings," At-Tibyan Forum, December 21, 2006, 10:49 p.m.

119. Abu Mus'ab al-Zarqawi, "Statement," Jihadist Websites, October 17, 2004, http://www.jamestown.org/single/?tx_ttnews%5Btt_news%5D=27305#.VowHJ5NcSko (accessed May 29, 2016).

120. *Compilation of Statements by Abu Mus'ab al-Zarqawi and Tawhed w'al Jihad.*

121. Osama bin Laden, "To the Muslims in Iraq and the Nation in General," As-Sahab Media, December 28, 2004.

122. Ibid.

123. Al-Zarqawi, "Statement."

124. For more, see Mohammed A. Hafez, "Takfir and Violence Against Muslims," in *Fault Lines in Global Jihad: Organizational, Strategic, and Ideological Fissures,* ed. Assaf Moghadam and Brian Fishman (London: Routledge, 2011), 25.

125. Abu Hamzah al-Baghdadi, *Why Do We Fight? Who Do We Fight?,* Islamic Renewal Organization website, October 2005, www.tajdeed.org.uk.

126. Ibid.

127. Abu Mus'ab al-Zarqawi, "Do You Know Better Than Allah?," Al-Qaeda in Iraq Media Section, October 7, 2005.

128. Al-Baghdadi, *Why Do We Fight?*

129. Al-Zarqawi, "Do You Know Better Than Allah?"

130. Ibid.

131. Hafez, "Takfir and Violence Against Muslims."

132. Abu Mus'ab al-Zarqawi, "Untitled Audio," Jihadist Websites, September 12, 2004.

133. Abu Mus'ab al-Zarqawi, "A Statement and Clarification by Abu Mus'ab al-Zarqawi on the Issues Raised by Sheikh al-Maqdisi in the Interview with Al Jazeera," Jihadist Websites, July 12, 2005.

134. Abu Mus'ab al-Zarqawi, "It is Allah Whom Ye Should Fear," Al-Furqan Media Establishment, October 14, 2005.

135. Abu Mus'ab al-Zarqawi, "You Will Not Be Harmed by Those That Failed You," Al-Furqan Media Establishment, September 5, 2006.

136. Abu Umar al-Baghdadi, "The Harvest of the Years in the Land of the Monotheists," Al-Furqan Media Establishment, April 17, 2007.

137. Zarqawi is not the only jihadi to take on this moniker. Abu Mus'ab al-Suri said his camp in Afghanistan was for Ghuraba, or "the strangers."

138. Abu Mus'ab al-Zarqawi, "They Will Not Be Harmed by Those Who Failed Them," World News Network, September 30, 2005.

139. Abu Mus'ab al-Zarqawi, "A Gift from al-Furqan Media," Al-Furqan Media Establishment, December 6, 2006.

140. See al-Maqdisi, "Zarqawi: Support and Advice, Pain and Hope"; Abu Anas al-Shami's real name was Umar Yusuf Jum'ah. See Faris Shar'an, "Killing of Abu Anas al-Shami a Strong Blow to Zarqawi," *Asharq al-Awsat,* September 24, 2004.

141. Shar'an, "Killing of Abu Anas al-Shami a Strong Blow to Zarqawi."

142. Abu Anas al-Shami, audio statement, Jihadist Websites, July 28, 2004.

143. Maysarah al-Gharib, "Zarqawi as I Knew Him," Al-Fajr Media Center, November 18, 2007.

144. Al-Zarqawi, "A Statement and Clarification by Abu Mus'ab al-Zarqawi on the Issues Raised by Sheikh al-Maqdisi."

145. Yasir Abu Hilalah (Al Jazeera bureau chief in Amman), "Interview with Abu Muhammad al-Maqdisi," Al Jazeera, November 5, 2005.

146. Abu Anas al-Shami Eulogy. Zarqawi quoted by an individual calling himself Commander Abu Azzam, Jihadist Websites, November 30, 2004; al-Gharib, "Zarqawi as I Knew Him."

147. For the best biography on Abu Abdallah al-Muhajir, see Kevin Jackson, "Abu Mus'ab al-Zarqawi Under Influence: One Mentor?," www.alleyesonjihadism.com, May 15, 2012 (accessed June 10, 2015).

148. For more on their opposition to suicide attacks in prison, see Wagemakers, A Quietist Jihadi, 213–217. Interestingly, Maqdisi later claimed he was not completely opposed to the use of suicide attacks and asserted that Zarqawi taught his "moderate" position in his Herat camp in Afghanistan. See Hilalah, interview, Al Jazeera, July 5, 2005.

149. Abu Mus'ab al-Zarqawi, "Clarification on the Issues Raised by Sheikh al-Maqdisi in the Interview with Al Jazeera," Jihadist Websites, July 12, 2005.

150. Abu Abdallah al-Muhajir was born Muhammad Ibrahim al-Saghir and widely used the name Abd al-Rahman al-Ali.

151. Mustafa Hamid described the Khaldan Camp as the most radical of all jihadi training centers in Afghanistan. See Mustafa Hamid, "Dialogue with Leah Farrell—5," www.allthingscounterterrorism.com (accessed May 28, 2016). The claim about Abu Abdallah al-Muhajir's belief that Shia are apostates comes from Zarqawi himself. See al-Zarqawi, "A Statement and Clarification by Abu Mus'ab al-Zarqawi on the Issues Raised by Sheikh al-Maqdisi."

152. Abu Bilal Badr Bin Musa'ed Al-Ruweili, Is Bin Laden Calling His Followers to the Gates of Hell?, www.almahdy.net (accessed June 9, 2006).

153. Alex Strick van Linschoten and Felix Kuehn, An Enemy We Created: The Myth of the Taliban–Al Qaeda Merger in Afghanistan (Oxford: Oxford University Press, 2012), 152–153; Anne Stenersen, "The Relationship Between al-Qaeda and the Taliban: Insights from Captured Documents," in Ten Years Later: Insights on al-Qaeda's Past and Future, ed. Lorry Fenner, Mark Stout, and Jessica Goldings (Washington, DC: Johns Hopkins University Center for Advanced Governmental Studies, 2012), 136–148.

154. Al-Zarqawi, "Clarification on the Issues Raised by Sheikh al-Maqdisi in the Interview with Al Jazeera."

155. Many hard-line salafis criticized al-Qaeda and bin Laden for supporting the Taliban. In 2003, a Kuwaiti salafi named Abu Bilal al-Ruweili wrote a scathing review of Osama bin Laden called Is Bin Laden Leading His Followers to the

Gates of Hell? that critiqued bin Laden's support for the Taliban. Al-Ruweili also criticized Abu Abdallah al-Muhajir, arguing (from the safety of Kuwait) that he softened his opposition to the Taliban under threat of expulsion from Afghanistan.

156. Ziad al-Zaatari, "Takfiri Literature Makes Headway in Lebanon," *al-Akhbar,* September 11, 2012; Jurgen Todenhofer, *My Journey into the Heart of Terror* (Vancouver/Berkeley: Greystone Books 2016), 172.

157. Al-Gharib, "Zarqawi as I Knew Him."

158. Abu Mus'ab al-Zarqawi, "The Descendants of Ibn al-Alqami Are Back," Al-Hesbah Forum, May 18, 2005; for more on jihadi views on "collateral damage," see Hafez, "Takfir and Violence Against Muslims."

159. Al-Baghdadi, *Why Do We Fight?*

160. Ibid.

161. Ibid.

162. This argument owes much to the work of Nelly Lahoud. See Nelly Lahoud, *The Jihadis' Path to Self-Destruction* (London: Oxford University Press, 2010).

163. Ibid.

164. For more on ISIS eschatology, see McCants, *The ISIS Apocalypse.*

165. "Dabiq Magazine," *Dabiq,* Vol.1, 1435 Ramadan.

166. See, for example, Abu Sa'd al-Amili, "May God Accept Your Sacrifice, al-Maqdisi," Jihadist Websites, June 13, 2010.

167. See Abu Muhammad al-Maqdisi, "Umar, You Have Brought Happiness into My Heart," Fallujah Forum, June 13, 2010.

168. Ibid.

169. Ayman al-Zawahiri, "Letter to Zarqawi," July 9, 2005.

170. Ibid.

171. Ibid.

172. Ibid.

173. His name was Abdullah Abu Azzam al-Iraqi. Bill Roggio, "Who Was Abdullah Abu Azzam al-Iraqi?," *The Long War Journal,* September 27, 2005.

174. Al-Zawahiri, "Letter to Zarqawi."

175. See, for example, Stephen Ulph, "Is al-Zawahiri's Letter to al-Zarqawi a Fake?," *Jamestown Monitor,* October 21, 2005; "Experts: Al-Zawahiri Letter Is Authentic," *ABC News,* October 19, 2005; Bruce Lawrence, "Fake Letter, Real Trouble?," *Los Angeles Times,* October 18, 2005.

176. Abu Maysarah al-Iraq, "Claims About 'Zawahiri's Message," World News Network, October 13, 2005.

177. They were Abd al-Rahman Hasan Abdallah, Abdallah Muhummad Hasan al-Sahli, and Ammar Ghazi al-Samarrai'i.

178. Indictment of twelve defendants for the Aqabah attack excerpted in Ahmad Kurayshan, "State Security Directs Charges of Terrorist Plotting and Possession of Explosive Charges," *Al-Ra'y,* March 15, 2006.

179. Joby Warrick, *The Black Flags: The Rise of ISIS* (New York: Doubleday, 2015), 139.

180. Hassan M. Fattah and Edward Wong, "U.S. Ships Target in Rocket Attack in Jordan's Port," *The New York Times,* August 20, 2005.

181. Kurayshan, "State Security Directs Charges of Terrorist Plotting."

182. "Bombers Kill 88 at Egyptian Resort," *The Guardian,* July 23, 2005. The Abdallah Azzam Brigades also claimed credit for Taba after a bombing in Cairo in April 2005. See "Statement by the Brigades of Abdallah Azzam—al-Qaeda in the Levant and Egypt," Al-Nahar, August 20, 2005; and "Statement on the Cairo Incidents," www.islam-minbar.net, April 30, 2005.

183. Al-Shami, "The Battle of the Parties in Fallujah."

184. "Biographies of Eminent Martyrs, Part IV."

185. Indictment of Abu Mus'ab al-Zarqawi, Sajidah al-Rishawi, Uthman Isma'il Fahd al-Dulaymi, Hiyam Khalid Hasan, Mazin Muhammad Farid Jamil Shihadah, Walid Khalid Ali Hasan, Nihad Fawwaz Atruz al-Rishawi, and Karim Jasim Muhammad al-Fahdawi, excerpted at length in Kurayshan, "State Security Directs Charges of Terrorist Plotting."

186. Marwan al-Mu'ashir, press conference, November 13, 2005.

187. Yasir Abu Hilalah, "Interview with Jamil Azar," Al Jazeera, November 15, 2005.

188. Abu Maysarah al-Iraqi, "Statement #1," Jihadist Websites, November 10, 2005.

189. Abu Maysarah al-Iraqi, "Statement #2," Jihadist Websites, November 10, 2005.

190. Abu Mus'ab al-Zarqawi, "Taste This! Truly You Were Might, Fully of Honor!," Al-Firdaws Forum, November 18, 2005.

191. Pew Global Attitudes Report, Pew Global Attitudes Project (Washington, DC: Pew Foundation, 2007), http://pewglobal.org/reports/pdf/257.pdf. (accessed June 4, 2016).

192. "Statement by Al-Khalayilah/Bani Hasan Tribes," *Al-Ra'y,* November 20, 2005.

193. Atiyah abd al-Rahman, "Note to Zarqawi," November 12, 2005, http://www.ctc.usma.edu/harmony/pdf/CTC-AtiyahLetter.pdf. (accessed April 9, 2015).

194. Ibid. Abu Yahya al-Libi again confirmed the validity of Zawahiri's letter to Zarqawi on November 20, 2005. Abu Yahya al-Libi, "A Message to Abu-Mus'ab Al-Zarqawi from Abu-Yahya," Jihadist Websites, November 20, 2005.

195. Al-Rahman, "Note to Zarqawi."

196. Eli Ashkenazi and Amos Ha'rel, "Israel Air Forces Attack Base in Lebanon," *Ha'aretz,* December 28, 2005.

197. Abu Maysarah al-Iraq, untitled statement, al-Qaeda in Iraq Media Organization, December 29, 2005.

198. For Lebanese army claim, see Radwan Aqil, "Security Official: No Training Camps, Crossings Controlled. Monitoring of Jubran Tuwayni Began in Paris," *Al-Nahar,* January 27, 2006; for Zarqawi claim, see Abu Mus'ab al-Zarqawi, untitled statement, *Al-Firdaws,* January 9, 2006.

199. AQI's claim of responsibility was largely ignored in the Western media but received extensive attention in the Arabic-language press. There are several exceptions, among them Ilene Prusher and Nicholas Blanford, "Al-Qaeda

Takes Aim at Israel," *The Christian Science Monitor,* January 13, 2006. For an example of Arab discourse, see "Has al-Qa'ida Reached Lebanon," Al-Arabiyah Television, January 13, 2006.

200. Attributed to Sayf al-Adl, published in Fuad Husayn, *Zarqawi . . . The Second Generation of al-Qaeda,* serialized in *Al-Quds al-Arabi,* May 13, 2005 to June 8, 2005.

201. Abu Maysarah al-Iraqi, untitled statement, Jihadist Websites, January 15, 2006.

202. For more, see Brian Fishman, "After Zarqawi: The Dilemmas and Future of al-Qaeda in Iraq," *The Washington Quarterly,* Autumn 2006.

203. See Brian Fishman, "Redefining the Islamic State: The Fall and Rise of al-Qa'ida in Iraq," The New America Foundation, August 2011.

204. Abdallah Rashid al-Baghdad, "The True Dawn Contest," Al-Meer Forum, January 20, 2005, www.almeer.net.

205. Statement on various Jihadi web forums, January 29, 2006.

206. Specifically, Zawahiri said that "the Muslim populace who love and support you will never find palatable . . . the scenes of slaughtering the hostages. You shouldn't be deceived by the praise of some of the zealous young men and their description of you as the Sheikh of the slaughterers, etc. They do not express the general view of the admirer and the supporter of the resistance in Iraq . . . we can kill the captives by bullet. That would achieve that which is sought after without exposing ourselves to the questions and answering to doubts. We don't need this."

207. Abu Qudamah al-Tunisi entered Iraq in 2003, not long after the U.S. invasion.

208. Muwaffaq al-Rubaie, press conference, *Al-Arabiyah,* June 28, 2006; "Tunisian Detainee from 'al-Qa'ida' Reveals Details of Bombings," *Al-Hayah,* June 29, 2006.

209. "Iraqi Police Find 53 Corpses in Baghdad," *Xinhua,* February 23, 2006.

210. Mujahidin Shura Council Statement, February 23, 2006; see also Craig Whiteside, "The Smiling, Scented Men: The Political Worldview of the Islamic State of Iraq, 2003–2013" (PhD diss., Washington State University, 2014), 147.

211. "Joint Statement 1920 Revolutionary Brigades, Islamic Army in Iraq, Islamic Front for Iraqi Resistance and Mujahdin Army," Jihadist Websites, February 28, 2006.

212. "Statement by 220 MPs Accuses US 'Mercenaries' of Mosque Bombing," Mehr News Agency, February 26, 2006; Ayatollah Ali Khamenei, "Speech with Governors General," Vision of the Islamic Republic, February 27, 2006.

213. Ali al-Sistani, statement, Al Jazeera, February 22, 2006.

214. See Abdallah al-Muhajir, "The Biography of Haytham al-Sab al-Badri, an Iraqi Field Commander," Al-Firdaws Forum, August 4, 2006; al-Rubaie, press conference.

215. Al-Rubaie, press conference; "Tunisian Detainee from 'al-Qa'ida' Reveals Details of Bombings."

216. Al-Rahman, "Note to Zarqawi."
217. Al-Qaeda's Special Committee on Iraq, "Letter to Abu Abdallah al-Shafi'i" (Letter to Shaykh Abu-'Abdallah al-Shafi'i), January 26, 2006, Bin Laden's Bookshelf (March 1, 2016 release).
218. "Letter from al-Qaeda's Special Committee on Iraq to Ansar al-Sunnah" (Letter to Special Committee of al-Jihads Qaida of the Mujahidin Affairs in Iraq and to the Ansar al-Sunnah Army), January 29, 2006, Bin Laden's Bookshelf.
219. Ibid.
220. There is some ambiguity about when Abd al-Hadi began his journey to Iraq. Al-Qaeda's letter to Ansar al-Sunnah suggests he was headed to Iraq as early as January 2006, but the U. S. Military Commission's charge sheet against Abd al-Hadi indicates he did not begin his journey until June 2006. It is hard to know what to make of this discrepancy. Perhaps al-Qaeda had made the decision to send him but still needed to work out the logistics; perhaps the charge sheet is predicated on intelligence that can carefully place Abd al-Hadi's whereabouts, as opposed to the letter to Ansar al-Sunnah, which offers more circumstantial evidence of his trip. (See Chapter 3.) *Referred Charge Sheet Abd al-Hadi al-Iraqi,* "Office of the Chief Prosecutor, Office of Military Commissions," February 3, 2014.
221. See, for example, Sabrina Tavernise and Dexter Filkins, "Local Insurgents Tell of Clashes with al Qaeda's Forces in Iraq," *The New York Times,* January 12, 2006; and Harmony Document NMEC-2007-637951.
222. Anonymous, "Smuggling, Syria, and Spending," in *Bombers, Bank Accounts and Bleedout,* ed. Brian Fishman (West Point, NY: Combating Terrorism Center, 2008).
223. Abu Mus'ab al-Zarqawi, "This Is a Declaration to the People," Mujahidin Shura Council, April 24, 2006, https://archive.org/details/newbkpvideo (accessed June 4, 2016).
224. Sean Naylor, *Relentless Strike* (New York: St. Martin's Press, 2015), 284.
225. "U.S.: Outtakes Show al-Zarqawi as Poor Gunman," CNN, May 4, 2006, http://www.cnn.com/2006/WORLD/meast/05/04/iraq.al.zarqawi/ (accessed February 2, 2016).
226. See Eric Schmitt and Thom Shanker, *Counterstrike: The Untold Story of America's Secret Campaign Against al-Qaeda* (New York: Henry Holt, 2011), 164–165.
227. Zarqawi had been remarkably clandestine until his death in June 2006, though he had several close calls. On February 20, 2005, U.S. troops established a roadblock on a lonely stretch of highway northwest of Ramadi hoping to stop Zarqawi. But Zarqawi's driver blew through the roadblock. Zarqawi made eye contact with the Special Operations troops manning the blockade. U.S. troops gave chase, and with a surveillance drone overhead had a great chance to capture or kill the terrorist leader before his greatest crimes could be committed. But Zarqawi fled the car on foot, and the drone's camera reset from

a tight focus on the fleeing terrorist to a wider-angle view. Naylor, *Relentless Strike*, 283.

228. Ibid., 279–288.

229. Ayman al-Zawahiri, "Eulogizing the Muslim Nation's Martyr and Commander of the Martyrdom Seekers, Abu Mus'ab al-Zarqawi," As-Sahab Media Foundation, June 24, 2006.

230. Ayman al-Zawahiri, "Eulogy for Abu Mus'ab al-Zarqawi," Jihadist Websites, June 24, 2006.

Chapter Three: The Stage of Standing Upright

1. Husayn, "Letter to Adnan and Jasim," Harmony Document NMEC-2007-658606.

2. Ibid.

3. "Statement," Media Commission of the Mujahidin Shura Council, June 12, 2006.

4. Abu Hamzah al-Muhajir's first official statement as emir of al-Qaeda in Iraq was made on June 13, 2006. See Abu Hamzah al-Muhajir, untitled statement, Media Commission of the Mujahidin Shura Council, June 13, 2006.

5. Harun Fadil, *The War Against Islam, Part Two* (distributed online). Available: https://www.ctc.usma.edu/posts/the-war-against-islam-the-story-of-fazul -harun-part-2-english-translation-2 (accessed June 2, 2016).

6. Ibid.

7. Al-Muhajir, "Statement," Media Commission of the Mujahidin Shura Council, September 7, 2006.

8. Ibid.

9. Sheikh Ahmed Naji al-Juburi, "Today's Harvest," Al Jazeera, September 26, 2006.

10. "Anbar Tribes Convene a 'War Council' to Evict al-Qa'ida," *Al-Bayinnah al-Jadidah,* September 13, 2006.

11. Ned Parker and Mohaned al-Kubacy, "Arm Tribes to Fight al-Qa'ida, Say Sunnis," *The Times* (London), September 13, 2006.

12. See Stephane Lacroix, *Awakening Islam: The Politics of Dissent in Contemporary Saudi Arabia* (Cambridge, MA: Harvard University Press, 2011).

13. A week before the ISI was declared, AQI announced the Mutayibeen Alliance (the Scented Ones Alliance), a group of insurgents and tribal leaders dedicated to fighting the U.S. occupation. The Alliance was named for an alliance made by the Prophet Muhammad's grandfather to maintain peace in Mecca. The original agreement was cemented when "signatories" dipped their hands in scented water at the Kaaba in Mecca. The modern participants replicated this process in Iraq.

14. "The Islamic State of Iraq," Media Commission of the Mujahidin Shura Council, October 15, 2006. Unlike the statement establishing the Mujahidin Shura

Council, which was attributed to Abu Maysarah al-Iraqi, the official spokesman of AQI, the formation of the ISI was announced by an Iraqi named Muharib al-Juburi, the first Shariah official of the new "state." See Cole Bunzel, "From Paper State to Caliphate," The Brookings Institution, Analysis Paper No. 19 (March 2015).

15. "Death Industry," *Al-Arabiyah*, May 7, 2010.

16. Ibid.

17. Abu Usama al-Iraqi, "Stages in the Life of Emir al-Baghdadi," June 9, 2012, https://www.mnbr.info/vb/showthread.php?t=11332&langid=3&styleid=18 (accessed June 4, 2016). Many thanks to Will McCants, whose use of this source allowed me to replicate after my original citation disappeared from the web.

18. For an excellent rundown on al-Qaeda's advocacy for declaring an Islamic state, see Bunzel, "From Paper State to Caliphate"; see also Brian Fishman, "Redefining the Islamic State: The Fall and Rise of al-Qa'ida in Iraq," The New America Foundation, August 2011.

19. There are very few references to the Islamic State of Iraq in Western media during October 2006. A notable exception is Stephen Negus, "Call for Sunni State in Iraq," *The Financial Times*, October 15, 2006.

20. "The Islamic State of Iraq," Media Commission of the Mujahidin Shura Council, October 15, 2006.

21. See "Audio Interview with the Minister of War of the Islamic State of Iraq," Al-Furqan Media Establishment, October 24, 2008; Abu Umar al-Baghdadi, "The Second Government of the Islamic State of Iraq," Al-Furqan Media Establishment, September 21, 2009; Joseph Felter and Brian Fishman, "Al-Qa'ida Foreign Fighters in Iraq: A First Look at the Sinjar Records," the Combating Terrorism Center at West Point, December 2007. See as well references to the Islamic State of Iraq's support for development efforts in certain tribal areas in Harmony Document NMEC-2007-005648.

22. In 2008, Abu Hamzah al-Muhajir responded to criticism that the Islamic State of Iraq was viable only on paper. When an interviewer explained that "some criticize the ministries of the Islamic State, making fun of it, like the Ministry of Agriculture and Marine Wealth," Abu Hamzah replied that "when we announced this ministry, we were, praise God, eager for it to be truthful. . . . Therefore it came to be limited in numbers . . . the Ministry of Agriculture and Marine Wealth . . . took about 500 fisheries in the south of Baghdad, Al-Mada'in, Diyala, and Salah al-Din as booty. . . . This land and orchards were distributed among Sunnis via contracts and we settled thousands of evicted families there. Additionally, this ministry . . . would dig small streams. For example it brought water to many orchards, which had not had running water under any regime in Iraq."

23. See, for example, "Reply of the Islamic Army of Iraq to the Transgressions of Brother Abu Umar al-Baghdadi," Jihadist Websites, April 4, 2007; Emir of the Islamic Army of Iraq, "The Killers," Jihadist Websites, December 29, 2006;

Ibrahim al-Shammari, "Without Borders Program," Al Jazeera, April 11, 2007; Hamid al-Ali, "Response to Question: 'Are Those Who Do Not Swear Allegiance to "The Islamic State of Iraq" Sinners?,'" Jihadist Websites, April 11, 2007.

24. For more on this debate, see Bunzel, "From Paper State to Caliphate."

25. "The Islamic State of Iraq," Media Commission of the Mujahidin Shura Council, October 15, 2006; see also Uthman bin Abd al-Rahman al-Tamimi, *Informing the People About the Islamic State of Iraq* (Iraq: Islamic State of Iraq Ministry of Shariah, 2006). Available: http://www.jihadica.com/wp-content/uploads/2014/08/ilam-al-anam.pdf (last accessed June 4, 2016).

26. Al-Tamimi, *Informing the People,* also reflected a very creative understanding of sovereignty and territorial control, arguing that most political entities considered "states" are not actually sovereign. "We find a clear question concerning the concept of control of the land! Who determines that a given government controls its land or not? . . . Many states suffer from turmoil and unrest, yet that does not prevent them from becoming states in the public opinion. The best examples are the states neighboring the Jewish-Israeli state. They are known internationally as states. . . . Yet we find that [they] are genuinely threatened by the Israeli Air Force. . . . Israel is capable of attacking any target that it wishes inside those states. . . . We can add to this example. . . . For example, commercial satellites are used by the developed states extensively without respect of the sovereignty of other states or their claimed control of the land. . . . They submit to the control and power of strong countries, meaning they also lack sovereignty to varying degrees."

27. Ibid., 41.

28. Ibid., 64–65.

29. Ibid., 65.

30. Abu Hamzah al-Muhajir, "The Command Is for None but God," Al-Furqan Media Establishment, November 10, 2006.

31. Yaman Mukhaddab, "Al-Qaeda Between the Last Stage and the One Announc[e]d by al-Muhajir," *Promise Keepers* (www.althabeton.co.nr), November 14, 2006 (accessed February 8, 2007).

32. Ibid.

33. See Bunzel, "From Paper State to Caliphate."

34. "Jihad and Reform Front, 22 May 2007," Bin Laden's Bookshelf, https://www.dni.gov/index.php/resources/bin-laden-bookshelf (accessed June 4, 2016).

35. M. Sait Unalan, "Summary of Proceedings Financial Crimes Directorate 2006/ Crime No. 765: Forging of Official Documents and Violating the 5682 Passport Law," *Anti-Smuggling and Organized Crime Directorate, Gazientep Police Department,* October 16, 2006, available as part of *United States of America vs. Abd al-Hadi al-Iraqi,* AE039 Government Motion in Limine to Consider Evidence During Preliminary Matters and to Admit Evidence for Trials on the Merits, April 22, 2015, Appendix 7A.

36. Ibid.

37. *Suspect's Deposition Record: Abdulrahman Son of Yar Mohammed*, October 16, 2006, available as part of *United States of America vs. Abd al-Hadi al-Iraqi*, AE039 Government Motion in Limine to Consider Evidence During Preliminary Matters and to Admit Evidence for Trials on the Merits, April 22, 2015, Appendix 9A.

38. Ibid.

39. *Suspect's Deposition Record: Sonia Zalmai*, October 16, 2006, available as part of *United States of America vs. Abd al-Hadi al-Iraqi*, AE039 Government Motion in Limine to Consider Evidence During Preliminary Matters and to Admit Evidence for Trials on the Merits, April 22, 2015, Appendix 18A.

40. Rusen Cakir, "The Story of al-Qaeda Militant Abd al-Hadi al-Iraqi, a Kurd from Mosul," www.rusencakir.com, November 25, 2014 (accessed September 22, 2015).

41. Kevin Bergner, MNFI press briefing, June 27, 2007, http://www.globalsecurity.org/military/library/news/2007/06/mil-070627-mnfi-b01.htm (accessed June 4, 2016).

42. Cakir, "The Story of al-Qaeda Militant Abd al-Hadi al-Iraqi."

43. Ibid.

44. "Letter to Special Committee of al-Jihads Qaida of the Mujahidin Affairs in Iraq and to the Ansar al-Sunnah Army," January 29, 2006, Bin Laden's Bookshelf.

45. Khalil Tawil, "Charge Sheet: Abd al-Hadi al-Iraq," February 3, 2014, http://www.mc.mil/Portals/0/pdfs/alIraqi/Hadi%20Al%20Iraqi%20Referred%20Charge%20Sheet.pdf (accessed June 4, 2016).

46. Cakir, "The Story of al-Qaeda Militant Abd al-Hadi al-Iraqi."

47. Ibid.

48. Trine Ostereng, "Violent Islamism in Turkey—an Overview," Norwegian Defence Research Establishment, April 2, 2013.

49. Karl Vick, "Suspect in al-Qaeda Bombings Disrupts Trial in Turkey," *The Washington Post*, March 21, 2006.

50. Senate Select Committee on Intelligence, "Committee Study on the Central Intelligence Agency's Detention and Interrogation Program," December 3, 2014, 161 (footnote 869).

51. "U.S. Says Two Turkish al-Qaeda Operatives Killed in Iraq," Reuters, June 27, 2007.

52. "3 al-Qaeda Terrorists Caught in Hakkari," *Hurriyet Daily News*, March 1, 2002.

53. Cakir, "The Story of al-Qaeda Militant Abd al-Hadi al-Iraqi."

54. "Turkish al-Qaeda Lawyer Killed in Aleppo Clashes," *Today's Zaman*, August 7, 2012.

55. Two other coalitions were important as well. The Jihad and Change Front was built around Iraq's Association of Muslim Scholars and espoused a nationalist-Islamist perspective. Hamas-Iraq captured a significant Muslim Brotherhood constituency from various existing militant groups but especially the 1920 Revolution Brigades.

56. See, for example, Muhammad Abu Rumman, "The Politics of Sunni Armed Groups in Iraq," Carnegie Endowment for International Peace, September 18, 2007.

57. "Interview with Dr. Ibrahim al-Shammari," Al-Boraq Islamic Network, October 5, 2006.

58. Abu Usamah al-Iraqi, "A Word of Truth—a Message to the Lion Leader Usamah bin Ladin, May God Protect Him," October 12, 2006. For more on al-Tatarrus, see Mohammed A. Hafez, "Takfir and Violence Against Muslims" in *Fault Lines in Global Jihad: Organizational, Strategic, and Ideological Fissures*, ed. Assaf Moghadam and Brian Fishman (London: Routledge, 2011).

59. "Ansar al-Sunnah Shariah Commission Letter to Emir of al-Qaeda in Iraq," January 22, 2007, https://web.archive.org/web/20100621083823/http://ctc .usma.edu/publications/pdf/AAS_Letter_to_AQI.pdf.

60. Harmony Document NMEC-2007-636898. See also Harmony Documents NMEC-2007-636880, NMEC-2007-636888, and NMEC-2007-636892.

61. Abu Hamzah al-Muhajir, "Letter to Ansar al-Sunnah," undated, but likely early 2007 (Harmony Document NMEC-2007-636878).

62. Abu al-'Abbas, "Letter to 'Raja,'" in "Dear Brother Abu al-'Abbas," Bin Laden's Bookshelf (released March 1, 2016), 1.

63. Atiyah abd al-Rahman, "Letter to Mustafa Abu Yazid ('My Dear Brother "Adnan"')," March 15, 2007, Bin Laden's Bookshelf.

64. Atiyah abd al-Rahman, "Letter to Mustafa abd al-Yazid (SOCOM-2012-0000011)," March 28, 2007 [in the English translation, this document is inaccurately dated as March 28, 2011], Bin Laden's Bookshelf; author and recipient identified in Ayman al-Zawahiri, "Testimony to End Bloodshed Among Mujahidin in the Levant," *Hanin*, May 2, 2014.

65. Atiyah abd al-Rahman (Raja), "Letter to Abu al-'Abbas," in "Dear Brother Abu al-'Abbas," April 5, 2007, Bin Laden's Bookshelf (released March 1, 2016), 1–2.

66. Ibid.

67. Ibid.

68. Ibid.

69. Abd-al-Wahab Ibn Muhammad al-Sultan (Abu Wa'el), "Ansar al-Sunnah Group and All Who Are Afilliated [*sic*] with It Announce Their Resignation from the Group," April 9, 2007; Brian Fishman, "Dysfunction and Decline," *Combating Terrorism Center at West Point*, March 16, 2009, https://www.ctc.usma.edu /posts/dysfunction-and-decline-lessons-learned-from-inside-al-qaida-in-iraq (accessed June 4, 2016).

70. See, for example, "The Book of Truth or Mirage of Illusion," Ansar al-Sunnah Shariah Commission, August 5, 2007; "The Book of Truth," Media Diwan Ansar al-Islam, July 14, 2008; "Ansar al-Sunnah: Chronology, Call and Jihad," Media Office of the Ansar al-Sunnah Group, June 9, 2010; "Ansar al-Islam: From the Date of the First Banner of Jihad to Enabling the Emirate in Iraq," Media Office of Ansar al-Islam, September 8, 2010.

71. "The Story of the Conspiracy," Global Islamic Media Front, April 6, 2010; Huthaifa Azzam tweets, compiled by @sha___me, July 20, 2015; see also Aron Lund, "As Rifts Open Up in Syria's al-Qaeda Franchise, Secrets Spill Out," *Syria in Crisis,* August 10, 2015, http://carnegieendowment.org/syriaincrisis/?fa =60973 (accessed September 13, 2015); "The Book of Truth or Mirage of Illusion." Ansar al Sunnah Shariah Commission, August 5, 2007.

72. No less an authority than Huthaifa Azzam praised Hardan's character and credentials. William McCants, "The Believer," The Brookings Institution, September 1, 2015; Huthaifa Azzam tweets, compiled by @sha___me, July 20, 2015; see also Lund, "As Rifts Open Up in Syria's al-Qaeda Franchise."

73. Muhammad Abu Rumman, "The Politics of Sunni Armed Groups in Iraq," Carnegie Endowment for International Peace, September 18, 2007, http://carnegieendowment.org/sada/?fa=20836 (accessed June 4, 2016).

74. Colin Powell, "Remarks to the United Nations," February 5, 2003, http://www.cnn.com/2003/US/02/05/sprj.irq.powell.transcript (accessed June 4, 2016).

75. Abu Umar al-Baghdadi, Al-Furqan Media Establishment, April 17, 2007.

76. Ibid.

77. Harmony Document NMEC-2007-636898. See also Harmony Documents NMEC-2007-636880, NMEC-2007-636888, and NMEC-2007-636892.

78. Abu Hamzah al-Muhajir, "Letter to Abu Abdallah al-Shafi'I," April 29, 2007 (Harmony Document NMEC-2007-636898).

79. Ibid.

80. Peter Beaumont, "Saddam Aide in Exile Heads List of Most Wanted Terrorists," *The Guardian,* October 16, 2004.

81. Daniel Voll, "The Hunter Becomes the Hunted," *Esquire,* February 17, 2011.

82. Ali Fadhil, "Reviving the Iraqi Ba'ath: A Profile of General Muhammad Yunis al-Ahmad," *Jamestown Terrorism Monitor* 7, no. 3 (February 10, 2009).

83. Voll, "The Hunter Becomes the Hunted."

84. Joe Klein, "Saddam's Revenge," *Time,* September 18, 2005.

85. See "Ba'ath Representative: Extraordinary Conference in Damascus Was a Hybrid Bloc That Does Not Represent the Party," *Al-Quds al-Arabi,* January 30, 2007; Hayyan Nayyuf, "Ba'ath Vow to Avenge Saddam," Al-Arabiyah Net, January 7, 2007; Usama Mahdi, "Al-Douri's Announcement of Decision to Dismiss 30 Leading Members Discloses Their Identity to Occupation," *Ilaf,* May 2, 2007; "Al-Douri Becomes Secretary General of the Ba'ath Party," *Al-Hayah,* June 23, 2007.

86. Peter Spiegel and Ned Parker, "Divide Is Seen Within Iraq's Ba'ath Party," *Los Angeles Times,* April 25, 2007.

87. Izzat al-Douri, "Statement by Izzat Ibrahim al-Douri," *Ilaf,* January 1, 2007.

88. Hugh Naylor, "Syria Is Said to Be Strengthening Ties to Opponents of Iraq's Government," *The New York Times,* October 7, 2007.

89. Saddam's Fedayeen, "Campaign of Revenge for Saddam," Jihadist Websites, January 4, 2007.

90. See Michael Knights, "The JRTN Movement and Iraq's Next Insurgency," *CTC Sentinel*, July 1, 2011; Kyle W. Orton, "Izzat al-Douri and ISIS," *Baghdad Invest*, July 4, 2015, http://www.baghdadinvest.com/izzat-ad-douri-isis/ (accessed August 9, 2015).

91. Basim al-Radi al-bu Mahal, Samran Mikhlif al-bu Mahal, and Muhammad Husayn al-Shufayr Jughayfi, "Analysis of the State of the ISI," https://www.ctc.usma.edu/posts/analysis-of-the-state-of-isi-english-translation-2 (Harmony Document NMEC-2007-612449).

92. Ibid.

93. Ibid.

94. See Bill Roggio, Daveed Gartenstein-Ross, and Tony Badran, "Intercepted Letters Shed Light on State of Network in Iraq," Foundation for Defense of Democracies, September 12, 2008.

95. Al-bu Mahal, al-bu Mahal, and Jughayfi, "Analysis of the State of the ISI."

96. Ibid.

97. See Jarret Brachman, Jeff Bramlett, Joseph Felter, Brian Fishman, James Forest, Lianne Kennedy-Boudali, Bill Perkins, and Tom Stocking, "Harmony and Disharmony," Combating Terrorism Center at West Point, February 14, 2006, https://www.ctc.usma.edu/posts/harmony-and-disharmony-exploiting-al-qaidas-organizational-vulnerabilities. The sections and theory referenced here were developed primarily by Jacob Shapiro. See also Jacob Shapiro, *The Terrorist's Dilemma* (Princeton, NJ: Princeton University Press, 2013).

98. See Abd-al-Karim Hammadi, "Interview with Abd al-Rahim al-Rawi (Reputed Emir of the Islamic State of Iraq)," Al-Iraqiyah, May 12, 2010; see also Harmony Document NMEC-2007-637927.

99. See Felter and Fishman, "Al-Qa'ida Foreign Fighters in Iraq," and Brian Fishman, ed., *Bombers, Bank Accounts, and Bleedout: Al-Qa'ida's Road in and out of Iraq* (West Point, NY: Combating Terrorism Center, 2008).

100. See Pete Mansoor, *Surge: My Journey with General David Petraeus and the Remaking of the Iraq War* (New Haven, CT: Yale University Press, 2013).

101. Islamic Army of Iraq, "Reply of the Islamic Army in Iraq to the Speeches of Brother Abu Umar al-Baghdadi," Al-Boraq Media Center, April 5, 2007.

102. See al-Baghdadi, Al-Furqan Media Establishment, April 17, 2007.

103. Harmony Document: 100607 Jaysh al-Muj (Dr. Abu Ghofran, "Letter to Sheikh").

104. Harmony Document 100607 Jaysh al-Muj.

105. Richard Oppel, "Number of Unidentified Bodies Found in Baghdad Rose Sharply in May," *The New York Times*, June 1, 2007.

106. The local commander's name was Abu Hasan Safir.

107. Harmony Document NMEC-2007-637011.

108. Ibid.

109. "Al-Baghdadi Orders His Soldiers to Stay in Their Strongholds, Issues Fatwa Calling Islamic Army Elements 'Inviolable,'" *Quds Press,* June 2, 2007; Harmony Document NMEC-2007-639155.

110. Ibrahim Al-Shammari, Interview with Abd-al-Samad Nasir, Al Jazeera, June 1, 2007. The Islamic Army's repeated access to Al Jazeera in moments of crisis is indirect evidence of the group's ties to Gulf governments, particularly Qatar, which was trying to legitimize some Sunni opposition groups as a bulwark against the Islamic State of Iraq and Shia influence in Iraq.

111. "Jihad and Reform Front 22 May 2007," Bin Laden's Bookshelf.

112. Damien Cave and Ahmad Fadam, "Iraq Insurgents Employ Chlorine in Bomb Attacks," *The New York Times,* February 22, 2007.

113. Charles Faddis, who ran the CIA's effort to find the ISI's chlorine, said, "The attacks are not being particularly successful. The people are dying in the blast, but fortunately nobody is dying from chlorine." Peter Bergen, "Al Qaeda's Track Record with Chemical Weapons," CNN, May 7, 2013.

114. James Glanz, "Iraq Toll at 250 in the Deadliest Attack of the War," *The New York Times,* August 16, 2007; Damien Cave and James Glanz, "Toll Rises Above 500 in Iraq Bombings," *The New York Times,* August 22, 2007; "General Calls Attack on Yazidis 'Ethnic Cleansing,'" NPR, August 15, 2007.

115. "The Book of Truth or Mirage of Illusion."

116. Uthman Al-Mukhtar, "What Is Going On in Algeria Is Stupid and the Al-Qa'ida Organization in the Arab Maghreb Is Controlled by Teenagers," *Al-Arab* (posted on the Al-Hanein website, February 12, 2008).

117. Ibid.

118. Ibid.

119. "Press Briefing with Brigadier General Kevin Bergner," July 18, 2007, http://www.globalsecurity.org/military/library/news/2007/07/mil-070718-mnfi-b01.htm (accessed September 25, 2015); "Insurgents Killed While Rigging Trucks with Explosives," CNN June 27, 2007, www.cnn.com/2007/world/meast/06/27/ireg.main/index.html?eref-rss_latest.

120. "Return to the Mountains," Al-Furqan Media Establishment, March 14, 2007; "Press Briefing with Brigadier General Kevin Bergner."

121. Atiyah Abd al-Rahman, "Congratulations to the Iraqi Mujahidin," Jihadist Websites, December 13, 2006.

122. Mashadani was previously a member of Ansar al-Sunnah and served as its military emir in Baghdad. See Abu Waleed al-Salafi, "Complete History of Ansar al-Islam," translated by Aymenn Jawad al-Tamimi, http://www.aymennjawad.org/2015/12/a-complete-history-of-jamaat-ansar-al-islam (accessed January 3, 2016).

123. Malcolm Nance, *The Terrorists of Iraq: Inside the Strategy and Tactics of the Iraq Insurgency, 2003–2014,* 2nd ed. (New York: CRC Press, 2015), 287.

124. Dean Yates, "Senior al-Qa'ida Figure in Iraq a Myth: U.S. Military," Reuters, July 18, 2007; Nance, *The Terrorists of Iraq,* 286–288.

125. When American forces raided an ISI outpost near Sinjar in September 2007, Abu Sulayman's name was listed on a roster of foreign fighters who had joined the cause. Harmony Document NMEC-2007-657716. Al-Utaybi's pseudonym Muhammad Bin-Su'ud Bin-Mas'ad al-Thubayti appears thirty-second in a list of fighters that joined the cause. Wasim al-Dandashi, "A Saudi Who Did Not Complete His Studies Becomes the Judge of the Islamic State of Iraq," *Ilaf,* April 25, 2007.

126. The Global Islamic Media Front emphasized that point when it eulogized Abu Sulayman as "a scholar and a mujahid who lived and worked according to Islam, and set a prime example when he rushed to the battlefield to protect the land of Islam." "The General Command Eulogizes Sheikh Abu-Sulayman al-Utaybi, and Sheikh Abu-Dujanah al-Qahtani, May God Accept Them Among the Martyrs," Global Islamic Media Front, May 12, 2008.

127. Office of the Emir of the Believers, untitled statement, Ministry of Information of the Islamic State of Iraq, August 25, 2007. For public statements, see Abu Sulayman al-Utaybi, "Preserving the Truth," Al-Furqan Media Establishment, April 6, 2007, and Abu Sulayman al-Utaybi, "Why We Perform Jihad," Al-Firdaws, April 9, 2007.

128. Office of the Emir of the Believers Islamic State of Iraq, untitled statement, August 25, 2007.

129. Those letters were declassified and released to *The Long War Journal* and then subsequently translated by the Foundation for Defense of Democracies. Roggio, Gartenstein-Ross, and Badran, "Intercepted Letters Shed Light on State of Network in Iraq"; Abu Sulayman al-Utaybi, "Letter," Ana al-Muslim Forum, November 24, 2013. A bulletized version of this release was also posted to Just Paste It, http://justpaste.it/fhsu (accessed July 14, 2015).

130. Abu Sulayman left Iraq in August 2007 with another defector, Abu Dujanah al-Qahtani, and traveled across Iran with the assistance of Ansar al-Sunnah, the jihadi group that was abandoning the ISI.

131. "Letter to Abu Abdallah al-Hajj," Bin Laden's Bookshelf, December 17, 2007.

132. See Roggio, Gartenstein-Ross, and Badran, "Intercepted Letters Shed Light on State of Network in Iraq."

133. Ibid.

134. Ibid.

135. Ibid.

136. "U.S.: Letters Show Infighting over al-Qaeda in Iraq's Mission," CNN, September 11, 2008.

137. Al-Zawahiri, "Dear Honorable Brother Sheikh Azmaray," March 5, 2008, Bin Laden's Bookshelf (released March 1, 2006), 3–4.

138. "A Statement from the Al-Fajr Media Center Regarding the Martyrdom of the Two Jihad Leaders Sheikh Abu-Sulayman al-Utaybi and Sheikh Abu-Dujanah

al-Qahtani, May God Accept Them Among the Martyrs," Al-Fajr Media Center, May 11, 2008.

139. See, for example, untitled statement, Mujahidin Shura Council, September 18, 2006.

140. For a detailed discussion of the Islamic State's eschatology, see William McCants, *The ISIS Apocalypse: The History, Strategy, and Doomsday Vision of the Islamic State* (New York: St. Martin's Press, 2015).

141. "Interview with Adam Gadahn," *Resurgence*, special issue (Summer 2015).

142. Ayman al-Zawahiri, "Testimonial to Preserve the Blood of Mujahidin in al-Sham," *Markaz al-Sham*, May 3, 2014, https://pietervanostaeyen.wordpress .com/2014/05/03/dr-ayman-az-zawahiri-testimonial-to-preserve-the-blood-of -mujahideen-in-as-sham/ (accessed December 5, 2015).

143. "Jihad and Reform Front 22 May 2007," Bin Laden's Bookshelf.

144. Ibid.

145. Abu Umar al-Baghdadi, "For the Scum Disappears Like Froth Cast Out," Al-Furqan Media Establishment, December 4, 2007.

146. Ayman al-Zawahiri, "A Review of Events," As-Sahab Media Establishment, December 16, 2007.

147. For bin Laden notes, see Harmony Document SOCOM-2012-0000019.

148. Harmony Document SOCOM-2012-000004.

149. See Daniel Kimmage and Kathleen Ridolfo, "Iraqi Insurgent Media: The War of Images and Ideas," Radio Free Europe/Radio Liberty, June 26, 2007, 14–15; the IAI eventually set up a new al-Boraq with a similar url.

150. See Will McCants, "Islamic State of Iraq Online Media Distribution," *Jihadica*, June 24, 2008.

151. Thomas Hegghammer, "The Rise of Muslim Foreign Fighters," *International Security* 35, no. 3 (Winter 2010/2011), 53–94.

152. See Felter and Fishman, "Al-Qa'ida Foreign Fighters in Iraq," and Fishman, *Bombers, Bank Accounts, and Bleedout.*

153. "Twenty-one countries were listed in the Sinjar Records as the origin of one or more fighter. Saudi Arabia contributed the most fighters; Libya contributed the second highest number of fighters. Of the 576 fighters that listed their nationality, 41 percent (237) were of Saudi Arabian origin, and 19.2 percent (111) were Libyan. Syria, Yemen, and Algeria were the next most common origin countries with 8.1 percent (46), 8 percent (44), and 7.1 percent (41), respectively. Moroccans accounted for 6.1 percent (36) of the fighters and Jordanians 1.9 percent (11). Nearly all of the home countries listed were in the Middle East or North Africa, though the sample does include individuals from France (2), Great Britain (1), and Sweden (1)." Fishman, *Bombers, Bank Accounts, and Bleedout,* 34. The vast majority of fighters arriving in Iraq listed no useful skills. Of the 595, only 87 listed their skills. Of those, 11 listed computer skills, 10 mentioned weapons, and 6 described prior military experience.

154. Ibid., 45.

155. "2011 Libya Civil War Fast Facts," CNN, updated April 1, 2015, http://www.cnn .com/2013/09/20/world/libya-civil-war-fast-facts/ (accessed July 20, 2015).

156. For more, see Jean-Pierre Filiu, "Ansar al-Fatah and 'Iraqi' Networks in France," in *The Evolution of the Global Terrorist Threat,* ed. Bruce Hoffman and Fernando Reinares (New York: Columbia University Press, 2014); Sarah White and John-Thor Dahlburg, "Terrorist Bomb in Paris Subway Kills 4; Injures 62," *Los Angeles Times,* July 26, 1995; Craig Whitney, "2 Die as Bomb Rips Train at a Paris Station," *The New York Times,* December 4, 1996; Anneli Botha, "The 2007 Suicide Attacks in Algiers," in Hoffman and Reinares, *The Evolution of the Global Terrorist Threat;* Felter and Fishman, "Al-Qa'ida Foreign Fighters in Iraq."

157. See George Packer, "The Lesson of Tal Afar," *The New Yorker,* April 10, 2006.

158. Abu Ghadiyah's real name was Badran Turki Hishan al-Mazidh. He should not be confused with Sulayman Khalid Darwish, who used the same moniker but was killed in 2006. This mistake is common. See Reese Ehrlich and Peter Coyote, "The Murders at al-Sukariya," *Vanity Fair,* October 2009; "Who Is Abu Ghadiyah," Al-Boraq.Info, November 6, 2008; and "Biographies of Eminent Martyrs Version 22," Media Commission of the Mujahidin Shura Council, August 15, 2006.

159. "Who Is Abu Ghadiyah."

160. Thomas Joscelyn, "Blowback in Syria," *The Weekly Standard,* July 24, 2012.

161. "Treasury Designates Members of Abu Ghadiyah's Network Facilitates Flow of Terrorists, Weapons, and Money from Syria to al Qaida in Iraq," U.S. Treasury Department, February 28, 2008; NAJM, "Arrest of Abu Talhah al-Kuwaiti," Al-Fallujah Islamic Forum, http://www.al-faloja.info/vb/showthread.php?t =58871 (accessed June 16, 2009).

162. U.S. Treasury Department, February 28, 2008.

163. Joseph Felter and Brian Fishman, "Becoming a Foreign Fighter: A *Second* Look at the Sinjar Records," in Fishman, *Bombers, Bank Accounts, and Bleed-out,* 46.

164. See Laura Rozen, "Syriana, the Rendon Group Edition," *Mother Jones,* May 6, 2008.

165. "Stolen Honda Used in Attack on U.S. Vehicle," *The Daily Star,* January 16, 2008.

166. Hani Bathish, "FBI Team Arrives to Aid in Probe of Karantina Blast Site," *The Daily Star,* January 18, 2008; "Shattered Glass, Bloodied Bystanders Mark Site of Latest Bombing," *The Daily Star,* January 15, 2008.

167. See Harmony Document NMEC-2007-639306.

168. Ibid.

169. Ayman al-Zawahiri, "Open Meeting with Ayman al-Zawahiri," As-Sahab Media Center, April 2, 2008. Specifically, Zawahiri explained: "[I spoke indirectly because the] brothers in Fatah al-Islam were being accused by the agents of America of being a branch of al-Qaida, and the brothers were denying that, so

I feared that if I supported them openly, I would cause difficulties for them at a time when we were unable to extend to them a helping hand."

170. See Bernard Rougier, *Everyday Jihad: The Rise of Militant Islam Among Palestinians in Lebanon* (Cambridge, MA: Harvard University Press, 2007).

171. Bernard Rougier, *The Sunni Tragedy in the Middle East* (Princeton, NJ: Princeton University Press, 2015).

172. Sami Haddad, "The Inside Story of Fatah al-Islam's Shakir al-Absi," *Ya Libnan*, June 16, 2007.

173. Ibid.

174. Abu Abdallah al-Maqdisi, "Open Conversation with Abu Abdallah al-Maqdisi," Shmukh Islamic Forum, August 14, 2007.

175. Ibid.

176. "Charges Pressed Against 59 Individuals from Fatah al-Islam That Include 25 in Custody in the Events of Nahr al-Barid for Crimes Against State Security, Committing Terroris[t] Acts, and Killing Members of the Army," Lebanese National News Agency, September 20, 2007.

177. A Fatah al-Islam release listing its battlefield losses noted thirty-nine people who had been killed in the group's service. Of those whose nationality was listed or whose names clearly suggested a nationality, the proportions are similar to those listed in the Lebanese indictment. The one exception is the number of Tunisians who were indicted. This discrepancy reinforces other anecdotal evidence that Tunisians often operated as logisticians rather than frontline fighters. Syrian: 17; Lebanese: 2; Saudi: 2; Algerian: 1; Tunisian: 1; Yemeni: 1; Jordanian: 3; Palestinian: 5; Libyan: 1. "Fatah al-Islam Caravan of Martyrs," *Midad al-Suyuf*, January 3, 2008.

178. Abd al-Rahman, "Letter to Mustafa Abu Yazid ('My Dear Brother "Adnan"')."

179. "The Martyrs of the Nahr al-Barid Battle, Part Three," Fatah al-Islam Media Division, July 15, 2008; "The Martyrs of the Nahr al-Barid Battle, Part Two," Fatah al-Islam Media Division, June 30, 2008; "The Martyrs of the Nahr al-Barid Battle, Part Five," Fatah al-Islam Media Division, July 30, 2008.

180. "The Martyrs of the Nahr al-Barid Battle, Part Three."

181. Posted by "Abu-Mas'ub al-Masry," "Caravan of Martyrs," *Midad al-Suyuf*, January 3, 2008, www.almedad.com/vb.

182. Bilal Y. Sa'ab, "Al-Qa'ida's Presence and Influence in Lebanon," *CTC Sentinel* 1, no. 12 (November 2008).

183. For example, see Harmony Documents NMEC-2007-657976, NMEC-2007-658005, NMEC-2007-658007, and NMEC-2007-658014.

184. See Zeina Karam and Qassim Abdul-Zahra, "Al Qaeda's Nusra Front Leaders Stays in Syria's Shadows," *The National*, November 4, 2013; Pieter Van Ostaeyen, "An Alleged Biography of Abu Muhammad al-Julani—Some Ideas," Pietervanostaeyen.wordpress.com, December 16, 2013; Truls Hallberg Tonnessen, "Heirs of Zarqawi or Saddam? The Relationship Between al-Qaida in Iraq and the Islamic State," *Perspectives on Terrorism* 9, no. 4 (2015).

185. "Gunmen Attack U.S. Embassy in Damascus," Associated Press, September 12, 2006.

186. "Interview with Abu Abdallah al-Maqdisi," Shmukh Islamic Forum, August 14, 2007.

187. Ibid.

188. Sa'ab, "Al-Qa'ida's Presence and Influence in Lebanon."

189. Husayn, "Letter to Adnan and Jasim."

190. Al-Absi did release several public statements during this period, most notably in early January 2008. Shakir al-Absi, "Statement," Hanin Net, January 7, 2008.

191. Rif Naffa, "Fatah al-Islam: Dream of Emirate Built on Sand," *Sada al-Balad*, January 30, 2008.

192. Abu Usama al-Maqdisi, "Fight the Chiefs of Unfaith," Fatah al-Islam Media Division, Jihadist Websites December 19, 2007.

193. Husayn, "Letter to Adnan and Jasim."

194. Abu Umar al-Baghdadi, "Religion Is Sincere Advice," Al-Furqan Media Establishment, February 14, 2008.

195. The other jihadi with Abu Talhah was Muhsin al-Fadhli, who was so deeply tied into al-Qaeda that he was suspected of being one of the few jihadis that knew of 9/11 beforehand. Al-Fadhli was ultimately killed in Syria in 2014. "Treasury Targets Key al-Qa'ida Funding and Support Network Using Iran as a Critical Transit Point," U.S. Treasury Department, July 28, 2011. https://www.treasury.gov/press-center/press-releases/Pages/tg1261.aspx.

196. Abu Talhah al-Kuwaiti was also known as Muhammad al-Dawsari. Husayn al-Harbi, "The Wanted Men Left Kuwait for Iran by Sea," *Al-Ra'y*, November 30, 2008; Husayn al-Harbi, "Abu Talhah al-Dawsari Arrives in Afghanistan," *Al-Ra'y*, November 22, 2008.

197. Radwan Murtada, "Abu Talhah al-Dawsari: al-Qaeda's Representative in Roumieh," *Al-Akhbar*, August 17, 2011. There is conflicting information about the exact date of Abu Talhah's arrival in Lebanon, but it appears to have been either May or June 2009.

198. "Beirut Court Sentences Three in UNIFIL Plot," UPI, January 8, 2010.

199. "Lebanon Arrests Islamists Plotting Attacks," *Al-Arabiya*, July 21, 2009.

200. Abu Talhah al-Kuwaiti, "A Story of Escape from the Roumieh Central Prison in Lebanon," *Al-Fida*, September 28, 2011.

201. Ibid.

202. "Doctors Held in Bomb Attack Probe," BBC, July 2, 2007.

203. Andrew Alderson, Ben Leach, and Duncan Gardham, "Bilal Abdulla; Doctor by Day, Terrorist by Night," *The Telegraph*, December 20, 2008.

204. Thanks to Shiraz Maher for sharing his recollection of Bilal Abdulla and Kafeel Ahmed.

205. Rafaello Pantuc'i, "The Islamist Terrorist Threat to Europe After Osama bin Laden's Death," Chatham House, July 1, 2011, https://www.chathamhouse.org

/sites/files/chathamhouse/public/Research/International%20Security
/010811wr_terrorism.pdf (accessed June 1, 2016); Raymond Bonner, Jane Perlez, and Eric Schmitt, "British Inquiry of Failed Plots Points to Iraq's Qaeda
Group," *The New York Times,* December 14, 2007.

206. Bonner, Perlez, and Schmitt, "British Inquiry of Failed Plots Points to Iraq's
Qaeda Group."
207. "Audio Interview with the Minister of War of the Islamic State of Iraq," Al-
Furqan Media Establishment, October 24, 2008.
208. Husayn, "Letter to Adnan and Jasim."
209. Despite these setbacks, however, the ISI was deeply resilient. Captured rosters
of fighters reveal thousands of names across the country, lending credence to
Abu Hamzah al-Muhajir's claim of 12,000 fighters under arms when the
Islamic State of Iraq was originally declared. See, for example, Harmony Documents MNFV-2007-000418, MNFV-2007-000422, MNFV-2007-000414,
MNFV-2007-000413, and MNFV-2007-000409.
210. Harmony Document MNFA-2007-000566.
211. Ibid.
212. See Harmony Document MNFA-2007-000572.
213. See Harmony Document MNFA-2007-000573; for a roster of individuals paid
according to these rules, see Harmony Document MNFA-2007-000562.
214. Harmony Document MNFA-2007-000566.
215. See Harmony Documents MNFV-2007-000424 and MNFV-2007-000428.
216. For a much more detailed breakdown of the ISI's fundraising and spending
patterns during this period, see Patrick Johnston et al., *Foundations of the Islamic State: Management, Money, and Terror in Iraq* (Santa Monica, CA: RAND
Corporation, 2016).
217. Harmony Document MNFA-2007-000566.
218. Michael Silverman, *Awakening Victory* (Philadelphia: Cassmate, 2011),
151–154.
219. The author was "Abu Tariq," emir of the al-Layin and al-Mashahdah sectors.
Harmony Document MNFT-2007-005648.
220. Abu Hamzah al-Muhajir, "Instructions to Emirs," September 23, 2007; Abu
Hamzah al-Muhajir, "Instructions to Soldiers," September 23, 2007; transla-
tions by the Global Islamic Media Front.
221. "Instructions to Emirs," September 23, 2007.
222. Scott Helfstein, ed., *Making the Grade: Assessing al-Qa'ida's Learning and Adap-
tation* (West Point, NY: Combating Terrorism Center, 2009).
223. Anonymous, "On the Ground from Syria to Iraq," in Fishman, *Bombers, Bank
Accounts, and Bleedout.*
224. Jonathan Finer, "Among Insurgents in Iraq, Few Foreigners Are Found," *The
Washington Post,* November 17, 2005; anonymous, "On the Ground from Syria
to Iraq."

225. Bradley Klapper, "Thousands of Christians Flee Mosul," Associated Press, October 11, 2008.

226. Jane Arraf, "As Iraq Calms, Mosul Remains a Battle Front," *Christian Science Monitor*, December 17, 2008; Michael Gordon, "Pushed Out of Baghdad, Insurgents Move North," *The New York Times*, December 6, 2007.

227. Rod Nordland, "Exceptions to Iraq Deadline Are Proposed," *The New York Times*, April 27, 2009.

228. Pascale Combelles Siegel, "Coalition Attack Brings an End to the Career of al-Qaeda in Iraq's Second-in-Command," *Jamestown Terrorism Monitor* 6, no. 21 (November 7, 2008).

229. Complaint in *U.S.A. v. Faruq Khalil Muhammad 'Isa*, January 19, 2011; Thomas Renard, "Moroccan Crackdown on Salafiya Jihadiya Recruitment of Fighters for Iraq," *Jamestown Terrorism Monitor* 5, no. 27 (July 23, 2008).

230. Ernesto Londono, "No. 2 Leader of al-Qaeda in Iraq Killed," *The Washington Post*, October 16, 2008; "Al Baghdadi Confirms the Death of Al Qaeda's Second-in-Command," CBS News, October 23, 2008.

231. Harmony Document NMEC-2009-602125.

232. Harmony Document NMEC-2007-000566.

233. "ISIS Renaming Mosul Neighborhoods and Mosques After Killed Jihadis," *Rudaw*, May 17, 2015.

234. See Harmony Document NMEC-2009-600863.

235. See Harmony Documents NMEC-2009-602764 and NMEC-2010-198564.

236. Jonathan S. Landay and Nancy A. Youssef, "CIA Led Mystery Syria Raid That Killed Terrorist Leader," *McClatchy Newspapers*, October 27, 2008, http://www.mcclatchydc.com/news/nation-world/world/article24507010.html (accessed October 2, 2015).

237. Sean Naylor, *Relentless Strike* (New York: St. Martin's Press, 2015), 322.

238. Eric Schmitt and Thom Shanker, *Counter Strike: The Untold Story of America's Secret Campaign Against Al Qaeda* (New York: Macmillan, 2011).

239. Mitchell Prothero and Peter Beaumont, "Dam[a]scus Car Bomb Kills 17," *The Guardian*, September 27, 2008.

240. Raed Rafei, "Babylon and Beyond Blog," *Los Angeles Times*, November 7, 2008, http://latimesblogs.latimes.com/babylonbeyond/2008/11/syria-tv-confes.html (accessed August 2, 2015); and Khaled Yacoub Oweis, "Syria Says Fatah al-Islam Group Behind Bombing," Reuters, November 6, 2008.

241. Nicholas Blanford, "Syrian Bombing: A Jihadi Attack?," *Christian Science Monitor*, September 29, 2008.

242. "Fatah al-Islam Leader Believed Dead," Al Jazeera, December 11, 2008, http://www.aljazeera.com/news/middleeast/2008/12/2008121017402963336.html (accessed August 3, 2015).

243. Ibid.

244. Complaint in *U.S.A. v. Faruq Khalil Muhammad 'Isa*, January 19, 2011.

245. Sam Dagher, "Suicide Attack Kills 5 G.I.'s and 2 Iraqis in Northern Iraq City," *The New York Times*, April 10, 2009; Complaint in *U.S.A. v. Faruq Khalil Muhammad 'Isa*, January 19, 2011.

246. Complaint in *U.S.A. v. Faruq Khalil Muhammad 'Isa*, January 19, 2011.

247. Karen DeYoung, "Iraq Militant Group's Pipeline Through Syria Revives After Long Gap," *The Washington Post*, May 11, 2009.

248. See Bill Roggio, "Senior al Qaeda Leader Leaves Pakistan, Directs Iraq Operations from Syria," *The Long War Journal*, August 21, 2009; "Treasury Targets Key al-Qa'ida in Iraq Operative," United States Department of Treasury, May 14, 2009.

249. Atiyah abd al-Rahman, "Our Respected Sheikh," August 22, 2009, Bin Laden's Bookshelf (released March 1, 2006).

250. DeYoung, "Iraq Militant Group's Pipeline Through Syria Revives."

251. Complaint in *U.S.A. v. Faruq Khalil Muhammad 'Isa*, January 19, 2011.

252. Al-bu Mahal, al-bu Mahal, and Jughayfi, "Analysis of the State of the ISI."

253. Muhammad Khalil al-Hakaymah, *Towards a New Strategy in Resisting the Occupier*, www.althabeton.co.nr, September 11, 2006. (Originally accessed: March 1, 2007.) A replica of the original links to this text can be accessed at: https://web.archive.org/web/20070222070122/http://altabetoun.110mb.com /news.php?action=view&id=135 (many thanks to Brinjar Lia's *Architect of Global Jihad: The Life of al-Qaida Strategist Abu Mus'ab al-Suri* for this citation).

254. Al-Zawahiri, "Dear Honorable Brother Sheikh Azmaray," Bin Laden's Bookshelf. The author of this letter does not name himself, but context reveals it to be Zawahiri. See in particular his reference to responding to questions from followers on jihadi websites. Zawahiri's response was released a month after this letter is dated. See Ayman al-Zawahiri, "Open Meeting with Sheikh Ayman al-Zawahiri."

Chapter Four: The Stage of Recuperation

1. Daniel Williams, "Fighters' Camp Hit by Major U.S. Strike," *The Washington Post*, June 14, 2003; Tom Lasseter and Drew Brown, "U.S. Attack Threatens to Make Thousands of New Iraqi Enemies," Knight-Ridder, June 13, 2003; David Rohde, "After the War: Hussein Die-Hards; Carnage and Clues Are Left in Camp Destroyed by U.S.," *The New York Times*, June 13, 2003.

2. Abu Ubayda is generally known as Ghassan al-Rawi.

3. Ken Ballen, *Terrorists in Love* (New York: Free Press, 2011), 64–70; "2 Americans Among 22 Killed in Baghdad," MSNBC News Services, May 8, 2005, http://www.nbcnews.com/id/7721003/ns/world_news-mideast_n_africa/t /americans-among-killed-baghdad/#.VdJiDxNVikp (accessed August 17, 2015).

4. Abd al-Karrim al-Hammadi, "Interview with Manaf Abd al-Rahim, the Baghdad Emir," Exclusive Interview, al-Iraqiyah, May 12, 2010.

5. Bisan al-Sheikh, "Whoever Went to Iraq from Lebanon Will Not Do It Again Because Greater Syria Has Become 'War Battleground,'" *Al-Hayah*, April 13, 2007.

6. Mohammed Hafez, *Suicide Bombers in Iraq* (Washington, DC: United States Instiute of Peace Press, 2007), 182.

7. Al-Hammadi, "Interview with Manaf Abd al-Rahim, the Baghdad Emir."

8. For more, see Harmony Documents NMEC-2009-602764 and NMEC-2010-174915. The Baghdad emir is called Haji Abd al-Wahid and was in conflict with an individual named 'Aqil. Other documents indicate that a conflict between "Abu Aqil" and "Abu Sulayman" should lead to Abu Sulayman's dismissal.

9. Salam Faraj, "Iraq Broadcasts Truck Bomber Confession," *Sydney Morning Herald*, August 24, 2009; Sam Dagher, "2 Blasts Expose Security Flaws in Heart of Iraq," *The New York Times*, August 19, 2009.

10. Jane Arraf, "Baghdad Bombing Leaves Hole in Diplomatic Corps," *The Christian Science Monitor*, August 24, 2009.

11. "Deadly Bombings Worst Iraq Attack in Two Years," CNN, October 25, 2009.

12. Khalid al-Ansary, "Iraq's Maliki Blasts Foreign Support for Bombings," Reuters, December 9, 2009.

13. Brian Fishman, "Redefining the Islamic State: The Fall and Rise of al-Qaeda in Iraq," New America Foundation, August 2011.

14. Craig Whiteside, "War Interrupted, Part I: The Roots of the Jihadist Resurgence in Iraq," *War on the Rocks*, November 5, 2014.

15. Greg Bruno, "Finding a Place for the 'Sons of Iraq,'" Council on Foreign Relations, January 9, 2009, http://www.cfr.org/iraq/finding-place-sons-iraq /p16088.

16. Craig Whiteside, "The Smiling, Scented Men: The Political Worldview of the Islamic State of Iraq, 2003–2013" (PhD diss., Washington State University, 2014), 158.

17. Arraf, "Baghdad Bombing Leaves Hole in Diplomatic Corps."

18. Al-Rawi also described the relationship between Abu Umar and Abu Hamzah: "Al-Baghdadi was not a war commander. He was higher in rank than Abu-Hamzah but the latter is responsible for military affairs."

19. Al-Hammadi, "Interview with Manaf Abd al-Rahim, the Baghdad Emir."

20. The initial U.S. read on these attacks jibes with al-Rawi's explanation. In August 2009, a U.S. spokesman explained, "Our evidence points so far to elements here in Iraq; where the bombs were built, those kinds of things." Also, in September 2009: "I will tell you that we believe many of these recent high-profile attacks are signature al Qaeda attacks." See press conference with Major General John Johnson, OSD-PA, August 27, 2009, http://www.globalsecurity .org/military/library/news/2009/08/mil-090827-dod01.htm; and press conference with Lieutenant General Charles Jacoby, OSD-PA, September 10, 2009, http://www.globalsecurity.org/military/library/news/2009/09/mil-090910 -dod02.htm.

21. Jihad al-Juburi (Ministry of Interior), Press Conference, Al-Sharqiyah Television, December 9, 2009.

22. United States of America and Republic of Iraq, "Agreement Between the United States of America and the Republic of Iraq on the Withdrawal of United States Forces from Iraq and the Organization of Their Activities During Their Temporary Presence in Iraq," November 17, 2008.

23. Karen DeYoung, "Obama Sets Timetable for Iraq Withdrawal, Calling It Part of Broader Middle East Strategy," *The Washington Post*, February 28, 2009.

24. Joel Rayburn, *Iraq After America: Strongmen, Sectarians, Resistance* (Stanford, CA: Hoover Institute Press, 2014), 214–215.

25. Thanks to Douglas Ollivant for discussions on this issue.

26. Haider Najm, "Government Crackdown and Feuds Weaken Awakening Councils," *Niqash*, September 30, 2009.

27. Geoff Ziezeluwicz, "Empowered by the U.S., Imprisoned by the Iraqis," *Stars and Stripes*, September 24, 2009; "Al Qaeda Chief Who Supported U.S. Forces Sentenced to Death," *The Telegraph* (United Kingdom), November 19, 2009.

28. See Harmony Document NMEC-2010-186334; Ben Bahney, Patrick Johnston, and Patrick Ryan, "The Enemy You Know and the Ally You Don't," *Foreign Policy*, June 23, 2015.

29. See also Nawzat Shamdeen, "Blackmailing the Government in Mosul," *Niqash*, January 25, 2012.

30. Harmony Document NMEC-2010-186334.

31. Ernesto Lodono, "Iraq Reports Arrest of Mastermind of '09 Bombing," *The Washington Post*, April 22, 2010.

32. Press conference with General Ray Odierno, OSD-PA, October 1, 2009, http://www.globalsecurity.org/military/library/news/2009/10/mil-091001-dod01.htm.

33. Al-Hammadi, "Interview with Manaf Abd al-Rahim, the Baghdad Emir."

34. Qassim Abdul-Zahra, "Militant Led Iraqis to al-Qaida Chief," Associated Press, April 30, 2010.

35. Waleed Ibrahim, "Al Qaeda's Two Top Iraq Leaders Killed in Raid," Reuters, April 19, 2010.

36. For a nice rundown, see Scott Steward, "Jihadist in Iraq: Down for the Count?," *Stratfor*, April 29, 2010.

37. "Press Conference with General Ray Odierno," OSD-PA, June 4, 2010, http://www.globalsecurity.org/military/library/news/2010/06/mil-100604-dod01.htm.

38. See Bill Roggio, "Iraqi Forces Arrest Leader of Ansar al-Islam," *The Long War Journal*, May 4, 2010; Abu Waleed al-Salafi, "Complete History of Jamaat Ansar al-Islam," trans. Aymenn Jawad al-Tamimi, December 15, 2015, http://www.aymennjawad.org/2015/12/a-complete-history-of-jamaat-ansar-al-islam.

39. "Press Conference with Brigadier General Robert Brown," OSD-PA, October 20, 2009.

40. "Press Conference with General Ray Odierno," OSD-PA, October 1, 2009.

41. "Press Conference with General Ray Odierno," OSD-PA, February 22, 2010.

42. "Letter to Sheikh Abu Abdallah dtd 17 July 2010," Bin Laden's Bookshelf.

43. For example, "Jaysh al-Umma Offers Condolences to the Islamic Umma on the Leaders of Global Jihad," Al-Fallujah Forum, April 25, 2010; "From Jaysh al-Umma to the Islamic State of Iraq, May God Keep It," Al-Fallujah Forum, May 2, 2010; "A Statement on the Martyrdom of the Amir Al-Baghdadi and His Minister of War, al-Muhajir," Al-Fajr Media Network, April 26, 2010; "The Moroccan Condolence," Al-Fallujah Forum, May 4, 2010.

44. "Eulogizing the Two Leaders: The Commander of the Faithful Abu-Umar al-Baghdadi and the Minister of War Abu-Hamza al-Muhajir," As-Sahab Media Foundation, May 24, 2010.

45. "Press Conference with General Ray Odierno," OSD-PA, June 4, 2010.

46. There are a range of jihadi biographies of Ibrahim bin Awad. For a good retelling, see Pieter van Ostaeyen, "Abu Bakr al-Baghdadi—A Short Biography of the ISIS Sheikh," pietervnostaeyen.wordpress.com, July 15, 2013 (accessed June 1, 2016).

47. See Aron Lund, "Who Will Succeed Abu Bakr al-Baghdadi? (And Does He Need a Successor?)," Carnegie Endowment for International Peace, May 14, 2015.

48. William McCants, "The Believer," Brookings Institution, September 1, 2015.

49. See Volkmar Kabisch, Amir Musawy, Georg Mascolo, and Christian Baars, "On the Trail of the IS Leader," ARD, February 18, 2015; Loveday Morris of *The Washington Post* provides a useful summary of the documents as well. See Loveday Morris, "Is This the High School Report Card of the Head of the Islamic State?," *The Washington Post*, February 19, 2015.

50. McCants, "The Believer."

51. *Ibrahim Awad Ibrahim Detainee Record,* U.S. Army Corrections Command; declassified as a result of a Freedom of Information Act request by *Business Insider.* See Hunter Walker, "Here Is the Army's Declassified Iraq Prison File on the Leader of ISIS," *Business Insider,* February 18, 2015.

52. See Abu Muhammad al-Maqdisi, "Umar, You Have Brought Happiness into My Heart," Al-Fallujah Forum, June 13, 2010.

53. Martin Chulov, "ISIS: The Inside Story," *The Guardian,* December 11, 2014.

54. Ibid.

55. Ibid.

56. See Richard Barrett, "The Islamic State," The Soufan Group, November 2014; Jawad al-Bulani (Iraqi interior minister), press conference, December 2, 2010, broadcast on Al-Iraqiyah, December 2, 2010, https://www.rewardsforjustice.net /english/abu_dua.html.

57. "Al Qaeda Facilitator Likely Dead in Coalition Air Strike," American Forces Press Service, October 26, 2005, http://archive.defense.gov/news/newsarticle .aspx?id=17963 (accessed January 21, 2016).

58. In addition to statements posted to various jihadi web forums, the Army of the Followers of the Sunnah developed a main website at www.alsaleeb.com. The

site appeared in late 2005 and was essentially unused by the end of 2006. Nonetheless, it includes numerous political and ideological statements.

59. Central Committee of Ahl al-Sunnah wa'al Jammah, "A Military Statement: The Revolutionary Brigade Arrests Gang of Iranian Intelligence in Diyala," Jihadist Websites, January 19, 2006.

60. Central Committee of Ahl al-Sunnah wa'al Jammah, "Military Statement: Ahl-al-Sunnah wa-al-Jama'ah Army; Killing the Deputy Military Leader of Al-Mahdi Army in the Governorate of Diyala," Hanein Islamic Forum, January 5, 2006.

61. Central Committee of Ahl al-Sunnah wa'al Jammah, "The General Plan," https://web.archive.org/web/20060107182138/; http://www.alsabeel.net/index .htm (accessed August 20, 2015).

62. Chulov, "ISIS: The Inside Story."

63. See Harmony Document NMEC-2009-602125-HT; credit to Patrick Johnston, Jacob N. Shapiro, Howard J. Shatz, Benjamin Bahney, Danielle Jung, Patrick K. Ryan, and Jonathan Wallace *Foundations of the Islamic State: Management, Money, and Terror in Iraq, 2005–2010* (Santa Monica, CA: RAND Corporation, 2016), 6.

64. Marc Lynch, "AQ-Iraq's Counter Counter-Insurgency Manual," *Foreign Policy*, March 17, 2010.

65. Uthman bin Abd al-Rahim al-Tamimi, "Informing the People About the Islamic State of Iraq," Al-Furqan Media Establishment, December 2006.

66. Ibid.

67. "A Statement of the Islamic State of Iraq's Shura Council," Shura Council of the Islamic State of Iraq, May 16, 2010. Unlike propaganda released by the Islamic State of Iraq, which was usually attributed to the al-Furqan Media Establishment, administrative matters were often attributed to the Shura Council of the Islamic State of Iraq.

68. Hani Nasirah, "New al-Qaeda Leadership in Iraq," *Al-Hayah*, May 21, 2010.

69. Letter from Atiyah abd al-Rahman to ISIS, April 21, 2010, quoted in Ayman al-Zawahiri, "Testimonial to Preserve the Blood of Mujahidin in al-Sham," Markaz al-Sham, May 3, 2014, https://pietervanostaeyen.wordpress.com/2014 /05/03/dr-ayman-az-zawahiri-testimonial-to-preserve-the-blood-of-mujahideen -in-as-sham/ (accessed December 5, 2015).

70. "Tunis," undated Bin Laden's Bookshelf, released March 1, 2016.

71. Letter from "an ISIS Sheikh to Atiyah," October 2010, quoted in Ayman al-Zawahiri, "Testimonial to Preserve the Blood of Mujahidin in al-Sham."

72. Osama bin Laden to Atiyah abd al-Rahman, July 16, 2011 (Harmony Document SOCOM-2012-0000019). The date is not included in the original document but is referenced in Zawahiri, "Testimonial to Preserve the Blood of Mujahidin in al-Sham."

73. "Letter to Sheikh Abu Abdallah dtd 17 July 2010."

74. Abu Muhammad al-Adnani, "The Islamic State of Iraq Will Remain," Al-Furqan Media Establishment, August 7, 2011.

75. Haji Bakr's true name was Samir Abu Muhammad al-Khilifawi. Abu Ahmad, "The Hidden Truths About Baghdadi's State," Jihadist Websites, April 7, 2014; some versions of the story suggest that Haji Bakr proved his loyalty to Abu Bakr by revealing information about Ba'athist networks in Iraq. "@Wikibaghdady Tweets," December 14, 2013, translated and collected by Yousuf bin Tafshin, http://justpaste.it/e90q (accessed January 20, 2016).

76. Letter from "an ISIS Sheikh to Atiyah," spring 2011, quoted in Ayman al-Zawahiri, "Testimonial to Preserve the Blood of Mujahidin in al-Sham."

77. Ahmad, "The Hidden Truths About Baghdadi's State."

78. For example, he asserted that Abu Bakr never studied for his PhD at Saddam Islamic University in Baghdad, when numerous witnesses, including his dissertation advisor, claim that he did. See William McCants, *The ISIS Apocalypse* (New York: St. Martin's Press, 2015), 76; Aaron Y. Zelin, "Abu Bakr al-Baghdadi: The Islamic State's Driving Force," BBC News, July 31, 2014, www.bbc.com /news/world-middle-east-28560449.

79. Letter from "an ISI communication representative to Atiyah," May 2011, quoted in Zawahiri, "Testimonial to Preserve the Blood of Mujahidin in al-Sham."

80. Zawahiri, "Testimonial to Preserve the Blood of Mujahidin in al-Sham."

81. Specifically, Zawahiri explains that "when ISI was announced, the leadership of al-Qaeda Central (AQC) under Sheikh Osama was not asked for permission, consulted, or even made aware of it! Abu Hamza al-Muhajir sent a letter to the central leadership justifying the creation of a state and that its allegiance was to AQC. And that the brothers in their Shura took an oath on Abu Omar al-Baghdadi that his leader is OBL and that ISI is part of AQ. And the brothers decided to work like this but not announce it publicly due to certain political aspects as they saw it. . . . The brothers in the leadership of AQ and ISI used to work on the basis that ISI was a part of AQC [al-Qaeda Central]." Zawahiri, "Testimonial to Preserve the Blood of Mujahidin in al-Sham"; Zawahiri goes on to cite several documents that the United States captured during the raid on Osama bin Laden's hideout in Abbottabad, specifically Harmony Documents SOCOM-2012-0000019 and SOCOM-2012-0000012.

82. If the correspondence Zawahiri cites is authentic, it contradicts General Odierno's October 2009 assertion that communication between the ISI and al-Qaeda Central had been "severed." "Press Conference with General Ray Odierno," OSD-PA, October 1, 2009.

83. The biography of Abu Bakr al-Baghdadi is usually attributed to Turk bin 'Ali, head of ISIS Shariah Committee, but the version I used is officially unattributed. "The Biography of Sheikh Abu Bakr al-Baghdadi Amir of the Islamic State in Iraq and Al-Sham," Archive.org/thebiographyofsheikhababubakralbaghd adi (accessed June 12, 2015).

84. Abu Hamzah al-Baghdadi, *Why Do We Fight? Who Do We Fight?*, Islamic Renewal Organization website, October 2005. A good example of this thinking is Bidun Mujamalah, "In Support of Abu Muhammad al-Adnani's Address: A Message to the Lions of Monotheism in Iraq," Shmukh Islamic Network, August 11, 2011.

85. Ellen Knickmeyer, "Al-Qaeda Web Forums Abruptly Taken Offline," *The Washington Post*, October 18, 2008.

86. Ellen Nakashima, "Dismantling of Saudi-CIA Website Illustrates Need for Clearer Cyberwar Policies," *The Washington Post*, March 19, 2010.

87. The jihadi community often referred to President Barack Obama by the derogatory term "house slave." "YouTube Campaign," Mujahidin Electronic Network, November 24, 2015.

88. "Al-Nusrah 3: Blog Raid," Jihadist Websites, November 17, 2009.

89. Abu Salim Mustafa al-Kinani, "The Third Phase of the Facebook Campaign," al-Fallujah Forum, April 21, 2009.

90. "The Alternative Is the Jihadist Shmukh al-Islam Web Forum, a Site That Makes You Love Martyrdom," Jihadist Websites, September 25, 2008.

91. Joseph Felter and Brian Fishman, "A First Look at the Sinjar Records," Combating Terrorism Center at West Point, December 2007; Kevin Peraino, "The Jihadist Riddle," *Newsweek*, April 19, 2008.

92. Zawahiri's change of heart was dramatic. In August 2009, he said that "the regime in Egypt and in most Arab-Islamic countries cannot be changed except by force. The regime in Egypt will not submit to any peaceful attempt for change, and Husni Mubarak and his son will not cede power except by force." Ayman al-Zawahiri, "The Facts of Jihad and the Lies of Hypocrisy," As-Sahab Media Foundation, August 3, 2009.

93. See Brian Fishman, "At a Loss for Words," *Foreign Policy*, February 15, 2011.

94. "To Our Muslim Family in Beloved Egypt," Ministry of War, the Islamic State of Iraq, February 8, 2011, http://jihadology.net/2011/02/08/al-fajr-media-presents-a-new-statement-from-the-islamic-state-of-iraq-al-qa%E2%80%99idah-to-our-muslim-family-in-beloved-egypt/ (accessed August 22, 2015).

95. Syria's digital revolutionaries called for protests on February 5, 2011, but those efforts fizzled. "Syrians Call for Facebook Revolution," *Damascus Bureau*, February 2, 2011; reposted by Vampire, "Syrians Call for Facebook Revolution," February 5, 2011, http://sawte.com/showthread.php?t=8616&s=1232b7ccae7c3e9ab5741ed5b1fff25c.

96. Hugh Macleod, "Syria: How It All Began," *Global Post*, April 25, 2011.

97. The Shura Council member was Abu Ubaydah abd al-Hakim al-Iraqi. "Interview with Abu Ubaydah Abd al-Hakim al-Iraqi," Jihadist Media Elite and Al-Furqan Media Establishment, April 11, 2011.

98. Ibid.

99. Jim Garamone, "Bombings Bear Signs of al-Qaida in Iraq, General Says," American Forces Press Service, August 15, 2011.

100. Abu Hamzah al-Muhajir, "The Command Is for None but God," Al-Furqan Media Establishment, November 10, 2006; "The Names of al-Qaeda Members" (Harmony Document AFGP-2002-600046), https://www.ctc.usma.edu /v2/wp-content/uploads/2013/10/List-of-Names-of-Al-Qaida-Members -Translation.pdf (accessed December 8, 2015).

101. See Fishman, "Redefining the Islamic State."

102. Timothy Williams and Omar al-Jawoshy, "Top Insurgents Escaped Prison Days After Iraq Took Over," *The New York Times*, July 23, 2010.

103. "Al-Qaeda Suspects Among Dozens of Escapees in Deadly Iraq Prison Break," Associated Press, September 28, 2012; "Death Row Inmates in Iraq Prison Break," Al Jazeera, March 24, 2012; Joel Wing, "Iraqi Forces Suspected in Escape of Al Qaeda Officials from Basra Prison," *Musings on Iraq,* January 21, 2011.

104. "The Islamic State of Iraq in Five Years," Al-Furqan Media Establishment, August 21, 2011.

105. Peter Bergen, *Manhunt* (New York: Random House, 2012), 100.

106. See Yassin Musharbash, "Bin Laden: Al-Qaeda Chooses an Interim Emir," *Der Spiegel,* May 17, 2011; Peter Bergen, "Egyptian Saif al-Adel Now Acting Chief of al-Qaeda, Ex-Militant Says," CNN, May 17, 2011; Vahid Brown, "Sayf al-Adl and al-Qaeda's Historical Leadership," *Jihadica,* May 18, 2011, http:// www.jihadica.com/sayf-al-adl-and-al-qaidas-historical-leadership/ (accessed June 5, 2016).

107. For much more, see Brown, "Sayf al-Adl and al-Qaeda's Historical Leadership"; Senate Select Committee on Intelligence, "Committee Study on the Central Intelligence Agency's Detention and Interrogation Program," December 3, 2014, 374 (footnote 2114).

108. Syed Saleem Shahzad, "How Iran and al-Qaeda Made a Deal," *Asia Times,* April 30, 2010.

109. For a description, see Brown, "Sayf al-Adl and al-Qaeda's Historical Leadership." For rundowns on al-Adl's later writing, see Vahid Brown, "Al-Qaeda Revisions: The Five Letters of Sayf al-Adl," *Jihadica,* February 10, 2011, http:// www.jihadica.com/al-qa%E2%80%99ida-revisions-the-five-letters-of-sayf-al -%E2%80%98adl/ (accessed June 5, 2016); William McCants, "Crowdsourcing the Revolution," *Jihadica,* May 9, 2011, http://www.jihadica.com/crowd sourcing-the-revolution/ (accessed June 5, 2016).

110. Scott Shane, "Bin Laden Daughter in Iran Seeks Refuge," *The New York Times,* December 23, 2009.

111. Brian T. McHugh, Michael Butsch, and Nehad Abu Suneima, "Statement of Sulayman Abu Ghaith," March 6, 2013, http://kronosadvisory.com /Kronos_US_v_Sulaiman_Abu_Ghayth_Statement.1.pdf (accessed June 1, 2015).

112. Abd al-Sattar Hatitah, "All Egyptians Will Return to Homeland Before End of This Year," *Sharq al-Awsat,* August 19, 2011.

113. See Musharbash, "Bin Laden: Al-Qaeda Chooses an Interim Emir"; Bergen, "Egyptian Saif al-Adel Now Acting Chief of al-Qaeda, Ex-Militant Says."

114. Leila Fadel, "Syria's Assad Moves to Allay Fury After Security Forces Fire on Protesters," *The Washington Post,* March 26, 2011; Alexandra Sandels, "Syria: More Than 200 Political Prisoners Released," Babylon & Beyond, *Los Angeles Times,* March 26, 2011; Katherine Marsh, "Syria's Political Prisoners: 'It's Hard to Imagine How I Got Through It,'" *The Guardian,* April 25, 2011.

115. Charles Lister, "Evolution of an Insurgency," *Foreign Affairs,* March 14, 2016.

116. Ben Taub, "Journey to Jihad," *The New Yorker,* June 1, 2015.

117. See Brian Fishman, "The Evidence of Jihadi Activism in Syria," *CTC Sentinel* Vol. 5, Issue 5 (May 22, 2012).

118. Fadel, "Syria's Assad Moves to Allay Fury After Security Forces Fire on Protesters"; Raniah Salloum, "From Jail to Jihad: Former Prisoners Fight in Syrian Insurgency," *Der Spiegel,* October 10, 2013.

119. "Jund al-Sham, Fatah al-Islam Organizations Accused of Deraa Events," All4Syria, March 21, 2011, http://all4syria.info.

120. Abu Hurayra al-Badawi, Khattab al-Maqisi, and Khadim al-Ghuraba, "Fatah al-Islam: Victory to Our Brothers in the Syria of Islam," Shumukh al-Islam, March 23, 2011.

121. For more on the Syrian revolution's impact on Lebanon, and vice versa, see Bilal Saab, "The Syrian Spillover and Salafist Radicalization in Lebanon," *CTC Sentinel* Vol 6, Issue 7 (July 23, 2013).

122. In 2010 several senior Fatah al-Islam leaders escaped Roumieh, and, following prisoner riots in April 2011, dozens of experienced Fatah al-Islam operatives were released. Abu Talhah al-Kuwaiti, "A Story of Escape from the Roumieh Central Prison in Lebanon," Al-Fida Islamic Network, September 28, 2011; "Prisoners Riot in Lebanon's Main Jail," *NOW Lebanon,* April 2, 2011, https://now.mmedia.me/lb/en/archive/prisoners_riot_in_lebanons_main_jail_ ; "An 'Operations Room' Coordinated Protests by Roumieh Inmates and Their Families," *NOW Lebanon,* April 13, 2011, https://now.mmedia.me/lb/en/archive/rifi _an_operations_room_coordinated_protests_by_roumieh_inmates_and _their_families.

123. Abu Talhah al-Kuwaiti, "A Story of Escape from the Roumieh Central Prison in Lebanon," Al-Fida Islamic Network, September 28, 2011.

124. Ibid.

125. "Islamist Militants Break Out of Lebanon Prison," Agence France Presse, August 13, 2011.

126. Barack Obama, Statement on Syria, August 18, 2011, https://www.whitehouse .gov/blog/2011/08/18/president-obama-future-syria-must-be-determined-its -people-president-bashar-al-assad (accessed August 15, 2015).

127. Josh Rogin, "Is Robert Ford Trying to Get Thrown out of Syria?," *Foreign Policy,* August 23, 2011.

128. Attributed to Sayf al-Adl, published in Fuad Husayn, *Zarqawi . . . The Second Generation of al-Qaeda,* serialized in *Al-Quds al-Arabi,* May 13, 2005 to June 8, 2005.

129. Lawrence Wright, "The Master Plan," *The New Yorker,* September 11, 2006.

130. Paul Cruickshank and Mohannad al Hage, "Abu Mus'ab al-Suri: Architect of the New al-Qaeda," *Studies in Conflict and Terrorism* 30 (2007): 1–14.

131. William Maclean, "Al-Qaeda Ideologue in Syrian Detention—Lawyers," Reuters, June 10, 2009.

132. Ibid.

133. Even Muhammad Khalil al-Hakaymah, reputed to be Abu Bakr Naji, got in on the action. See Muhammad Khalil al-Hakaymah, *Toward a New Strategy,* September 11, 2006, https://web.archive.org/web/20070222070122/; http://altabetoun.110mb.com/news.php?action=view&id=135; Muhammad Khalil al-Hakaymah, *How to Fight Alone,* 2006, http://www.transasianaxis.com/showthread.php?52-The-Religion-of-Peace/page4 (accessed June 6, 2016). For a detailed jihadi plan to encourage recruiters operating independently in "occupied" countries, see Abu Amr al-Qa'idi, *A Course in the Art of Recruitment,* https://archive.org/details/ACourseInTheArtOfRecruiting-RevisedJuly2010 September 2008, and Brian Fishman and Abdullah Warius, "A Jihadist's Course in the Art of Recruitment," *CTC Sentinel* Vol 2, Issue 2 (February 2009).

134. Scott Shane, *Objective Troy* (New York: Tim Duggan Books, 2015).

135. Abu Mus'ab al-Suri's book *Lessons Learned from the Jihad Ordeal in Syria* was often recommended on jihadi web forums. As an example: Abu Abdallah al-Qasimi, "Al-Qasimi's Letter to the Proud People of the Levant," Al-Nur Media Establishment, February 6, 2011; Abu Mus'ab al-Suri, *Lessons Learned from the Jihad Ordeal in Syria,* https://www.ctc.usma.edu/posts/lessons-learned-from-the-jihad-ordeal-in-syria-english-translation-2 (Harmony Document: AFGP-2002-600080) (accessed December 8, 2015).

136. Abu Mus'ab al-Suri, *Lessons Learned from the Jihad Ordeal in Syria.*

137. Ibid.

138. Ibid.

139. Al-Suri's writing about deterrence was resurrected by al-Qaeda in the Arabian Peninsula's English-language magazine *Inspire* in spring 2013. See Abu Mus'ab al-Suri, "The Strategy of Deterring with Terrorism," *Inspire,* No. 10 (March 2013).

140. Rania Abouzeid, "The Jihad Next Door," *Politico,* June 23, 2014.

141. Ibid.

142. "Al Qaeda in Iraq, Becoming Less Foreign," Radio Free Europe / Radio Liberty, November 18, 2009.

143. In 2009, a Pakistan-based al-Qaeda leader named Issa al-Masri arrived in Syria to coordinate operations in Iraq and the Levant. An Egyptian, before 9/11 he had taught at the "Syrian guesthouse in Kabul," which was run by Abu Mus'ab

al-Suri and his deputy, Abu Khaled. Syrian forces, however, quickly arrested al-Masri, and another al-Qaeda effort to directly control events in Iraq fizzled. In 2014, Zawahiri cited a 2010 letter allegedly written by an ISI Shura member to al-Qaeda saying that "if anyone is sent from you . . . to take over the leadership, then we have no problem with that and we will be HIS SOLDIERS, and this is agreed upon by Abu Bakr and the Majlis Shura." If authentic, this must have frustrated al-Qaeda no end. Bill Roggio, "Senior al Qaeda Leader Leaves Pakistan, Directs Iraq Operations from Syria," *The Long War Journal*, August 21, 2009; Abul Hameed Bakier and Erich Marquardt, "An Ideological and Operational Threat: Abu 'Amr Sheikh 'Isa," *CTC Sentinel* (July 15, 2008); see Letter from "an ISI communication representative to Atiyah," May 2011, quoted in Zawahiri, "Testimonial to Preserve the Blood of Mujahidin in al-Sham."

144. The dispute was specifically about whether or not such revenue constituted Fay', a concept of peaceful plunder from apostates that the Qu'ran (Al-Hashr 59:7) dictates should be distributed to the needy.

145. Letter from Mosul Sector to ISI Leadership (Harmony Document NMEC-2010-186331), undated.

146. Ibid.

147. Huthaifa Azzam Tweets, compiled by @sha___me, July 20, 2015; see also Aron Lund, "As Rifts Open Up in Syria's al-Qaeda Franchise, Secrets Spill Out," *Syria in Crisis*, August 10, 2015, http://carnegieendowment.org/syriaincrisis/?fa =60973 (accessed September 13, 2015).

148. See Huthaifa Azzam Tweets, compiled by @sha___me, July 20, 2015; Aymen Jawad al-Tamimi, "A Jaysh al-Mujahideen Amir's Testimony on Abu Bakr al-Baghdadi," December 12, 2014, http://www.aymennjawad.org/2014/12/a -jaysh-al-mujahideen-amir-testimony-on-abu-bakr (accessed September 13, 2015).

149. The document lists "Ansar al-Sunnah" rather than the "Ansar al-Sunnah Shariah Commission." This is because the Shariah Commission took the Ansar al-Sunnah name in 2008 after its former allies reverted to their original group name of Ansar al-Islam.

150. Harmony Document NMEC_191107_Request for Assassination, February 2, 2007 (estimate).

151. "Untitled List of Names," Jihadist Websites, July 23, 2010.

152. Huthaifa Azzam Tweets, compiled by @sha___me; see also Lund, "As Rifts Open Up in Syria's al-Qaeda Franchise, Secrets Spill Out."

153. "Interview with Sheikh Abu-Wa'il Abd-al-Wahab Bin-Muhammad al-Sultan," Hanein Islamic Forum, December 8, 2008.

154. Huthaifa Azzam Tweets, compiled by @sha___me. This claim was made first by Huthaifa Azzam, son of Abdallah Azzam, and was echoed by Salih al-Hawami and Abu Mariyah al-Qahtani.

155. See Steve Coll, *Ghost Wars* (New York: Penguin, 2004).

156. For an excellent review of this phenomenon, see Elizabeth Dickinson, "Playing with Fire: Why Private Gulf Financing for Syria's Extremist Rebels Risks Igniting Sectarian Conflict at Home," Brookings Project on U.S. Relations with the Islamic World, *Analysis Paper* No. 16, December 2013.

157. "Annou[n]cing Jabhat al-Nusrah for the People of the Levant," Al-Manarah al-Bayda Media Establishment, January 23, 2012.

158. Ayman al-Zawahiri, "Testimonial to Preserve the Blood of Mujahidin in al-Sham."

159. "Annou[n]cing Jabhat al-Nusrah for the People of the Levant," Al-Manarah al-Bayda Media Establishment.

160. "Message from One of Sheikh Hamid's Students," undated (Bin Laden's Bookshelf, released March 1, 2006).

161. Abu Muhammad al-Adnani, "Now Time for Fighting Has Come," Al-Furqan Media Establishment, January 12, 2012.

162. Both Omar Bakri, a leading salafist in Lebanon, and Abu Basir al-Tartusi, a longtime jihadi critic of the Islamic State of Iraq, suggested they did not know the group. Abu Muhammad al-Shafi'i, "Islamists and Free Syrian Army Share Suspicions About the Organization That Took Credit for the Damascus Bombing," *Asharq al-Awsat*, March 22, 2012.

163. The JaN explained that the group's statements were numbered sequentially, which is true. The "claim of responsibility" was an obvious fraud because it was numbered "4" despite the fact that JaN had already released a "Statement 4" (and Statements 5, 6, and 7 as well). The JaN disavowed several other major bombings, including May and October strikes in Damascus. See "Denying Responsibility for the Criminal Bombing in the al-Zuhur Neighborhood and Promising Revenge," Jabhat al-Nusrah—Media Statement 2, October 27, 2012.

164. "An Alert About the Palestine Branch's Fake Statement Attributed to Jabhat al-Nusrah," Jabhat al-Nusrah—Media Statement 8, May 13, 2012.

165. "Raid to Avenge the Free Women of Syria," Al-Manarah al-Bayda Foundation for Media Production, February 26, 2012.

166. "To the al-Nusrah Front," Ansar al-Mujahidin Network, February 11, 2012.

167. Noman Benotman and Roisin Blake, "Jabhat al-Nusra: A Strategic Briefing," Quilliam Foundation, http://www.quilliamfoundation.org/wp/wp-content/uploads/publications/free/jabhat-al-nusra-a-strategic-briefing.pdf (accessed December 10, 2015). Interestingly, this approach reflects the practice of al-Qaeda in pre-9/11 Afghanistan.

168. Whereas JaN leaders described their constituency as "Muslims," Ahrar al-Sham focused on "Syrians" who were "Sunnis." See Abu Fatimah al-Halabi, "Al-Jazeera Hosted by Jabhat al-Nusrah in Syria," Al Jazeera, November 18, 2012.

169. Hazim al-Amin, "Idlib: Ahrar al-Sham Brigades' Hinder Joining Global Jihad," *Al-Hayah*, August 21, 2012.

170. Ivan Watson and Samya Ayish, "Ex-Syrian Ambassador Calls for Foreign Military Intervention," CNN, July 15, 2012; Ruth Sherlock, "Exclusive Interview: Why I Defected from Bashar al-Assad's Regime, by Former Diplomat Nawaf Fares," *The Telegraph* (United Kingdom), July 14, 2012.

171. Justin Vela and Liz Sly, "In Syria, Group Suspected of al-Qaeda Links Gaining Prominence in War to Topple Assad," *The Washington Post,* August 19, 2012; "In Syria, Islamic Militants May Complicate Uprising," *Los Angeles Times,* August 25, 2012; Mark Hosenball, "As Militants Join Syria Revolt, Fears Grow over Arms Flow," Reuters, June 22, 2012; Regan Doherty and Amena Bakr, "Secret Turkish Nerve Center Leads Aid to Syria Rebels," Reuters, July 27, 2012; Chris Zambelis, "Foreign Fighters Bring a Global Agenda to Syria," *Jamestown Terrorism Monitor* 10, no. 17 (September 13, 2012).

172. Jonathan Landay and Hannah Allam, "U.S. Might Name Syrian Rebel Nusra Front a Foreign Terrorist Group," *McClatchy Newspapers,* December 4, 2012.

173. "Chief of Syrian Rebel Joint Military Council on 'Unification of Military Groups,'" Al Jazeera, December 10, 2012.

174. "Syria: FSA Chief of Staff Condemsn [sic] Adding Jabhat al-Nusrah to US Terrorism List," *Zaman al-Wasl,* December 11, 2012.

175. "Signs of Mounting Criticism of U.S., Support for Syrian Jihadi Group Jabhat al-Nusra, Following Its Designation as Terrorist Organization by Obama Administration," Middle East Media Research Institute, *Special Dispatch No. 5089* (December 11, 2012).

176. Aaron Zelin wrote a useful contemporaneous analysis on Syrian reaction to the designation. See Aaron Zelin, "Rally 'Round the Jihadis," *Foreign Policy,* December 11, 2012.

177. Landay and Allam, "U.S. Might Name Syrian Rebel Nusra Front a Foreign Terrorist Group."

178. Scott Wilson and Joby Warrick, "Assad Must Go, Obama Says," *The Washington Post,* August 18, 2011.

179. "Dozens of Syrian Troops Killed in Iraq After Seeking Refuge," Associated Press, March 4, 2013.

180. "Statement on the Blessed Raid," Ministry of Information—Islamic State of Iraq, March 11, 2013. For a useful contemporary analysis, see Michael Knights, "Syrian and Iraqi Conflicts Show Signs of Merging," POLICYWATCH 2042, Washington Institute for Near East Policy, March 7, 2013.

181. "Statement Regarding the Dissemination of the Production of the Al-I'tisam Establishment for Media Production," Ministry of Information—Islamic State of Iraq, February 21, 2013.

182. "Pounding the Fortresses," Al-I'tisam Establishment for Media Production, March 7, 2013.

183. "The Secrets of Baghdadi's State," *Al-Akhbar,* January 10, 2014.

184. Abu Bakr al-Baghdadi, "Declaration of Establishing 'Islamic State of Iraq and the Levant'—A Statement by the Emir of the Believers, Abu Bakr al-Baghdadi," Al-Furqan Media Establishment, April 9, 2013.

185. Abu Muhammad al-Jawlani, "Important Audio Statement on the Levant Battlefield by Conqueror Sheikh Abu Muhammad al-Jawlani," Al-Manarah al-Bayda Media Establishment, April 10, 2013.

186. Ayman al-Zawahiri, "Testimonial to Preserve the Blood of Mujahidin in al-Sham."

187. The private correspondence between Zawahiri and Abu Bakr is referenced in a later letter from Zawahiri on September 4, 2013. Ayman al-Zawahiri, "Letter to Abu Suhayb," September 4, 2013, included in tweet by @asrarwk on August 22, 2015, most likely a whistleblower with access to ISIS own records. The letter is attributed to "Abu Fath," a pseudonym used by Zawahiri.

188. Ayman al-Zawahiri, "Letter to Abu Bakr al-Baghdadi al-Husayni and Abu Muhammad al-Jawlani," Al-Fajr Media Center, May 23, 2013.

189. Aron Lund, "Who and What Was Abu Khaled al-Suri? Part 1," *Syria in Crisis*, February 24, 2014.

190. Charles Lister, *The Syrian Jihad* (London: Hurst Publishers, 2015), 107–109.

191. Prior to Zawahiri's statement, Jawlani directed commanders to abide by Zawahiri's proclamation—and avoid conflict with ISIS. Abu Muhammad al-Jawlani, "To the Regional Emirs and Leaders of Jabhat al-Nusrah," tweeted by @kooka605 on June 7, 2013.

192. Abu Bakr al-Baghdadi, "It Remains in Iraq and the Levant," Al-Furqan Media Establishment, June 15, 2013.

193. Abu Muhammad al-Adnani, "So Leave Them and Their Inventions Alone," Al-Furqan Media Establishment, June 19, 2013.

194. Ayman al-Zawahiri, "Letter to Abu Suhayb," September 4, 2013, included in tweet by @asrarwk on August 22, 2015.

195. For an extensive retelling of this back and forth, see McCants, *The ISIS Apocalypse.*

196. Al-Zawahiri, "Letter to Abu Suhayb," September 4, 2013.

197. Taub, "Journey to Jihad."

198. The al-Absi brothers share a surname with Shakir al-Absi, founder and emir of Fatah al-Islam, but their relationship is unclear. Shakir was of Palestinian descent, whereas the two brothers were born in Saudi Arabia.

199. Ahmad al-Masri, "The Free Syrian Army Assassinates Head of the Mujahdin Shur Council of the Islamic State at Bab al-Haw Crossing," *Al-Quds al-Arabi*, September 4, 2012; Lorenzo Cremonesi, "How the Syrian Guerillas Hunt the al-Qaeda Men," *Corriere della Sera*, September 10, 2012; "The Belgian Brigade," *Storify* (tweets by Daniele Raineri) by flr666, https://storify.com/flr666/t.

200. Romain Caillet, "The Islamic State: Leaving al-Qaeda Behind," Carnegie Endowment for International Peace, December 27, 2013.

201. Taub, "Journey to Jihad."

202. For more on Haji Bakr, see Kyle Orton, "The Riddle of Haji Bakr," The Syrian Intifada, November 10, 2015, https://kyleorton1991.wordpress.com/2015/11/10/the-riddle-of-haji-bakr/ (accessed January 20, 2016).

203. "@Wikibaghdady Tweets," December 14, 2013.

204. Aaron Y. Zelin, "ICSR Insight: Up to 11,000 Foreign Fighters in Syria; Steep Rise Among Western Europeans," International Centre for the Study of Radicalisation, December 17, 2013.

205. "The Islamic State of Iraq and al-Sham Executes Three Men in Raqqa in Retaliation for the Banias Massacre," Brown Moses Blog, http://brown-moses.blogspot.co.uk/2013/05/the-islamic-state-of-iraq-and-al-sham.html, May 14, 2013.

206. McCants, The ISIS Apocalypse.

207. Ake Sellstrom, Scott Cairns, and Maurizio Barbeschi, "Report of the United Nations Mission to Investigate Allegations of the Use of Chemical Weapons in the Syrian Arab Republic on the Alleged Use of Chemical Weapons in the Ghouta Area of Damascus on 21 August 2013," United Nations General Assembly, September 16, 2013, https://disarmament-library.un.org/UNODA/Library.nsf/78ocfafd472b047785257b1000501037/e4d4477c9b67de9085257bf800694bd2/$FILE/A%2067%20997-S%202013%20553.pdf (accessed October 1, 2013).

208. President Barack Obama, "Remarks to the White House Press Corps," August 20, 2012, https://www.whitehouse.gov/the-press-office/2012/08/20/remarks-president-white-house-press-corps (accessed October 1, 2015).

Chapter Five: The Stage of Declaring the State

1. Anthony Cordesman and Sam Khazai, "Iraq in Crisis," Center for Strategic and International Studies, May 2014.

2. Yochi Dreazen and John Hudson, "U.S. Won't Ship Iraq the Weapons It Needs to Fight al-Qaeda," The Cable, Foreign Policy, January 7, 2014.

3. "Iraq Violence: US Speeds Up Supply of Military Equipment," BBC, January 7, 2014; Ahmed Rasheed, "Iraq Signs Deal to Buy Arms, Ammunition from Iran—Documents," Reuters, February 24, 2014.

4. "Iraqi Attacks: Fear, Sectarianism Behind Iraq Army Collapse," Associated Press, June 13, 2014.

5. Harith al-Dari Interview on Al Jazeera, January 22, 2014.

6. Abdullah Mustafa, "Sheikh Rafi al-Rifa'i, the Sunni Grand Mufti of Iraq . . . Described the Events in Fallujah as 'Genocide,'" Asharq al-Awsat, February 24, 2014.

7. Abu Waleed al-Salafi, "Complete History of Ansar al-Islam," in Aymenn Jawad al-Tamimi, *A Complete History of Jamaat Ansar al-Islam,* December 15, 2015, http://www.aymennjawad.org/2015/12/a-complete-history-of-jamaat-ansar-al -islam.

8. "Rise of the Islamic State and the Fading Away of the Rest of the Iraqi Insurgency: Interview with Aymenn Jawad al-Tamimi," *Musings on Iraq,* May 4, 2015, http://musingsoniraq.blogspot.com/2015/05/rise-of-islamic-state-and-fading -away.html.

9. David Remnick, "Going the Distance," *The New Yorker,* January 27, 2014.

10. Ibid.; Glenn Kessler, "Spinning Obama's Reference to Islamic State as a 'JV' Team," Fact Checker, *The Washington Post,* September 3, 2014.

11. For more, see J. M. Berger, "War on Error," *Foreign Policy,* February 5, 2015.

12. For more discussion of the ISI flag and its adoption by jihadi groups around the world, see William McCants, *The ISIS Apocalypse* (New York: St. Martin's Press, 2015).

13. Carl von Clausewitz, *On War,* trans. Michael E. Howard and Peter Paret (Princeton, NJ: Princeton University Press, 1989).

14. See Howard Shatz and Erin Elizabeth-Johnson, "The Islamic State We Knew: Insights Before the Resurgence and Their Implications," RAND Corporation, 2015; Brian Fishman, "Redefining the Islamic State: The Fall and Rise of al-Qaeda in Iraq," The New America Foundation, August 2011 Vol. 7, Issue 3.

15. Abu Abdallah Muhammad al-Mansur, "The Islamic State Between Truth and Illusion," Shariah Commission of the Mujahidin Army, February 2014.

16. Abu Muhammad al-Adnani, "A Scout Never Misleads His Followers," Al-Furqan Media Establishment, January 7, 2014.

17. Martin Chulov, "ISIS Kills Hundreds of Iraqi Sunnis from Albu Nimr Tribe in Iraq," *The Guardian,* October 30, 2014.

18. "Interview with Abu Samir al-Urduni," *Dabiq 10* (September 2015).

19. "Statement of the Islamic State of Iraq and the Levant, al-Raqqah Governorate on Incidents in the City," The Islamic State of Iraq al-Raqqah Governorate, January 13, 2014.

20. "In Response to the Admission of the State-Faction That It Killed Sheikh Abu Sa'd al-Hadrami—Jabhat al-Nusrah's Emir in Raqqah," Al-Manarah al-Bayda Media Establishment, January 15, 2014.

21. Abu Khaled al-Suri, "Sheikh Abu Khaled al-Suri on the Current Events in Syria," January 16, 2014. Justpaste.it link posted by Twitter User @Khaled852111. Originally available at: http://t.co/7SIXQMZoov (accessed March 20, 2014).

22. Abu Khaled al-Suri, "A Message of Glad Tidings: al-Baghdadi's State Will Fail and the State of Islam Is Coming," uploaded to YouTube, January 13, 2014, https://www.youtube.com/watch?v=zdqkb4iHHco (no longer available; accessed April 3, 2014).

23. "Al-Qaeda—General Command: Statement on al-Qaeda's Relationship with ISIS," Al-Fajr Media Center, February 3, 2014.

24. "Treasury Designates al-Qaeda Supporters in Qatar and Yemen," U.S. Department of Treasury, December 18, 2013.

25. Thomas Joscelyn, "Al Qaeda's Chief Representative in Syria Killed in Suicide Attack," *The Long War Journal*, February 23, 2014.

26. Spanish intelligence officials, who knew Abu Khaled well from his years living in Spain, eventually declared that they were sure ISIS ordered the hit. This report also claimed that Spanish intelligence officers were planning to meet with Abu Khaled al-Suri in Turkey. Nelly Lahoud and Muhammad al-'Ubaydi, "The War of Jihadists Against Jihadists," *CTC Sentinel* Vol. 7, Issue 3, March 26, 2014; Jose Maria Irjuo, "Resident in Spain, al-Qaeda's Mediator," *El País*, August 2, 2015.

27. Abu Muhammad al-Jawlani, "If Only You Were Eulogizing Me," Al-Manarah al-Bayda Media Establishment, February 24, 2014.

28. Ibid.

29. Muhammad al-Najjar, "Al-Maqdisi Calls on Jawlani to Cancel Ultimatum to ISIS," Al Jazeera, March 2, 2014.

30. Abu Mus'ab al-Suri, *Lessons Learned from the Jihad Ordeal in Syria;* see Harmony Document AFGP-2002-600080.

31. Al-Suri, "A Message of Glad Tidings."

32. "Where Has Jabhat al-Nusrah's Military Commander Gone?," *Al-Safir*, October 18, 2014.

33. Ben Hubbard, "Deaths Reported in Syria of Top Figures in Group Affiliated with Al Qaeda," *The New York Times*, March 6, 2015.

34. Abu Hammam al-Suri, "Testimonies Before the Ultimatum of Mubahalah," Al-Basirah Media Establishment, May 9, 2014.

35. Ibid.

36. Ibid.

37. Ibid.

38. "Dawn of Tidings: Messages from the Land of Epics 21," Al-Furqan Media Establishment, March 21, 2014.

39. Abu Hammam al-Suri, "Testimonies Before the Ultimatum of Mubahalah."

40. Ibid.

41. The nine obligations are: (1) proselytizing a vision of Islam and shariah based on seventh-century social concepts; (2) adjudicating civil disputes; (3) appointing judges and local rulers; (4) releasing Muslim prisoners and protecting Muslim women; (5) imposing *hudud* (mandatory punishments); (6) attacking enemies and fortifying towns; (7) raising funds; (8) supporting the families of martyrs, soldiers, prisoners, and the weak; (9) appointing qualified people to positions of authority. See Uthman bin Abd al-Rahman al-Tamimi, *Informing the People About the Islamic State of Iraq* (Al-Furqan Media Establishment, December 2006).

42. Ibid.

43. Ibid.

44. See "Statement from the Governor of Aleppo Province" (Specimen 7F), October 2013, http://www.aymennjawad.org/2015/01/archive-of-islamic-state -administrative-documents (accessed October 20, 2015); original at http:// justpaste.it/aleppowalioct2013 (accessed October 20, 2015).

45. "List of *Hudud* Punishments" (Specimen 1C), March 2014, http://www .aymennjawad.org/2015/01/archive-of-islamic-state-administrative-documents (accessed October 20, 2015).

46. Jacob Siegel, "Islamic Extremists Now Crucifying People in Syria—and Tweeting Out the Pictures," *The Daily Beast,* April 30, 2014.

47. See Rori Donaghy and Mary Atkinson, "Crime and Punishment: Islamic State vs Saudi Arabia," *Middle East Eye,* January 20, 2015.

48. "Saudi Arabia: Rampant Executions Fuelled by Justice System 'Riddled with Holes,'" Amnesty International, August 25, 2015; Adam Taylor, "How Saudi Arabia and the Islamic State Find Common Ground in Beheadings," *The Washington Post,* January 4, 2016.

49. *Criminal Complaint in United States of America v. Nicholas Michael Teausant,* United States Department of Justice, March 16, 2014, https://www.justice.gov /sites/default/files/usao-edca/legacy/2014/03/17/Teausant%20Complaint%20 .pdf.

50. Ibid.

51. Ibid.

52. Ibid.

53. Ibid.

54. For a fascinating retelling of Awlaki's radicalization and the campaign to kill him, see Scott Shane, *Objective Troy* (New York: Tim Duggan Books, 2015).

55. *Criminal Complaint in United States of America v. Nicholas Michael Teausant,* March 16, 2014; *The Lone Mujahid Pocketbook,* Al-Malahem Media Foundation, spring 2013, http://jihadology.net/2013/03/02/al-mala%E1%B8%A5im-media -presents-a-new-booklet-from-al-qaidah-in-the-arabian-peninsula-the-lone -mujahid-pocketbook/.

56. Randal M. Bundy, "Al Qaida Nicholas Teausant Convert to Islam Arrested at Canadian Border," YouTube, March 17, 2014, https://www.youtube.com/watch ?v=qYhRHFqw_3s (accessed October 21, 2015).

57. "Nicholas Teausant YouTube Page," https://www.youtube.com/user/nickteau sant (accessed October 21, 2015).

58. *Criminal Complaint in United States of America v. Nicholas Michael Teausant,* March 16, 2014; *The Lone Mujahid Pocketbook,* Al-Malahem Media Foundation.

59. The Sacramento Bee, "Terror Suspect Teausant Breaks Silence," YouTube, August 26, 2014, https://www.youtube.com/watch?v=d7nssHW5yFg (accessed October 21, 2015).

60. Confidential informants have emerged as key law enforcement tools in fighting domestic terrorism cases. For more, see Peter Bergen, *United States of Jihad: Investigating America's Homegrown Terrorists* (New York: Crown, 2016).

61. "Nicholas Teausant Charged with Attempting to Aid al-Qaeda Fighters from California," Associated Press, March 27, 2014.

62. The Sacramento Bee, "Terror Suspect Teausant Breaks Silence"; Aaron Zelin, "Up to 11,000 Foreign Fighters in Syria; Steep Rise Among Western Europeans," International Centre for the Study of Radicalisation and Political Violence, December 2013.

63. "Al-Qaeda—General Command: Statement on al-Qaeda's Relationship with ISIS," Al-Fajr Media Center, February 3, 2014; Liz Sly, "Al-Qaeda Disavows Any Ties with Radical Islamist ISIS Group in Syria, Iraq," The Washington Post, February 3, 2014.

64. See "Individuals and Entities Designated by the State Department Under E.O. 13224," State Department—Bureau of Counterterrorism, http://www.state.gov /j/ct/rls/other/des/143210.htm (accessed October 22, 2015).

65. Criminal Complaint in United States of America v. Nicholas Michael Teausant, March 16, 2014.

66. "Terrorist Designations of Groups Operating in Syria," Department of State— Office of Spokesperson, May 14, 2014, http://www.state.gov/r/pa/prs/ps/2014 /05/226067.htm (accessed October 23, 2015).

67. Sam Stanton and Denny Walsh, "Lodi Area Man Who Tried to Join Islamic State Sentenced to 12 Years in Prison," Sacramento Bee, June 7, 2016.

68. "Clanging of the Swords—Part 1," Al-Furqan Media Establishment, June 30, 2012.

69. "Clanging of the Swords—Part 4," Al-Furqan Media Establishment, May 14, 2014. For an early take recognizing the importance of the "Clanging of Swords" series to ISIS general strategy, see Bryan Price, Dan Milton, and Muhammad al-'Ubaydi, "Al-Baghdadi's Blitzkrieg, ISIS Psychological Warfare, and What It Means for Syria and Iraq," CTC Perspectives, June 12, 2014.

70. Sameer Yacoub, "Iraqi Militants Attack Anbar University, Take Students Hostage," Associated Press, June 7, 2014; "Bombs Kill 52 as Gunmen Storm University in Iraq," The Daily Star, June 8, 2014.

71. Ned Parker, Isabel Coles, and Raheem Salman, "Special Report—How Mosul Fell: An Iraqi General Disputes Baghdad's Story," Reuters, October 14, 2014.

72. "Raid to Avenge Our People in Mosul," Islamic State of Iraq—Baghdad Province (as tweeted by @fawaresbaghdad), June 8, 2014.

73. Parker, Coles, and Salman, "Special Report—How Mosul Fell."

74. See, for example, https://www.youtube.com/watch?v=frKoXLY3oWI (accessed October 28, 2015).

75. "ISIS Issues '10 Commandments' for Islamic Rule," Hurriyet Daily News, June 13, 2014.

76. Dominic Evans and Isra' al-Rube'i, "Convert, Pay Tax, or Die, Islamic State Warns Christians," Reuters, July 18, 2014; Abdelhak Mamoun, "URGENT: ISIS Destroys the Virgin Mary Church in Mosul," Iraqi News, July 26, 2014; "ISIS Destroys Shrines, Shiite Mosques in Iraq," Al Arabiya, July 5, 2014.

77. "Iraq Crisis: Islamists Force 500,000 to Flee Mosul," BBC, June 11, 2014.

78. Matt Bradley, "Insurgents in Iraq Seizing Advanced Weaponry," *Wall Street Journal*, July 6, 2014.

79. Brett McGurk, "Statement to the Senate Foreign Relations Committee," July 24, 2014, http://www.foreign.senate.gov/imo/media/doc/McGurk%20Testimony%20072414-Final%20Version%20REVISED.pdf.

80. Borzou Daraghi, "Biggest Bank Robbery That 'Never Happened'—$400m ISIS Heist," *Financial Times*, July 17, 2014.

81. Tim Arango, "Escaping Death in Northern Iraq," *The New York Times*, September 3, 2014.

82. "Sunni Tribes Will Totally Control Anbar Within 'Two Days,'" *Asharq al-Awsat*, June 23, 2014.

83. Ibid.

84. Luke Harding and Fazel Hawramy, "New Militant Group Replacing ISIS in Mosul, Says City Governor," *The Guardian*, July 18, 2014; Jessica Lewis, "The Islamic State of Iraq and al-Sham Captures Mosul and Advances Toward Baghdad," Institute for the Study of War, June 11, 2014.

85. Izzat al-Douri, "Full Audio Message of Izzat Ibrahim al-Douri," Al-Basrah Net, July 12, 2014.

86. Ibid.

87. Christopher Reuter, "The Terror Strategist: Secret Files Reveal the Structure of the Islamic State," *Der Spiegel*, April 18, 2015.

88. See Jarret Brachman, Jeff Bramlett, Joseph Felter, Brian Fishman, James Forest, Liane Kennedy-Boudali, Bill Perkins, Jacob Shapiro, and Tom Stocking, "Harmony and Disharmony," CTC at West Point, February 14, 2006.

89. Truls Hallberg Tonnessen, "Heirs of Zarqawi or Saddam? The Relationship Between al-Qaida in Iraq and the Islamic State," *Perspectives on Terrorism* 9, no. 4 (2015).

90. Abu Muhammad al-Adnani, "Eulogy for Abu Abd al-Rahman al-Bilawi al-Anbari," June 10, 2015; translation in Romain Caillet, "From the Ba'th to the Caliphate: The Former Officers of Saddam and the Islamic State," Norwegian Peacebuilding Resource Centre, June 2015.

91. Mostafa Nasser, "Iraq: Signs of Disagreement Emerge Between ISIS an[d] the Ba'ath," *Al-Akhbar*, June 16, 2014; Mushreq Abbas, "Iraq's 'Sunni' Rebellion Shows Splits Between ISIS, Others," *Al-Monitor*, June 20, 2014.

92. Hani al-Sibai, "A Special Sermon on the Liberation of Mosul—Victories for Iraq's Sunnis: Hopeful Moments and Fears," YouTube, June 13, 2014.

93. Email from Fuad Husayn to Brian Fishman, August 12, 2015.

94. Abu Muhammad al-Adnani, "The Promise of Allah," Al-Furqan Media Establishment, June 29, 2014.

95. Ibid.

96. Ibid.

97. Ibid.

98. Abu Bakr al-Baghdadi, "A Message to the Mujahdin and the Muslim Umma in the Month of Ramadan," Al-Furqan Media Establishment, July 1, 2014.

99. For more on this tension, see Nelly Lahoud, *The Jihadis' Path to Self-Destruction* (London: Oxford University Press, 2010).

100. Abu Bakr Al-Baghdadi, "Friday Sermon and Prayer at the Grand Mosque in Mosul; Delivered by Our Imam, the Commander of the Faithful," Al-Furqan Media Establishment, July 5, 2014.

101. "Egypt's Al-Azhar Denounces ISI 'Criminals,'" *As-Safir,* September 10, 2014, translated by Al-Monitor.

102. Thomas Hegghammer and Aaron Y. Zelin, "How Syria's War Became a Holy Crusade," The Washington Institute for Near East Policy, July 7, 2013.

103. Shafiq Mandhi, "Muslim Leaders Reject Baghdadi's Caliphate," Al Jazeera Online, July 7, 2014, http://www.aljazeera.com/news/middleeast/2014/07 /muslim-leaders-reject-baghdadi-caliphate-20147744058773906.html.

104. Cole Bunzel, "From Paper State to Caliphate: The Ideology of the Islamic State," The Brookings Institution Project on U.S. Relations with the Islamic World, Analysis Paper No. 19, March 2015.

105. Maqdisi's criticisms included that the caliphate was premature, lacked scholarly support, and abused Christians before they could pay the *jizya,* a special tax for Christians and Jews. Muwaffaq Kamal, "DA'ISH Supporters in Jordan Pledge Allegiance to al-Baghdadi," Al-Ghadd Online, July 23, 2014.

106. "Maqdisi Criticizes ISIS," *Ammun News,* July 3, 2014.

107. Abu Muhammad al-Maqdisi, "Statement," *Arin al-Mujahidin,* June 29, 2014; Abu Muhammad al-Maqdisi, "We Sent You Not, but as Mercy for All Creatures," YouTube video posted by "Almaqdisi," August 15, 2014.

108. "The Torches of Knowledge to Aid the Islamic Caliphate," signed by fifty-seven jihadi scholars; widely distributed on Twitter, November 7, 2014.

109. For an excellent discussion, see Cole Bunzel, "The Caliphate's Scholar-in-Arms," *Jihadica,* July 9, 2014, http://www.jihadica.com/the-caliphate%E2% 80%99s-scholar-in-arms/.

110. "In the Words of the Enemy," *Dabiq* 1 (1435 Ramadan), 32–33, quoting Douglas Ollivant and Brian Fishman, "State of Jihad: The Reality of the Islamic State in Iraq and Syria," *War on the Rocks,* May 21, 2014.

111. Abu Bakr al-Baghdadi, "A Message to the Mujahdin and the Muslim Umma in the Month of Ramadan."

112. Ibid.

113. *U.S. Interrogation Report 003,* Spring 2007–Early 2008, https://www.ctc.usma .edu/v2/wp-content/uploads/2013/10/Redacted-Intelligence-Report-003 -Summary.pdf (accessed June 2, 2015).

114. Ibid. Several declassified interrogation reports describe similar consternation from Iraqis. See *U.S. Interrogation Report 28,* https://www.ctc.usma.edu/v2/wp -content/uploads/2013/10/Redacted-Intelligence-Report-028-Summary.pdf; *U.S.*

Interrogation Report 23, https://www.ctc.usma.edu/v2/wp-content/uploads/2013
/10/Redacted-Intelligence-Report-023-Summary.pdf (accessed June 2, 2015).

115. *U.S. Interrogation Report 23.*

116. Hala Jaber, "Hezbollah Elite Help Assad Retake Strategic Town," *The Sunday Times,* May 26, 2013.

117. Hanna Batatu, "Shi'i Organization in Iraq: Al-Dawah and al-Mujahidin," in *Shi'ism and Social Protest,* ed. Juan Cole and Nikkie Keddie (New Haven, CT: Yale University Press, 1986), 179–200.

118. Fail Jamali claims that there were 896 Iranians (665 from the Indian subcontinent) and 326 Iraqis (47 from Syria or Lebanon, and 20 from Bahrain and smaller Shia communities). Aziz quotes Fail Jamali, "The Theological Colleges of Najaf," *Muslim World* (Hartford, CT) 50, no. 1 (January 1960): 15.

119. T. M. Aziz, "The Role of Muhammad Baqir al-Sadr in Shii Political Activism in Iraq," *International Journal of Middle Eastern Studies* 25, no. 2 (May 1993): 207–222.

120. See Magnus Ranstorp, *Hizb'allah in Lebanon: The Politics of the Western Hostage Crisis* (New York: Palgrave Macmillan, 1997), 27; Aziz, "The Role of Muhammad Baqir al-Sadr in Shii Political Activism in Iraq."

121. Nicholas Blanford, *Warriors of God: The Inside Story of Hezbollah's Relentless War Against Israel* (New York: Random House, 2011), 35; Bruce Hoffman, "Recent Trends and Future Developments in Iranian Sponsored Terrorism," RAND Corporation, March 1990; Martin Kramer, "The Oracle of Hizbullah: Sayyid Muhammad Husayn Fadlallah," in *Spokesmen for the Despised: Fundamentalist Leaders in the Middle East,* ed. R. Scott Appleby (Chicago: University of Chicago Press, 1997), 83–181.

122. Islamic Jihad was little more than a "telephone organization . . . used by those involved to disguise their true identity." The group was composed of Hizballah's core security section—led by Imad Mugniyah and Husayn Musawi—and the most militant remnants of the Iraqi Dawah Party. Islamic Jihad went on to commit numerous other terrorist attacks during the 1980s, including airline hijackings ostensibly executed to ransom the fighters imprisoned by Kuwait for the December 1983 attack. Ranstorp, *Hizb'allah in Lebanon,* 63; Hoffman, "Recent Trends and Future Developments in Iranian Sponsored Terrorism," 20; Richard Halloran, "Weir Says Captors Want 17 Released," *The New York Times,* September 20, 1985; Bureau of Intelligence and Research, *Current Reports,* December 15, 1983 (declassified for National Security Archive, January 17, 2001); Claude van England, "Who Are the Terrorists Behind Planning, Execution of the Kuwaiti Airliner Hijacking?," *The Christian Science Monitor,* December 10, 1984.

123. Blanford, *Warriors of God,* 52–53.

124. The U.S. ambassador requested additional security measures prior to the event and was denied. Stanley Brooks, "Interview with Ambassador Francois Dickman," February 9, 2001, Foreign Affairs Oral History Collection of the Association for Diplomatic Studies and Training, http://www.adst.org/OH%20TOCs

/Dickman,%20Francois%20M.toc.pdf; "Trial of Embassy Bombing Suspects," *KUNA*, February 11, 1984.

125. Kenneth Dam, "Memo for the President," December 12, 1983 (declassified for National Security Archive, January 17, 2001).

126. CIA cable, "Kuwait: Terrorist Bombings," December 13, 1983 (declassified for National Security Archive, January 17, 2001).

127. Robert Fisk, "The Invasion of Kuwait: Iraq May Have Released Prisoners," *The Independent*, August 5, 1990.

128. "Mustafa Amine Badreddine Fact Sheet," Special Tribunal for Lebanon, 2014.

129. "FSA: Mustafa Badreddine Leading Hizballah Operations Near Qusayr," *Naharnet*, May 20, 2013; Ronen Bergman, "The Hezbollah Connection," *The New York Times*, February 10, 2015.

130. Bergman, "The Hezbollah Connection."

131. The Kuwaiti indictment refers to al-Muhandis and Badreddinne as Jamal Jaf'ar Muhammad and Elias Fuad Sa'ib, respectively, both known aliases for the men. See "Profiles of Accused at the Rafik Hariri Trial at the Hague," BBC News, January 16, 2014; Anne Barnard and Sewell Chan, "Mustafa Badreddine, Hezbollah Military Commander, Is Killed in Syria," *The New York Times*, May 13, 2016.

132. Concern about terrorism from "Islamic Jihad" against U.S. diplomatic targets was rampant in 1983. A Kuwaiti newspaper in October 1984 reported that the CIA warned diplomats about the possibility of "kamikaze" strikes using hijacked aircraft in suicide attacks on U.S. facilities. The report is poorly sourced, but it belies the notion that such attacks could not be envisioned before the September 2001 attack. The article is worth quoting at length: "The CIA warned the Reagan Administration in a special report prepared and submitted to the White House several days ago of a suicide operation that would be executed by a small aircraft against an important U.S. target in one of the Middle East countries. The source explained that the CIA received information from various parties in the region, including Israeli intelligence, saying that elements opposing U.S. policy are preparing to attack one of the U.S. embassies or the house of one of the U.S. ambassadors in the region following the style of the Japanese pilots who used to crash their planes into American warships during . . . World War II; they were called kamikaze pilots." "Suicide Attack on U.S. Facility Expected," *Al-Qabas*, October 26, 1984, in FBIS Daily Report, October 29, 1984.

133. CIA, *Possible Outcomes and Implications of the Iran-Iraq War*, May 17, 1982 (declassified for National Security Archive, August 12, 2002).

134. See Joseph H. Felter and Brian Fishman, *Iranian Strategy in Iraq: Politics and "Other Means"* (West Point, NY: Combating Terrorism Center, 2009).

135. Michael Gordon and Bernard Trainor, *The Endgame: The Inside Story of the Struggle for Iraq from George W. Bush to Barack Obama* (New York: Random House, 2012), 104.

136. Sami al-Askari, a key advisor to then Iraqi prime minister Nouri al-Maliki, re-counted a story whereby Khazali, when challenged by a British commander to prove his influence, made a single phone call from prison, and "within two weeks, the attacks stopped." Babak Dehghanpisheh, "Special Report: The Fighters of Iraq That Answer to Iran," Reuters, November 12, 2014.

137. USFZ-2010-M00043-D2C00000234, www.ctc.usma.edu.

138. Ibid.

139. See FSEC-2008-08000016, www.ctc.usma.edu.

140. The Khazalis' release was also tied to a prisoner exchange for several British hostages seized by AAH in 2007. Martin Chulov, "Qais al-Khazali: From Kidnapper and Prisoner to Potential Leader," *The Guardian*, December 31, 2009; Elie Chalhoub, "Interview with Qays Khazali," *Al-Akhbar*, January 21, 2012, http://english.al-akhbar.com/node/3556 (accessed June 4, 2015).

141. Jane Arraf, "US Likely to Release Insurgent Accused of Killing Five U.S. Soldiers," *The Christian Science Monitor*, June 11, 2009; Ned Parker and Saad Fakhrildeen, "Iraq Frees Shiite Militant in Exchange for Briton," *Los Angeles Times*, January 6, 2010.

142. See OFAC list at http://www.treasury.gov/ofac/downloads/sdnlist.txt; see also "Treasury Designates Individual, Entity Posing a Threat to Stability in Iraq," U.S. Department of the Treasury, July 2, 2009.

143. Charlie Savage, "Prisoner in Iraq Tied to Hezbollah Faces U.S. Military Charges," *The New York Times*, February 23, 2012; *Ali Musa Daqduq al-Musawi Charging Sheet, Office of Military Commissions*, January 3, 2013, https://assets.documentcloud.org/documents/302052/daqduq-tribunal-chargesheet.pdf.

144. "Iraq Releases Suspect Hezbollah Operative Daqduq," Reuters, November 16, 2012. For a useful time line of Daqduq's life, see Stephen Wicken and Kim Dudine, "Timeline: Ali Mussa Daqduq," The Institute for the Study of War, November 21, 2012; "Treasury Sanctions Hezbollah Leadership," U.S. Department of the Treasury, August 22, 2013; David Barnett, "Treasury Designates 4 Members of Hezbollah's Leadership," *The Long War Journal*, August 22, 2013.

145. For excellent details, see Phillip Smyth, "The Shiite Jihad in Syria and Its Regional Effects," The Washington Institute Policy Focus 138 (February 2015).

146. See Phillip Smyth, "From Karbala to Sayyida Zaynab: Iraqi Fighters in Syria's Shia Militias," *CTC Sentinel* Vol. 6, Issue 8, August 27, 2013; Jeffrey White, "The Qusayr Rules: The Syrian Regime's Changing Way of War," The Washington Institute, May 31, 2013.

147. Qassim Abdul-Zahra, "Shiite Cleric Issues Fatwa in Support of Fighting in Syria War: Grand Ayatollah Kazim al-Haeri Supports Assad," Associated Press, December 19, 2013; Samia Nakhoul and Suadad al-Salhy, "Thousands of Shi'ites Ready to Fight in Syria, Iraqi Says," Reuters, June 21, 2013.

148. See https://www.youtube.com/watch?v=OKVNSGaLHDo, and "Hezbollah Man Dies on 'Jihad Duty' in Iraq," Al Jazeera, July 31, 2014. Ibrahim al-Haj was a Hizballah fighter killed near Mosul. He had previously participated in one of

Hizballah's most consequential raids—a 2006 cross-border kidnapping of two Israeli soldiers, which led to the disastrous 2006 war between Israel and Hizballah. Hugh Naylor, "Hizbollah Increases Number of Fighters in Syria," *The National*, July 6, 2014; "Hezbollah Commander Killed in Iraq," *The Daily Star*, August 1, 2014; Mustafa al-Kadhimi, "Will al-Sistani Be Able to Control the Popular Mobilization Forces?," *Al-Monitor*, March 12, 2015.

149. James Gordon Meek, Brian Ross, Rym Momtaz, and Alex Hosenball, "'Dirty Brigades': US-Trained Iraqi Forces Investigated for War Crimes," ABC News, March 11, 2015; Zaid al-Ali, "Tikrit: The Abandoned City," *The New York Review of Books*, May 4, 2015.

150. Haidar Sumeri photograph via Twitter feed, February 28, 2015, https://twitter .com/iraqisecurity/status/571930950029991936 (accessed June 4, 2015); "Photos: Soleimani in Battle for Tikrit," United States Institute of Peace (The Iran Primer), March 10, 2015, http://iranprimer.usip.org/blog/2015/mar/10/photos -soleimani-battle-tikrit.

Chapter Six: The Stage of Absolute Confrontation

1. Abu Umar al-Baghdadi, "The Harvest of the Years in the Land of the Monotheists," Al-Furqan Media Establishment, April 17, 2007.

2. *Dabiq*, Vol. 5, 1436 Muharram.

3. Abu Bakr al-Baghdadi, "And Wait, for We Are Also Waiting," Al-Furqan Media Establishment, December 26, 2015.

4. "Foreign Fighters: An Updated Assessment of the Flow of Foreign Fighters into Syria and Iraq," The Soufan Group, December 2015.

5. Rukmini Callimachi, "How ISIS Built the Machinery of Terror Under Europe's Gaze," *The New York Times*, March 29, 2016.

6. Abu Muhammad al-Adnani, "Indeed Your Lord Is Ever Watchful," Al-Furqan Media Establishment, September 22, 2014 (translated by Pieter van Ostaeyen), https://pietervanostaeyen.wordpress.com/2015/01/26/audio-statement-by-is -spokesman-abu-muhammad-al-adnani-as-shami-say-die-in-your-rage/ (accessed December 23, 2015).

7. Fuad Husayn, "The Second Generation of al-Qaeda Part 14 and Part 15" (attributed to Sayf al-Adl), serialized in *Asharq al-Awsat*, May 28, 2005.

8. Abu Bakr Naji (Muhammad Khalil al-Hakaymah), *The Management of Savagery*, 2004, translated by William McCants for the John M. Olin Center for Strategic Studies, Harvard University, May 23, 2006. Available: https://azelin.files .wordpress.com/2010/08/abu-bakr-naji-the-management-of-savagery-the -most-critical-stage-through-which-the-umma-will-pass.pdf.

9. Erika Solomon, "The ISIS Economy: Meet the New Boss," *The Financial Times*, January 5, 2015.

10. Richard Spencer, "Islamic State Issues New School Curriculum in Iraq," *The Telegraph*, September 16, 2004.

11. See Ayman Jawad al-Tamimi, "The Evolution in Islamic State Administration: The Documentary Evidence," *Perspectives on Terrorism* 9, no. 4 (2015). The Islamic State of Iraq named two cabinets. The first was named in April 2007 and included ministers of war, legal commissions, public relations, security, information, detainee affairs, petroleum, agriculture and marine wealth, health, and a first minister to support the emir. The second cabinet shuffled these roles a bit. It replaced the minister of agriculture and marine wealth with a minister of treasury. See "Announcing the Second Cabinet of the Islamic State of Iraq," Al-Furqan Media Establishment, September 21, 2009, and "Announcing the Cabinet of the Islamic State of Iraq," Al-Furqan Media Establishment, April 19, 2007.

12. See Harmony Document NMEC-2009-602125.

13. See Harmony Document NMEC-2007-000566; Michael Silverman, *Awakening Victory: How Iraqi Tribes and American Troops Reclaimed al-Anbar and Defeated al-Qaeda in Iraq* (Philadelphia: Casemate, 2011), 151–154.

14. Aaron Zelin, "The Islamic State of Iraq and Syria Has a Consumer Protection Office," *The Atlantic*, June 13, 2014; Aaron Zelin and Oula A. Alrifai, "The Islamic State in Southern Syria," *CTC Sentinel* Vol. 8, Issue 11, special issue on Islamic State (December 15, 2015).

15. Abu Hamzah al-Baghdadi, *Why Do We Fight? Who Do We Fight?*, Islamic Renewal Organization website, October 2005.

16. Tore Hamming, "The Extremist Wing of the Islamic State," *Jihadica*, June 9, 2016, http://www.jihadica.com/the-extremist-wing-of-the-islamic-state/; "The Just Path: Between the Extremes of Excessiveness and Negligence," Islamic State Shariah Ministry, May 29, 2016, https://ansarukhilafah.wordpress.com /2016/06/08/the-just-path-between-the-extremes-of-excessiveness-negligence / (accessed June 12, 2016).

17. See Harmony Documents SOCOM-2012-0000005, SOCOM-2012-0000016, and SOCOM-2012-0000017. See also "Letter Addressed to Atiyah," Bin Laden's Bookshelf. For more, see William McCants, *The ISIS Apocalypse* (New York: St. Martin's Press, 2015).

18. Usama bin Laden, "Private Letter to Atiyah" (Letter to Atiyah), Bin Laden's Bookshelf, undated.

19. Abu Hamzah al-Muhajir, "To Those Entrusted with the Message," Al-Furqan Media Establishment, September 15, 2010 (released posthumously).

20. "Iraqi Students Learn Patriotism Is Kufr," Middle East Online, October 5, 2014; Ali Mamouri, "IS Impose New Rules on Education in Syria, Iraq," *Al-Monitor*, October 21, 2014.

21. Aymenn Jawad al-Tamimi has done critical work collecting and archiving primary source data on the Islamic State governance. See http://www .aymennjawad.org/2015/01/archive-of-islamic-state-administrative-documents (accessed December 29, 2015).

22. Brett McGurk, "Statement to the Senate Foreign Relations Committee," July 24, 2014.

23. Aymenn Jawad al-Tamimi, "The Archivist: Unseen Islamic State Financial Accounts for Deir az-Zor Province," Jihadology, October 5, 2015.

24. "The Islamic State," The Black Flags Series, 2015, 52. https://archive.org/details /EBooksBlackFlagSeriesAllzip-53mb (accessed February 2, 2016).

25. "Islamic State Monthly Revenue Totals $80 Million, IHS Says," IHS Janes press release, December 7, 2015. Available: http://press.ihs.com/press-release /aerospace-defense-security/islamic-state-monthly-revenue-totals-80-million -ihs-says (accessed June 16, 2016).

26. Adam Szubin, "Remarks by Acting Under Secretary Adam Szubin at Chatham House," U.S. Department of the Treasury, December 10, 2015, https://www .treasury.gov/press-center/press-releases/Pages/jl0299.aspx.

27. Erika Solomon and Sam Jones, "ISIS Inc. Loot and Taxes Keep Jihad Economy Churning," The Financial Times, December 14, 2015.

28. "The Jizyah," Al-Battar Media Foundation, August 21, 2014, reprinted in "Heroes of Syria: Shuhada Stories from al-Sham" (this is an e-book compiled by English-speaking supporters of the Islamic State).

29. See Ahmed Rasheed and Ned Parker, "In Mosul, Islamic State Turns Captured City into Fortress," Reuters, January 22, 2015; Damian Paletta and Adam Entous, "Militants in Iraq Siphon State Pay," Wall Street Journal, March 23, 2015; "Iraq MP: Mosul Salaries Might Be Aiding ISIS," Rudaw, August 27, 2015.

30. Solomon and Jones, "ISIS Inc. Loot and Taxes Keep Jihad Economy Churning."

31. Daveed Gartenstein-Ross, "Oil Sales," The Cipher Brief, January 13, 2016; Matthew M. Reed, "Revealed: Assad Buys Oil from ISIS," The Daily Beast, December 10, 2015, http://www.thedailybeast.com/articles/2015/12/10/isis-is-the-con -ed-of-syria.html; "Inside ISIS Inc.: The Journey of a Barrel of Oil," The Financial Times, http://ig.ft.com/sites/2015/isis-oil/ (accessed June 2, 2016); Martin Chulov, "Turkey Sends in Jets as Syria's Agony Spills Over Every Border," The Guardian, July 25, 2015.

32. Szubin, "Remarks by Acting Under Secretary Adam Szubin at Chatham House." There is even some evidence that ISIS oil has been exported from Turkey for refining and sale elsewhere. An analysis of oil shipped out of the Turkish port of Ceyhan in late 2014 and early 2015 suggests that Islamic State oil may be shipped through the Kirkuk-Ceyhan pipeline for broader distribution. George Kiourktsoglou and Alec D. Coutroubis, "ISIS Export Gateway to Global Crude Oil Markets," Marsec Review, http://www.marsecreview.com/wp-content /uploads/2015/03/PAPER-on-CRUDE-OIL-and-ISIS.pdf.

33. "Draft of the Wealth Management Plan," Islamic State, Deir al-Zour Financial Ministry, February 5, 2015, in Aymenn Jawad al-Tamimi, "The Archivist: Unseen Islamic State Financial Accounts for Deir az-Zor Province," Jihadology, October 5, 2015.

34. "Administrative Order Number 5," Islamic State General Committee, September 15, 2015, available in Andrew Keller, "U.S. Department of State: Documenting

ISIS's Antiquities Trafficking" (PowerPoint), U.S. Department of State, September 29, 2015.

35. Emily Glazer, Nour Malas, and Jon Hilsenrath, "U.S. Cut Cash to Iraq on Iran, ISIS Fears," *Wall Street Journal,* November 3, 2015; Nibras Kazimi, "The Islamic State's Sovereign Wealth Fund," Talisman Gate, Again, December 11, 2015.

36. *Final Report of the National Commission on Terrorist Attacks upon the United States* (Washington, DC: Government Printing Office, 2004), Executive Summary.

37. See http://www.mass.gov/bb/gaa/fy2015/. The population is also similar to that of the Southeast Asian nation of Laos, which claims a budget of about $2 billion per year. "Laos to Borrow 263 Miln USD due to Budget Deficit," *Xinhua,* December 24, 2013.

38. Many thanks to Reid Sawyer, who pointed to this dynamic more than a decade ago.

39. Charles Tilly, "War Making and State Making as Organized Crime," in *Bringing the State Back In,* ed. Peter Evans, Dietrich Rueschemeyer, and Theda Skocpol (Cambridge: Cambridge University Press, 1985), 170–187.

40. Ibid.

41. "The Rise of the Khilafah—Return of the Gold Dinar," Al-Hayat Media Center, August 29, 2015.

42. "Announcement Concerning the Minting of a Currency Specific to the Islamic State," Islamic State—Finance Ministry, November 13, 2014.

43. "Questions and Answers Regarding Captives and Slaves," Al-Himma Library (Islamic State Publishing), October/November 2014, http://www.memrijttm .org/islamic-state-isis-releases-pamphlet-on-female-slaves.html (accessed December 26, 2015); "Fatwa Number 64," Islamic State Committee for Research and Fatwas, January 29, 2015.

44. Rukmini Callimachi and Mauricio Lima, "ISIS Enshrines a Theology of Rape," *The New York Times,* August 13, 2015.

45. "General Notification," Islamic State–Aleppo Province, February/March 2015, http://justpaste.it/aleppogeneralnote (accessed December 26, 2015); translation available at http://www.aymennjawad.org/2015/01/archive-of-islamic-state -administrative-documents (accessed December 26, 2015).

46. Abu Hamzah al-Muhajir, "Interview with the Minister of War of the Islamic State of Iraq," Al-Furqan Media Establishment, October 24, 2008.

47. "Letter to Hatim" (HADI-1-018398—HADI-1-018416), *USA v. Abd al-Hadi al-Iraqi,* AE35, Part 3.

48. Barack Obama, "Remarks on Martha's Vineyard," August 20, 2014, https:// www.whitehouse.gov/the-press-office/2014/08/20/statement-president (accessed June 17, 2016).

49. Jacob Prousther, "In Nations with Significant Muslim Populations, Much Disdain for ISIS," Pew Research, November 17, 2015; Katie Halper, "45 Examples of Muslim Outrage About Charlie Hebdo Attack That Fox News Missed," *AlterNet,*

January 9, 2015, http://www.alternet.org/media/45-examples-muslim-outrage
-about-charlie-hebdo-attack-fox-news-missed (accessed June 16, 2016); Elisa
Oddone, "Jordanian Jihadist Leader Condemns ISIS Caliphate," *Al-Monitor,*
July 7, 2014.

50. Ascribed to an "ISIS Mujahid" on www.invitetoislam.org, included in "The Islamic State," *The Black Flags Series.*

51. Charlie Winter, "The Virtual 'Caliphate': Understanding Islamic State's Propaganda Strategy," The Quilliam Foundation, July 2015.

52. Bruce Hoffman, *Inside Terrorism* (New York: Columbia University Press,
2006), 37.

53. Winter, "The Virtual 'Caliphate.'"

54. Aaron Zelin, "Picture or It Didn't Happen: A Snapshot of the Islamic State's
Official Media Output," *Perspectives on Terrorism* 9, no. 4 (2015).

55. Winter, "The Virtual 'Caliphate.'"

56. Greg Miller and Souad Mekhennet, "Inside the Surreal World of the Islamic
State's Propaganda Machine," *The Washington Post,* November 20, 2015.

57. For example, see "Paid, Owned and Earned Media Framework," Change Conversations, http://conversations.marketing-partners.com/2011/01/paid-owned
-earned-media-channels-are-you-in-the-right-place/ (accessed December 30,
2015).

58. Zelin, "Picture or It Didn't Happen."

59. Mike Arsenault, "How Valuable Is Amazon's 1-Click Patent? It's Worth Billions," Conversion Sense, July 13, 2012, http://blog.rejoiner.com/2012/07
/amazon-1clickpatent/ (accessed June 16, 2016).

60. "Denying Responsibility for the Criminal Bombing in the Al-Zuhur Neighborhood and Promising Revenge," Jabhat al-Nusrah—Media Statement 2, October 27, 2012.

61. J. M. Berger and Jonathon Morgan, "The ISIS Twitter Census," The Brookings
Project on U.S. Relations with the Islamic World, Analysis Paper No. 20,
March 2015.

62. "Combating Violent Extremism," Twitter Blog, February 5, 2016, https://blog
.twitter.com/2016/combating-violent-extremism (accessed February 16, 2016).

63. Daniel Heinke and Jan Raudszus, "German Foreign Fighters in Syria and Iraq,"
CTC Sentinel Vol. 8, Issue 1, January 22, 2015; Robin Simcox, "We Will Conquer
Your Rome," Henry Jackson Society, September 29, 2015. The Sinjar Records
revealed that only a handful of nearly 600 fighters who traveled to fight in Iraq
in 2006 and 2007 mobilized online. Felter and Fishman, "Al-Qaeda's Foreign
Fighters in Iraq: A First Look at the Sinjar Records," December 2007.

64. For a regularly updated map of foreign fighter numbers, see "Foreign Fighters
in Iraq and Syria: Where Do They Come From?," Radio Free Europe/Radio
Liberty, http://www.rferl.org/contentinfographics/foreign-fighters-syria-iraq
-is-isis-isil-infographic/26584940.html (accessed December 31, 2015).

65. Ibid.

66. Eric Schmitt and Somini Sengupta, "Thousands Enter Syria to Join ISIS Despite Global Efforts," *The New York Times,* September 26, 2015.

67. "Understanding Jihadists in Their Own Words," *Quantum White Papers,* No. 2 (March 2015).

68. Ibid.

69. Rohit Kachroo, "Belgium Delivers Verdicts in Massive Trial of Alleged Islamist Extremists," NBC News, February 11, 2015.

70. Abu Amr al-Qa'idi, *A Course in the Art of Recruitment,* 2009, https://archive.org /details/ACourseInTheArtOfRecruiting-RevisedJuly2010 (accessed June 16, 2016); Brian Fishman and Abdullah Warius, "A Jihadi's Course in the Art of Recruitment," *CTC Sentinel* Vol. 2, Issue 2 (February 2009).

71. Rukmini Callimachi, "ISIS and the Lonely Young American," *The New York Times,* June 27, 2015; Kimiko De Freytas-Tamura, "Teenage Girl Leaves for ISIS, and Others Follow," *The New York Times,* February 24, 2015.

72. Scott Shane, *Objective Troy* (New York: Tim Duggan Books, 2015).

73. *United States of America v. Enrique Marquez, Jr. Criminal Complaint,* December 17, 2015, http://www.justice.gov/opa/file/800606/download (accessed January 9, 2016).

74. The Islamic State regularly releases magazines in English (*Dabiq, Islamic State Report, Islamic State News*), French (*Dar al-Islam*), Russian (*Istok*), and Turkish (*The Conquest of Constantinople*).

75. "Homegrown Extremism Project," New America, International Security Program (accessed November 20, 2015). Abu 'Amr al-Qa'idi warned in *A Course in the Art of Recruitment* that new recruits would want to travel for jihad rather than fight in their home country. Julian Hattem, "FBI: More Than 200 Americans Have Tried to Fight for ISIS," *The Hill,* July 8, 2015.

76. Shiraz Maher, "From Portsmouth to Kobane: The British Jihadis Fighting for ISIS," *New Statesman,* November 6, 2014.

77. Mary Ann Weaver, "Her Majesty's Jihadists," *The New York Times,* April 14, 2015.

78. "Syria Regional Refugee Response," UNHCR Inter-Agency Information Sharing Portal, http://data.unhcr.org/syrianrefugees/regional.php (accessed December 31, 2015).

79. Borzou Daraghi, "This Is How ISIS Has Spread Beyond Syria and Iraq," *Buzzfeed,* December 12, 2015, https://www.buzzfeed.com/borzoudaragahi/this -is-how-isis-has-spread-beyond-syria-and-iraq?utm_term=.uclZxeXMV#.wiZ xO3zm5.

80. Benedetta Berti and Zach Gold, "Hamas, the Islamic State, and the Gaza-Sinai Crucible," Carnegie Endowment for International Peace, January 12, 2016; Daniella Peled, "ISIS in Egypt: Al-Sissi Locked in Bloody Battle with Islamic Extremists," *Ha'aretz,* December 3, 2015; "Factions Close to State of Sinai and ISIS Spread in Gaza," *Al Arabiya,* September 29, 2015.

81. Felter and Fishman, "Al-Qaeda's Foreign Fighters in Iraq."

82. David D. Kirkpatrick, Ben Hubbard, and Eric Schmitt, "ISIS' Grip on Libyan City Gives It a Fallback Option," *The New York Times,* November 28, 2015; "Until They Saw Clear Evidence," Al-Furqan Media Establishment, April 29, 2015; "Egypt Bombs ISIS Targets in Libya," *Asharq al-Awsat,* February 16, 2015.

83. The group has several notable foreign fighters, including Abu Muhammad al-Maqdisi's brother. "An Interview with the Mujahid Brother Salah al-Din al-Maqdisi," Al-Battar Media Establishment, April 24, 2014; Don Rassler, "Situating the Emergence of the Islamic State of Khorasan," *CTC Sentinel* 8, no. 3 (March 2015).

84. "O Victorious Umma: Mobilize, Wage Jihad, Rejoice," *Al-Nafir,* May 2014.

85. There are competing versions describing the actual date of Mullah Omar's death. Some say January 2013, others April 2013. See Sami Yousafzai, "Inside the Mysterious 'Death' of Taliban Leader Mullah Omar," *Newsweek,* July 29, 2015; Rod Nordland and Joseph Goldstein, "Taliban Leader Mullah Omar Died in 2013, Afghans Declare," *The New York Times,* July 29, 2015.

86. The Islamic State ridiculed Mullah Omar—and, by extension, al-Qaeda—in a July 2015 *Dabiq* article, citing his penchant for Afghan nationalism and lack of Qurayshi lineage. "A Fatwa for Khurusan," *Dabiq* 10 (1436 Ramadan).

87. Fuad Husayn, "The Second Generation of al-Qa'ida" (attributed to Sayf al-Adl), serialized in *Asharq al-Awsat,* May 30, 2005.

88. In 2005, Abu Abd al-Rahman al-Iraqi threatened attacks against the West—specifically the Vatican—but AQI subsequently clarified that it was not actually a threat. See Abu Abd al-Rahman al-Iraqi, "Here I Am at Your Service, Abu Mus'ab," Islamic Renewal Organization, April 30, 2005.

89. Abu Muhammad al-Adnani, "Indeed Your Lord Is Ever Watchful," Al-Furqan Media Establishment, September 22, 2014; Abu Mus'ab al-Zarqawi, "Do You Know Better Than Allah?," Al-Qaeda in Iraq Media Section, October 7, 2005.

90. Basim al-Radi al-bu Mahal, Samran Mikhlif al-bu Mahal, and Muhammad Husayn al-Shufayr Jughayfi, "Analysis of the State of the ISI," https://www.ctc.usma.edu/posts/analysis-of-the-state-of-isi-english-translation-2 (Harmony Document NMEC-2007-612449).

91. Callimachi, "How ISIS Built the Machinery of Terror Under Europe's Gaze."

92. David Chazan, "Brussels Museum Shooting Suspect 'Beheaded Baby,'" *The Telegraph,* September 7, 2014.

93. Henry Samuel and Patrick Sawer, "Charlie Hebdo Attack: The Kouachi Brothers and the Network of French Islamists with Links to the Islamic State," *The Telegraph,* January 8, 2015; "Yes We Can: A Bullet a Day Keeps the Infidel Away," *Inspire,* No. 10 (March 2013).

94. Bob Fredericks, "Charlie Hebdo Suspects, Kosher-Market Gunman Killed; 4 Hostages Die in Rescue Attempt," *New York Post,* January 9, 2015.

95. Paul Cruickshank, "Inside the ISIS Plot to Attack the Heart of Europe," CNN, February 13, 2015.

96. Guy van Vlierden, "Profile: Paris Attack Ringleader Abdelhamid Abaaoud," *CTC Sentinel*, Vol. 8, Issue 11, special issue on Islamic State (December 15, 2015).

97. "Interview with Abu Umar al-Baljiki," *Dabiq* 7 (February 2015).

98. Ibid.

99. David Gauthier-Villars, Stacy Mechtry, and Matt Bradley, "Abdelhamid Abaaoud, Alleged Ringleader of Paris Attacks, Was 'Emir of War' in Syria," *Wall Street Journal*, November 19, 2015.

100. Abu Muhammad al-Adnani, "So They Slay and Are Slain," Al-Furqan Media Establishment, March 12, 2015.

101. Rukmini Callimachi, "US Seeks to Avoid Ground War Welcomed by Islamic State," *The New York Times*, December 7, 2015; Graeme Wood, "What ISIS Really Wants," *The Atlantic*, March 2015.

102. Al-Qaeda in the Arabian Peninsula republished al-Suri's argument in 2013 prior to the formal split between the Islamic State and al-Qaeda. Abu Mus'ab al-Suri, *Lessons Learned from the Jihad Ordeal in Syria*, https://www.ctc.usma .edu/posts/lessons-learned-from-the-jihad-ordeal-in-syria-english -translation-2 (accessed June 17, 2016); Abu Mus'ab al-Suri, "The Jihadi Experiences: The Strategy of Deterring with Terrorism," *Inspire*, No. 10 (March 2013).

103. Fuad Husayn, "The Second Generation of al-Qa'ida" (attributed to Sayf al-Adl), serialized in *Asharq al-Awsat*, May 30, 2005.

104. Abu Muhammad al-Adnani, "Indeed Your Lord Is Ever Watchful," Al-Furqan Media Establishment, September 22, 2014.

105. Lauren Carroll, "What Barack Obama Said About ISIS Being Contained," Politifact, November 15, 2015.

106. Neil MacFarquhar, "Russia Allies with France Against ISIS, Saying Jet That Crashed in Sinai Was Bombed," *The New York Times*, November 17, 2015; Barbara Starr, "Russian Plane Crash: ISIS Chatter Supports Bomb Theory, Officials Say," CNN, November 9, 2015.

107. "Foreword," *Dabiq*, Vol. 12 (1437 Safar): 2–5.

108. Anne Barnard and Hwaida Saad, "ISIS Claims Responsibility for Blasts That Killed Dozens in Beirut," *The New York Times*, November 12, 2015.

109. Rukmini Callimachi, Katrin Bennhold, and Laure Fourquet, "How the Paris Attackers Honed Their Assault Through Trial and Error," *The New York Times*, November 30, 2015.

110. Andrew Higgins, "Inquiry into Paris Terror Attacks Widens to Eastern Europe," *The New York Times*, December 4, 2015.

111. Vikram Dodd, "Call for Urgent Security Review of How Paris Attacks Ringleader Got Ferry to UK," *The Guardian*, January 10, 2016.

112. "Three Hours of Terror in Europe, Moment by Moment," *The New York Times*, November 15, 2015.

113. "Paris Attacks: Who Were the Victims?," BBC News, November 27, 2015.

114. Callimachi, Bennhold, and Fourquet, "How the Paris Attackers Honed Their Assault Through Trial and Error."

115. Michael Stothard, "Hard-Drinking 'Cowgirl' Killed Alongside Paris Attack Ringleader," *The Financial Times*, November 20, 2015.

116. "Kill Them Wherever You Find Them," Al-Furqan Media Establishment, January 20, 2016.

117. Ibid.

118. Steven Erlanger and Alissa Rubin, "Salah Abdeslam, Suspect in Paris Attacks, Is Captured in Brussels," *The New York Times*, March 18, 2016.

119. Anwar al-Awlaki, "A Message to the American People and Muslims in the West," March 2010, http://anwar-awlaki.blogspot.com/2011/10/message-to-american-people.html (accessed June 17, 2016).

120. "The Extinction of the Grayzone," *Dabiq*, Vol. 7 (1436 Rabi' al-Akhar): 54–64.

121. "Foreword," *Dabiq*, Vol. 12 (1437 Safar): 2–5.

122. "Islamic State Group Claims Saudi Mosque Suicide Blast," BBC News, August 6, 2015, http://www.bbc.com/news/world-middle-east-33805901; "Islamic State Attack on Saudi Mosque Kills One: Ministry," Reuters, October 26, 2015; Ben Hubbard, "ISIS Turns Saudis Against the Kingdom, and Families Against Their Own," *The New York Times*, March 31, 2016.

123. Dion Nissenbaum, Ayla Albayrak, and Gordon Lubold, "Turkey Blames Islamic State in Istanbul Attack," *The Wall Street Journal*, January 12, 2016; Daren Butler and Humeyra Pamuk, "Islamic State Is Prime Suspect in Turkey Bombing, as Protests Erupt," Reuters, October 13, 2015.

124. *United States of America v. Enrique Marquez, Jr. Criminal Complaint*, December 17, 2015.

125. Emma Reynolds, " 'It's Their Right to Kill You': Bloggers Sent Death Threats and Abuse by IS-Linked Militants," news.com.au, December 20, 2015, http://www.news.com.au/world/middle-east/its-their-right-to-kill-you-bloggers-sent-death-threats-and-abuse-by-islinked-militants/news-story/dfca25dfce959cfee840d7d7fb65fo4d.

126. "Interview with Abu Muhammad al-Maqdisi," Ru'ya Television, February 6, 2015.

127. "Foreword," *Dabiq* 7 (1436 Rabi al-Akhar).

128. "The Evil of Division and Taqlid," *Dabiq* 11 (1436 Dhul Qa'dah): 10–13.

129. "The Extinction of the Grayzone."

130. See, for example, Petya Petrov, "Message from the Sheikh Mujahid Ali Abu Mukhammad al-Dahistani—Amir of Islamic Imarat Kavkaz—to the Islamic Umma," YouTube, January 11, 2015.

131. Andrew H. Kydd and Barbara F. Walter, "The Strategies of Terrorism," *International Security* 31, no. 1 (Summer 2006): 49–80; Clint Watts, "ISIS and

al-Qaeda in a Race to the Bottom," Snapshot, *Foreign Affairs*, November 23, 2015, https://www.foreignaffairs.com/articles/2015-11-23/isis-and-al-qaeda-race-bottom; Daveed Gartenstein-Ross, Jason Fritz, Bridget Moreng, and Nathaniel Barr, "Islamic State vs. al-Qaeda: Strategic Dimensions of a Patricidal Conflict," New America International Security Program, December 2015.

132. Ayman al-Zawahiri, "Letter to Abu Bakr al-Baghdadi," September 4, 2013, included in tweet by @asrarwk on August 22, 2015.

133. Rukmini Callimachi and Eric Schmitt, "Iran Released Top Members of Al Qaeda in a Trade," *The New York Times*, September 17, 2015; "Terror Fears as Iran Frees Al Qaeda Members," Sky News, September 14, 2015.

134. The five reportedly released were al-Aruri, Shihab, al-Adl, Abu Muhammad al-Masri, and Abu Khayr al-Masri. According to a Zarqawi supporter imprisoned in Iran, al-Aruri and Shihab (Suhayb al-Urduni) were the only two Zarqawi supporters in Iran who did not swear *bayah* to Osama bin Laden after Zarqawi did in October 2004. Interestingly, both the Islamic State and AQAP publicly mentioned the individuals released by Iran during the negotiations. Abu Jarir Ash-Shamali's article in *Dabiq*, released in late December 2014, mentioned Aruri and Shihab twice. Likewise, AQAP obsequiously praised al-Adl, Abu Muhammad al-Masri, and Abu Khayr al-Masri in a May 2015 statement. With the exception of al-Adl, none of these characters were common figures in jihadi propaganda. Abu Jarir ash-Shamali, "Al-Qaeda of Waziristan," *Dabiq* 6 (1436 Rabi al-Awwal): 40–55, and Khalid bin Umar Batarfi, "Victory and Martyrdom," Al-Malahim Media Establishment, May 8, 2015.

135. Eric Schmitt, "Al Qaeda Turns to Syria, With a Plan to Challenge ISIS," *The New York Times*, May 15, 2016.

136. Sayf al-Adl, "Abu Khaled al-Suri: May God Have Mercy on You, Lion of Jihad Wahl," Al-Bushrayat Group, dated February 2014, released August 2015. In September 2015, al-Adl's introduction to a collection of essays written by Atiyah abd al-Rahman generated buzz among jihadis. Sayf al-Adl, "Introduction to the Complete Works of the Sheikh, Imam, and Martyr, and Mujahid, Atiyatallah al-Libi," September 2015. Tweeted by @nukhba_alfeker, September 26, 2015.

137. See Tim Lister, "Al-Qaeda Leader to ISIS: You're Wrong, but We Can Work Together," CNN, November 15, 2015, http://www.cnn.com/2015/09/14/middleeast/al-zawahiri-al-qaeda-isis-olive-branch/.

Chapter Seven: The Stage of Final Victory

1. "The Future of World Religions: Population, Growth Projections, 2010–2050," Pew Research Center, April 2, 2015, http://www.pewforum.org/files/2015/03/PF_15.04.02_ProjectionsFullReport.pdf (accessed June 16, 2016).

2. See Nelly Lahoud, *The Jihadis' Path to Self-Destruction* (London: Oxford University Press, 2010).

3. For a forceful version of this argument, see Bruce Hoffman, "The Coming ISIS-Al-Qaeda Merger," *Foreign Affairs Snapshot*, March 29, 2016, https://www .foreignaffairs.com/articles/2016-03-29/coming-isis-al-qaeda-merger.

4. Clint Watts, "ISIS and al Qaeda Race to the Bottom," *Foreign Affairs*, November 23, 2015, https://www.foreignaffairs.com/articles/2015-11-23/isis-and-al-qaeda-race-bottom. Daveed Gartenstein-Ross and Nathaniel Barr, "Neither Remaining nor Expanding: The Islamic State's Global Expansion Struggles," *War on the Rocks*, February 23, 2016, http://warontherocks.com/2016/02/neither-remaining -nor-expanding-the-islamic-states-global-expansion-struggles/.

Appendix: The 2005 "General Plan"

1. I am grateful to Alexander Key of Stanford University for translating this statement.

INDEX